MAN OF WARS

William Howard Russell of
The Times

To F. R. Poskitt
who taught me to enjoy history

'I suppose there is no absolute truth in any history.'
(W. H. Russell's diary, 4 July 1883)
'A good book of biography is one in which the book vanishes and the man remains;
not the man who wrote the book, but the man about whom it was written.'
(G. K. Chesterton)

MAN OF WARS

William Howard Russell of
The Times

Alan Hankinson

Heinemann

LONDON

Heinemann Educational Books Ltd
22 Bedford Square, London WC1B 3HH
LONDON   EDINBURGH   MELBOURNE   AUCKLAND
HONG KONG   SINGAPORE   KUALA LUMPUR   NEW DELHI
IBADAN   NAIROBI   JOHANNESBURG
EXETER (NH)   KINGSTON   PORT OF SPAIN

Hankinson, Alan
  Man of wars.
  1. Russell, William Howard
  2. Journalists—Great Britain—Biography
  I. Title
  070'.92'4   PN5123.R

  ISBN 0-435-32395-4

Phototypesetting by Parkway Group, London and Abingdon
Printed and bound in Great Britain by
Biddles Ltd, Guildford and King's Lynn

Contents

23   The Last Years   251
24   Final Reckoning   267

     Notes   271
     Bibliography   280
     Index   283

List of Maps and Illustrations

Acknowledgements

So much of the source material for this book rests, as it should, in the Archives of *The Times* that it would have been pointless to have tried to write it without the co-operation of the newspaper and its Archivist, Mr Gordon Phillips. I have had much more than that. Mr Phillips made all the relevant documents readily available, took an encouraging interest in my progress, indicated fresh lines of inquiry and checked the finished work. It was help far beyond the call of his duty and I am deeply grateful.

'Billy' Russell built his success on his reputation as 'a truth-telling man' and it is pleasant to be able to report that his descendants, living today, have a similar respect for the truth. None of them tried to obstruct or deflect my researches in any way. One great-grandchild, Mrs David Simonds of Pangbourne, Berks., gave me access to the family papers in her possession. Another, Colonel R. J. Longfield of Lower Silton, Dorset, allowed me to study the large collection of documents in his keeping and gave generous encouragement, support and hospitality as well. A granddaughter, Miss Violet Howard-Russell of West Kirby in the Wirral, poured out her memories freely, though unfortunately all her family documents were destroyed in the bombing of Liverpool in the Second World War.

Several libraries were called into service: the London Library, the Bodleian Library in Oxford, the Harris Library in Preston, the central libraries in Chelsea and Newcastle-upon-Tyne, and my local library at Keswick in Cumbria. I was given expert assistance by the staff of Staffordshire Record Office and the General Register Office in London and by the Assistant Registrar of the Royal Archives, Windsor Castle. I am indebted to the gracious permission of Her Majesty the Queen for quotations from documents in the Royal Archives.

My thanks are due to many others: Mr Rupert Furneaux, a previous biographer of Russell; Dr Hew Strachan of the Royal Military Academy, Sandhurst; Mr Martin Crawford of the Department of American Studies at Keele University; Sir Ronald L. Prain of Weybridge, Surrey; Ms Elizabeth Parry of Sumner Place, Kensington; Mrs Kathleen Tillotson and Mr Graham Storey of the Pilgrim Edition of the letters of Charles Dickens; Dr Clifford Mawdsley of Winchburgh, West Lothian; Mr Richard Fawkes, the biographer of Dion Boucicault; Mr Frank Singleton, the Librarian of *The Guardian;* Miss Helen Gane of Fulham who helped with some of the research and took some photographs; Mr Richard Hall, journalist and author of *Lovers on the Nile;* and Doctors Michael and Jim Cox of Caldbeck who gave valuable medical advice.

My greatest debt, as ever, is to my wife who gave selfless and invaluable help throughout and who, when the chapters were being written, checked everything with the utmost care, pointed out mistakes and flaws mercilessly and suggested countless improvements. If it was sometimes annoying at the time, it was entirely beneficial to this book.

Bassenthwaite,
Cumbria

November 1981

Author's Note

There is of necessity much quotation in this book. I have tried to give the originals exactly as they first appeared, retaining their spelling of place-names (for example) even where it differs from the spelling in the text. There is, I think, no danger of confusion.

With Russell's diaries, which he often wrote hurriedly and without punctuation, I have inserted an occasional dash or comma to make his meaning more immediately clear.

Russell was a compulsive as well as a 'special' correspondent and many of his private letters have survived. It was necessary to distinguish between them and the Letters he sent to *The Times* and other papers for publication. I have done this by using a capital initial letter for all the Letters meant for publication.

I

Victorian Man

When William Howard Russell was born in March 1820 Princess Victoria was ten months old. Four years after her accession to the throne in 1837 he began work as a reporter for *The Times*, covering the turbulent elections in his native Ireland. For the next six decades of her reign, years which saw Britain rise to the peak of her industrial and imperial might, he was active as an observer and chronicler of great events. When she died in January 1901 his own life's work was over and he had only six more years to live.

His life encompassed the Victorian age and to a great extent reflected it and even in some measure, influenced it. He was the leading newspaper writer of the day, 'the father of war correspondents', and he remains the only journalist whose work can be said to have led directly to the downfall of a British government. His reputation was such that Prime Ministers and proconsuls sought his advice; kings and generals took him into their confidence; the Queen herself was—sometimes painfully—aware of him. He gossiped with Abraham Lincoln in the White House and quarrelled with Bismarck at Versailles.

There was probably no other man who saw so much of the Victorian age in such a variety of its aspects, at such close quarters, over so comprehensive a period. And in many ways he personified Victorian man.

In religion, after a brief spell of Protestant zeal of the Irish kind, he settled down to a comfortable, tolerant, middle-of-the-road Anglicanism. He went to church when it was not too inconvenient, presided over family prayers in the mornings and felt slightly guilty when he played cards on the Sabbath. He had little regard for the pomp of High Church Ritualism and less for the blinkered Puritanism he found among Nonconformist missionaries. He believed in the Christian God and shared much of Christ's compassion and had an abiding respect for the language of the Prayer Book but beyond that, like many Victorians, he ran into doubts.

His politics were those of enlightened Conservatism, acutely portrayed by the historian G. M. Young:

In the mid-Victorian years we settled down into an easy genial compromise between progress and tradition—years when a candidate, being asked about his political opinions might reply, and very often did reply 'Sir, I am a liberal Conservative,' which meant 'our old institutions have served us well. . . . But I have an open mind, and if there are any improvements which public opinion demands, then I am ready to consider them.' (1)

On the one occasion when he ran for Parliament Russell put himself forward as 'a Conservative on independent Liberal principles'. He was a pragmatic man, distrustful of dogma, always more concerned with the practical effects of policies than with political theory. He was grateful to live in the security of a settled and hierarchical society and even more grateful that he lived in a land where ideas could be freely exchanged and the way laid open for controlled reform.

He accepted the rigid codes and conventions of his time, social and sexual, without demur. If he departed from the paths of righteousness at any time, he was careful—and this, too, was a very Victorian trait—to cover his tracks. For a man who spent so much of his life on campaign with soldiers and in the London clubs, he was surprisingly prudish. He strongly disapproved of the conduct of many of his fellow members of the Prince of Wales' set and was often embarrassed by their talk: 'The Prince came in with his evil genius Duppy and told me a beastly story,' he wrote in his diary. 'I am so sorry he should say such things and say them to *me*.' (2)

But Russell was a convivial man, by all accounts the best of company with a ready wit and a fund of anecdotes and a pleasing baritone voice. He devoured the massive meals of the time and all too often drank far too much, and the most insistent theme of his personal diary is that of morning-after remorse. He spent much time playing billiards and lost a lot of money at the whist table. He was an inveterate traveller and a man of protean interests—political and military affairs, history and natural history, art and literature, the theatre and the opera.

He was a loving if largely absentee husband, a strict but caring father. In his personal relationships he was inclined to be emotional to the point of sentimentality. There was much about him of the redoubtable Mr Pooter, the central figure of the late-Victorian classic *The Diary of a Nobody*. He was liable to social discomfitures of a minor kind and had a strong penchant for weak puns. His grasp on the practical details of daily life was unsure. For all his travelling he could never master the railway time-tables and rarely reached his destination with all his luggage. There was endless trouble with servants and with horses. His earnings were high but his affairs were always in disorder and he was continuously in debt.

The shaping of his career was typically Victorian too, and might have formed the basis for many a Sunday School homily. In accordance with the tenets of Samuel Smiles, the apostle of self-help, he owed his success not to any advantages of birth or upbringing or to any extraordinary natural abilities but to qualities of character—a capacity for concentrated hard work, dedication to the job in hand, respect for the truth and high moral courage. He did his research thoroughly and when he took up his pen it was with no thought of supporting his paper's line or glorifying his own role or displaying his erudition. He made his reports as truthful as he could and sought to set the event he was describing in its historical context, assessing its significance, looking for any lessons that might be learnt. Many of his rival correspondents were better educated than Russell and some of them wrote prose that was wittier and more elegant. But he surpassed them all in the clarity of his observation, the critical intelligence he brought to bear, and above all in courage—the fact that he was never afraid to speak and write his mind whatever the dangers might be to his career or his popularity or even his personal safety.

Such independence of spirit can also be accounted a characteristic Victorian attribute, but two of the ways in which it was manifested distinguished Russell from the majority of his contemporaries.

In the first place, although he was undoubtedly a 'man of wars' in the sense that he saw much fighting in many parts of the world, he did not like war. He could be impressed by acts of heroism and moved by the sight of masses of men wheeling into battle, but he was more moved and impressed by the horrors and futilities of war—the sufferings of the soldiers, the follies of their commanders, and the debasing effect on men's humanity. No other journalist of the nineteenth century—no other British writer of any kind—insisted so powerfully on 'the pity of war'. The great majority of them, from Tennyson to Kipling among the poets, from G. A. Henty to Winston Churchill among the journalists, continued to see it chiefly in terms of gallantry and glory. But Russell wrote in his diary during his second big campaign, the suppression of the Indian Mutiny, 'War, war, let no women or poets deify thee—womanhood and poetry die in thy bloody strife', (3) and throughout his career he never spared his readers the knowledge, often in gory detail, of what war really meant for those who were involved. 'Queen Victoria's reign,' he cried in his diary, 'has been an incessant record of bloodshed.' (4)

The other important way in which Russell found himself at odds with his age concerned the outbreak of colonial expansion which marked the closing decades of Queen Victoria's reign. Most of his contemporaries saw this as the expression of their natural superiority over other peoples, especially those of other races and religions. Russell did not. He saw it as an expression of greed and arrogance. He found little evidence that the British were morally or temperamentally superior to the 'lesser breeds without the law' and, even if he had, he would not have concluded that this gave them the right to conquer and annex. He may have owed something of this feeling to the fact that he was born and brought up in Ireland, where British rule had signally failed to make itself acceptable to most of the people over many centuries. He owed more, probably, to his sense of history which told him that the British empire could not and would not last and that, as long as the British failed to recognize this, it would involve them in continuous trouble and expense.

He conducted a one-man campaign against imperialism and intensified it in his later years as Britain's involvements multiplied. With tireless fervour he argued the case of the exploited people—Egyptian, Zulu and Boer, Maori, Burmese and

Afghan. And he hated colonialism most of all when it was supported, as it frequently was, by claims of racial or religious superiority.

Russell was not entirely free of racial prejudice. Occasional entries in his diary reveal a general dislike for Jews and Jewishness though he never allowed the feeling to show in his more public writings. This apart, however, his attitude belonged much more to the latter half of the twentieth century than to the century in which he lived. And while his was not the only voice raised at the time against British pretension and colonialism, it was certainly a lone voice in the circles in which he mostly moved—those of journalism and the London clubs and the higher reaches of society.

He touched the life of his times at so many points that it is necessary to look at how matters stood for Britain and the world when Russell was born.

In 1820 Britain was, in the memorable words of *1066 and All That*, 'top nation' in Europe, which meant 'top nation' in the world. The country had emerged from the long wars against Napoleon with the prestige of the victor, an effective army and a triumphant navy. Unlike most of Europe the homeland had not been ravaged by invading soldiers, and in many parts of the world—India and Africa, the Mediterranean and the Caribbean—territories had been acquired which were to form the basis of the new empire. For four decades after Waterloo the chief concern of the British army would be the defence and, in India, the extension of this empire.

There was no nation to challenge Britain's supremacy. France was beaten and exhausted. Germany and Italy were still broken up into patchworks of independent states. The great empires of Eastern Europe, Austria and Russia were weakened by continual fighting and distracted by the problems of controlling their own subject peoples. The Turkish empire was beginning to totter under the burden of its own incompetence and corruption and the strain of maintaining its rule in the Balkans, the Near East and Egypt. Across the Atlantic the United States of America turned its attention away from the Old World towards the virgin land to the west.

For all its predominance, however, Britain had serious problems. The population of the United Kingdom, which included the whole of Ireland, was about twenty million. Numbers had been growing steadily from the middle of the previous century and would continue to grow. But it was a population on the move—from the countryside to the new industrial centres, from the British Isles to the more spacious opportunities of North America and Australasia. The Napoleonic Wars had brought economic hardships and these, together with the dissemination of revolutionary notions of liberty and equality, created unrest especially among the emerging classes of the industrial areas. Pressure for the recognition of these social forces, particularly for the extension of the vote, came up against an almost immovable object—a Tory government which had held power for twenty years and whose attitudes were conditioned by the fear of French ideas. The conflict came to a head at St Peter's Fields in Manchester on

16 August 1819 when a large crowd which had gathered to hear speeches demanding Parliamentary reform was charged by men of the regular and the Yeomanry cavalry, their sabres swinging. Eleven people were killed and more than a hundred injured. Seven months later, on the day William Howard Russell was born, the two main stories in *The Times* dealt with the trial of a group of working class activists in York and the trial in London of the Cato Street conspirators who had been plotting to blow up the entire government.

Ireland, an integral part of the United Kingdom since 1800, was passing through a period of comparative calm. Even so, a large part of the British army had to be garrisoned there to keep the peace, and all the ills that were to afflict the country throughout the century were already present: extreme poverty; dependence on one crop, the potato; hatred between the Irish Roman Catholic majority and the enclave of Protestants who had been transplanted from Scotland to Ulster; widespread distrust, among the Catholics, of government and landlords; a vein of savagery which had been made endemic by centuries of repression and frustration. Russell spent the first twenty years of his life in Ireland and he never lost his interest in the fortunes of 'John Bull's Other Island'. It was a constant source of distress to him that the two countries he loved most could not resolve their differences.

When Russell was born *The Times* was thirty-five years old. Founded in 1785 by a Lloyd's underwriter called John Walter, it had quickly shown an independence that was rare in the London press of those days. During the Napoleonic Wars John Walter II, the founder's son, improved the news-gathering and printing facilities so effectively that it became the country's leading daily paper with a circulation, by 1820, of over 6,000 copies—more than twice that of its nearest rival. Thomas Barnes, a literary man of great pugnacity, had been appointed editor in 1817 and lost no time in showing his contempt for the repressive government. He gave full coverage to the killings in St Peter's Fields and, when Tory Ministers accused him of dangerous Radicalism, said: 'There is nothing they so much dread as a free journal, unattached to any other cause than that of the truth, and given to speak boldly of all parties.' Barnes was editor for twenty-four years, a period during which the paper acquired its enduring nickname 'The Thunderer' and came to be respected and feared as the leading journal of Europe.

By modern standards, however, *The Times* of 1820 was poor value for money. It sold at 7d a copy, the equivalent of more than 35p in the mid-1970s. And all it offered for that was four pages of tightly-packed print, two of them entirely given over to small advertisements. A hundred and sixty years later the paper cost 20p and consisted of thirty-two pages, more than half of them offering a wide variety of news and opinion and pictures.

But the comparison is misleading. The greater part of the price of 1820 was due to taxes imposed by a government which was determined to discourage the publication of independent views—a Stamp Duty of 4d on every copy printed as well as taxes on paper and advertisements. These 'taxes on knowledge', as

Gladstone later called them, applied to all newspapers and magazines. The *Manchester Guardian* when it first appeared, as a weekly, in May 1821 cost 7d. The stamped edition of Cobbett's *Political Register* cost a shilling and sometimes more. They were only able to survive because production costs were low, they attracted advertisers, and a high proportion of their purchasers were not individuals but groups and associations which made copies available to many subscribing members. The Stamp Duty, once paid, enabled a newspaper to be sent through the post free of charge so that the same copy would be posted from reader to reader until it was hopelessly out of date. There was a national appetite for news. The papers went into clubs, business and coffee houses, as well as to 'newsrooms' specially created for the purpose in towns all over Britain. If the price of a paper was higher than at any other time, so was the number of readers per copy, which meant that the circulation figures were not so derisory as they might seem to twentieth-century eyes.

Most of Russell's journalistic work and all of his best work was done for *The Times* and the title that gave him the greatest pleasure was 'Mr. Russell of *The Times*'. In the course of his long life, however, he collected a number of titles and nicknames. When he was making his name during his first major campaign he became widely known as 'Crimea Russell' and then 'Balaclava Russell'. A few years later another battle gave him another nickname, 'Bull Run Russell', though this was a term of abuse rather than praise in Yankee mouths. His correct title by this time was Doctor Russell, for his old university, Trinity College, Dublin, had made him an honorary Doctor of Literature. And Dr Russell he remained —sometimes deploring the title, sometimes insisting on it—until he was knighted and became Sir William for the last few years of his life. But throughout it all, from his schooldays in Dublin to the days of his fame, he was known to his friends—who were legion—simply as Billy. 'There's Russell! Billy, is that you?' was the cry he heard one afternoon in the Rue Castiglione: 'It was the Prince of Wales with H. Farquhar and Macduff. He stood for a quarter of an hour or twenty minutes chaffing. He had been playing baccarat and won.'(5)

That was in Paris in April 1878. But the story begins fifty-eight years earlier.

2

The Formative Years, 1820–41

'Sixty-six or sixty-five years ago I was born at Lily Vale, Jobestown, County Dublin, at the house of my grand-father maternal, Captain Jack Kelly, and my mother then a young thing of eighteen or so, my father some three or four years older. I always thought it was in 1821 till I had an extract from the Register which makes it 1820 but I have not seen the original.' Russell wrote this in his diary in 1886 on his birthday, 28 March. The day of his birth never seems to have been in any doubt but he spent much of his adult life uncertain whether the year was 1820 or 1821 and inclined, for a long time, to favour the latter. By the time he wrote this entry, however, he was reluctantly coming to accept the burden of that extra year. The question was resolved soon after—he was born in 1820.

His parents, who married in June 1819, represented Ireland's sectarian divide. His father's family were devout Protestants with strong evangelical instincts, his mother's were Roman Catholic. Such marriages were common enough in Ireland at that time and his parents adopted the customary compromise: 'It had been arranged that the sons of my parents' marriage should be brought up in their father's faith and that the daughters should be Roman Catholics, but that was viewed with disfavour by the grandparents on both sides, and over my unconscious body waged an acrimonious controversy.' (1)

He was not left unaware of the family antagonism for very long. Most of his childhood and the whole of his adolescence were spent under the powerful influences, alternately, of each set of grandparents, and both did their best to indoctrinate him while they had the chance.

He arrived in the world at a moment when the fortunes of both sides of his family were in decline. His father, John Russell, who claimed descent from an old County Limerick family which numbered sea captains and several Church of Ireland clergymen in its ranks, was in a small way of business and lacked the qualities that might have brought success. Russell described him as 'a large-limbed, solid, joyous man, in some way agent for a great Sheffield firm, Waterhouse and Co., and deep in speculations which were not successful.' (2)

Soon after Russell's birth there was a financial crisis and the family sailed to Liverpool where his father launched another, unspecified venture. A second son,

John, was born in 1823. But Russell was to see little of his brother. The family's affairs prospered no better in Liverpool than they had in Ireland and it was not long before the elder boy was sent back across the water to live at Lily Vale.

The difficulty in dealing with the first twenty years of Russell's life is that Russell himself is virtually the only source of information. Most of the evidence is to be found in an autobiographical essay he wrote in his late sixties which he called *Retrospect*. It was never published and all but a few typescript pages have now disappeared altogether. Fortunately, however, it was available in full to Russell's first biographer, J. B. Atkins, who quoted from it liberally in his opening chapters. Russell's style in *Retrospect* is impressionistic rather than factual. He gives few dates or details but offers instead a lively picture of his upbringing and the contrasting characters who dominated it. An Irishman by origin and a journalist by profession, he was unlikely, on either count, to let his story suffer from understatement. But he was a fundamentally truthful man too and even less likely to distort or misrepresent the facts to any serious extent.

His earliest memories were of the time when he lived at Lily Vale. The background of his mother's family, the Kellys, was one of violent action, sometimes with the British army, sometimes in insurrectionary action against it. One ancestor, Major Felix Kelly, had been 'killed in the Low Countries'. Another, a grand-uncle, had been hanged as a rebel on the bridge at Wexford when General Lake won the battle of Vinegar Hill in 1798.

When the young William Howard Russell joined the household in 1824 or thereabouts its central figure was his grandfather, Captain Jack Kelly, who was passionately devoted to fox hunting. More than seventy years later Russell remembered him as 'a handsome grey-haired man, red-faced, with a pig-tail, top boots, yellow waistcoat, blue cut-away coat and brass or gilt buttons'. (3) Russell never learned what his grandfather had been a captain of, but there was no doubt what he was Master of—the Tallaght pack of fox-hounds:

All my early memories relate to hounds, horses and hunting: there were hounds all over the place, horses in the fields and men on horseback, galloping, blowing of horns, cracking of whips, tallyho-ing, yoicksing and general uproar. If the weather was fine on a hunting morning, Capt. Jack was in fine spirits. His voice could be heard above the tumult outside the house, front and rear, as he sang:—

Tally ho, my boys! These are the joys
That far exceed the delights of the doxies!
Hark to those hounds! Hark to those sounds!
The huntsman is on before with the hounds. (4)

The Captain was 'a severe Catholic' but the boy's spiritual guidance was left to the women of the house:

I was taught my prayer and rudimentary spelling by my grandmother Kelly. I was also taught to cross myself and pray to the Virgin. I was taken to Mass and could prattle Paternosters and Ave Marias. I had been baptised as a Protestant, yet I was started with every chance of running in the race of life as a Roman Catholic. (5)

But once again a financial crisis changed the course of his life. Captain Kelly's neglect of his farm during the hunting season and a drop in livestock prices created a situation so desperate that the boy's belongings were packed up once more and he was moved, despite the danger to his soul, to No. 40 Upper Baggot Street, the Dublin home of his paternal and very Protestant grandparents.

Russell does not say how old he was when the move was made but he was probably six or seven. He spent the rest of his childhood and the whole of his adolescence at Upper Baggot Street, and his adult character owed more, in manner and attitudes, to the Protestant influence than to the Catholic.

A high proportion of the Russells and their friends were clerics of the Church of Ireland or related sects:

My grandfather William Russell in Dublin was very different from the tenant of Lily Vale. He was lame, but withal very active and alert; a short, stout, silver-haired, ruddy-cheeked man, clean-shaven and bright-eyed, with a stentorian voice and quick temper which flamed out like gunpowder when the gout was in possession and his 'leg was bad'. . . . There was no fiercer man in politics or religion. He had been a Moravian [a Protestant sect noted for austerity and missionary zeal], but my grandmother made a condition that he should adjure that belief as she did not approve of the 'kiss of peace to sisters in the faith'; so he established a chapel, in which he was his own Pope. He was not altogether cut off from the Church of Ireland. (6)

The chief activities of Mr Russell's sect were the abuse of Papists and the support of the Protestant ascendancy. The tone of the house was serious and sober, and the boy was taught to respect the Puritan virtues—honesty and reliability, hard work and self-control, propriety in behaviour and the courage to stand by his beliefs. It must have been a shock to move so suddenly from Lily Vale to Upper Baggot Street but the new life was far from being joyless. The house looked towards the sea and was close to meadows, hills and woods. The boy spent long hours exploring the countryside, fishing the streams and shooting small game. He watched his clerical relatives—'long, lean gentlemen in knee breeches and black gaiters, frock coats and shovel hats' (7)—practising with boomerangs in a nearby field. He was introduced to the worlds of literature and learning.

A near neighbour for a while was the poet Mrs Hemans* who became, with her sons—she was already separated from her husband—a regular visitor:

> She wore robes of a classical type, and to me there was something very stately and imposing in her slow, measured steps, her eyes which were bright and sad, her sweet smile and her gentle voice. And what touched me most was the superiority of the children—the youngest a little older than I was. It was first brought home to me by their mother; she was reading for us the life of Spagnoletto out of 'Triumphs of Genius and Perseverance,' and she asked: 'Willie, what is genius?' I had not the least idea, but I fancied it must have some connection with another book 'Tales of the Genii.' I dared not say so. 'And what is perseverance?' Silence. 'Now, boys, what do you say?' They appeared to know all about it. And I could not tell what a 'substantive' or an 'adjective' was. One of the boys played the guitar and sang, another drew trees and houses and animals, and a third wrote in a book 'things out of his head.' They said French lessons and German lessons, and were learning Latin, botany, history and geography. (8)

By the time he was nine, though, Billy Russell had acquired some social accomplishments. When the Hemans family were leaving the district his rendering of 'Love not, love not, the thing you love may die' moved the impressionable lady to sobs.

His first school was Miss Steadman's Day School for Young Ladies which apparently found room for a few boys as well. He moved on to the Reverend Richard H. Wall's school in Hume Street. Its prospectus claimed a remarkably wide-ranging education but Russell remembered it only for the regular beatings he was given by a sadistic teacher. Within the year he moved again, this time to the Reverend E. J. Geoghegan's school which was also in Hume Street. He spent the rest of his schooldays there, six years or so as a day boy, and never ceased to be grateful for the experience: 'In that house I spent some of the happiest years of my life, and assuredly it was my own fault that I didn't turn to good account the teaching of one of the kindest of friends and most indulgent of masters. How deeply I am indebted to that just, considerate and inflexible man, perhaps I do not, with all my gratitude, understand.' (9)

There was corporal punishment here too—what was called 'pandying', a beating on the hands with a cane or strap—and a good deal of violence outside the classroom as well. His memories of his schooldays were much concerned with fighting: 'St. Stephen's Green was the great battlefield of the schools—Wall's, Huddart's, Geoghegan's etc.—in those days. Black eyes were as plentiful as blackberries, and I had my share.' (10)

---

* Felicia Dorothy Hemans (Hemans (1793–1835) wrote verse which was widely popular in her day, especially in America. She is remembered now only for the opening lines of *Casabianca*—'The boy stood on the burning deck . . .'

He showed an early interest in the military life:

I was always very fond of soldiering, and used to get up early and set off from
our house in Baggot Street to watch the drills in the mornings at the Biggar's
Bush Barracks. I used to get cartridges from the soldiers which caused my
people much annoyance. Yet not so much as they did the old watchman in his
box at the corner of Baggot Street. We found him asleep one night,
discharged a shot or two inside, and pitched him and his box over into the
canal. He escaped, but we did not, for we caught it severely and deserved it.
(11)

In 1835 when Sir George de Lacy Evans was raising a force to go to Spain and
fight for Queen Isabella against the Carlists, Russell pleaded to be allowed to
enlist. It was in vain. He was to spend many years of his life marching with armies,
but this was his only attempt to join one.

Towards the end of his life Russell gave one or two reminiscent hints in his
diary that tenderer feelings were also stirred at this time, particularly by one of the
headmaster's daughters, 'a little pretty ringletted child I used to love to see waiting
for me as I trotted in at the schoolroom door in Hume Street': 'She was a phantom
of delight as a child of ten when she sat on the stairs at No. 8 Hume Street to see
me come to school, *aetatis* nine. And we exchanged kisses.' (12)

Among the boys at the school were some who became life-long friends. One of
them, Henry de Bathe, was to become a general. Another, Obé Willans, became
a colonel in the Army Pay Department and helped Russell for many years by
keeping his financial affairs in order. Almost exactly contemporary with Russell
was a boy called Dion Boucicault who was to become a leading and formative
figure in the Victorian theatre.* Russell remembered him as 'a very cantankerous
boy though unquestionably plucky. I remember he fought a big fellow named
Barton . . . with one arm tied behind his back, and took a licking gallantly. He was
always considered a gallant fellow; but oh how he used to romance.' (13)

The education which Dr Geoghegan instilled was broad and intensive. The
boys were given a firm grounding in the ancient languages and their literatures,
some knowledge of science and mathematics, geography and history, and
sufficient introduction to modern languages to make it a comparatively simple
matter for Russell to master conversational French, German and Italian in later
life. Most important of all from Russell's point of view, they were drilled in the
disciplines of their own language. Russell was naturally articulate, even voluble.

---

* Dionysius Lardner Boucicault (1820–90) was a skilful adapter of other men's work for the stage, an
actor-manager, an inventive producer and a clever dramatist. His best-known plays, still occasionally
revived, are *London Assurance* (1841) and *The Shaughraun* (1875). Like Russell, he was unsure of the
year of his birth but his latest biographer, Richard Fawkes, has little doubt that it was 1820.

The flow of words and images came to his mind with an ease that might have been dangerous had it not been controlled. But Dr Geoghegan imparted the laws of the English language so successfully that it became almost impossible for Russell to write an ungrammatical sentence. He wrote many millions of words in his career—often at speed and in distracting circumstances, sometimes when he was ill or exhausted—yet there is scarcely a sentence, even among the hastily-scrawled entries in his diaries, that is incomplete or unclear in meaning.

At school he read the classics of Greek, Latin and English literature—Dr Geoghegan was the editor of textbook editions of Xenophon and Caesar and Alvarez's *Prosody*. At home his reading was mainly devotional. About the time of his sixteenth birthday he discovered, by chance, the delights of the moderns. Charles Dickens' first major work *The Posthumous Papers of the Pickwick Club* began to appear in monthly numbers at one shilling each in the spring of 1836. Russell's eye was caught by the sporting scene on the cover of the first issue:

> I bought the number in full confidence that it related to sport, angling etc., and was disappointed to find that it was what appeared to me at first glimpse a foolish story, 'The Theory of Tittlebats,' 'The Pond at Hampstead' and so on. It was a shilling lost. But I carried my book to a bench in St. Stephen's Green for further examination. In five minutes a new world was open to me. (14)

He had already made his own first modest venture into print. More than sixty years later he described the incident for a reporter from a Dublin newspaper:

> I, then a boy of 15, was out shooting larks in the stubble. I brought home a miscellaneous collection, and my grandfather picked out one lark with a large tuft, which I had remarked when I picked it up, and asked if it was among the other larks. He told me to take it to a Mr. Colville, a member of the Royal Dublin Society, to whom I was accustomed to take any birds I did not know, and he immediately declared it was a crested lark. He got down a volume of Buffon, illustrated, and with the plate compared my bird and found it identical with the *Alauda cristata*. I made a tracing of the bird and filled it in, and sent it to the *Dublin Penny Journal*. I can remember my pride and pleasure at seeing the reproduction. (15)

His sketch of the bird, accompanied by a short account of where he found it, what it looked like and his researches into its identity, made minor ornithological history. The bird is rarely seen anywhere in the British Isles but it was, on the sole strength of Russell's evidence, admitted to the Irish list by more than one authority. Whether it was in fact a crested lark or some misleading deviant must remain forever in doubt. Its identification can neither be proved nor disproved. When the Dublin reporter asked Russell what had become of the specimen, he got the reply, 'We probably ate him.'

It was intended all along that he would go on from school to study at Trinity College, Dublin, a stronghold of the Protestant ascendancy. When he was seventeen, though, his Russell grandfather died, leaving very little money and none at all for Billy. Other possible sources proved equally disappointing: 'My aunt Stanistreet,' he wrote, 'left me a sum of money in her will, but it could never be found anywhere else.' (16) The college career was threatened. He had an anxious summer working as a tutor in County Leitrim and studying for the college examination. He won admission but not a scholarship. The family rallied round and somehow the money was found for his continued education. Judging from Russell's account of his student days, it seems doubtful whether they got their money's worth:

> I entered Trinity College in 1838. . . . There were glorious doings during
> election times, when the Trinity College students—who were mostly
> Orangemen—met the Roman Catholics and engaged them in battle; but, alas!
> they were tyrannous and strong. The coal porters were there—'the descendants
> of the Irish Kings from the coal quay', as Daniel O'Connell called them, and
> sometimes we had to seek safety at the college gates. Sometimes we had it all
> our own way, and made the most of it. Away we would go to King William's
> statue on College Green, shouting 'Down with the Pope! Down with the
> Pope!' . . . We frequently parted with broken heads. We were often triumphant,
> though. (17)

This is the only description Russell left of his life as a student. He had no particular plans for the future. There was some idea that he might read for the Bar. There were hopes that he might be awarded a Fellowship by the college. One of his cousins, a surgeon in the army, tried to interest him in that as a career but a single visit to a dissecting room was enough to scotch the notion. He was in his third year at the university and still undecided what to do with his life when the immediate problem at least was settled for him.

The story can be pieced together from scattered notes in a later diary. (18) At the beginning of 1841 he was in Liverpool, presumably paying a New Year visit to his father and brother—his mother, Mary, had died nine months before. On 12 January he noted: 'Sailed at 8 a.m. from Liverpool by the *Medina* and arrived with ten shillings in my pocket in Dublin. Quartered with Robert Russell.' Robert, a cousin, was already working for *The Times* of London. The diary for 14 January records that Russell attended a protest meeting at one of the Dublin theatres, followed by the line: 'My first attempt to report.' Nothing more is known of this first attempt but it looks as if Robert Russell was trying him out as a reporter.

That summer, when a general election was called and *The Times* gave Robert the job of organizing its coverage in Ireland, one of the first things he did was look up his cousin Billy:

He found out where I was and came one night to the third floor No. 17 Botany to make an astounding proposal. He wanted some young fellows to go to various places where the contests promised to be of interest who could write plain trustworthy accounts of what they saw at the Elections. 'You will have a pleasant time of it. Letters to the best people—a guinea a day and your hotel expenses. Will you go next week?' The prospect of such a plunge into a world of which I knew so little was entrancing. I did not hesitate for a moment. (19)

Although he took the decision without thinking, it was a key moment in Russell's life. He enjoyed the reporting work and was pleased to find he had some aptitude for it. Even so, it was only a temporary job and when the election was over he was still far from sure that the reporter's life was the one for him. But he did not return to Trinity College to complete his course and take a degree, and though he tried his hand at more than one profession in the next few years, he was unable to stick at any of them for long. It took him some time to realize it but he had already found his *métier*.

He was twenty-one years old and his basic character was formed.

By all the shibboleths of twentieth-century psychology, it was a disastrous upbringing: born into a family that was religiously divided and financially insecure; his mother so remote and shadowy a figure that she is hardly mentioned in his autobiographical writings and never with any hint of affection; an ineffectual father, confirmed in failure; from the arms of these parents 'untimely ripp'd' at an early age to be moved between grandparents who had nothing in common beyond the intensity of their conflicting faiths and their determination to infect him with their own bigotries; an education attended throughout by violence, in the classroom and in the streets; and all this in a country which was riven by discord of every kind. It was a background that might have been specifically contrived to turn any normally sensitive boy into an embittered zealot with strong destructive tendencies.

Yet with Billy Russell it did nothing of the kind. In fact, he emerged from it all unusually well-balanced and sensible. Physically he was of medium height and sturdy build, inclined to overweight but with impressive reserves of strength. His character was extrovert and sociable. He inherited his father's natural cheerfulness and something of his grandfather Russell's quick temper. From his mother's side of the family he derived a relish for the eccentricities and absurdities of human behaviour and a love of country pursuits. Good-natured, generous and affection-ate, direct and open in manner, he could get along well with men of all kinds and classes even those with whom he wholeheartedly disagreed. There was no rancour or malice in his nature though he could be fierce if he thought his honour impugned.

At school and college in Dublin he had not distinguished himself either as a scholar or as a sportsman. For a man who was to make himself eminent by his pen he did remarkably little writing in his formative years. If there were any youthful literary endeavours, he successfully destroyed all traces of them. They are unlikely to have had any great merit. Russell had no talent for imaginative writing; he was not of the cast of mind that can tease out a line of thought or fantasy and make it fascinating. He needed reality to work from, pictures from life and preferably events of drama and colour. Given these and the chance to describe them while the impression was still fresh on his mind he was in his element.

In the summer of 1841 the chance came.

3

'Mr. Russell of The Times'

R ussell was excited at the prospect of reporting the election in Ireland:

> It seemed as if that day would never come when I was to take my place on the box of the mail for Longford, where Mr. Lefroy was to fight the battle of the Constitution, church and state etc. against the powers of darkness. To hear my name as 'Mr. Russell of *The Times*' pronounced by an anxious agent as the coach pulled up at Sutcliffe's Hotel in the dirty dismal little town, this indeed was fame! (1)

The 1841 general election was called for entirely English reasons, chiefly because of growing pressure for the repeal of the Corn Laws which protected English farming and kept the price of bread artificially high for everyone by imposing duties on imported corn. The issue was of no concern to the Irish, whose staple was the potato and who had vital interests of their own to pursue.

Things had been generally quiet in Ireland since the passing of the Emancipation Act in 1829 which finally made it possible for Roman Catholics to become judges, army officers and Members of Parliament. The Act was a triumph for Daniel O'Connell and his policy of pursuing his ends by mobilizing and demonstrating the strength of Irish feeling without resort to violence or illegal activities of any kind. During the 1830s successive Whig administrations were careful to do nothing provocative and to consult O'Connell regularly. By the end of the decade, however, it was clear that the period of Whig rule was nearly over and the Catholics knew they could expect no concessions from a Tory government unless they could exert enormous pressure. O'Connell began to organize his next great campaign through the National Loyal Repeal Association, whose aim was the repeal of the Act of Union—independence for Ireland. The movement was under way in 1841 but not sufficiently established to play an active role in the election. Ireland returned one hundred members to the House of Commons in Westminster but, despite the extended franchise of the Reform Act, most Catholics were too poor to qualify to vote. Those who had the vote would naturally support Whig candidates. The rest would do what they could to discourage the Tories and make things awkward for the authorities.

Russell's sympathies lay firmly with the Tories: 'Of political principles I had none except a vague attachment to the Orangeism of Baggot Street which represented Protestant ascendancy in Church and State, the "Glorious Pious Immortal Memory", and a prompt participation in any rows with Repeal mobs and the coal porters.' (2)

The town of Longford, where he was sent first, lies in the centre of Ireland. Some of the events he saw there may have reminded him of the comic election at Eatanswill in *The Pickwick Papers;* others were more like the scenes of war he was to see so often in later life. For a man who was to be a war correspondent, it was an appropriate introduction to his craft.

He arrived at Longford on a July evening in 1841 and was made welcome by the Tory candidate, Mr Lefroy, and his lieutenants. He sat through a long dinner and longer speeches, and was 'blooded' in the cause when a paving stone 'the size of a penny roll' crashed through the window behind him and hit him on the back of the head. The Tories, Russell among them, rushed out to the street to disperse their attackers, then adjourned for further drinking and smoking and speech-making: 'Before the night was over I found myself clouded with tobacoo smoke and reeking with whisky punch, addressing a convivial assemblage about Magna Charta (an eminently Protestant document!), the Bill of Rights, the Defence of Derry, the Inquisition, the Barn of Scullabogue,* Peter Dens' theology.† What a headache I had in the morning!' (3)

There was much fighting on the outskirts of the town that night and Russell's task next morning, despite his headache, was to piece together some account of the action. He was particularly proud of the way he solved the problem: 'my Irish wit told me that in an Irish Election most of the free and independent electors generally had to come to hospital. So I sat there until they all came in to get their heads bandaged, and so I got quite a dramatic account of it all.' (4)

He sent his first report to *The Times* on Thursday 15 July and it appeared in the paper five days later among a number of Irish election stories. Under the modest heading 'Longford (County)' with the by-line '(From our own reporter)', it illustrates the partisan ferocity of his prentice work to the full:

> I have this moment returned from a visit to the Infirmary and never was I more affected than I was by the horrid sights I witnessed there. With countenances crushed and bruised out of all the lineaments of humanity and bathed in blood are lying a number of poor fellows, some of whom it is to be feared are fast

---

* More than two hundred Protestants were said to have been killed in the Barn during the Wexford rebellion of 1798.

† The extremist writings of Peter Dens—reputed to be a Catholic theologian though some Catholic bishops disavowed him—had been circulated to stir up Protestant anger.

hastening to another world. One or two of these suffered in the town but the greater number were attacked on their way home. . . .

To the scenes of violence I have already witnessed I regret to say that I have to record an atrocious attack made this day upon a harmless young gentleman named King, who while standing near his own house in the middle of the day not twenty yards from the barracks and within a hundred yards of an immense force of military and police was attacked by a number of pitiless miscreants, beaten, trampled under foot and left helpless on the road. He is now, or rather his inanimate body is lying in the Infirmary, his life despaired of. This is the manner in which these sanguinary ruffians have carried out the principles of their revered pastors' admonitions. How much have those pastors to answer for, what a sea of blood lies at their door!

The report goes on to abuse a Church of Ireland Dean for voting for the Whigs and to accuse Whig voters of taking bribes. Russell left his readers in no doubt which side he was on: 'It being extremely dangerous to leave the parts of the streets lined with the military,' he wrote, 'I cannot procure accurate information as to the state of the suburbs; in fact, I have been warned that I am a marked man.'

Though the final note is reminiscent of the brasher reaches of twentieth-century journalism, the partisanship of the account rings shockingly in modern ears. There was nothing shocking or even unusual about it at the time. Men read the papers to have their prejudices reinforced and their feelings stirred, and journalists were expected to express themselves forcefully. The news columns of the papers reflected opinion as openly and powerfully as the leading articles. The high-minded notion that news should be given impartially and kept clearly separate from comment, which C. P. Scott propounded in the *Manchester Guardian* eighty years later, weighed no more with the British journalist of the 1840s than it has with most journalists at any time. Throughout his career, in fact, Russell never hesitated to let his views and feelings show through his reports, though they were never again expressed quite so ferociously as in his first despatches.

At any rate *The Times* entirely approved. The paper had a new editor, John Thadeus Delane, but he was still feeling his way into the job and effective control lay with the experienced Chief Proprietor, John Walter II, who took a keen and passionately anti-Catholic interest in Irish affairs.

The Times was prompt with its praise. Russell remembered: 'It would be impossible to describe my delight when by next post came a letter from Robert Russell—"Your work is capital—a most effective description." But that was nothing to my feelings when *The Times* (24 July) appeared with a leader on my burning words.' (5) In fact the leader dealt with the whole of what it called 'the sanguinary and shocking . . . election conspiracy in Ireland', but it quoted generously from Russell's Longford report and concluded:

To details like these we can add nothing. Any attempt to embellish or exaggerate such facts would be to weaken their effect. We will not be guilty of thus distorting or diluting the truth. We will not fritter away the strength of the most scandalous enormity that ever defiled the law and disgraced the government of a country pretending to civilisation.

Russell was ordered to Carlow 'where a great fight was expected' but his departure was delayed: 'my career was very nearly ended that same night. As I was crossing the street to Sutcliffe's between two lines of policemen, a mob charged down on the barrier. I turned to see what was the matter and received a kick which sent me flying, as if from a catapult, into the Hotel. I was put to bed and "fomented".' (6) The quotation comes from the autobiography which Russell hoped to publish. His diary was not so delicate: 'JULY 18 Suffering great pain from kick in scrotum which led to swollen testicle.' Many years later he added another line: 'Now if that kick had been a little stronger I might have been spared all family afflictions.'

He was soon on the road again:

... flying from one election to the other. . . . At Athlone I had a horrible experience. The Tory candidate, Major Beresford, was at Ally Gray's where I put up also. As I was speaking to him and to County Inspector Colclough a multitude of women, old, middle-aged and young, screaming and yelling came upon us. I was seized as by a shoal of octupuses, receiving slaps and scratches and spiteful kisses, the wretches spitting on me as they dragged me towards the bridge to 'give him a shiver in the Shannon'. A party of police rescued me, but I was in such a state that it was necessary to be 'wiped down' like a horse in the stableyard ere I could go to my rooms to change my clothes. (7)

It was rough work but Russell enjoyed it: 'I threw neutrality to the winds, plunged into the excitement of these contests with the greatest ardour, and kicks and blows . . . stimulated my energies. I was elated by the praise and comforted by the prospects that were opened before me.' (8) There was the money too—£4 a week plus expenses: 'I revelled in riches which seemed to me inexhaustible,' he said.

The experience unsettled him. When the election was over he abandoned all thoughts of trying for a Trinity Fellowship, which would have afforded him free board and lodging and £40 a year, and went to Printing House Square in London to discuss his future with the treasurer of *The Times*, W. F. A. Delane:*

---

* William Frederick Augustus Delane had managed the financial affairs of *The Times* since 1831. He left the paper in 1847 when irregularities came to light in the way the accounts had been kept, though there was no suggestion of dishonesty, and became manager of the *Morning Chronicle*. He had nine children, the second of whom was John Thadeus Delane, editor of *The Times* from 1841 to 1877.

He asked me friendly questions about my plans and prospects. I told him frankly how I was situated, all my hopes and fears, that I wished to take my degree and be called to the Bar etc., but that I could not live without working. He suggested that I should transfer myself bodily to London, get a transfer *ad eundem in statu pupillari* to Caius College, Cambridge, and hold myself at the disposal of *The Times* which had need of a young gentleman with my readiness and knowledge of Ireland, but he did not make any definite proposal. (9)

It was a characteristically cautious offer but Russell found it attractive enough to induce him to leave Dublin which had been his home almost all his life and move to London which was to be his home for the rest of his life. He took lodgings in Great College Street, Westminster, and almost immediately fell seriously ill with pleurisy. When the danger was past an old family friend arranged a convalescent cruise for him along the coasts of Portugal and Spain to Gibraltar.

He returned to London to join his cousin Robert in comfortable rooms at No. 3 Plowden Buildings. He went to Cambridge to organize his transfer to Caius but decided, with shrewd self-knowledge, that life by the Cam would be too dangerous: 'I saw temptations to expense I might be unable to resist, and if I yielded the result would be ruinous. I knew that I was not apt to resist.' (10)

So he went back again to London where Robert Russell, who was now on *The Times* Parliamentary staff, encouraged him to opt for a journalistic career: 'You have only to learn shorthand,' he told him, 'study composition and style, and send in articles to papers and magazines regardless of rejection. If you put your heart and soul into it, I am certain you will do well; you can keep your terms and go to the Bar just the same.' (11)

He took the advice which was reinforced by a letter from Dr Geoghegan, his old headmaster:

January 8th, 1842

My dear Russell,

You tell me that you are looking for a situation as reporter to a newspaper, and it seems to me that you have hit upon the very thing for which you are best fitted. You possess, I know, a good store of classical and general information, which united to suitable natural talents and quickness of perception, ought to make you a first-rate person in that department of literary labour. I hope sincerely that you may succeed in obtaining the object of your wishes, and if my testimony as to your qualifications for the office can be of the least service to you you may command it at any time, for I could say with perfect truth that I believe you to possess the very qualities requisite to form a good reporter. (12)

Russell applied himself assiduously to the task:

In 3 Plowden Buildings I found rest, quiet, books—I practised shorthand, attended lectures, busied myself in composition—wrote tales, essays, a poem and a play, but none of my productions ever saw print, except some sketches in the *Sporting Magazine*. Occasionally Delane asked me to describe some meeting or pageant or dinner for which I received a few guineas. It was a miserable year, and yet I was not unhappy. Indeed my cousin upbraided me for my cheerfulness. (13)

The Delane he was dealing with now was John Thadeus Delane, recently appointed editor of *The Times* at the age of twenty-three. John Walter's choice of Delane, who had worked less than a year on the paper, was bolder than his appointment of Thomas Barnes had been and even more successful. Barnes had built the paper up into the most popular and influential daily not only in Britain but in the whole of Europe. By 1841 its circulation had risen to 20,000 copies a day, more than double that of all its London rivals added together. When Barnes died Charles Greville, Clerk of the Council and a tireless observer of the political scene, had written in his diary: 'The vast power exercised by *The Times* renders this a most important event, and it will be curious to see in what hands the regulating and directing power will hereafter be placed.' (14)

Delane had read Classics at Magdalen Hall, Oxford, taken his degree in 1839 and joined *The Times* in July 1840. Ten months later he became editor. He held the post for more than thirty-six years and was arguably the best editor any British newspaper has ever had—quick in apprehension, generally sound in judgement, the centre of a network of highly-placed informants, shrewd in choosing men and adept in handling them, totally dedicated to the paper. 'No-one,' Russell wrote, 'has seen so many sunrises in London as Delane; he takes a pure delight in walking out of Printing House Square to Blackfriars Bridge and looking at London in the early morning. Then he saunters to his house in Serjeant's Inn and settles down to rest, having first sent off all the necessary letters to leader-writers and reporters.' (15)

It was only occasionally during 1842 that Delane could find work for Russell and he was very short of money. But he was one of those for whom cheerfulness was always breaking through. Some of his Dublin friends were now in London, the circle extended and they had a sociable time. Russell worked for one term as mathematics teacher at Kensington Grammar School but his real interest —judging from his memoirs—centred on his night life among the clubs and taverns of Covent Garden and St Martin's Lane: 'We used to adjourn for supper at the Cock, and finally I would set out for Kensington just as the sun was rising. I do not care to remember how often I repeated that morning walk.' (16)

Towards the end of the year, when he had achieved the required shorthand speed, Delane offered him work on a more regular basis as a Parliamentary reporter. It was not as exciting as the Irish elections but there were impressive precedents—Delane had worked briefly in the Press Gallery, Charles Dickens was there ten years before, and, in the previous century, no less a figure than Samuel Johnson—and it enabled Russell to study the workings of the Commons at a tim when the House was under the businesslike management of Sir Robert Peel. If it sometimes seemed very like drudgery to Russell it gave him training in the basic skills of his craft, accuracy and speed.

He mastered the work quickly and felt confident enough within a few months to ask for a rise. Delane's diplomatic reply is the first surviving letter of their long correspondence:

My dear Sir,
 After giving your letter all consideration, and without at all detracting from the merit you justly claim for your zealous services, we are of the opinion that we cannot in justice to your colleagues make a permanent addition to your present salary. In acknowledgement, however, of the zeal and ability you have displayed during the recess, I have the pleasure to request your acceptance of the enclosed cheque.
Believe me ever,
Yours faithfully,
John T. Delane. (17)

In the autumn of 1843 Russell was sent back to Ireland where events were moving towards another crisis. Peel had made it clear that the Act of Union would never be repealed under his government. O'Connell, idolized by the Irish as 'The Liberator', organized a massive reply to the man he derided as 'Orange Peel'. The Repeal Association held open meetings—at Cork in May, Clare in June, Tara in August—and hundreds of thousands gathered to hear O'Connell speak and to sign the petition for Ireland's independence. Receipts from subscriptions—at a penny per month per member—rose from £680 a week in May to £2,200 in June. The Orange authorities were disturbed by the size of the movement and even more by its legality. For a few remarkable months agrarian outrages and crime and even drunkenness almost disappeared, and the Lord Chancellor of Ireland was moved to remark that 'the peaceable demeanour of the assembled multitudes is one of the most alarming symptoms'.

The Times was against repeal and so, too, was Russell though he found himself, for all his Orange sympathies, highly impressed by the new movement. He was at Leinster for a great meeting at the Rath of Mullaghmast and two days later his report, one and a half columns long, appeared in the paper, describing O'Connell's triumphant progress through the countryside and giving a full account of his speech and its rapturous reception. Decades later, writing *Retrospect*, he remembered it vividly:

The scene at the first 'monster' meeting I attended was one never to be forgotten. It was at the Rath of Mullaghmast, where tradition had it that a treacherous slaughter of the Irish was perpetrated in the reign of Elizabeth. O'Connell made the most of the story, revelling in details. He described a massacre—which was, he said, perpetrated by Cromwell, when 300 women were slaughtered round the Cross of Christ in Wexford—with dramatic power beyond compare. 'They prayed to Heaven for mercy! he exclaimed. 'I trust they found it! They prayed to the English for pity, and Cromwell slaughtered them! We were a paltry remnant then! We are millions now!' The men yelled, and danced with rage; the women screamed and clapped their hands. The vast multitude—I believe there were really 100,000 present—moved and moaned like a wild beast in agony.

I have never heard any orator who made so great an impression on me as O'Connell. It was not his argument, for it was often worthless, nor his language, which was frequently inelegant. It was his immense passion, his pathos, his fiery indignation. At first sight one was tempted to laugh at the green cloth cap with the broad gold band set on top of his curly wig—his round chin buried deep in the collar of a remarkable compromise between a travelling cloak and a frock, green and ornamented with large gilt buttons; but when he rose to speak with imperious and imperial gesture for silence, and was 'off,' in a few minutes the spell began to work, the orator was revealed. As a speaker addressing a mob—a meeting of his own countrymen—I do not believe anyone equalled or that anyone will equal O'Connell. (18)

The reporter's job was not as dangerous as Russell had found it during the elections two years before, but it was difficult enough:

It was no unusual experience for the 'press gang', as O'Connell called the editors and reporters, to travel to and fro between the meetings and their offices by hack cars, post chaises and the like, and to write out their notes as they were jolted along as best they might, and some of the bills I sent in to *The Times* afforded curious illustration of the straits we were put to. (19)

O'Connell was unfailingly polite to Russell: '"Let Mr. Russell past, boys!" he would call out. "He is no relation of Lord John.* The young gentleman, I daresay, does not like being a *Times*-server after all."' (20) Russell, in his turn, warmed towards the repealers as people though he could not approve their principles: 'When I found myself amid avowed "disunionists", Repealers and Roman Catholics, I felt at first very much, I suppose, as a Puritan would have done in the company of Malignants; but after a while I made them out to be, apart from politics, as pleasant as other people; though I could not for some time get over the shock of seeing Protestants or non-Catholics . . . cheering in the wake of the Liberator's car.' (21)

---

* Lord John Russell (1792–1878) was the leader of the Whigs by this time, having steered the first Reform Bill through the House of Commons. He was Prime Minister twice and held several other high government offices.

On one occasion, when Russell's coach broke down on the road from Athlone to Dublin, O'Connell made one of his lieutenants travel outside his carriage so that Russell could sit inside:

> It was a very interesting journey; one perpetual hurray from the fields, from the streets mile after mile; men, women and children cutting turf and digging potatoes—no matter what they were doing—rushed off to the roadside to see O'Connell and to cheer for Repeal; priests and farmers in every town thronged round the coach if it halted for a moment to shake hands with him, and when we got to Dublin too late to think of getting to Kingstown for the mail boat, O'Connell said, 'Now come in to dinner. You can do nothing more. You won't mind our coachload sitting down without dressing for it after we have washed our hands.' And it was a very pleasant and excellent dinner, though I was a veritable fly in amber to company. (22)

But admiration and even liking for its leader did not convert Russell to repeal. Nor did the fact that he spent much time among the repealers inhibit him from the plain expression of his views in his reports. On 2 October 1843 he sent an article to *The Times* about a mass meeting planned for Clontarf on the northern outskirts of Dublin the following Sunday:

> A second metropolitan monster meeting, which threatens to be a far more formidable display of physical force than the comparatively harmless display at Donnybrook last summer, is to be held under the very nose of the executive authorities, who will no doubt rest perfectly satisfied with playing the parish constable, waiting for the blow to be struck ere the spirit shall move him to take the offender into custody. (23)

But he was wrong. The authorities were poised to act. The army garrison in Ireland had been strengthened to 35,000 men. On Saturday the Lord-Lieutenant issued a proclamation forbidding the Clontarf meeting. Next morning there was a formidable force of soldiers in the area, including the 11th Hussars and their contentious commanding officer, Lord Cardigan, whom Russell was to see in action at Balaclava eleven years later.* Trouble was averted when O'Connell, anxious to preserve the peaceful reputation of his movement, ordered his supporters to disperse quietly and they obeyed.

The Times was delighted: 'We rejoice at this unhoped-for display of Ministerial vigour'. (24) A few days later O'Connell and five of his lieutenants were arrested and charged with seditious conspiracy.

The Times took the trial very seriously—John Walter's anti-Catholic feelings saw to that. Russell was retained in Dublin to send daily reports of the proceedings,

---

* Lord Cardigan had already offered to arrest O'Connell. 'Leave him to me,' he is said to have told the Duke of Wellington, the army's Commander-in-Chief, 'and I'll nab him at the outset. My life on it!' The offer was declined.

and elaborate measures were taken to make sure the paper would be first with the result. There was a proud tradition to be maintained in this respect. Since the early days of Barnes' editorship it had been accepted that *The Times* would get any vital news not only ahead of its rival papers but often ahead of the government too. Now a special train was kept in readiness at Westland Row in Dublin; a steamship, the *Iron Duke*, lay in Kingstown Harbour with her steam up; and there was another special train at Holyhead for the run to London. The *Morning Herald*, the chief rival, had a steam yacht waiting at Kingstown.

They all had to wait a long time. Though its outcome was not in doubt, the trial went on for twenty-three days. There were six accused and many counts against each of them and the lawyers and jurymen took full advantage of the opportunities for confusion. It was not until late in the afternoon of Saturday, 10 February 1844 that the jury finally retired. A few hours later they filed back but only to seek clarification on certain points of law. Then they returned again, this time to seek clarification of the clarification. It was well after midnight when the verdicts were pronounced and Russell was able to set off on the race to London:

At Westland Row there was a delay. They had given up any expectation of the train being needed. The steam was blown off, the engineer had gone off to sleep or to beer, but at last the express rattled out of the dirty suburb and the whistles of the engine soon were disturbing the curlew and barnacle on the shore at Booterstown. I stepped out on the platform at Kingstown with all my baggage, a large note-book full of caricatures and facetiae, notes and observations, and a light overcoat in my hand. There was no one to receive me at the station—no boat at the stairs; but one of the police on the quay showed me the lights of the *Iron Duke*. The harbour was soon vocal with that name, '*Iron Duke*,' and many 'Ahoys,' till just as I sank into hoarse silence a lantern was waved over the counter and an 'Aye, aye' came shorewards over the water. Presently a boat came off for me, and as I stepped on deck of the steamer I was received with the remark, 'We gave you up after midnight and banked up, but will be off in less than half an hour.' One way or another an hour was lost ere we left Kingstown Harbour; but the *Iron Duke* made a rapid run across the Channel, and in a few minutes after landing I was on my way to London the bearer of exclusive news to Printing House Square.

I had been sitting all day and night in boots inclined to tightness. I was very tired, and as I tried to get a little sleep in the train, I kicked them off with some difficulty. I was awakened by a voice in my ear. 'Jump out, sir. The cab is waiting—not a minute to lose.' We were at Euston. The man who spoke was the *Times* office messenger. He saw my boots on the floor of the carriage. 'You get in and put them on in the cab! They're in a dreadful state, waiting at the office.' How I did struggle with those boots. It is a most difficult thing to put on a boot in a cab in motion, but I persevered, and got one on in less than half an hour. Then the vehicle stopped in a small square of houses, one side of which was a blaze of lights from top to bottom. The messenger opened the cab door. 'I'll tell the editor you've come,' said he, and vanished through the door, outside which stood some men in their shirt sleeves. As I alighted one of them in my ear said, 'We are very glad to hear they've found O'Connell guilty at last.' I did not reflect—thought it was one of the office people, and answered, 'Oh, yes! All guilty, but on different counts.' And then, with one boot under my arm and my coat over it, I entered the office.

Here I was met by the messenger, 'This way, sir, Mr. Delane is waiting for you. This way!' There were printers at counters in the long room which I now entered, and as I hurried along I was aware that every one of them had his eye on my bootless foot and its white stocking. I passed out of the office through a short corridor. The door of the editor's room opened, and I made my bow to the man who had much to say, I believe, to the leaps and bounds by which the *Times* had become the leading journal of England: a broad-shouldered man with a massive head and chin, square jaws, large full-lipped firm mouth, and keen light luminous eyes. He was shading his face with his hand from the lamp. His first words were, 'Not an accident, I hope?' as he glanced at the unfortunate foot. 'No, sir!' 'Is it all written out?' I handed him my narrative. 'Tell Mr. — to let me have slips as fast as he can! Now, tell me all about the verdict.' And he listened intently. The first slip interrupted us; then came a second and a third, and so on till I sank to sleep in my chair. I was awakened by a hand on my shoulder. The room was empty: only my friend the messenger. The clock marked 4.20. There was a hotel in Fleet Street, to which my guardian messenger sent off a printer's devil to order a room, and to it I drove with my overcoat and boot *pour tout butin*, and slept till noon next day. My waking was not pleasant. A fiery note from the manager: 'You managed very badly. The *Morning Herald* has got the verdict! This must be inquired into.'

It turned out that my pleasant interlocutor at the entrance to the office was an emissary of the enemy. (25)

Next morning, Monday 12 February 1844, *The Times* came out with an almost verbatim account of the final day's proceedings, covering more than fourteen columns, under the heading 'The Verdict—Express from Dublin'. In the manner of the time there was no attempt at an introductory paragraph to outline the main points of the story. It simply gave a chronological report of everything that had been said in court on the Saturday. The story was so long and its legal complications were so tangled and obscure that it must have taken the fullest concentration of the most serious-minded reader to make out what the verdicts had been. Nontheless, *The Times* had the full story and one day ahead of all other London papers.

The fact that the *Morning Herald* had been able to give the main verdict, though no further details, on the Monday morning was not taken lightly at Printing House Square. Russell was summoned to the office of Delane *père* and made to recall every incident and encounter on his journey to London. They soon realized it was Russell's casual remark at the doorway that had given the game away:

> Delane thumped the table. 'The confounded miscreants! But it was sharp of them! And now, my young friend, let me give you a piece of advice. As you have very nearly severed your connection with us by your indiscretion, and as you are likely, if you never repeat it, to be in our service, let me warn you to keep your lips closed and your eyes open. Never speak about your business. Commit it to paper for the editor, and for him alone. We would have given hundreds of pounds to have stopped your few words last night.' (26)

Russell went back to Dublin at the end of May for the delivery of the judgements. O'Connell was sentenced to a year's imprisonment but his appeal to the House of Lords was upheld and he and his lieutenants were free by September. Yet it was a victory, of a kind, for the Dublin establishment. O'Connell was nearly seventy by now and tired and sick. He no longer had the vigour for inspirational leadership and there was no one to take his place. His great constitutional movement for repeal, one of the most hopeful movements in Ireland's troubled history, withered miserably away.

4

Reporter at Large

On one of his visits to Dublin in 1843 Russell became acquainted with a leading family of Catholic repealers, the Burrowes, and among them he met the girl he was to marry. Her great-uncle, Peter Burrowes, had been one of Grattan's companions in the days when Ireland had its own Parliament and was one of the first Catholics to be appointed a judge after the Emancipation Act. The must have been a tolerant family for they gave generous hospitality to Russell even though he was working for the anti-repeal cause:

> I became intimate with the family of this man's [Judge Burrowes'] son, and at the charming house in Leeson Street I made the acquaintance of two daughters of Judge Burrowes' nephew. I became engaged to one of these, Mary Burrowes, and the strangest thing of all was that the relations and friends of the lady who was willing to link her fate with mine did not set their faces resolutely against such a wild and ill-considered match. (1)

The match was unsuitable for more than just the reasons of political and religious discrepancy. Mary Burrowes was nineteen. Russell left no description of her at this time but—reading between the lines of his later letters and diaries—she seems to have been one of those pretty, unassertive, rather helpless young women that men of vigour often find attractive. Russell, four years older, had no paper qualifications, no settled prospects, still no clear idea what his career would be. His work for *The Times* was on a freelance basis and the end of the O'Connell trial meant the end of regular employment. He returned to London, took chambers in the Middle Temple and divided his time between reading for the Bar, doing occasional reports and reviews for Delane and enjoying a full social life. The only fixed thing about his income was that he consistently lived beyond it.

For the next ten years, until the outbreak of the Crimean War in 1854, little is known of the detail of his life. Hardly any of his letters have survived from this period and none of his diaries. Those passages of *Retrospect* that have been spared are largely unrevealing. *The Times*' records, too, are scanty. Yet it was an important time in Russell's life. He married and fathered four children; he did a lot of journalistic work, including his first war reporting; he met many eminent men and made friends with some of them; he completed his law studies and was called to the Bar. The decade was not so much directionless as moving in several directions at once and he was still—at the end of it—by no means certain where he was heading.

In later life he remembered it as a period of parties. 'What a Bohemian I was then!' he recalled in his diary. Most of his friends were struggling young writers and lawyers, short of money but full of *joie de vivre*. And there were forays into more elevated circles. Russell went regularly to Gore House in Kensington where Lady Blessington, the friend of Byron and Count Alfred d'Orsay, gave receptions for leading and not-so-leading authors and artists. At one of these he was introduced to Prince Louis Napoleon,* who had already made two unsuccessful attempts to seize power in France, and the Prince gave him a lift back to town in his brougham and quizzed him closely about *The Times* and the way it was run.

Sometimes Delane sent him tickets for a play and Russell would review it. He became a keen opera-goer and was always proud of the fact that —standing in for a friend who was music critic for *The Observer*—he was the only reviewer in London to acclaim the melodic profusion of a work called *Ernani* by an unknown Italian composer. It was London's first experience of a Verdi opera.

He resumed work as a parliamentary reporter for *The Times* and 'soon acquired the reputation of a very active and clever young journalist'. (2) Delane was sufficiently impressed with his work to put him in charge of the paper's coverage of the House of Commons sub-committees set up in 1845 to assess the claims of rival railway companies and award concessions for new lines.

This was the time of the great railway mania. Everyone realized that railway traffic was expanding and would continue to expand and that this would be gratifyingly reflected in share values and dividends. There was a stampede to invest and a mushrooming of companies clamouring for the rights to lay permanent ways in all directions. Samuel Smiles described the symptoms of the speculation fever:

> A reckless spirit of gambling set in. . . . The mania was not confined to the precincts of the Stock Exchange, but infected all ranks. It embraced merchants and manufacturers, gentry and shopkeepers, clerks in public offices, and loungers at the clubs. . . . Folly and knavery were, for a time, completely in the ascendant. The sharpers of society were let loose, and jobbers and schemers became more and more plentiful. They threw out railway schemes as a lure to catch the unwary. They fed the mania with a constant succession of new projects. The railway papers became loaded with their advertisements. (3)

* Charles Louis Napolean Bonaparte (1808–73), a nephew of Napoleon I, returned to France after the 1848 revolution, was elected President, assumed complete control in 1851 and was proclaimed Emperor Napoleon III the following year.

The daily newspapers, too, began to draw rich revenues from encouraging the mania and printing company prospectuses in their advertising columns. *The Times* was alone among the national dailies in refusing to be swept along by the avalanche. It had built up a high reputation for financial probity and it now denounced the railway press as corrupt, and repeatedly pointed out that most of the would-be investors were doomed to disappointment. A supplement was published proving that the competing railway schemes—there were more than a thousand of them in 1845—presupposed the spending of more money than there was in the whole of the country.

Delane was paying Russell a considerable compliment by putting him in charge of such an important and delicate story. It was a more responsible role than any he had been given so far and it was one for which he was in some ways poorly suited. He was never particularly adept at handling other men's work and he knew little of the complex operations of high finance—he could never even master his own modest finances. And the task was made harder by the physical conditions in which he and his team of reporters had to work. The Palace of Westminster was being rebuilt following the fire ten years before which had destroyed almost everything except Westminster Hall. The sub-committees were housed in temporary out-buildings:

> I have seen the rain streaming in on their honourable heads, and also on the tables at which they were seated in the wooden sheds told off for the sittings. . . . The corridors, the lobbies and approaches to the committee rooms were thronged with a crowd of promoters, witnesses, parliamentary agents, solicitors, engineers, traffic takers. The sheds were packed to suffocation. Counsel who had the reputation for skill in private bills business commanded whatever fees they or their clerks asked. (4)

Delane's orders were clear: 'You will have only one committee to attend personally. You are to read the copy of the other reporters and exercise unlimited and merciless power in dealing with it, suppressing all suspicious adjectives and all statements not connected with actual fact.' (5) He kept a sharp eye on Russell's work from the spring to the autumn of 1845. Two of his notes to Russell have survived:

> The complaint I make against the reports is that occasionally the man will persist in reporting cumulative evidence. It is much better in such cases to state the general purport of the facts to be proved and, if they are not too many, the names of the witnesses called to prove them; but not to give the evidence of each witness separately.
>
> You have been unfortunate in entrusting the most important of the committees—Group X—to the worst man, Mr. Ley. Pray attend it in future yourself and let it have the larger amount of report and closer attention than any of the others. (6)

But Russell had one vital virtue. He was an honest man—an unusual and important quality in such shark-infested corridors. He was surrounded daily by multitudes of men on the make, most of whom would gladly pay for the favourable presentation of their case in the press. Though Delane had increased his pay for the duration of the sub-committees, Russell remained short of cash. But there was no bribing him. It was not long before he was introduced to the 'Railway King', George Hudson. Several times he was invited to dine with the great man at Albert Gate:

> One night *en petit comité*, the Railway King said: 'Will you tell us why you were so down in *The Times* on the Cambridge and Lincoln in Group X? I was told you had a large interest to support there.' I answered: 'If anyone told you I had an interest to the extent of one shilling in that or any other railway in Group X, he told you what was untrue.' 'Dear me,' he said, 'is that so! I am very sorry to hear it, for your sake.' (7)

The railway committees concluded their work towards the end of the year and Russell was sent once more across the Irish Sea. In August *The Times* had appointed what it grandly called its own Irish Commissioner, a barrister, Thomas Campbell Foster, who travelled about Ireland and sent the paper detailed accounts of the social conditions he found. His reports were shocking. He went to Derrynane in County Kerry where O'Connell himself owned an estate and found 'The Liberator's' tenants living in conditions that were deplorable even by Irish standards. When his description was published, O'Connell denounced Foster as the 'villain father of lies . . . a malignant hireling of the infamous *Times*', and maintained his assault so fiercely that Delane thought it would be wise to get a second opinion. Russell was sent to confirm or repudiate Foster's findings:

> Accordingly, I went and saw the place, and found that no partisanship could overpaint the truth. Derrynanebeg was an outrage on civilisation. Cabins reeking with fever exhalations, pigs, poultry, cattle standing deep in the oozy slough, the rafters dripping with smoky slime, children all but naked, women and men in rags. (8)

Russell's continued association with the anti-O'Connell cause did nothing to smooth the path of his love. He had declared his feelings to Mary Burrowes by this time and had not been repudiated. But some members of her family, particularly her elder brother Waldron, had objections to the match. At the end of November 1845 Russell was moved to send a firm letter to his prospective father-in-law:

> Sir,
> . . . A gentleman by birth and education with a character and position which may safely set slander and calumny at defiance, I consider myself in no way

unauthorised to solicit your sanction to my union with your daughter Mary whom I have long esteemed although I did not declare it until very recently. Honourably connected with the leading journal of Europe as Parliamentary reporter I have an income exceeding £400 a year with a propect of an increase, whilst I have every reason to believe that my future career at the Bar may not be profitless. . . .

I feel it is to my most painful and imperative duty to repudiate and denounce the cowardly and insidious attempts which have been made to blast my character as a man of honour and a gentleman. . . . Your eldest son, who sought my friendship and intimacy and abused both, has recently assailed my character in a manner which would be ludicrously contemptible were it not that it was malignant and mischievous . . . I trust you will not refuse me the opportunity of showing that he has been as false to you as he has been to me, and that in no way am I unsuited for the relationship I seek with you, and in that trust,

I subscribe myself,

Your very obedient faithful servant,

W. H. Russell. (9)

The letter shows the pride he took in his connection with *The Times* but he was not starry-eyed about it. He speaks of an income of £400 a year—equal to more than £5,000 in the mid-1970s—but he was still not on the staff, merely hired on short-term contracts for specific tasks. There had grown up a mystique that working for *The Times* was not a job so much as a way of life, akin to membership of some exclusive and dedicated order, implying a prestige that far outweighed any shortcomings in pay. The notion was naturally fostered by the management. But it failed to impress Russell, whose need for ready money was chronic and all the more pressing now he wanted to marry. He had been writing for *The Times* for more than four years and in positions of increasing responsibility. Yet it had failed to offer him what he most needed, the security of a staff appointment. For all his respect and liking for Delane, he felt no special debt of loyalty: 'I was ready to fight,' he said, 'for the side which paid me the highest salary.' (10)

He was well known in the London newspaper world, and the offers came. His cousin Robert had left *The Times* to join the team which Charles Dickens was recruiting to launch his new paper, the *Daily News*. Russell was offered seven guineas a week to join them. Then an established daily, the *Morning Chronicle*, offered him a staff job at nine guineas a week. He wrote to Delane to say he was going to the *Chronicle*. Delane replied with the hope, which he clearly thought beyond all possibility of fulfilment, that he would not regret the move.

The *Morning Chronicle* sent Russell back to the Press Gallery where he covered the months of debate and manoeuvre which ended with the repeal of the Corn Laws and the destruction of the old Tory party.

Russell was beginning to develop his taste for foreign travel. In January 1846 he had a few days in Boulogne and was 'much pleased with theatre, cafés, *bal masqué'*. He paid another visit to Boulogne four months later and on the journey home struck up a friendship that was to be lifelong.

Max Müller, only twenty-three but already deeply read in philosophy, philology and oriental languages, was on his way from Germany to London to study manuscripts in the library of the East India Company with a view to editing the Rig-Veda, the oldest Hindu scriptures. It was his first sea voyage and he felt very sick. More than fifty years later he recalled his first meeting with Russell:

> There a young fellow traveller saw the poor bundle of misery and tried to comfort me, and brought me what he thought was good for me, not, however, without a certain merry twinkle in his eye and a few kindly jokes at my expense. We landed at the docks in London, a real drizzly day, rain and mist, and such a crowd rushing on shore that I missed my cheerful friend and felt quite lost. In addition to all this a porter had run away with my portmanteau, which contained my books and MSS, in fact all my worldly goods. At that moment my young friend reappeared and, seeing the plight I was in, came to my assistance. 'You stay here,' he said, 'and I will arrange everything for you,' and so he did. He fetched a four-wheeler, put my luggage on the top, bundled me inside, and drove me through a maze of London streets to his rooms in the Temple. Then, still knowing nothing about me, he asked me to spend the night in his rooms, gave me a bed and everything else I wanted for the night. The next morning he took me out to look for lodgings, which we found in Essex Street. . . . He came every day to show me things which I ought to see in London, and brought me tickets for theatres and concerts, which he said were sent to him. His name was William Howard Russell. . . . He remained my warm and true friend through life, and even now when we are both cripples, we delight in meeting and talking over very distant days. (11)

According to Russell's recollections—also written down half a century later—Müller was a rewarding companion:

> It was the custom at the time for students after dining in hall at the Temple to go off to their rooms with a friend or two, and others dropped in. Max Müller was always the most welcome guest at mine, and he provided strange and wonderful entertainment for the company. For the first time the Temple was enlivened by the strains of *Edite, bibite, conviviales, Crambambuli*, and other *Studenten-Lieder*. One *morceau* of surpassing excellence, as we all thought, we always encored, and Max smilingly complied. It was an imitation of a whole orchestra—trumpets, drums, bassoons and goodness knows what besides!—delivered with the greatest precision. (12)

By the spring of 1846 Russell had overcome the last of the Burrowes family's opposition to his marriage to Mary. He spent his Easter holiday at Howth on the northern side of Dublin Bay, saw Mary daily and was very happy: 'I was full of life and hope. Sanguine and thoughtless, I revelled in the prospect of breasting the waves of the world.' (13) The wedding was arranged for 16 September.

In July, however, he heard from the *Morning Chronicle* that, as part of a general retrenchment, his salary was to be cut by one-third—to six guineas a week—with effect from September. It was a hard knock. As usual Russell had debts and he was sending regular sums of money to help his brother John through Cambridge where he was a sizar, a poor scholar, at St John's. Nevertheless, the wedding plans went ahead. William Howard Russell and Mary Burrowes were married at the parish church in Howth. The had a week's honeymoon at an hotel in Malahide. Then, as he wrote in his diary, 'To London to begin the battle of life.'

Almost immediately he was sent back to Ireland where for many people the battle of life had become a struggle for survival. Much of the previous year's potato crop had been destroyed by a fungus. In the west and south-west particularly, millions were threatened with starvation. The problem was too big for any measures now taken by the authorities to be more than palliative. And the potato harvest of 1846 was even more disastrously blighted than that of the previous year.

Russell's orders were to describe conditions in the famine-stricken areas. His journey made an impression he never forgot:

> In all my subsequent career—breakfasting, dining and supping 'full of horrors,' in full tide of war—I never beheld sights so shocking as those which met my eyes in that famine tour of mine in the West. They were beyond not merely description, but imagination. The effects of famine may be witnessed in isolated cases by travellers in distant lands, but here at our doors was a whole race, men, women and children, perishing round Christian chapels and churches. . . . I was indignant at what I saw, but I could not say with whom the blame lay. The children digging up roots, the miserable crones and the scarecrow old men in the fields, the ghastly adults in the relief works—all were heart-rending. One strange and fearful consequence was seen in the famished children: their faces, limbs, and bodies became covered with fine long hair; their arms and legs dwindled, and their bellies became enormously swollen. They were bestial to behold. Hunger changed their physical nature as it monopolised all they had of human thought—'Give us something to eat!' (14)

Soon after his return to London from this assignment Russell's engagement with the *Morning Chronicle* came to an end. Relations between them had not been happy and early in 1847, when Russell's doctor ordered him to rest after a brief illness, the editor told him to return to work immediately. Instead, Russell resigned and entered on a period that was more than usually uncertain and difficult.

He picked up reporting and writing jobs when he could and went on studying law. He and Mary moved about from one lot of rented rooms to another, in the

Kensington area and around the Vauxhall Road. In May 1847 his brother John died. One month later Mary gave birth to their first child, a girl they called Alice. Russell wrote to a relation:

> She is very fair, and on the whole, not a bad sort of little thing. Big blue eyes, larger and darker than Mary's, with very long eyelashes, a very pretty mouth, dark hair, a bullet head, rather snub nose in its present development, and to complete all is as fat as butter, and no wonder, for she never stops tormenting her mother to feed her. And Mary is a regular slavey to it, and hides herself in dark and out-of-the-way corners with it from morning to night and cares for no earthly thing in this world beside, so that I begin to get jealous of my own little baby. (15)

In April 1848 Russell was one of those—Prince Louis Napoleon was another—who enrolled as special constables in case of civil disorder during the Chartists' march to Westminster. Their help was not needed. Although this was a year of revolutionary ferment throughout Europe, the Chartist leaders—demanding better conditions for the poor and a reformed Parliament with votes for all men—dared not risk a direct confrontation with the authorities. The march took place but the numbers were disappointingly small and the people of London unwelcoming.

In the autumn of that year Russell returned to *The Times*, this time as a staff man. It was something of an achievement. The paper was not in the habit of re-employing men who had been wilful enough to leave its service for a rival. But there is evidence that Delane had wanted to retain Russell two years before by offering him a permanent post, and Delane's position at Printing House Square was now much stronger. He offered a regular job and it was immediately accepted.

Russell found things greatly changed at *The Times*. The three men who were to control its fortunes for the next twenty-five years had taken their appointed places: John Walter III as Chief Proprietor; John Thadeus Delane as Editor; Mowbray Morris as Manager. They made a formidable triumvirate—'the three ruling officers' as *The History of The Times* called them—and their rule carried the paper to the summit of its prestige and influence.

Delane had been editor for more than seven years. He had worked out his period of probation with conspicuous success. At the close of 1845 he pulled off his first great political scoop by breaking the news that Peel's Cabinet had decided on the repeal of the Corn Laws.* The incident demonstrated two of Delane's invaluable attributes—reliable sources in high places, and the nerve to publish when he was sure in his own mind that his information was authentic.

But even at the height of his power, which came some years later, Delane was no absolute ruler. He could never take the acquiescence of the Chief Proprietor for

---

* Delane's source for this information was the Foreign Secretary, Lord Aberdeen, who was in almost daily contact with him.

granted. For John Walter III,* despite his responsibilities as an M.P. and a considerable landowner, kept a critical eye on all aspects of the paper's affairs and this included Delane's domain. Delane and his Assistant Editor, George Dasent,† did not like it but they had to put up with it. Their private nickname for John Walter was 'The Griff' which was short for 'griffin', a vigilant guardian of grim aspect.

John Walter's first important act when he became Chief Proprietor in 1847 was the appointment of Mowbray Morris as Manager.‡ Morris, a man of Byronic good looks, was a highly conscientious and efficient administrator. For the next twenty-five years he was to play a significant part in Russell's life, organizing his travel, advising and encouraging and cajoling, struggling to unravel the tangles of his claims for expenses. Despite all this—perhaps because of it—Russell never really liked the man, finding him cold and sometimes coarse.

These four were to shape *The Times* for the next generation. They were all young: Delane was thirty-one, John Walter thirty, Morris twenty-nine, Russell twenty-eight. They were all university men though Morris, like Russell, had left without taking a degree. They had all studied law—Russell was the only one among them who had not yet been called to the Bar. There were marked differences between them, in character and interests and attitudes, and they did not feel, their work apart, particularly close—Russell and Delane were the only two who became friends. But they could work together and they each had the vital qualities—integrity, vigour, dedication to the paper and a high concept of its role in the affairs of the nation.

A few years later, when it was accused by Lord Derby of seeking to usurp the powers of statesmen without acknowledging their responsibilities, *The Times* spelt out its view of the press in successive leading articles. (16) 'The press lives by disclosures; whatever passes into its keeping becomes a part of the knowledge and the history of our times; it is daily and for ever appealing to the enlightened force of public opinion—anticipating, if possible, the march of events—standing upon the breach between the present and the future, and extending its survey to the horizon of the world.' It was the newspaper's purpose to seek out 'the earliest and most correct intelligence of the events of the time, and instantly, by disclosing them, to make them the common property of the nation.' It was the journalist's job 'to investigate truth and to apply it on fixed principles to the affairs of the world.'

---

* John Walter III (1818–94), his father's eldest son, has been educated at Eton and Exeter College, Oxford, and called to the Bar in 1847. He was a High Anglican and an ardent supporter of the Oxford Movement.

† George Webbe Dasent read classics at Magdalen Hall, Oxford, and became a leading authority on Scandinavian languages and mythology. He was Assistant Editor of *The Times* from 1845 to 1870. He was married to Delane's sister Mary.

‡ Mowbray Morris (1819–74) was educated at Trinity College, Cambridge, and called to the Bar in 1841. He was Manager of *The Times* from 1847 to 1873. He was closely related to Delane by marriage: his second wife was Delane's sister Emily; his sister married Delane's brother George.

Delane had planned to send Russell to the Press Gallery but in the event his first assignment took him back to the courtrooms of Ireland. He went to Clonmel where four men who had staged a pathetic attempt at insurrection were found guilty of treason and sentenced to be hanged, drawn and quartered. The sentences were later commuted to transportation for life. In October he moved to Dublin to report the trial and acquittal of Charles Gavan Duffy, charged with treason for advocating the use of force to end the Union and secure a separate Irish Parliament.

Back in London he took up his duties as a parliamentary and general reporter. In March 1849 his second child was born, a son named William. Soon after he was in Norwich to cover a murder trial. Between journalistic and domestic duties, he continued his legal studies and was finally called to the Bar at the Middle Temple in June 1850. Delane attended his celebration dinner at the London Tavern, where speeches were made predicting a distinguished forensic future.

Russell never quite abandoned the notion that he might have made a great barrister but all the evidence suggests—and he himself more than suspected—that this was unlikely. He was an articulate man but his milieu was the small social gathering, the friendly intimate atmosphere with food and drink to hand. On grander, more formal occasions he was inclined to be nervous and, when this was overcome, to grow pompous and long-winded. On his very few appearances in court he was—to judge from his own account in *Retrospect*—almost farcically incompetent.

It was fortunate for his career that one month after being called to the Bar he was sent to cover his first war.

5

Reporter at War

A t this time there was no such thing as a 'war correspondent'. The term had not been coined and, when it was, Russell did not think much of it. He always considered himself a newspaper reporter who had developed into a special correspondent with an aptitude for 'descriptive letters' and who, by chance rather than anything else, had come to be associated primarily with the reporting of war.

His first venture into the field was neither particularly important nor particularly auspicious. In July 1850 Delane sent him to cover the conflict over Schleswig-Holstein.

For many centuries the King of Denmark had been also the Duke of Schleswig and Holstein, the two small provinces which lay across the neck of the Danish peninsula. The people of Holstein, however, were entirely German and those of Schleswig were predominantly so, and in 1848, when national sentiment found violent expression all over Europe, they had made it clear that they resented Danish rule. By 1850, with some stiffening from Prussian 'volunteers', they had built an army of 30,000 men. The Danes decided the time had come to reassert their authority.

As the emissary of *The Times*, Russell was received with great respect by the commander of the Holstein army, General Willisen. His first report, date-lined 'Schleswig, July 22' and published in London five days later, described the disposition of the Holstein army but refrained from detail: 'I do not give the numbers of each brigade, nor the strength of the different arms composing it, for special reasons. They were stated to me, but on the understanding that they should not be made public while there was a chance of the details reaching the enemy before an engagement.'

The battle took place at the village of Idstedt on the 25th. Russell was busy all day collecting information and eye-witness accounts. At one stage he came under fire himself and received a slight flesh wound. Next day he compiled a full account, one and a half columns which appeared in *The Times* of 29 July under the heading 'Defeat and Retreat of the Schleswig-Holstein Army'. It is a detailed but dry description that does not come to life even when Russell was most closely involved:

About 11 o'clock a most fearful cannonade commenced on both sides. . . .
Individual instances of courage were shown that would appear almost
incredible. . . . The most determined courage of the whole army was, however,
of no avail against the superior force the Danes at this time brought into action.
They were also deficient in ammunition. About 2 o'clock the Danes made
another attack, but being myself at this time obliged to withdraw, I was no longer
an eye-witness of what occurred. Soon after, however, individual soldiers were
seen running along the Chaussée in the direction of Schleswig, followed soon
after by larger masses, spreading the mournful news that the Danes had broken
through our centre . . .

Russell concluded, correctly, that the battle had been 'decisive for the present
fate of the Duchies' and returned to London. There had been nothing in his
despatches to suggest that here was a great war reporter in the making. He was, of
course, dealing with a subject that was completely new to him and must have been
inhibitingly aware that he could not hope to understand all that happened. He was
probably inhibited, too, by some sense of obligation towards General Willisen.
Even his first biographer, J. B. Atkins, an unstinting admirer of Russell's work, felt
constrained to criticize: '. . . probably because he was conscious that he was
expressing himself in unfamiliar terms, he allowed himself less freedom in his
writing than he had allowed himself in much of his previous work. We miss the
flexibility, the audacity, and the warm touches of enthusiasm or indignation which
glowed later in his Crimean pages.' (1)

Nonetheless, Russell now found himself being used by Delane increasingly in
the role of descriptive reporter. He went to Cherbourg for the naval review before
Louis Napoleon, who had become President of France and was to be Emperor and
virtual dictator before the next year was out. He accompanied the Hungarian rebel
leader, Kossuth, on his triumphant tour of English cities and, though *The Times*
took a disapproving view of all revolutionaries and made no exception of Kossuth,
found himself admiring and liking the Magyar patriot. He described a *bal masqué*
at Vauxhall, the rise of the Crystal Palace and preparations for the Great
Exhibition of 1851, and won the praise of Charles Dickens for his portrait of
Greenwich Fair in a rainstorm. In 1852 he was, he claimed, the first journalist ever
to be invited to a dinner of the Royal Academy. (2) At the end of the year he
received a £50 bonus from *The Times* with an explanatory note from Mowbray
Morris: 'The paper, thanks to the exertions of all connected with it, has been
unusually prosperous this year, and it is the intention of the proprietors to give a
share of their abundance to those who have chiefly contributed to secure it.' (3)

But his spending continued to out-run his income and he sought aid, as
journalists will, in freelance work. He wrote pieces for *Indépendence Belge* and the
Edinburgh *Witness*. He played a part in the launching of the Dublin *Daily Express*
in 1851. He had been struck, he said, by 'the want of a sound Conservative organ
in Ireland.' He declined the editorship but became the paper's London

correspondent at £400 a year: 'The work of the new newspaper taxed me very heavily. I was obliged in the morning to wait till the first papers were brought to my chambers, go through them, write my letter and have it delivered at a quarter to eight at W. H. Smith's in the Strand, and then I had to look over parliamentary papers, blue books and the like, and prepare another letter to post in the evening.' (4) His annual earnings had grown dramatically but his debts were mounting too. He had something of his father's gift for unlucky speculation, but the chief cause of the trouble was undoubtedly his active social life.

He had many friends, among them the two literary lions of the day, Thackeray and Dickens. They met at the Fielding Club, long since defunct, which had rooms in Henrietta Street in Covent Garden and later moved to the Coalhole in Maiden Lane:

> It was very pleasant in its lifetime, with just a suspicion of the sea-coast of Bohemia among the *habitués*—artists, actors, guardsmen, men about town, and journalists . . . there was a set dinner at some moderate price at six o'clock, and there was a supper, boundless as to time, limited as to oysters, grills, lamb's head, cow heel and tripe, kidney *à la Massol* (so called from a Belgian singer), and other subtleties of devilry. Supper would last commonly till the early milkman cast long shadows on the pavement and the thrush in the public house on the corner began to trill its early lay. Each M.F.C. could take in a friend, and when the opera was over the room was crowded, every seat at the long table filled, and amid the noise of glasses, knives, forks and tongues, clouds of tobacco smoke poured out from every window. The existence of the Fielding, like that of some other clubs, was due to the conservatism of the dear old Garrick. (5)

He was elected to the Garrick Club in November 1853. He was to remain a member all his life and be an active one for most of it, sitting on the committee for several years, wining and dining there frequently and all too well, becoming acquainted with many of the eminent men of the time, entertaining distinguished friends, losing money at the whist table with depressing regularity: 'No more delightful club was ever invented or maintained for the intercourse of moderately intellectual, entirely convivial, beings than the old Garrick. It was Tory of Tory; there was no comfort for strangers; they were admitted, indeed, to dine to a limited number in the parlour, but they were not permitted to smoke. . . . But *per contra* the guests enjoyed the best dinner that could be cooked of the kind, and admirable wine.' (6)

The Garrick Club had been founded in 1831 to establish a society 'in which actors and men of education and refinement might meet on equal terms'. Named after the eighteenth-century actor David Garrick, it was dedicated to the principle that actors are not necessarily disreputable, a radical idea at a time when clubs like the Beefsteak specifically excluded them from membership. Its founder members included William Macready, Charles Kemble and many lesser Thespians; Sir John Soane the architect and collector; Samuel Rogers the poet, Theodore Hook the humorous writer, and the Reverend Richard Barham, author of *The Ingoldsby Legends;* Lord John Russell the Whig leader and other noblemen; painters, journalists and theatre managers. Lord Melbourne soon joined. Thackeray became a member in 1833 and rapidly established himself as the presiding spirit, the *genius loci*, a position he held till his death thirty years later. Dickens joined in 1837 and became notorious for the regularity with which he resigned and was re-elected.

London was still small enough—and its leading artistic spirits were still sociable enough—for the great majority of them to know each other well and to enjoy, for the most part, each other's company. Russell's membership of the Garrick was to bring him into companionable contact with a remarkable range of men. Something of the relaxed, cheerful spirit that animated them is suggested by one of his diary entries:

> X. asked a party to Watford to shoot. There were only hares and rabbits to be sure, but what more could be expected in April? The sportsmen among whom I had the honour to be numbered were of the Winkle order: Thackeray, Dickens, John Leech, Jerrold, Lemon, Ibbotson and others were invited and carriages were reserved to Watford. As we were starting, a written excuse was brought from Dickens to be conveyed to Mrs. X. by Thackeray. The party drove up to the house and, after compliments, Thackeray delivered the billet. The effect was unpleasant. Mrs. X. fled along the hall, and the guests heard her calling to the cook, 'Martin, don't roast the ortolons; Mr. Dickens isn't coming.'
> Thackeray said he never felt so small. 'There's a test of popularity for you! No ortolans for Pendennis!' (7)

Another popular resort was Chertsey, where the genial Albert Smith entertained his friends generously: 'Generally for the convenience of his many theatrical intimates, male and female, a tent was erected on the lawn on Sundays, and this was devoted to an interminable luncheon-dinner-supper—oysters, lobster, salad, cold fowl, lamb and peas—till it was time to rush for the last train to Waterloo.' (8)

Smith was an odd highly-extrovert character who had trained to be a doctor, found he enjoyed the life of a humorous writer a good deal more, then discovered his true *métier* as the presenter of vivid and eccentric travel lectures. He had been fascinated all his life by the high mountains of the Alps, particularly the highest of them all, Mont Blanc, and in August 1851 he achieved his ambition and reached the summit. As mountaineering feats go, it was significant only for the fact that it was probably the most extravagant expedition the mountain had ever endured —four guides to each climber and twenty porters laden with crates of wine and a variety of meats and cheeses. It soon became the best-publicized expedition in history. On his return to London Smith commissioned a series of dioramic pictures and in March 1852 launched his lecture, *The Ascent of Mont Blanc*, at the Egyptian Hall in Piccadilly. It was part lecture, part pantomime, part icy horror show. It played to full houses, at 2s 6d a seat, for six years and made Smith famous and wealthy.

Smith was far from being everyone's favourite. He was boisterous, unsophisticated and given to practical jokes. Some Garrick Club members despised him as a vulgar showman. Douglas Jerrold said his initials 'conveyed only two-thirds of the truth'. Russell, while conceding that Smith's 'voice was strident and high pitched, and his laugh rang like the clatter of a steam shuttle', liked him for his energy and goodness of heart. In the autumn of 1852 they went to the Alps together for a walking holiday. It was brought to an end by an urgent summons from Delane. The Duke of Wellington had died and Russell was needed to describe the funeral for *The Times*.

Russell had never met the Duke but had heard him speak movingly, at the Royal Academy dinner, about the disciplined behaviour of the soldiers on the *Birkenhead*,* and had seen him frequently: 'Often and often had I stopped in the street and taken off my hat as the well-known figure of the Duke of Wellington caught the eye as he rode from the Horse Guards to the House of Lords; the thin form in the plain blue frock coat, with white stock and buckle showing above the neck, and white duck trousers strapped over the boots which bore his name. Never, as far as I could see, did he omit to raise his right hand to the brim of his hat as a return to the salutations of the people.' (9)

The Duke's body lay in state for many weeks to enable the people to pay their last respects to the man who had led them to victory against Napoleon and helped to hold the nation steady in the contentious years of peace. The funeral, a heraldic state funeral designed by the Prince Consort, took place on 18 November.

Russell was now living in Bedford Row near Gray's Inn and his first concern was how he would get to St Paul's: 'I had a sleepless night, and before dawn a dull noise like that of the surf beating on a distant shore came through the night air; it was the tramp of feet in the direction of St. Paul's. The job-master in the neighbouring mews had asked £8 for a brougham or a cab, and he had come to me later to say that he could not drive me for less than £10 and compensation for damages to horse or vehicle.' (10)

So he walked across Lincoln's Inn Fields to Fleet Street where he joined the main current: '. . . it was full, it was strong, but it was not rapid. As the boom of the guns, fired to mark the progess of the funeral car, reached the ears of the vast mass that filled the streets, there was a movement as though the multitude had become a living entity, with every muscle vibrating, as though it formed a great python.' (11)

---

* The *Birkenhead*, a British troopship, sank off the coast of South Africa on 26 February, 1852. The soldiers maintained their ranks on deck while the women and children were taken off in the boats. Four hundred and thirty-six officers and men were drowned.

As soon as the Cathedral service was over Russell hurried through the dispersing crowds to Printing House Square to begin work, assembling and rewriting other reporters' accounts of the scenes along the funeral route and appending his own description of the scene in St Paul's. The following morning's paper carried more than seven unbroken columns—about 16,000 words—of detailed description. It began:

> Yesterday the mortal remains of Arthur Duke of Wellington were conveyed from the Horse Guards to the Cathedral of St. Paul's, and there buried by the side of Nelson. A million and a half of people beheld and participated in the ceremonial, which was national in the truest and largest sense of the word.

The procession was described almost step by step:

> On no occasion in modern times has such a concourse of people been gathered together, and never probably has the sublimity which is expressed by the presence of the masses been so transcendently displayed. The progress, too, of the procession imparted to it in this respect an almost dramatic unity and completeness, for, from the regions of palaces and great mansions, and from the assemblages of the wealthy, the titled, and the great, it passed, first, among great gatherings of the middle classes, then through thoroughfares swarming with myriads of the people, and finally closed its course at the lofty threshold of the metropolitan cathedral, the centre of London, now engaged by a new tie to the affections of the country by having deposited under its dome the ashes of England's greatest son.

The piece runs through a thesaurus of reverential superlatives. It has many of the qualities of Russell's style at its worst—heavy, slow, spattered with commas and dependent clauses, with few of the telling details that can bring such a picture to life. To the modern taste, accustomed to newspaper writing of an altogether brisker kind, it seems repetitious and often turgid. Yet in a way it suited the occasion. In the broad sweep of its description, in its banal high-flown generalizations, it caught and reflected the mood of the nation. One passage read: 'When the independence of England and of the world was assailed Providence sent us a champion, and as the myriads of his countrymen yesterday watched with the deepest interest the transit of his body to the tomb, many a heartfelt prayer must have been uttered that, should days of darkness again come and this land of freedom be once more threatened, God may grant us another Wellesley to lead our armies and win our battles.' Within eighteen months England was at war again and, though it was hardly a war on the Napoleonic scale, she was to feel the need of a leader of Wellington's calibre very bitterly.

The Crimean War began as an obscure quarrel between Christian monks over who should hold the keys to some of the ancient shrines in Jerusalem. The Czar of

Russia, Nicholas I, saw it as his duty to protect the right of the Greek Orthodox Church. The Emperor of France, Napoleon III, who was looking for a military adventure that would enhance his prestige without engaging France too closely, supported the Roman Catholic claims. Each put pressure on the Sultan of Turkey, whose empire extended to the Holy Land as well as far into Europe, to declare in favour of his co-religionists. The Sultan struggled to placate each in turn but found it impossible as their demands grew.

No British interests were seriously threatened but gradually, as Russia and Turkey moved towards another of their recurrent conflicts, Lord Aberdeen's pacific government was forced towards war by the pressure of public opinion. Many Britons hated the Czar as the personification of reaction and tyranny. Some feared that any Russian gains from the Turks would upset the delicate balance of European power. And there was another, more elemental factor—the simple fact that a generation brought up on tales of victories over Napoleon I and bubbling with confidence had been denied any military expression of its strength for nearly forty years.

At first *The Times* stood firmly behind the government's determination to keep clear of trouble. Lord Aberdeen, the Prime Minister of the coalition government, was Delane's most valuable contact in high places. The Foreign Secretary, Lord Clarendon, was a close friend of the paper's chief leader-writer Henry Reeve. But Aberdeen's position was not secure even inside his own Cabinet and as the year moved on events in Eastern Europe made his position increasingly hard to hold. Russian and Turkish troops were fighting north of the Danube in October 1853. Next month the Russian fleet attacked and destroyed the Turkish Black Sea fleet at the port of Sinope. Public feeling in Britain was inflamed. It was widely feared that Russia's next advances might give her control of the Bosphorus and access to the eastern Mediterranean, which would endanger the fast route to India. In December *The Times* switched, and called on the government to declare war on Russia.

War had not, however, been declared when Delane sent for Russell:

When the year of grace 1854 opened on me I had no more idea of being what is now—absurdly, I think—called a 'war correspondent' than I had of becoming Lord Chancellor—nay, far less; for I confess I had at times visions of the Woolsack such as, I suppose, float in the air before the mind's eye of many sanguine barristers. . . . As I was sitting at my desk in *The Times* office one evening in February 1854, I was informed that the editor, Mr. Delane, wished to see me, and on entering his sanctum I was taken aback by the announcement that he had arranged a very agreeable excursion for me to go to Malta with the Guards. The Government had resolved to show Russia that England was in earnest in supporting the Sultan against aggression, and that she would, if necessary, send an expedition to the East. It was decided, he said, that I was the best man to represent the paper on the occasion. Lord Hardinge

[Commander-in-Chief of the British army] had given an order for my passage with the Guards from Southampton, and everything would be done to make my task agreeable: the authorities would look after me—my wife and family could join me—handsome pay and allowances would be given—in fact, everything was painted *couleur de rose*. When I made some objection on the score of losing my practice at the Bar, Mr. Delane said, 'There is not the least chance of it; you'll be back by Easter, depend on it and you will have a pleasant trip for a few weeks only.' (12)

Little of this came about. The military authorities did not look after him. His wife and family—there were now four children, two girls and two boys*— did not join him. He was away from home not for two months but for nearly two years. But when he left England he was nothing more than one member of a team of *Times* reporters assigned to cover all aspects of the impending war. When he came back he was famous.

* A second daughter, Alberta, was born in February 1853; a second son, John, one year later.

6

To the Crimea

The prospect of war was greeted by the British people with an enthusiasm that did not wane even when the Chancellor, Mr Gladstone, doubled income tax from 7d to 14d in the £ and increased the duties on spirits, sugar and malt. The soldiers were cheered to the docks and *The Times* praised 'the finest army that has ever left these shores'. It was certainly a fine looking army, brilliantly dressed and fiercely disciplined, but in the long history of British unreadiness for war it is doubtful whether the army had ever been worse prepared for a major conflict.

There were many reasons for this. Great victories do not encourage a nation to reform its forces. After 1815 the Duke of Wellington, convinced that the army would not be called upon for anything more serious than minor colonial campaigns for many years, presided over the rundown of ancillary arms, supply and transport and medical services. The politicians, usually eager to reduce defence spending in times of peace, kept the purse strings tight. Control of the army's affairs was divided between seven separate and largely autonomous authorities—some military, some civilian. They did not meet to co-ordinate their efforts and often operated as jealous and parsimonious rivals. The soldiers came from the lowest levels of society. Convicted criminals were often given the choice between prison and signing on for ten years in the army. The men were poorly paid, atrociously housed and greatly given to drunkenness. The death rate among British infantrymen from disease was twice that of civilians of comparable age. Commissions up to the rank of Lieutenant-Colonel were bought and above that promotion was by seniority; so command was the preserve of the wealthy and high command largely confined to the elderly.

Wellington's influence lay heavily on the years between 1815 and 1852 and he was opposed in principle to any reform. The man who succeeded him as Commander-in-Chief in 1852, Lord Hardinge, saw the need for change, but the Crimean War came too quickly for him to effect any great improvement. One measure of his did play an important part—the introduction of a new French-designed rifle, the Minié, which fired a blunt lead bullet through a grooved bore and proved more accurate than the rifles of the Russian infantry.

In contrast to the army, *The Times* was in better shape than ever before. The triumvirate of John Walter, Delane and Mowbray Morris was in assured control. A reduction in Stamp Duty had made it possible to cut the price from 7d to 5d. The railways had brought every city and town of Britain within reach of Printing House Square on the day of publication. The paper's circulation, some 40,000 copies a day, had doubled in a decade and was four times bigger than the combined sales of its chief competitors, the *Morning Chronicle*, the *Morning Herald* and the *Morning Post*. Its network of contacts and correspondents worked so well it became axiomatic that important news would be known to Delane before it reached the government. Many politicians feared that 'the fourth estate', as represented by *The Times*, would swallow up the other three.

Delane prepared to give his readers a more comprehensive account of the coming campaign than any newspaper had ever attempted. This was not difficult since little effort had been made to report previous wars. *The Times* had sent a man to cover the Peninsular campaign in 1808 and the *Morning Post* made a similar move in the Carlist War in Spain in 1837, but neither correspondent stayed long enough in the field to make an impression. For the rest, the British press traditionally relied on official despatches, on what it could pick up from foreign papers and on occasional letters from serving officers, usually those with a grievance. The Duke of Wellington accused the press, with some self-contradiction, of getting its facts almost invariably wrong and of giving vital information to the enemy. He would not allow journalists near his army and did all he could to discourage officers from writing to the papers.

Now that the Duke's obstructing hand was stilled at last, Delane and Mowbray Morris could make their dispositions with confidence. They had Thomas Chenery in Constantinople; they sent a young officer on leave from the East India forces, Lieutenant Charles Nasmyth, to accompany the Turkish army on the Danube; they gave a roving role to an adventure-loving Hungarian called Ferdinand Eber; and William Howard Russell was ordered to follow the fortunes of the British expeditionary force.

Russell's salary was doubled to twelve guineas a week and, since his living and travel expenses were to be met by the paper, he was in the happy position of being able to leave all his pay at home. It was arranged that half the money would go to his family, who went to live on the island of Guernsey where they had friends. The other half would be managed by Russell's old school friend, Obé Willans, who was deputed to pay off Russell's debts as the money accumulated. Everyone was agreed that it would be unwise to leave the handling of the whole income to Mary.

From now on, through those letters of Russell to Mary that have survived, we begin to get a clearer picture of their life together. The letters are full of affection and concern for his family. He used a battery of nicknames for Mary—most often 'deenyman' or 'Bucky' but also 'Dot' and 'Dotty' and 'dotterel'. Sometimes he lapses into baby-talk. There are old family jokes—his tendency to grow fat, her cold nose. He is constantly eager for news of home and often disappointed by her failure to provide it. None of Mary's letters has survived but from his the shortcomings of her character begin to emerge. She was, it seems, extremely timid and nervous, shy of company, inclined to indiscretion, impractical in everyday affairs, a doting mother but subject to periods of inertia.

The day before he left home Mary gave him a Book of Common Prayer. (1) A small stout volume, bound in leather with a metal edge and clasp, it also contained the Psalms and the Revised Version of The New Testament. Russell carried it with him throughout the Crimean campaign and on all his subsequent travels.

His friends gave him a farewell party at the Albion on the evening of 19 February 1854. The company included Dickens and Thackeray, Douglas Jerrold, Wilkie Collins, Mark Lemon, Shirley Brooks, Tom Taylor and Albert Smith, as well as other literary men and journalists and a few army officers. Doggerel verses were composed and sung in his honour.

As soon as he set off he received an early warning of the sort of obstructionism he would have to live with throughout the next two years. Lord Hardinge had assured Delane that Russell would be allowed to sail with the Guards from Southampton, but when he got there Russell found the order had not been passed down and no one was prepared to find room for him on the ships. So he made his own way, overland across France then by sea to Valetta to join the army in Malta. He had a busy few days, talking to officers and men, soldiers and sailors, about their voyage from England and from their stories he composed his first Letter to The Times, dated 6 March and published nine days later. This news-gathering technique was to serve him often and well in the coming months, especially in piecing together accounts of the great battles where it was impossible for one man to see everything. His pleasant amusing manner won him the confidence of the junior officers. He had no difficulty getting them to talk and enough common sense to know when they were trying to use him to promote their personal vanities or prosecute private feuds.

No one expected to stay long in Malta but the days lengthened into weeks and no sailing orders came. Russell practised his revolver shooting and visited the various officers' messes. But the inactivity made his job hard. He was never a natural penny-a-liner—a writer, that is, who is paid according to the number of words he produces and is consequently at pains to stretch things out as wordily as he can. Russell needed events and facts to work on and they were in scant supply these first weeks. He had a struggle, which sometimes showed, to give his employers their money's worth. His early Letters were sometimes verbose and on the whole genial, even chauvinistic, in tone. But there were hints of things to come. His first Letter spoke of some regiments coming ashore to find they had no means of heat or light in their quarters and inadequate food for men and horses:'. . . if the complaints to which I have alluded are well-founded,' he wrote, 'serious blame rests in some quarter or another . . .' Although his next Letter admitted that the complaints had been exaggerated, it was a warning shot, a signal that mismanagement would not go unreported.

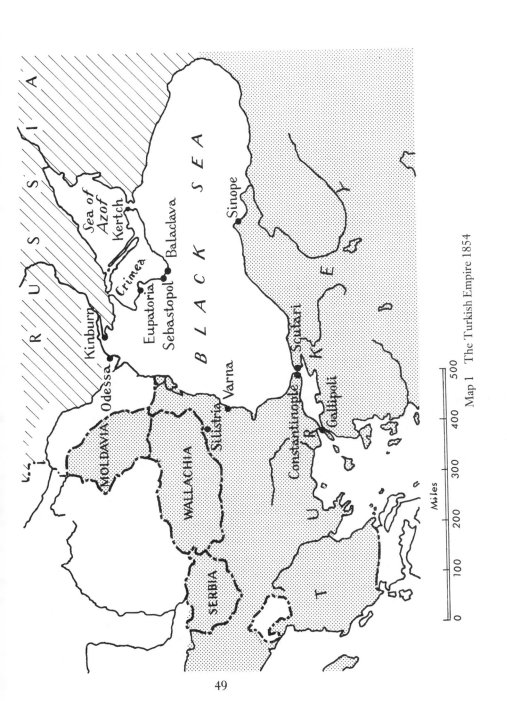

Map 1   The Turkish Empire 1854

RUSSIA

Sea of
Azof

Kertch

Crimea

Kinburn

Odessa

Eupatoria

Sebastopol

Balaclava

BLACK SEA

Sinope

Varna

Silistria

MOLDAVIA

WALLACHIA

SERBIA

Constantinople

Scutari

Gallipoli

TURKEY

Miles

0   100   200   300   400   500

49

Nearly two weeks after arriving in Malta he wrote to Mary:

My dearest deenyman, my own dear dotterel,
    I trust and pray that you and our dear little children are well. . . . I am *burning* with anxiety to hear from you. . . . We are very grand and stupid here. I have been introduced to the Governor—have dined at the Palace—very magnificent and very dull. . . . I have bought you a handsome gold bracelet of the finest Maltese workmanship—a gold Cup ditto—and a silver bracelet ditto, and I intend to buy you a cameo—I wish you were by my side with your dear old red nose to choose one for yourself. . . . I am horribly uneasy about my affairs for on looking to my diary I find I did not arrange one half of what ought to have been arranged. *Do not*—however kind any person may be to you—talk too much or let them know too much of our private affairs particularly as they are in such a shuck position . . . (2)

His next letter showed how right he was to worry about her capacity for indiscretion:

My dearest old Dotty,
    Don't be afraid for one moment that I was in the least angry with you for your slip of the tongue. I can only attribute it to the same cause that made you so unwise and so foolish as to love me. But I am almost afraid nevertheless to write to you secretly on *many matters* lest you *should* let my letter lie about, or slip out something or other to offend one of our friends . . . (3)

Later in the same letter he revealed his Victorian belief in the need for sexual discipline, among women especially: 'You are quite right my dear Dot too in objecting to Mrs. W. for using such a very coarse word as that you indicated with "R—s" and I trust you will never use it unless to make *me* laugh sometimes. A woman after all *cannot* be *too* pure and *too* guarded in conversation and the world puts the most monstrous construction on any looseness of words in the sex. I think it a blot in her character, above all as she is an Irishwoman.'
    In the third week of March contingents of the French army arrived in Malta and Russell reported 'the most perfect good feeling' between the new-found allies. In the Danubian provinces, territory which is now part of Rumania, the Russians and Turks continued to fight in a rather desultory fashion. The two western powers sent Russia an ultimatum which was designed to be unacceptable and was duly rejected. Emperor Napoleon III declared war on 26 March 1854. The next day the British government followed suit.
    But the allied forces were still in Malta at the end of the month. Russell told his readers that the *entente* remained *cordiale*, the Guards were practising with their new Minié rifles, the British were pleased to have 'good English porter' in camp. His Letter of 31 March, however, mentioned several matters that were to become

important later. He commented on the unsuitability of many of the British uniforms for active service. He described the blinkered insistence of many senior officers on a regulation turn-out regardless of conditions, their stolid resistance to the growing of beards and moustaches. Most prophetic of all, he reminded his readers that the army's chief enemy was disease:

> What we have most to fear in an encampment is an enemy that musket and bayonet cannot meet or repel. We have a fearful lesson in the records of the Russo-Turkish campaign of 1828–9, in which 80,000 men perished by 'plague, pestilence and famine,' and let any one who has the interests of this army at heart just turn to Moltke's history of that miserable invasion, and he will grudge no expense, and spare no precaution, to avoid, as far as human skill can do it, a repetition of such horrors. Let us have plenty of doctors. Let us have an overwhelming army of medical men to combat with disease. Let us have a staff—full and strong—of young and active and experienced men. Do not let our soldiers be killed by antiquated imbecility.

Russell's main anxiety was whether he would be allowed to go with the army when it sailed East. The precedent, his journey to Malta, was not reassuring. 'How was I to move?' he wrote many years later, 'I have no *locus standi* (or sitting); the ships were under Government orders and charters. But I had a friend in the dockyard in high place, and one evening, as I was telling him of my difficulties, he said: "I'll manage a passage for you all right! But you must be ready to start at a moment's notice, for I can't tell myself when the first transport will go to the Dardanelles." I packed up my kit, engaged a Maltese body-servant, and rode at single anchor.' (4)

The call came on the night of 30 March 1854 just as Russell was about to be initiated into the Freemasons at the Lodge of St Peter and St Paul. He rushed to the steamer the *Golden Fleece* which was due to sail at midnight and was already packed with men of the Rifle Brigade, a detachment of engineers and the headquarters staff of the Light Division. The Maltese servant, who had begged an advance of wages to maintain his family during his absence, disappeared with the bulk of Russell's effects.

During the voyage Russell got his first taste of the sort of treatment he might expect from the army commanders. General Sir George Brown, commander of the Light Division (Infantry), was sixty-four and the archetype of those senior officers who believed nothing had changed since the days half a century before when they had fought under Sir John Moore and the Duke of Wellington, a brave reactionary martinet of the old school. Sir George did not take kindly to the presence of a journalist: 'I was not introduced to Sir George by anyone,' Russell wrote to Delane, 'and he took no notice of me the whole time he was on board except one day to take wine with me and to say "Well, Sir, I'm off now" the day he was going on shore. He offered me no facilities and I did not ask for any and his staff etc., of course, are afraid of acting when they see the Chief so taciturn.' (5)

They anchored off Gallipoli on 5 April and the soldiers started going ashore three days later. Russell's Letter to *The Times*, dated 8 April and published on the 24th, made no mention of Sir George's behaviour but was critical on other counts. The French had landed before them and commandeered all the best quarters. And Russell wondered what the armies were doing there, too far south to defend Constantinople and hundreds of miles from the fighting:

> Unless there is danger of the forces of His Imperial Majesty the Emperor of All the Russias getting by some means or other down on the very shores of the Dardanelles, the advantage of fixing our position at Gallipoli does not strike the unprofessional critic very forcibly. . . . Would it not be better to . . . march at once to aid the Turks on the Danube, if we seriously intend to strike a blow for them?

At the same time Russell sent a private letter to Delane, inaugurating the system by which he informed his editor of the state of affairs as he saw it with a strength of language and a degree of personal detail that might seem too forceful or vindictive in his Letters for publication:

> My dear Sir,
> . . . There is but scanty water and no shelter on the site of the encampment—neither tree nor blade of grass. The management is infamous and the contrast offered by our proceedings to the conduct of the French most painful. Would you believe it?—the sick have not a bed to lie upon. They are landed and thrust into a ricketty house without a chair to sit upon or a table in it. The French with their ambulances, excellent Commissariat staff, and *boulangerie* etc. in every respect are immeasurably our superiors. While these things go on Sir George Brown only seems anxious about the men being clean shaved, their necks well stiffened up and their waist belts tight. He insists on officers and men being in full fig, no loose coats, jackets etc. His wonderful pack kills the men, as the weight is so disposed as to hang from instead of resting on the shoulders. . . .
> I run a good chance of *starving* if the army takes the field, for the Commissary will give me *no rations without an order from Head Quarters*, and well disposed and kind as the officers are they have little enough for themselves in their own allowance. I have no *tent* nor can I get one without an order, and even if I had one I doubt very much if Sir George Brown would allow me to pitch it within the camp. . . . I am living in a pig stye—a mud-walled room without chair table stool or window glass—and an old hag of 60 to attend on me who does not understand a word I say. I live on eggs and brown bread—some Tenedos wine and onions and rice. The French have got all the place to themselves. I am told if the army marches I must get a bullock waggon as the Commissariat won't allow my things to go on the Government

waggons *without an order*. Again I am told that they will not allow my things to be taken charge of by the rear guard and come in the baggage train *without an order!*

The letter mentions all the themes that were to become insistent in Russell's reports—poor management, shortage of medical facilities, the breakdown of the Commissariat, the preoccupation of the British generals with anachronistic regulations, the 'red-tapery' that ruled their juniors, the superiority of the French in every aspect of the armies' affairs.

His next Letter, dated 10 April, described Gallipoli as: 'a wretched place——picturesque to a degree, but, like all picturesque things or places, horribly uncomfortable. The French came first and, like all first-comers, they are the best-served.' Preparations for the reception of the British had been hopelessly inadequate:

The only steps taken by the authorities were to send two commissary officers, without interpreters or staff, to the town a few days before the troops actually landed, to make provision for them. These officers could not speak the language, nor were they furnished with any facilities for making themselves intelligible. . . . While our sick men have not a mattress to lie down upon, and are literally without blankets, the French are well provided for. We have no medical comforts—none were forwarded from Malta—and so, when a poor fellow was sinking the other day, the doctor had to go to the General's and get a bottle of wine for him.

Three days later he fired another broadside:

Amid the multitude of complaints which meet one's ear from every side, the most prominent are charges against the commissariat; but I am satisfied that the officers here are not to blame. The persons really culpable are those who sent them out without a proper staff, and without the smallest foresight or consideration. Early and late I find them toiling amid a set of apathetic Turks and stupid araba [cart] drivers, trying in vain to make bargains and give orders in the language of signs.

And now he made direct reference to Sir George Brown's preoccupation with his men's appearance: 'No-one under his command need dread the fate of Absalom. His hatred of hair is almost a mania. . . . The stocks [close-fitting leather neck bands], too, are to be kept up, stiff as ever. On the march of the Rifles to their camp at least one man fell out of the ranks senseless; immediate recovery was affected by the simple process of opening the stock.'

Russell was getting into his stride. The honeymoon days of Malta were over. The move to Gallipoli had uncovered the key weaknesses of the British army and he was not the man—whatever the cost to his personal convenience—to hide the facts. Within a few weeks his Letters assumed the style that was to characterize them throughout the campaign—detailed, observant, informed, confident and frequently critical.

His Letters were not works of literary art; they were not carefully shaped or neatly rounded or, for the most part, particularly elegant in style. But in a sense these defects were strengths. For his readers it was like getting long letters, hastily but honestly set down, from a soldier son who was fair-minded and fearless, who had an insatiable appetite for information of all kinds and a lively no-nonsense way of putting it down on paper. The very fact that Russell was always ready to correct any mistakes he made—to set the record right in subsequent Letters—increased the trust of his readers. Here was a man, they felt, whose overriding concern was to tell the truth. This reliability was his strongest weapon. His Letters were also fluent and clear and, as the pace of events quickened, crammed with facts and comment and ideas. No newspaper had ever before provided such a vivid and complete account of a British army overseas. Suddenly Russell found himself, for all the anxieties about his relations with the army, in a powerfully influential position—the sole correspondent with the army of the country's greatest newspaper, with much to tell. Without any deliberate calculation on his part, simply by virtue of his straightforward attitude to his job, he was able during these weeks to create a formidable following in Britain and build a foundation of faith in his reporting that was to stand him in good stead in the harsher months to come.

He wrote something every day, or every other day, and despatched his package twice a week when the vagaries of the postal system allowed. Often several packets would arrive at Printing House Square on the same day. But Delane, knowing what his readers wanted, would print the lot immediately, sometimes giving a whole page or more to Russell's reports. Within a few weeks 'Our Own Correspondent with the British troops at Gallipoli' was essential reading for all who would be well informed.

The Letters were more than a catalogue of complaints. They described the landscape and the local people, the movements and parades of the soldiers. There were anecdotes of daily life in camp, sometimes cumbrously facetious, garnished with literary allusions, classical and Biblical. But it was the criticisms that attracted most attention.

Delane not only printed the Letters in full, he ordered his leader-writers to follow up important points and acquainted his political contacts with the stronger comments he was getting from Russell privately.

The government responded promptly. The Duke of Newcastle, Secretary of State for War, told the House of Lords: 'As to the statements respecting the treatment of the sick and the total want of medical comforts for them, the whole thing is so monstrous that I cannot for a moment believe it to be true.' Lord Lovaine demanded to know 'how the person who reported to *The Times* newspaper' had obtained his passage to Gallipoli. A leading article on 3 May gave the details of Russell's journey and added grandly: 'If it seems necessary to the

1a *The Times* offices at Printing House Square 1847

1b　John Thadeus Delane

1c　Mowbary Morris

2a   The allied commanders in conclave in the Crimea

2b   British shipping in Balaclava Harbour

Enthusiasm of Paterfamilias on reading the Report in the *Times* of the Grand Charge of British Cavalry.

(Reproduced by kind permission of the proprietors of "Punch.")

3   *Punch* cartoon portraying the impact of Russell's Balaclava despatch

conductors of this journal that somebody should represent them and the public at Gallipoli or elsewhere, he may be very sure that there "Our Own Correspondent" will be found. If he were excluded from all the ships of war and transports which float upon the sea, there he would be found at the time appointed.'

By mid-April the allied armies were assembled in Gallipoli. The French Commander-in-Chief was Marshal Saint-Arnaud, an ambitious man who had fought with the Foreign Legion in Algeria and helped Napoleon III seize power in 1851. His British counterpart was Lord Raglan.

Raglan had been given the command because he was the only officer with the necessary qualifications who was under the age of seventy. He was in fact sixty-six but still strong and fit. He had been an officer for fifty years, one of the Duke of Wellington's aides-de-camp during the Peninsular campaign and at Waterloo. His bravery was a legend—unruffled under fire and capable of great fortitude. At Waterloo, when his right elbow was smashed by a musket ball, he walked quietly back to the field hospital and made no moan as the arm was cut off below the shoulder without benefit of anaesthetic. As the surgeon went to throw it away, Raglan called out, 'Hey, bring back my arm. There's a ring my wife gave me on the finger.' He was intelligent, diligent, devoted to the service and capable of enormous charm. He had a clearer grasp of military realities than most of the Crimean commanders. Yet he was ill-suited for the command of an army of 30,000 men. He had never commanded so much as a battalion in the field. Like Sir George Brown, his active service had consisted of taking and relaying the orders of 'The Great Duke'. Since then, he had spent forty years without active service of any kind, as Military Secretary at the Horse Guards, later as Master-General of the Ordnance. During the Crimean campaign he was hobbled, in a sense, by his own gentlemanliness. In councils of war with his fellow commanders, though he was often right when they were wrong, he lacked the force of will to carry the argument. He hated scenes and was determined, above all, to avoid serious conflict with his allies. There was nothing showy or inspirational about his leadership. On the march, or in camp, he was too reticent to make any display of himself. On the battlefield, he was chary of giving orders. He suffered, too, from the venerable belief that awkward problems will go away if you ignore them long enough. It was this attitude that prompted his policy, or non-policy, towards Russell and the other press correspondents who had joined the army.

The Duke of Wellington would have ordered the expulsion of all journalists. But that was an altogether simpler matter in his day. In the half century since then British public opinion had grown, through the widening of the franchise, into a powerful force and the press, *The Times* particularly, saw itself as the voice of the people. Any attempt to exclude reporters from the field of action would certainly have led, in the 1850s, to public outcry and great trouble and embarrassment in the corridors of power.

The alternative was to institute a system of field censorship, ostensibly to stop any leakage of information to the enemy, in practice to muzzle—or at least to muffle—criticism. No doubt there would have been strident protests against this too, particularly from *The Times* which believed it had a God-given duty to get information and publish it. But a sound case could have been made and a workable system set up. It would have meant issuing orders, though, and a certain amount of bother, and Raglan chose instead to try to freeze the journalists out. He never spoke to them, gave them no information and encouraged his *aides* and subordinate commanders—by example, not by orders—to give them no help. It was the policy of the ostrich and it was to cost him dearly.

Lord Raglan landed at Gallipoli on 2 May 1854, took a characteristically unobtrusive look round and sailed the same night for the Bosphorus. He had been given Russell's name before he left London, presumably by Lord Hardinge, but made no attempt to see him.

A few days later Russell took passage to Constantinople, stayed a few days at Missirie's Hotel, then crossed the Bosphorus to Scutari where the Guards were camped.

He was beginning to form a household. He had bought a tent, a horse and a pony, and hired an Italian servant, Angelo Gennaro. They pitched the tent alongside the Coldstreams' camp but a few days later Russell returned from an evening ride to find his tent dismantled and four hundred yards away. '*Un officiale brutale*,' Angelo told him, and thrown them out. This was on the orders of Brigadier-General Sir Henry Bentinck, Commander of the Guards Brigade. Copies of *The Times* with the Gallipoli reports were now circulating in the army; the Raglan attitude was filtering down the ranks; the cold official shoulder was turning icy.

Russell made strenuous efforts to improve his relations with the army authorities. He wrote to Delane:

> I have crossed over every day in the hope of seeing Lord Raglan especially, and three times I have written my name in his book. Yesterday I heard he was going to Varna today, and I went over at 8 o'clock. First he was at breakfast, then he had a Council of War. I waited on patiently till 4 o'clock—from 8 am till 4 pm—but as there were others, French Generals etc. still waiting to see him, I consented to see Col. Steele, Military Secretary, and had a disagreeable interview. I had to explain who I was, why I called, what I wanted etc. and finally Col. Steele requested me to 'write a letter' stating what I required, but at the same time he expressed an opinion that it would be impossible to give me or my horse rations. . . . I fear the promises made at home will not be kept abroad. . . . I fear to pitch my tent in camp till I see Lord Raglan, lest I should be ordered away. (6)

But there were consolations. For one thing, he was not alone in his troubles. Other journalists had arrived on the scene, among them Nicholas Woods for the *Morning Herald*, Joseph Crowe for the *Illustrated London News*, Captain Blakeley for the *Morning Chronicle* and Lawrence Godkin for the *Daily News*. And a steady flow of encouragement came from Printing House Square. There had been trouble in early May when Russell suspected that the financial arrangements were not being fully honoured. He complained to Delane and said that if he had misunderstood their agreement 'I must beg you to allow me to return as soon as you may find it convenient to send a person to take my place.' (7) Delane quickly settled the matter, reassured Russell about it and the well-being of his family, sympathized with his sufferings and said how much *The Times* appreciated his work.

By the end of May some of Russell's problems were solved. The army had at last accepted the job of supplying rations and transport for him, his servant and the horses. He was attached, loosely, to the Light Division. His chief worry was whether he would be allowed to accompany the army when it went into action.

This concern arose not so much from Lord Raglan's attitude, which remained one of passive resistance to the reporters, as from fears that the French commander, Marshal Saint-Arnaud, might bring his influence to bear. The French army, though more democratic than the British in some ways and certainly more open to claims of merit in the matter of promotion, held its attendant journalists under tight censorship. Napoleon III had no intention of allowing the French press the sort of influential licence *The Times* enjoyed in England. Russell warned his readers:

> I regret to have to inform you it is very generally rumoured that Marshal St.
> Arnaud has expressed his determination to prevent any newspaper
> correspondent accompanying the army, and that he has been persuading Lord
> Raglan and Omar Pasha [the Turkish commander] to come to a similar
> resolution. Such a course of conduct may be suited to the notions of military
> propriety entertained by our gallant allies, but it is not at all in consonance with
> the spirit of our institutions or with the feelings of the public in England. There
> can be no desire, on the part of any British subject, to pry into secrets, or to
> publish what ought to be concealed. All that a newspaper correspondent wants
> is to see what is done, and to describe it to the best of his ability. (8)

The allied armies sailed once more, this time to Varna on the western shore of the Black Sea, much closer to the fighting. Seventy miles to the north the Turks, vigorously assisted by *The Times* correspondent Charles Nasmyth, were defending the town of Silistria from the besieging Russians. If the Russians were to take the town and advance towards Constantinople, there would be fighting enough for everyone.

Enlivened by the prospect of action, the soldiers were in high spirits. The weather was fine, the countryside was lush and beautiful and rich in game. Rations were supplemented by fishing and hunting and bartering with Bulgarian villagers. Anglo-French relations remained good. It was an idyllic interval for the soldiers and for Russell, who wrote to Mary: 'All my difficulties have vanished now. . . . I am great friends with all the Generals and officers. . . . the more I rough it the better I am. I am as brown as a berry—have a great beard and am cropped to the very roots of the hair. I always go about with sabre and pistol, so you would scarce know the little fellow. . .' (9)

The euphoria was soon over. In the third week of June the Russians abandoned their siege of Silistria and withdraw northwards. With their hopes of action disappointed, the soldiers called themselves 'the army of no occupation'. Idleness bred indiscipline and severe punishments were invoked. The weather grew sultry, tempers shortened and the British generals passed the time in issuing complicated and sometimes conflicting orders on questions of turn-out—whether the soldiers should be excused stocks or not, how much latitude officers should be given in their off-parade dress, whether to permit moustaches, or beards, or neither. Russell found a new subject for attack in 'the abominable shako', the tall cylindrical hat with a peak and pompom, and suggested an alternative: '. . . in war everything should be sacrified to utility. A stout forage cap, with the peak of the shako put on, and a roll of linen round it, turban fashion, would be far more suitable to this climate.' (10)

Sir George Brown ordered that stocks would not be worn on the march. One of his brigadiers objected and incurred the weight of Russell's ridicule:

> He is a very gallant and excellent officer, but he actually has an affection for a 'common soldier's stock,' and never wears anything else; *ergo*, because he, riding at his ease, on a fine soft-going charger, without anything on his shoulders, and being spare withal, feels no annoyance from this singular anti-pneumonic apparatus, Private Peter Brown, No. 1 company, with 56 lb. on his back, 50 rounds of Minié cartridge, a close coatee, a water canteen, a shako, etc., must positively like to wear a similar article in a little march over a Bulgarian sand common, with the thermometer at 110°. (11)

The army's vital problems remained unsolved and Russell worried away at them in his Letters—the shortage of transport, rigid red-tape attitudes, the lack of field ambulances and hospitals. His unpopularity with the generals returned. Once again his tent was ordered out of the lines, this time by the Commander of the First Division, the Duke of Cambridge, a cousin of the Queen. He moved to the Light Division's area near Devno, ten miles from Varna. Sir George Brown received him with a poor grace and shouted after him one day, 'You see your Gallipoli letters and a Russian speech in Parliament are the only extracts quoted by the Russians.' (12)

This was an increasingly tender point. Although the Letters took ten to fourteen days to reach London by sea, they were published immediately on arrival and all important points could be transmitted to Moscow by telegraph within the day. Among the senior officers the conviction grew that Russell was helping the enemy with information and encouraging him by continually harping on the British army's difficulties.

The Times did not budge from its belief that the *raison d'être* of newspapers was disclosure. In a leading article on 29 May 1854 it told its readers there was serious danger that the correspondents would be expelled from the army and warned the government that any attempt to do so would be fiercely resisted:

> If a regiment cannot move for want of horses or ammunition; if the sappers and miners find themselves without tools; if some other needful preparation has been omitted, we may be sure that Government will have a much better chance of hearing it through 'Our Own Correspondent' than through its own despatches, if, indeed, the information comes at all before it is too late. We can easily understand why a certain class of officers should like no tale told but their own; and why Government should wish a veil to be thrown over its possible neglects; but the people of England will look for safety in publicity rather than in concealment.

Delane could already point to some successes for his policy. He had campaigned for a more unified control for the army and in June the government created a new ministerial post, Secretary for War, and gave it to Lord Newcastle. For the first time all military departments came under a single supreme authority. Pressure from *The Times* also brought about some easing of antiquated regulations about uniforms.

So far the general health of the army had been good; boredom, drink and diarrhoea had been the chief complaints. But towards the end of July, there was ominous news from the allied camps. Cholera was prevalent throughout southern Europe that summer and it now spread quickly through the French then the British armies, then to the ships' crews on the Black Sea. Camps were moved to new sites where the air was thought to be healthier but the epidemic raged on. The French suffered most. In his Letter of 9 August 1854 Russell described a nightmare visit to the French general hospital at Varna:

> I rode up there at twelve o'clock the other night for medicine for an officer, a friend of mine, who was taken suddenly ill in the evening. Along two sides of the hospital was drawn up a long train of araba carts, and by the moonlight I could see that some of them were filled with sick soldiers. I counted thirty-five carts, with three or four men in each. These were sick French soldiers sent in from the camps, and waiting till room could be found for them in the hospital. A number of soldiers were sitting down by the roadside, and here and there the moonbeams flashed brightly off their piled arms. The men were silent; not a song, not a laugh! A gloom, which never had I seen before among French troops, reigned amid these groups of grey-coated men, and the quiet that prevailed was only broken now and then by the moans and cries of pain of the

poor sufferers in the carts. Observing that about fifteen arabas were drawn up without any occupants, I asked a *sous-officier* for what purpose they were required. His answer, sullen and short, was,—'*Pour les morts—pour les Français décédés, Monsieur.*'

The medical services were overwhelmed. Soldiers spent their days nursing sick comrades and digging graves. Russell reckoned the British lost about seven hundred men to cholera at this time, the French considerably more. Other soldiers went down with dysentery and fever. There was a sudden, alarming decline in the strength of the allied armies. On 19 August Russell wrote:

So completely exhausted, on last Thursday, was the Brigade of Guards, these 3000 of the flower of England, that they had to make two marches in order to get over the distance from Aladyn to Varna, which is not more than (not so much, many people say, as) ten miles. But that is not all. Their packs were carried for them. Just think of this, good people of England, who are sitting anxiously in your homes, day after day, expecting every morning to gladden your eyes with the sight of the announcement, in large type, of 'Fall of Sebastopol,' your Guards, your *corps d'élite*, the pride of your hearts, the delight of your eyes, these Anakim, whose stature, strength and massive bulk you exhibit to kingly visitors as no inapt symbols of your nation, have been so reduced by sickness, disease, and a depressing climate, that it was judged inexpedient to allow them to carry their own packs, or to permit them to march more than five miles a day, even though these packs were carried for them! Think of this, and then judge whether these men are fit in their present state to go to Sebastopol, or to attempt any great operation of war.

Russell's own health remained excellent. The rigours of camp life and the daily exercise which his job involved suited his constitution admirably. Throughout his campaigning life, which spanned more than a quarter of a century, he was generally much fitter in the field than he was at home in London where he could never resist the temptations of the table.

In a long letter to Mary, which is undated but which must have written in mid-August, he gave a picture of his daily life in camp with the Rifle Brigade. He had a second Italian servant by this time, Virgilio. And he was on the friendliest terms with his neighbours, Captain W. J. Colville and his two subalterns, Egerton and Lord Leveson-Gower, a son of the Duke of Sutherland. Russell would breakfast with them, then return to his own tent to write:

Lots of fellows come in and I have to keep a two-gallon vessel full of weak country wine, sugar and water for them which is emptied about twice a day. Sometimes I move beyond the precincts of our own camp, visit my horses and stroll over to the 77th, then go on to the 19th, then to the 23rd and so on through all the regiments, or I stop with someone or other and lunch on bread and cheese.

In the cool of the evening he would shoot birds for the pot, then back to Colville's tent for dinner: 'A large pot is brought into the tent full of soup made with rice and the meat boiled down. We fill our tin porringers and grub away like anything. Then the meat is eaten with bread, and once or twice a week we have a fowl curried or a boiled goose or turkey bought from the country people.' After coffee and a smoke and a chat, they would turn in about ten o'clock:

At night the dew is like a fall of rain. When I have groped over to my tent it is all wet outside. I open the flap, grope about in the dark, strike my light, pop goes a big beetle or a cloud of rum insects into it, while centipedes and all kinds of nasty things bundle away into the darkness. Then carefully keeping my legs from the ground, I undress and, thinking every night of my deenyman and children, soon add my snores to the tremendous chorus of the thousands around me.

The letter ends on an optimistic note:

We may expect soon to go to Sevastopol. I'll try to get on board some large steamer from which I can see all the fun without going into danger, and if Sevastopol is taken, as I expect it will, the war will be over for the year and I will get over for a few weeks to see my deenyman and children while the troops are in winter quarters.

A few days later, writing to Mary from on board an English man-of-war in Varna Bay, he was not so sanguine:

I am in excellent health, thank God, though I am somewhat moved of course by the ravages death is making around me. . . . I do not think it possible that the army here can do anything this year unless it becomes healthier and in better spirits than it is at present. . . . I hate seeing wounded men and the thought of the 'butcher's bill' we will have to pay at Odessa, Sevastopol or Cronstadt is not very pleasant to me, for I am now getting tired a good deal of what is called 'glory' from seeing the inner life of camps and fleets. (13)

Some move by the allies was now inevitable. To a man, the soldiers wanted to get away from the coast where cholera, though diminishing, still claimed many lives. There was little doubt what their objective would be.

Sebastopol, at the southern tip of the Crimean peninsula, was the base of the Russians' Black Sea fleet. It was from here that they had sailed to destroy the Turkish ships at Sinope. It was from here that any threat would come to Britain's links with the eastern Mediterranean and India. Orders came from London and Paris to go for Sebastopol and the three Commanders-in-Chief and their senior officers held a council of war.

Although they knew their own strength—some 30,000 French troops, 27,000 British, 7,000 Turks—they had no idea how many men the Russians had in the Crimea. Estimates ranged from 45,000 to 140,000. The allied navies had command of the Black Sea—the Russian ships were bottled up in Sebastopol harbour—so they could choose their point of landing and take the enemy by surprise. After that, though, it looked as if the odds might lie in the Russians' favour.

Lord Raglan asked Sir George Brown for his opinion and got a classic reply: 'You and I are accustomed, when in any great difficulty, or when any important question is proposed to us, to ask ourselves how the Great Duke would have acted under similar circumstances. Now I tell your Lordship that without more certain information than you appear to have obtained with regard to this matter, that great man would not have accepted the responsibility of undertaking such an enterprise as that which is now proposed to you.'

But the generals had no real choice. Their orders were clear and their men were eager to move. On 26 August 1854 Marshal Saint-Arnaud issued a general order couched in grandiose Napoleonic terms: '*L'heure est venue de combattre, et de vaincre.*' Lord Raglan, more phlegmatically, asked the Commissary-General 'to take steps to insure that the troops shall all be provided with a ration of porter for the next few days.'

Once more, Russell's problem was that of ensuring a passage for himself with the army. It was solved by General de Lacy Evans, Commander of the Second Division and much the most battle-experienced of the British generals, who found a berth for him on board the steamer *City of London*. But there was no room for his servants and horses, nor for his tent, nor for most of his baggage.

The army's spirits were high again. 'Nearly everyone,' Russell told his readers, 'looks with confidence to the result, and places full reliance on Lord Raglan's soundness of head and clearness of judgement.' (14)

The Great Battles—
September–November 1854

The allied fleets made a smooth crossing and the landings, at Kalamita Bay near Eupatoria, thirty-five miles north of Sebastopol, were unopposed.

The French were first ashore, at seven o'clock on the morning of 14 September. By mid-afternoon the British were disembarking. Sir George Brown advanced up the beach so briskly he was in serious danger of being killed or captured by a small group of mounted Cossacks who were watching the landings. This was to be a regular feature of the campaign. Time and again British generals would be found plunging ahead of their men, endangering themselves for no good reason except to show they were not afraid. They were certainly brave men and could not be accused, as their successors in the First World War often were, of sitting safely 'miles behind the line', but their courage was often pointlessly displayed and may have owed something to the high incidence, among them, of short-sightedness.

In the evening heavy rain set in and, without their tents, the British spent a miserable night. Russell was luckier than most. He found some friends of the 33rd, the Duke of Wellington's, and passed the night with them beneath an upturned cart, smoking his pipe and listening to the rain. At dawn he went back on board and settled down to describe the invasion for his readers.

'We are "an army of occupation" at last,' he wrote. 'The English and French armies have laid hold of a material guarantee in the shape of some score square miles of the soil of the Crimea, and they are preparing to extend the area of their rule in their progress towards Sebastopol.' (1)

He described the landing and gave the credit not to the commander of the British Fleet, Admiral Dundas, but to his deputy, Vice-Admiral Sir Edmund Lyons: 'In our fleet the whole labour and responsibility of the disembarkation rested with Sir E. Lyons. The Admiral remained aloof, and took no share in the proceedings of the day.' Sir Edmund was a man of Nelsonian vigour, as widely respected as the senior admiral was despised. In the weeks to come Russell's comments on Dundas were to grow critical to the point of bitterness.

He soon had other criticisms. In his Letter of 16 September he wrote:

A most extraordinary occurrence, which deserves severe censure, took place yesterday. Signal was made from the *Emperor* for all ships to send their sick on board the *Kangaroo*. In the course of the day the last-named ship was surrounded by hundreds of boats laden with sick men, and the vessel was speedily crowded to suffocation. . . . Many deaths occurred on board—many miserable scenes took place, but there is, alas! no use in describing them. It is clear, however, that neither afloat nor on shore is the medical staff nearly sufficient. I myself saw men dying on the beach, on the line of march, and in bivouac, without any medical assistance; and this within hail of a fleet of 500 sail, and within sight of head-quarters! We want more surgeons, both in the fleet and in the army. Often—too often—medical aid cannot be had at all; and it frequently comes too late.

Three distinguished visitors had arrived just in time to see the landings: the travel writer A. W. Kinglake, the excavator of Nineveh A. H. Layard, and Russell's editor J. T. Delane.

Delane found Russell on the beach on 15 September and they had a long talk. He was able to confirm for himself much of what Russell had been reporting, but was no more successful than Russell had been in getting access to the elusive Lord Raglan. He thought of marching with the army to see the taking of Sebastopol, than changed his mind and sailed the evening before the march began. He wrote home that he had found Russell 'fat and flourishing'. But Russell, waving goodbye from the shore, was far from confident: 'I saw my friends depart to their ships with feelings akin to those of one who is marooned and sees the boat rowing away from him. Truth to tell, there was not much to make me happy. I was not *en rapport* with any one. There was no cheeriness in the surroundings.' (2)

His position was unenviable. He had neither tent nor servant. A major battle was clearly imminent and his experience of war was limited to a single day's action at Idstedt four years before. He had no idea how he would stand up to the test of coming under heavy fire and little notion how to go about his job—where to station himself on the line of march, the best place to be when the fighting started. There were no precedents to guide him. He could be sure his presence would be resented by most of the generals and sure, too, that even those officers who had become friends would be too busy to spare time or thought for him. The soldiers had been trained for this moment and many of them had longed for it; they would have comrades and orders and objectives. Russell knew only that he would have to be in the thick of the action, that if he behaved well he could expect neither medals nor promotion, and if he were killed there would be no government pension for his wife and children. 'I was nobody's child,' he said, (3) and he felt it keenly.

His costume proclaimed his unattached condition: 'I wore a Commissariat officer's cap with a broad gold band; a Rifleman's patrol jacket, for which I had

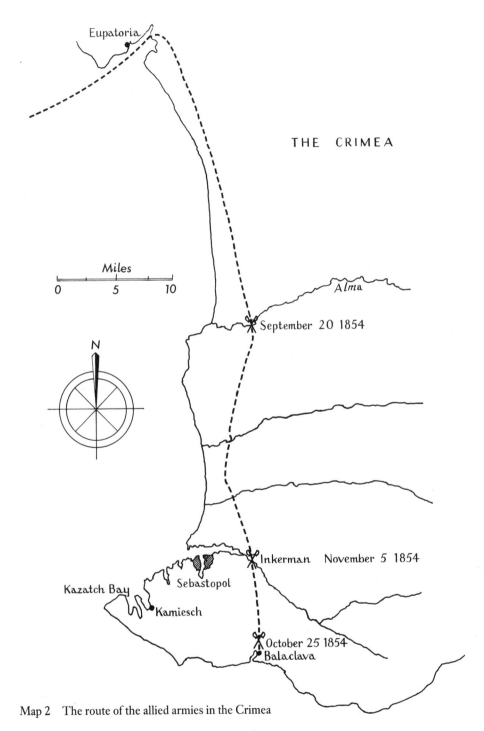

Eupatoria

THE CRIMEA

Miles
0   5   10

N

Alma

✗ September 20 1854

✗ Inkerman   November 5 1854

Kazatch Bay   Sebastopol
            • Kamiesch

✗ October 25 1854
Balaclava

Map 2   The route of the allied armies in the Crimea

given egregious *largesse* to the owner; cord breeches; a pair of butcher boots and huge brass spurs.' (4) At least his health was good and at the last moment he acquired a horse of sorts—'a fiddle-headed, ewe-necked beast—great bone and not much else—that Nolan imparted to me in exchange for twenty golden sovereigns.' (5) Captain Lewis Edward Nolan of the 15th Hussars, an old friend, had seized the horse on a foraging expedition inland.

The armies marched on 19 September, the Turks on the coast, the French in the centre, the British on the left with their cavalry protecting the exposed flank. Russell rode about, observing and making notes, struck—as he was to be many times in the years to come—by the splendour of the general spectacle and the pathos of much of its detail: 'It was a painful sight—a sad contrast to the magnificent appearance of the army in front, to behold litter after litter borne past to the carts, with the poor sufferers who had dropped from illness and fatigue.' (6)

As he crossed the front of the Second Division, he was challenged by an aide-de-camp and taken to see the Brigade Commander, Brigadier Sir John Pennefather:

> 'By —, sir!' exclaimed the General, when I had told him all I knew about myself; 'I'd as soon see the devil! What on earth do you know of this kind of work, and what will you do when we get into action?'
>
> 'Well, General,' I answered, 'it is quite true I have very little acquaintance with the business, but I suspect there are a great many here with no greater knowledge of it than myself.'
>
> He laughed. 'Bedad, you're right! You're an Irishman, I'll be bound! And what's your name, sir?'
>
> I told him.
>
> 'Are you from Limerick?'
>
> 'No, sir; but my family are.'
>
> 'Well, good-bye. Go to the rear, I tell you now! There will be wigs on the green to-day, my boy! So keep away from the front if you don't wish to have your notes cut short! Good morning!' (7)

They soon found the enemy, securely in position on steeply rising ground beyond the river Alma. The Russian guns covered the natural lines of ascent and stakes had been fixed into the ground to indicate the range. There was little natural cover for an attacking force. The Russian commander, Prince Mentschikoff, was so confident his position was impregnable that he had invited a number of officers' wives from Sebastopol to picnic on the heights and enjoy the slaughter of the invaders.

The allied commanders had no idea of the strength of the Russian forces and made no effort to study their dispositions and formulate a careful plan. Marshal Saint-Arnaud, a very sick man, proposed that the French should attack first on the coastal flank, covered by the ships' guns, and when they had gained sufficient height to fire along the line of the Russians, the British should attack frontally. Lord Raglan listened so taciturnly to the proposals that Saint-Arnaud was not sure he agreed and could only assume that near silence implied assent. In fact Raglan intended to honour the plan in so far as he understood it, though he knew it would fling his battalions against the strongest enemy formations in well-entrenched positions.

The battle was fought on 20 September 1854. The initial French attack met stiffer opposition than expected and the British, too far advanced under the Russian guns, had to wait patiently under a hail of artillery fire and then move into the attack without sufficient covering fire from the flank. It became a dogged pounding-match as Russell's friends of the Light Division, then the Guards and Highlanders of the First Division, stormed their way up hill to take the Russian strong-points and break the massed lines of Russian infantry beyond. Russell was frantically busy, just behind the leading troops, noting everything with his sharp eyes and ears, struggling to comprehend the pattern of the action, talking to the wounded, scribbling notes. When the Russians finally fled, virtually unpursued, he found himself at the top of the hill and anxiously aware that the chief part of his job was still to be done:

> Soldiers wild with victory, cheering 'like mad,' were narrating escapes and adventures; and I might as well have tried to get a consecutive narrative out of a whirlwind. 'Smiler' Bell told me how he had captured a gun; Lacy Yea how he had refused to let the Fusiliers retire (when I told him I had seen a sergeant and a lot of his men under the bank of the river, he shouted, 'Show the sergeant to me, and—I'll shoot him!'); and so forth!
>
> How was I to describe what I had seen?—where learn the facts for which they were waiting at home? My eyes swam as I tried to make notes of what I heard. I was worn out with excitement, fatigue, and want of food. I had been more than ten hours in the saddle: my wretched horse, bleeding badly from a cut in the leg, was unable to carry me. My head throbbed, my heart beat as though it would burst. I suppose I was unnerved by want of food and rest; but I was so much overcome by what I saw that I could not remain where the fight had been closest and deadliest. I longed to get away from it—from the exultation of others in which thought for the dead was forgotten or unexpressed.
>
> It was now that the weight of the task I had accepted fell on my soul like lead. It was time for me to set to work. I had the description of a battle to write! I felt not the least delight in the triumph. I knew it was a great victory; and though I did not feel, like little 'Emmeline,' that 'it was a very wicked thing' to win it, I did not share in the exultation of the conquerors. (8)

Wisely, he did not try to write his Letter that evening. Friends offered him a corner of their tent and he lay there through the night listening to the moans of the wounded. He started to write at first light, using a quill pen and the yellow pages of a Russian account book he had found. At first he wrote lying at full stretch on the ground, then a desk top was contrived for him by laying a plank across two casks. The story finished, he toured the broken slopes where the battle had been fought, and watched the removal of the wounded and the burial of the dead. He talked to dozens of officers and men and formed a clearer picture of what had happened, so decided to rewrite his Letter.

The result, published in *The Times* on 10 October, was a racy, vivid and coherent account and one that caught the character and shape of the battle with remarkable accuracy considering the conditions under which he worked. There were factual errors but they were, on the whole, minor ones and he scrupulously corrected them in later Letters. He concentrated on the British part of the action but this was understandable: it was what he knew about, it was what his readers wanted to hear about, and as it happened, it was the disciplined courage of the British infantrymen that had determined the issue. The chief fault of his Alma despatch lay in its tone which was dangerously like that of a rattling yarn in a boys' magazine. The British officers were unfailingly 'gallant'. The generals were portrayed as clear-headed and decisive and this was far from true. The soldiers were shown as brave and determined and this—as Russell knew—was not the whole truth. He described the final climax of the battle in these words:

> ... the Guards on the right of the Light Division, and the brigade of Highlanders, were storming the heights on the left. Their line was almost as regular as though they were in Hyde-park. Suddenly a tornado of round and grape rushed through from the terrible battery, and a roar of musketry from behind thinned their front ranks by dozens. It was evident that we were just able to contend against the Russians, favoured as they were by a great position. At this very time an immense mass of Russian infantry were seen moving down towards the battery. They halted. It was the crisis of the day. Sharp, angular and solid, they looked as if they were cut out of the solid rock. It was beyond all doubt that if our infantry, harassed and thinned as they were, got into the battery, they would have to encounter again a formidable fire, which they were but ill calculated to bear. Lord Raglan saw the difficulties of the situation. He asked if it would be possible to get a couple of guns to bear on these masses. The reply was 'Yes,' and an artillery officer, whose name I do not now know, brought up two guns to fire on the Russian squares. The first shot missed, but the next, and the next, and the next cut through the ranks so cleanly, and so keenly, that a clear lane could be seen for a moment through the square. After a few rounds the columns of the square became broken, wavered to and fro, broke, and fled over the brow of the hill, leaving behind them six or seven distinct lines of dead, lying as close as possible to each other, marking the passage of the fatal messengers. This act relieved our infantry of a deadly incubus, and they continued their magnificent and fearful progress up the hill.

If his first account of a great battle was entirely uncritical, Russell was quick to right the balance. In his next Letter, written on the following day, he described the horrific aftermath, the surgeons working 'with humane barbarity', and noted the continued absence of ambulances: 'Our men were sent to the sea, three miles distant, on jolting arabas or tedious litters. The French—I am tired of this disgraceful antithesis—had well-appointed covered hospital vans, to hold ten or twelve men, drawn by fine mules, and their wounded were sent in much greater comfort than our poor fellows, as far as I saw.' Admiral Dundas sent no sailors ashore to help with this work and Russell was scathing. He pointed out, too, how ridiculous it was that the senior British officers should attract fire to themselves on the field of battle by the flamboyance of their dress.

The battle laid Sebastopol wide open. The Russians were so shocked and demoralized by their defeat that the allies could, at comparatively little cost, have taken the naval base from the north within a few days. Lord Raglan wanted a prompt assault but Saint-Arnaud demurred, fearing that the enemy's defences might be too much for an allied army weakened by battle and disease. Concerned above all to keep the *entente* intact, Raglan reluctantly accepted an alternative plan—to march round to the south of Sebastopol, where its defences were thought to be minimal, and take it from the high ground there.

Russell saw very little of the flank march. Soon after it began, he went down with a delirious fever. Fortunately, his servants, Angelo and Virgilio, had caught up with him immediately after the Alma and they were able to look after him. He travelled on a truss of hay in the back of a cart and did not begin to recover until he was installed in a house in the little port of Balaclava. On 3 October he wrote to Delane:

> . . . I have lost all my baggage except bed, a coat, some paper. . . . There is no sign yet of the siege beginning. They are getting up the guns but slowly. Cholera is very bad. . . . Certainly we are giving the Russian every advantage in time and he is fortifying his weak points as hard as he can. The Admiral as usual aids the Czar as far as *he* can, and so between land and sea commanders it will be surprising if the Muscovite does not make a hard fight of it.

He worked hard the next few days, piecing together an account of the flank march, describing the situation of the allied forces, the landing of the siege guns and the frenzied efforts of the Russians to strengthen their southern defences. His Letter of 3 October announced that Marshal Saint-Arnaud was dangerously ill and had been replaced as French commander by another veteran of the Algerian wars, General Canrobert. It warned that Sebastopol was not besieged, only threatened on one side. It also said, 'The cholera continues its ravages.'

There was hundreds of sick men—not just from cholera, but dysentery and fever too—and there were no facilities at Balaclava to cope with them. They were crowded on to ships and transported to Scutari where an old Turkish army barracks had been taken over as the British hospital. It was a place of horror. With little or no equipment and a hopelessly inadequate staff, the patients lay in their own filth on the bare floors or on the ground outside and died in their hundreds. Russell has been praised as the man who exposed Scutari to the public, but he was not there and the credit is not his. His continuing criticism of the army's medical shortcomings had done something, no doubt, to prepare public opinion in England for the more terrible revelations of Scutari. But it was *The Times'* Constantinople correspondent, Thomas Chenery, who wrote a series of searing articles about the hospital. They were published in mid-October and led immediately to the appointment of Miss Florence Nightingale to lead a team of nurses to the stricken place, and *The Times* invited the public to subscribe to a Fund which would provide medical supplies and comforts to Scutari and Balaclava.

Lord Raglan established his headquarters at a farmhouse on the plateau above Sebastopol, four and a half miles north-west of Balaclava harbour. The British held the right of the allied line. The French, on the left, had supply harbours at Kamiesch and Kazatch and the complete protection of the Black Sea and the allied navies on their left flank. High ground to the north of Raglan's headquarters afforded a clear view of Sebastopol and every day the enemy could be seen at work building strong-points and fortifications under the expert guidance of Colonel Todleben. It was a worrying sight. Many British officers urged an immediate attack. Each day's delay, they argued, would mean the loss of scores, perhaps hundreds of allied lives. Lord Raglan was inclined to agree but once again allowed French counsels of caution to overrule his judgement. Canrobert said it would be a crime to ask the soldiers to attack without the support of heavy guns. So the siege guns were unloaded from the ships and man-handled into position while the soldiers dug trenches and waited.

For a while Russell found himself living virtually at headquarters. A friend on Raglan's staff offered him a corner of his tent. Lord Raglan continued to ignore him but he got to know most of the staff officers and made friends with the aides-de-camp.

The bombardment that was to open the way for the final assault began on the morning of 17 October 1854. The allies were confident that the perennial dream of the soldier—to get home for Christmas—would be realized. But it was soon apparent that the Russians had made excellent use of their breathing-space. A fierce artillery duel went on all day. At 8.30 that evening Russell wrote to Mary:

> I read your letter in the middle of the most tremendous tumult of battle that ever the ear of man has heard perhaps. . . . I fear these Russians will fight Sevastopol to the last. The scene today was terrible beyond all imagination. Our loss was very little, less than 100 men smashed by cannon shot and shell—about 200 French blown into the air and at least 1,000 Russians killed inside their batteries.

The bombardment was a failure. Most of the French guns, closer to the enemy than the British, were silenced. Lord Raglan still wanted to attack but was again dissuaded by the French. British disappointment turned to anger when copies of *The Times* of 2 October arrived proclaiming, nearly twelve months prematurely, that Sebastopol had fallen. The mistake was not Russell's—it seems to have sprung from over-optimistic Turkish interpretations of the victory at the Alma—but it did nothing to enhance his standing with the army.

On 25 October the Russians made their first attempt to smash the exposed British wing of the allied line. Their aim was to take the port of Balaclava and cut the British off from their supplies.

Russell watched the battle of Balaclava in almost ideal conditions. It was a fine clear day and from his position, high on a ridge overlooking the scene, he could study each movement and encounter as it took place. He had his watch and notebook, and frequent pauses in the action made it easy to keep full notes. He knew every British unit involved and many of the officers personally. The result was the best battle report he had written, comprehensive and colourful, precise and accurate. He caught the intense excitement of the day but was not carried away by it. He showed a sharp eye for the key moments and key questions of the battle and a remarkable ability to make an immediate and balanced appraisal of its significance. 'Don Quixote,' he wrote, 'in his tilt against the windmill was not near so rash and reckless as the gallant fellows who prepared without a thought to rush on almost certain death.' The last sentence of the Letter spoke of 'this melancholy day, in which our Light Brigade was annihilated by their own rashness'.

He began his Letter by sketching the background—the lie of the land over which the battle was fought, the resentment among British cavalrymen that they had seen little fighting so far.

In the early morning a large force of Russian cavalry, guns and infantry emerged from the valleys to the north and attacked the Turkish strong-points that formed the first line of Balaclava's defences. By the time Lord Raglan and his staff—and Russell too—had reached their vantage-point on the ridge, the Turks were being driven back by vastly superior forces: 'Never did the painter's eye rest on a more beautiful scene than I beheld from the ridge. The fleecy vapours still hung around the mountain tops, and mingled with the ascending volumes of smoke; the patch of sea sparkled freshly in the rays of the morning sun, but its light was eclipsed by the flashes which gleamed from the masses of armed men below.'

With the Turks routed, there was only one obstacle left between the advancing Russians and Balaclava—the 93rd Highlanders, drawn up in a line, two deep, under the command of Sir Colin Campbell, a veteran of wars in three continents.

The silence is oppressive; between the cannon bursts one can hear the
champing of bits and the clink of sabres in the valley below. The Russians on
their left drew breath for a moment, and then in one grand line dashed at the
Highlanders. The ground flies beneath their horses' feet; gathering speed at
every stride, they dash on towards that thin red streak topped with a line of steel.
The Turks fire a volley at eight hundred yards and run. As the Russians come

within six hundred yards, down goes that line of steel in front, and out rings a rolling volley of Minié musketry. The distance is too great; the Russians are not checked, but still sweep onwards through the smoke, with the whole force of horse and man, here and there knocked over by the shot of our batteries above. With breathless suspense every one awaits the bursting of the wave upon the line of Gaelic rock; but ere they come within a hundred and fifty yards, another deadly volley flashes from the levelled rifle, and carries death and terror into the Russians. They wheel about, open files right and left, and fly back faster than they came.

One phrase in this passage—'that thin red streak topped with a line of steel'—became part of the common currency of the language in a slightly altered form. Before long 'the thin red line' was a cliché of Victorian jingoism, expressing the controlled restraint of the British rifleman in the face of an enemy whose superiority in numbers could not outweigh his inferiority in discipline. The 93rd Regiment of Foot, who became the Sutherland Highlanders, took the words as the title of their regimental magazine.

The next phase of the battle brought the British cavalry into action at last when the Heavy Brigade, led by Brigadier-General Scarlett, charged a much larger body of Russian cavalry:

Lord Raglan, all his staff and escort, and groups of officers, the Zouaves, French generals and officers, and bodies of French infantry on the height, were spectators of the scene as though they were looking on the stage from the boxes of a theatre. Nearly every one dismounted and sat down, and not a word was said. The Russians advanced down the hill at a slow canter, which they changed to a trot, and at last nearly halted. Their first line was at least double the length of ours—it was three times as deep. Behind them was a similar line, equally strong and compact. They evidently despised their insignificant looking enemy, but their time was come. The trumpets rang out again through the valley, and the Greys and Enniskilleners went right at the centre of the Russian cavalry. The space between them was only a few hundred yards; it was scarce enough to let the horses 'gather way,' nor had the men quite space sufficient for the full play of their sword arms. The Russian line brings forward each wing as our cavalry advance, and threatens to annihilate them as they pass on. Turning a little to their left, so as to meet the Russian right, the Greys rush on with a cheer that thrills to every heart—the wild shout of the Enniskilleners rises through the air at the same instant. As lightning flashes through a cloud, the Greys and Enniskilleners pierced through the dark masses of Russians. The shock was but for a moment. There was a clash of steel and a light play of sword-blades in the air, and then the Greys and the redcoats disappear in the midst of the shaken and quivering columns. In another moment we see them emerging and dashing on with diminished numbers, and in broken order, against the second line, which is advancing against them as fast as it can to retrieve the fortune of the charge. It was a terrible moment. 'God help them! they are lost!' was the exclamation of more than one man, and the thought of many. With unabashed fire the noble hearts dashed at their enemy. It was a fight of heroes. The first line of Russians, which had been smashed utterly by our charge, and had fled off at one flank and towards the centre, were coming back to swallow up our handful of men. By sheer steel and sheer courage Enniskillener and Scot were winning their desperate way right through the enemy's squadrons, and already grey horses and red coats had appeared right at the rear of the second mass, when, with irresistible force, like one bolt from a bow, the 1st Royals, the 4th Dragoon Guards, and the 5th Dragoon Guards rushed at the remnants of the first line of the enemy, went through it as though it were made of pasteboard, and, dashing on the second body of Russians as they were still disordered by the terrible assault of the Greys and their companions, put them to utter rout. This Russian Horse in less than five minutes after it met our dragoons was flying with all its speed before a force certainly not half its strength.

It was still not ten in the morning. There was a long pause now before the incident for which the day is chiefly remembered.

The story of the charge of the Light Brigade has been told many times in varying ways, from the pounding doggerel of Tennyson to the detailed dissection of military historians. Few of the narrative accounts have been more vivid than the one Russell wrote that night:

At ten minutes past eleven, our Light Cavalry Brigade advanced. . . . As they rushed towards the front, the Russians opened on them from the guns in the redoubt on the right, with volleys of musketry and rifles. They swept proudly past, glittering in the morning sun in all the pride and splendour of war. We could scarcely believe the evidence of our senses! Surely that handful of men are not going to charge an army in position? Alas! it was but too true—their desperate valour knew no bounds, and far indeed was it removed from its so-called better part—discretion. They advanced in two lines, quickening their pace as they closed towards the enemy. A more fearful spectacle was never witnessed than by those who, without the power to aid, beheld their heroic countrymen rushing to the arms of death. At the distance of 1200 yards the whole line of the enemy belched forth, from thirty iron mouths, a flood of smoke and flame, through which hissed the deadly balls. Their flight was marked by instant gaps in our ranks, by dead men and horses, by steeds flying wounded or riderless across the plain. The first line is broken, it is joined by the second, they never halt or check their speed an instant; with diminished ranks, thinned by those thirty guns, which the Russians had laid with the most deadly accuracy, with a halo of flashing steel above their heads, and with a cheer that was many a noble fellow's death-cry, they flew into the smoke of the batteries, but ere they were lost from view the plain was strewed with their bodies and with the carcasses of horses. They were exposed to an oblique fire from the batteries on the hills on both sides, as well as to a direct fire of musketry. Through the clouds of smoke we could see their sabres flashing as they rode up to the guns and dashed between them, cutting down the gunners as they stood. We saw them riding through the guns, as I have said; to our delight we saw them returning, after breaking through a column of Russian infantry and scattering them like chaff, when the flank fire of the battery on the hill swept them down, scattered and broken as they were. Wounded men and dismounted troopers flying towards us told the sad tale—demi-gods could not have done what we had failed to do. . . . At thirty-five minutes past eleven not a British soldier, except the dead and dying, was left in front of those bloody Muscovite guns.

There was no doubt in the minds of the onlookers that what they had seen had been calamitous as well as courageous. In less than twenty-five minutes the Light Brigade had been destroyed—to no purpose at all. In the opening sentence of his Letter Russell called it a 'disaster'. His account dealt in detail with the immediate cause—the failure of Raglan's order to make it clear he wanted the Light Brigade to attack the Russian guns on the hill to their right, not those at the end of the long valley in front of them which was open to gunfire from three sides. Neither Raglan nor any of his staff realized that what was clear to them from their position on the ridge was hidden from the cavalry commanders in the valley. But Russell did not attempt to probe the powerful psychological forces that were at work. Captain Nolan, his friend, was among the most outspoken of those cavalry officers who were angry and ashamed that they had been 'kept in a bandbox' throughout the campaign, one of those who derided Lord Lucan, their commander, as 'Lord Look-on'. It was Nolan who was chosen to carry Raglan's vaguely-worded order to Lord Lucan. There was a brief altercation as Lucan strove to understand it. Then the order, still unclarified, was passed on to the Commander of the Light Brigade, Lord Cardigan. Cardigan's resentment and hatred of his brother-in-law, Lucan, was notorious and he was wild and wilful enough to lead his brigade to disaster for no better reason than to point the folly of his senior's order. As the charge got under way, Nolan galloped to the front waving his sword and trying, it seemed, to swing them to the right and towards their intended target. Cardigan ignored the 'impertinent devil' and rode straight on. A moment later Nolan was the first to be struck down by the Russian cannonade.

Further actions were fought before the battle subsided, leaving Balaclava harbour intact but the Russians holding high ground just to the north. Russell spent the remaining hours of daylight 'meandering about' in search of news and food. It was dark when he got back to his tent:

It was filled with officers discussing the events of the day, amid clouds of tobacco smoke. . . .

It was not a favourable place or moment for literary composition, and yet it was absolutely necessary to write, and that at once, for the mail would be leaving in a few hours! My head was aching and my heart was sore, but there was no help for it, and to work I went; my writing table was my knee, my seat a saddle, my lamp a commissariat candle stuck in a black bottle. . . . My companions were not inclined to silence, and they were full of information and of comment and advice—'Mind you put in this, etc. etc.,' 'Don't forget to say that, etc. etc.' But they had had a long day as well as myself. One by one the interlopers retired with friendly advice to me to 'Shut up and go to sleep,' and soon all the sound that came to my ears was the sonorous breathings—the *spiritus asper*—of my friends in the straw beside me, and I struggled on till my candle end disappeared in the bottle like a stage demon through a trap-door, and left me in darkness to settle down into my welcome blanket till *reveille* sounded. (9)

The Balaclava Letter was despatched next morning and published in *The Times* twenty days later together with a leading article which said: 'Few of our readers will hesitate to allow that they seldom read an incident of war described by so graphic a pen as that of our Correspondent in the Crimea.' Russell's reputation soared. *Punch* paid tribute to the impression he made in Britain (Plate 4). The circulation of *The Times* received fresh impetus. It had been rising fast in recent weeks—67,000 copies were sold on 2 October when the paper wrongly reported the fall of Sebastopol, more than 70,000 one week later when Russell's account of the Alma appeared.

Balaclava had been costly and inconclusive. It left the allied forces as much besieged as the Russians and more directly threatened. There was much sickness and official incompetence and winter was coming. Russell's despatches reflected the prevailing anxiety: 'The men are worn out'; (10) 'We must have more men and that speedily.' (11)

Before the plea could be answered, the Russians struck again. On 5 November, only eleven days after Balaclava, they attacked the British lines in the rough country above the Tchernaya valley near a place called Inkerman. The two battles could hardly have been more contrasting. Where the first was a matter of swift attack and counter-attack, involving cavalry rather than infantry and fought out in the clear light of a brilliant day, Inkerman was a long and bloody slogging-match of infantrymen, fighting at close quarters and often with the bayonet, in conditions of total confusion. The 'fog of war' was never foggier. There was thick early-morning mist when the battle began and it never lifted. No one could tell what was happening except in his own small corner of the battlefield and even there it was often impossible to distinguish friend from foe.

The British were commanded, in so far as any man could effectively command in such circumstances, by Brigadier-General Pennefather of the Second Division. Russell said later that Pennefather was 'only at his best in a Tipperary fight', (12) but that—on an enlarged scale—is exactly what Inkerman was. Russell's account was necessarily impressionistic:

> The battle of Inkerman admits of no description. It was a series of dreadful deeds of daring, of sanguinary hand-to-hand fights, of despairing rallies, of desperate assaults—in glens and valleys, in brushwood glades and remote dells, hidden from all human eyes, and from which the conquerors, Russian or British, issued only to engage fresh foes, till our old supremacy, so rudely assailed, was triumphantly asserted, and the battalions of the Czar gave way before our steady courage and the chivalrous fire of France. (13)

Despite the difficulties, he put together a coherent and accurate account, making it clear that although a victory of sorts had been won and against superior numbers, it was a hollow, possibly a Pyrrhic victory:

> A heavy responsibility rests on those whose neglect enabled the enemy to attack us where we were least prepared for it, and whose indifference led them to despise precautions which taken in time might have saved us many valuable lives, and have trebled the loss of the enemy, had they been bold enough to have assaulted us behind intrenchments. We have nothing to rejoice over, and almost everything to deplore, in the battle of Inkerman. We have defeated the enemy indeed, but have not advanced one step nearer towards the citadel of Sebastopol.

Ferdinand Eber, *The Times*' roving correspondent at the war, had joined Russell just before the battle and they spent the day together sharing a greater danger than Russell had ever experienced. He wrote to Delane:

> I gave Eber a shake-down the night before, and we were together nearly all day, and two very narrow escapes we both had. Once a shell burst and the fragments turned up the ground around us and threw the dirt all over Eber. I was in front of him, and a piece about the size of a tea-cup whistled over my head as I lay on the ground (for we saw the fellow coming towards us), rapped the earth within an inch of my hand, threw up the mound over Eber, who was likewise awaiting the explosion, and then went on its way rejoicing. (14)

Eber was exhilarated by danger and bloodshed but Russell was too empathetic a man to feel anything but pity and horror. Three days after Inkerman, he wrote to his wife:

> O dear Mary, the kind good friends I have lost, the dear companions of many a ride and walk and lonely hour—I have seen them buried as they lay all bloody on

the hillside amid their ferocious enemies, and I could not but exclaim in all bitterness of heart 'Cursed is he that delighteth in war'. . . . Our generals from Lord Raglan down are not worth a button except old General Evans. . . . I could not sleep in my tent last night owing to the groans of dying Russian prisoners outside. They are as thick on the field as sparrows on a hayrick. They literally die in heaps, and they are buried thirty together in holes in the ground. The air stinks of blood. . . . (15)

He was completely disillusioned with the British leadership, especially that of Lord Raglan. There was nothing malicious or vengeful about this. Raglan had treated him with a calculated disdain from the outset but Russell still hoped, patriotically, for inspired leadership and still convinced himself, in his account of the Alma, that Raglan was capable of it. Now he could do so no longer. On 8 November he wrote to Delane:

I am convinced from what I see that Lord Raglan is utterly incompetent to lead an army through any arduous task. He is a brave good soldier, I am sure, and a polished gentleman, but he is no more fit than I am to cope with any leader of strategic skill. . . . For a long time I was close to Lord Raglan on the 5th. He was wrong in two palpable respects: he exposed himself uselessly to fire, and he gave no directions whatever; he was a mere cool and callous spectator. But the most serious disadvantage under which he labours is that he does not go among the troops. He does not visit the camp, he does not cheer them and speak to them, and his person is in consequence almost unknown to them.

'Is that old gentleman with one arm the General?' asked a sergeant of the 23rd of another the other day when his lordship was riding through the lines. I may be wrong in all I say, and the conclusions I arrive at, but I do so honestly and I am sure of my facts.

Winter 1854–5

There was no hope now that the allies would be in Sebastopol by Christmas. The question, rather, was whether they would survive the coming winter, exposed on the plateau, virtually besieged by the enemy, weakened by their losses in battle and the continued ravages of disease.

Nine days after Inkerman the area was hit by a hurricane which flattened tents and flooded trenches and turned the track to deep mud. In the narrow waters of Balaclava harbour or anchored close inshore ships smashed into each other and into the harbour walls and on to the rocks. Many lives were lost and much valuable cargo.

The storm gave warning, soon to be fulfilled, that the Crimea was in for one of its occasional winters of great severity. For the soldiers, knee-deep in the mud of the trenches or crouched in their flimsy tents, there was no adequate clothing and rations were short. Even when they could get food they could not cook it because there was no fuel. They were under regular bombardment. It was a time for regret and recrimination. Why had they not seized Sebastopol when they had the chance? Why had the vital supply line, the track between Balaclava and the camps, not been turned into an all-weather road? Why were they left on the plateau instead of concentrated—as the Duke of Wellington would surely have done—into the comparatively sheltered area immediately around Balaclava? The British army, which had marched hard and fought three fierce battles in a few weeks, felt itself abandoned not only by the authorities in England but by its own commander and his staff.

After the great storm, when the tent he shared was blown down, Russell found new quarters in Balaclava. For all the smells and other inconveniences, his small room above some stables had notable advantages. It was beyond the range of the Russian guns. It enabled him to make friends among the ships' captains and he spent many evenings on board ship. It also helped him to extend his acquaintance among the army officers; all new arrivals passed through Balaclava and veterans from the camps visited the town regularly in search of provisions.

At this time a new source of evidence becomes available, Russell's personal diary. He had kept a diary for much, perhaps all, of his adult life but the earlier volumes have disappeared. From the first day of December 1854, however, and for the next half century the diaries have survived almost intact, fifty thick octavo-sized books. The first is a sturdy, leather-bound notebook with a metal locking clasp in which Russell entered the dates himself and often crammed two or three days' events on one page. From the beginning of 1857 onwards he used the printed Letts diary with a separate page for each day.

The handwriting is tiny but neat and generally legible. Sometimes he wrote in properly-constructed sentences, sometimes in disjointed phrases, but his meaning is always clear. There is scarcely a spelling mistake or an illiteracy or even a simple literal, certainly fewer than there are in the average published book of similar length today. It is a tribute to the literary training he received at Dr Geoghegan's school.

In some ways, though, the diaries are disappointing. Like most people's, they are intermittent—there are many blank days and weeks, occasional longer gaps, and the pages are often empty when his life was at its fullest. And Russell was not a self-regarding, self-analysing man. Insights into his character, revelations of his innermost feelings have to be sought not along the written lines but between them. For the most part the entries give little more than a factual, skeletal account of his days—where he went, who he met, what they talked about. Sometimes he gives brief expression to his feelings and opinions. When he tries, rarely, to reflect on his condition in a philosophical way, the results are usually forc_d and unrevealing. His concerns were those of a straightforward man—doing his job well, paying his debts, providing for his family. He was careful not to confide to the diary any guilty thoughts or shameful actions. Indeed, he seems to have been in the habit of leaving his diaries openly about for others to glance at *en passant*. He wrote some paragraphs in an indecipherable shorthand; some lines were later inked over; some pages were torn out: but judging from those instances where it is possible to make out something beneath the attempted obliterations, most of these entries were nothing worse than forceful comments on friends or relations. Some of the deletions probably date from 1880 when there was a move, which came to nothing, to prepare the diaries for publication.

The first entries show a compassion few of his companions felt for the captured Russians and the despised Turks as well as for the British soldiers:

DECEMBER 1 1854 With all our boasted humanity and kindness to prisoners I suspect the poor wounded Russians fare very badly. There are now only 21 of them left alive. . . .

The Turks are being turned into beasts of burden for us. . . . Our rations still continue short, rum particularly which is cruel in wet weather.

Lord Raglan . . . I don't hear that his Lordship visits Balaklava.

DECEMBER 5 Bitter cold last night . . . *Europa* came in with the 90th Regiment on board. We were long listening to their music with melancholy. Poor fellows, they will soon need all their wind to keep themselves alive. . . . The men still continue to eat half rations, to suffer and to die. . . . Rum, their great comfort, is not forthcoming, sometimes they get half rations. Sometimes none at all. And this is what John Bull is paying his money for! Oh Lord. Lord Raglan, true to his frigid nature, never stirs out among his men in all their distress and privations.

DECEMBER 7 It is one of the terrible consequences of knowing naval officers that you must lend them your horses for it is their nature to lame animals unrelentingly in their impetuous equitation. Let a sailor on horseback and he will ride to the Devil and no mistake. Mud and dirt increase and multiply. Poor horses suffer for it all.

On that same day, 7 December, two *Times* men, Thomas Chenery and Ferdinand Eber, arrived in Balaclava. Russell, who had a bad cold and was feeling 'seedy', seized his chance and sailed for Constantinople next day for a short holiday. He had distinguished travelling companions—Lord Cardigan, who had been wounded in the Light Brigade's charge and was on his way home with his civilian friend Hubert de Burgh. Cardigan, for all his prickly arrogance, had always been more ready than most of the generals to recognize Russell, and Russell enjoyed his eccentric company on the voyage:

DECEMBER 8 1854 . . . Lord Cardigan said when he went before the medical board he had to write down his complaints they were so numerous. It was the greatest fun I ever had to hear my Lord and de Burgh squabbling. Cardigan says he has a wound—and I've backed him up on it—from a lance in the rump.

DECEMBER 9 Writing all day—many letters etc. Dining with Lord Cardigan, Hamilton and de Burgh pleasantly enough in the evening. Afterwards Hamilton went to sleep, and Cardigan had a furious go in at Stafford* for visiting hospitals at Balaklava and writing soldiers' letters. . . . Cardigan fierce against doctors and paymasters. A weak, prejudiced, imperious, chivalrous fellow. Is the compound possible? . . . Cardigan is most amusing when with an awful toss of his head he speaks of 'my brother-in-law the Lieutenant-General Lord Lucan'—his hatred is sincere and uncompromising to the last degree.

Russell had two weeks in Constantinople, staying with John Macdonald who had been sent out to administer *The Times*' Fund and distribute its supplies. He visited wounded friends in Scutari hospital, bought supplies for himself and ordered a hut, and attended a succession of dinner parties: '. . . had much confounded carousing till all hours.'

He returned to Balaclava on Boxing Day to find many of his belongings stolen. He was increasingly suspicious of his servants, Angelo and Virgilio—'my drones' as the diary calls them.

---

* Augustus Stafford M.P. had been visiting the Crimea.

For several weeks Russell had been smarting under an insult in the *Daily News* which claimed that *The Times*' correspondent had bolted during the cholera epidemic at Varna. In the timeless traditions of gutter journalism, the statement was gratuitous, malicious and untrue. Russell himself would not stoop to such stuff and he had no intention of letting anyone else get away with it: 'I have written to the editor of the *Daily News*,' he told Delane in early November, 'to tell him I will trounce his lying correspondent within an inch of his life if I ever catch him, and I have written to the man himself to warn him what he has to expect if he meets me.' (1) Unfortunately, he sent his threatening letter to the wrong man, Lawrence Godkin. 'You are entitled to an apology,' he later wrote to Godkin, 'for my language and violent menace, and I beg to tender it to you and to assure you I never shall cease to remember the lesson I have received not to act on hearsay evidence.' (2) Now, on his return from Constantinople, he discovered the real culprit—Otto Wenkstein—and went to considerable trouble to hunt him down and extract a full apology.

The convenience of Russell's room for visitors to Balaclava proved a great inconvenience to Russell himself. Naturally generous and hospitable, he was conscientious too and the stream of interruptions made it hard for him to do his job:

JANUARY 13 1855 Very cross, especially against Colville who knows my troubles. Missed post completely . . . I must bar my door in future altogether. It is the only way. They put their cold noses at my window—there are two panes not of wood through which they see me. . . .

JANUARY 20 . . . trying to write, interrupted by idlers . . . very disagreeable. One man after another came to bore me.

JANUARY 22 Post night. Writing all day. Interrupted of course by fellows who don't mind a button the notice on my door—'Mr. Russell requests that he may not be interrupted except upon business!' And yet if I am savage and offend them they may go away without leaving me valuable information.

Information about the various units was vital to him now because there was one compelling story to tell. From mid-November when the hurricane flattened the camps, relentlessly on through the three terrible months that followed, his Letters played endless variations on a single theme, perhaps the most important message of his life—that the British army was in danger of perishing altogether.

Russell has been accused in the twentieth century of being insufficiently concerned with the sufferings of the common soldier. The charge does not stand up to a close study of his Letters, which showed a compassion far beyond anything any other correspondent expressed:

It is now pouring rain—the skies are black as ink—the wind is howling over the staggering tents—the trenches are turned into dykes—in the tents the water is sometimes a foot deep—our men have not either warm or waterproof clothing—they are out for twelve hours at a time in the trenches—they are plunged into the inevitable miseries of a winter campaign—and not a soul seems to care for their comfort or even for their lives. These are hard truths, but the people of England must hear them. . . . (NOVEMBER 25, 1854)

Although the men are only left for twelve hours in the trenches at a spell, they suffer considerably from the effects of cold, wet, and exposure. The prevalent diseases are fever, dysentery, and diarrhoea, and in the Light Division, on which a large share of the labour of the army falls, there were 350 men on the sick list a day or two ago. The men's clothes are threadbare and tattered, and are not fit to resist rain or cold. (NOVEMBER 27)

The army is suffering greatly; worn out by night-work, by vigil in rain and storm, by hard labour in the trenches, they find themselves suddenly reduced to short allowance, and the excellent and ample rations they had been in the habit of receiving, cut off or miserably reduced. For nine days there has been, with very few exceptions, no issue of tea, coffee, or sugar, to the troops. (DECEMBER 1)

. . . our army is rapidly melting away—dissolved in rain. At the present date there are no less than 3,500 sick men in the British camp before Sebastopol, and it is not too much to say that their illness has, for the most part, been caused by hard work in bad weather, and by exposure to wet without any adequate protection. (JANUARY 2 1855)

What has been the cost to the country of the men of the Brigade of Guards who died in their tents or in hospital of exhaustion, over-work, and deficient or improper nutriment? The brigade musters now very little over 400 men fit for duty. It would have been *cheap* to have fed those men who are gone on turtle and venison, if it could have kept them alive—and not only those, but the poor fellows whom the battle spared, but whom disease has taken from us out of every regiment in the expedition. It is the *men* who are to be pitied—the officers can take care of themselves; they have their bât-horses [baggage animals] to go over to Kamiesch and to Balaclava for luxuries; their servants to send for poultry, vegetables, wine, preserved meats, sheep, and all the luxuries of the sutlers' shops; and they have besides abundance of money, for the pay of the subaltern is ample while he is in the field. (FEBRUARY 11)

Russell's Letters were more than a mere catalogue of calamity. He looked, too, for the sources of the army's sufferings:

. . . though there is a cause, there is no excuse for the privations to which the men are exposed. We were all told that when the bad weather set in, the country roads would be impassable. Still the fine weather was allowed to go by, and the roads were left as the Tartar carts had made them. . . . (DECEMBER 1 1854)

In fact, we are ruined by etiquette, and by 'service' regulations. No one will take 'responsibility' upon himself if it were to save the lives of hundreds.

We are cursed by a system of 'requisitions,' 'orders,' and 'memos,' which is enough to depress an army of scriveners. . . . (JANUARY 2 1855)

In his Letters for publication he kept his criticisms general. He mentioned, for example, that the soldiers felt 'deprived of the cheering words and of the cheering personal presence and exhortations of their generals.' This was a considerate way of putting it. He expressed his feelings more forcefully in his letters to Delane and in his diary:

JANUARY 6 1855 I have a painful duty day after day recording the disappearance of our army, and yet the commanders are all apathy. . . Raglan one never sees and there is a joke in camp that there is a dummy dressed up at headquarters to look out of the window while the Commander-in-Chief is enjoying an *incognito* at Malta. Airey is laid up with sore eyes and lets the roads go to the deuce. Poor old Estcourt is absorbed in papers and writing. The 69th Regiment, which has disappeared except from the Army List, was obliged by old Dalbell to dig holes over which to pitch their tents before he would let them get their winter clothing . . . and the holes they dug were full of snow, mud and water. Not one of them could have on a dry stitch, and so they perished miserably, murdered slowly and in accordance with military discipline.

For all their restraint, his Letters to *The Times* made a tremendous impression in Britain. There was nothing new in the event—previous expeditionary forces had suffered just as much as the men in the Crimea from the ineptitude and indifference of their superiors. What was new was that the story was being told as it happened, and while there was still time to do something about it. 'What can any novelist write,' Thackeray asked a friend, 'so interesting as our own correspondent?' (3) Russell's accounts were corroborated by those of other correspondents and by letters home from the soldiers. But his was the strongest and clearest and most persistent voice, the one that demanded most fiercely that something should be done to save the army before it was too late.

It earned him no official thanks. The Queen raged against 'the infamous attacks against the army which have disgraced our newspapers.' The Prince Consort, deeply involved in the organization of the army, declared that 'the pen and ink of one miserable scribbler is despoiling the country of all the advantages which the heart's blood of twenty thousand of its noblest sons should have earned!!!' Government spokesmen continued to deny that anything had gone seriously wrong.

The Times had been, on the whole, favourably disposed towards the Aberdeen government. This changed dramatically on 23 December 1854. 'The noblest army ever sent from these shores,' *The Times* proclaimed, 'has been sacrificed to the grossest mismanagement. Incompetency, lethargy, aristocratic *hauteur*, official indifference, favour, routine, perverseness, and stupidity reign, revel and riot in the Camp before Sebastopol. . . . We say it with extreme reluctance, no one sees or hears anything of the Commander-in-Chief.' The next day the paper called for the complete reorganization of the War Office. And a few days later it declared: 'There are people who think it a less happy consummation of affairs that the Commander-in-Chief and his staff should survive alone on the heights of Sebastopol, decorated, ennobled, duly named in despatch after despatch, and ready to return home to enjoy pensions and honours amid the bones of 50,000 British soldiers, than that the equanimity of office and the good-humour of society should be disturbed by a single recall or a new appointment over the heads now in command.'

There was nothing half-hearted about *The Times* when it moved into action. Delane outlined his strategy to Russell:

> Probably before this reaches you, you will have heard that I have at last opened fire on Lord Raglan and the General Staff. According to all accounts, their incapacity has been most gross, and it is to that and to the supineness of the General that the terrible losses we have undergone are principally to be attributed. All this will, no doubt, make much commotion at the camp, but I appreciate your position too well to ask you to take any share in these dissentions. Continue as you have done to tell the truth, and as much of it as you can, and leave such comment as may be dangerous to us, who are out of danger. (4)

The Times kept up the pressure into the New Year and Lord Aberdeen's coalition Cabinet, never zealous for the war and now torn by discord, mounted only feeble resistance. On 23 January 1855 the Radical M.P., J. A. Roebuck, who hated inherited privilege and shared *The Times*' view that this was the chief cause of the soldiers' sufferings, introduced a motion in the House of Commons asking 'that a select committee be appointed to inquire into the condition of our army before Sebastopol, and into the conduct of those Departments of the Government whose duty it has been to minister to the wants of that Army.'

It amounted to a motion of no confidence in the government. One senior minister, Lord John Russell, resigned as soon as it was tabled. Everyone expected the motion to succeed but no one expected the extent of the victory—305 in favour, 148 against. M.P.s were so astonished that the announcement of the figures brought a moment's silence and then a roar of laughter from both sides instead of the customary cheers and cries of 'Resign'. The government resigned and Lord Palmerston, over seventy but still possessed of considerable bellicose energy, became Prime Minister.

More than any other single thing, it was Russell's Letters to *The Times* that had brought this about. 'It was you who turned out the government,' the Duke of

Newcastle, Aberdeen's War Secretary, told him in the Crimea a few months later. Other weighty factors were, of course, involved—the inherent weaknesses of the coalition, the power of *The Times*—but few journalists in history can claim to have exerted such an influence on great events.

Yet Russell was completely unmoved. There is no mention, even in his diary, of the fall of the Aberdeen government. The diary and his private letters make it clear that his mood at this time was closer to despair than to jubilation. 'There is no doubt about this,' he told his wife, 'that we are all heartily tired of war simply because we think the Government has not treated the army well and it is fearful to think of the lives which have been lost in consequence.' (5) And to Delane he wrote:

This army has melted away almost to a drop of miserable, washed-out, spiritless wretches, who muster out of 55,000 just 11,000 now fit to shoulder a musket, but certainly not fit to do duty against the enemy. . . . My occupation is gone; there is nothing to record more of the British Expedition except its weakness and its misery—misery in every form and shape except that of defeat; and from that we are solely spared by the goodness of Heaven, which erects barriers of mud and snow between us and our enemies. While the people expect every day to hear of fresh victories they would be astonished to hear there is not an officer in command of the trenches at night who does not think of an attack by the Russians with dread and horror. I cannot tell the truth now—it is too terrible. (6)

The Fall of Sebastopol, 1855

T hings had already begun to improve for the British army before the fall of the Aberdeen government. The authorities in London and the Crimea had been stung into action at last. Supplies and reinforcements poured into Balaclava. Work started on clearing up the town and its harbour and on building an all-weather road to the plateau. Engineers arrived to survey a railway line from the dockside to the camps.

Though this was largely due to Russell's work, he expected no gratitude from the British headquarters and received none. He wrote to Delane on 17 January 1855: 'I am told on good authority that Lord Raglan felt the remarks in the paper very keenly, and his staff very wisely evince their sense of the outrage by lowering their civility meter to freezing point.'

Raglan's chief concern, characteristically, was not the reflections on his own competence to command. He was upset by attacks on his senior staff officers, Estcourt and Airey, and defended them with determination. And he was worried that Russell's Letters to *The Times* were helping the Russians, encouraging them by continually harping on the poor condition of the army and giving them valuable information about the British dispositions and the allies' plans. Even now, however, he took no firm steps to control the correspondents. So Russell carried on with his work in the way he had done it so far and, despite the snubs and obstruction he had to endure, did not allow the least hint of personal rancour to sour his writing.

He was happy to record a gradual improvement in most aspects of the army's fortunes. Work on the road and the railway from Balaclava went rapidly ahead and by the beginning of March a steam engine was hauling supplies to the plateau. It was one of the remarkable features of this war that the allied supply lines, although they involved a long sea voyage, were vastly more reliable than the overland routes of the Russians.

'Lord Raglan now goes about frequently,' he wrote to *The Times* on 21 January, 'and rides through the various camps.' On 17 February he reported: 'Scarcely a day passes on which his Lordship does not now inspect some part or other of the lines.' And three weeks later: 'Lord Raglan is out and about the camps every day,

4a   'Returning from picket'

4b   'Dr Russell; or the troubles of a War Correspondent'

Sketches by Captain W. J. Colville

THE WAR IN THE CRIMEA.

THE OPERATIONS OF THE SIEGE.

[The following appeared in our second edition of yesterday:—]

(FROM OUR SPECIAL CORRESPONDENT.)

HEIGHTS BEFORE SEBASTOPOL, Oct. 19.

The enemy scarcely fired a shot during the whole of the 18th. Our batteries were equally silent. The French, on their side, opened a few guns on their right attack, which they had been working to get into position all night; but they did not succeed in firing many rounds before the great preponderance of the enemy's metal made itself felt, and their works were damaged seriously; in fact, their lines, though nearer to the enemy's batteries than our own in some instances, were not sufficiently close for the light team guns with which they were armed. At daybreak the firing continued as usual from both sides. The Russians, having spent the night in repairing the batteries, were nearly in the same position as ourselves, and, insulted or at least unassisted to the full extent we had reason to expect by the French, we were just able to hold our own during the day. Some smart affairs of skirmishers and sharp shooters took place in front. Our riflemen annoy the Russian gunners greatly, and prevent the tirailleurs from showing near our batteries. On one occasion the Russian riflemen and our own came came close upon each other in a quarry before the town. Our men had exhausted all their ammunition; but as soon as they saw the Russians they seized the blocks of stone which were lying about, and opened a vigorous volley on the enemy. The latter either had empty pouches, or were so much surprised that they forgot to load, for they resorted to the same missiles. A short fight ensued, which ended in our favour, and the Russians retreated, pelted vigorously as long as the men could pursue them. The coolness of a young artillery officer, named Maxwell, who took some ammunition to the batteries through a tremendous fire along a road so exposed to the enemy's fire that it has been called "the Valley of Death," is highly spoken of on all sides. The blue jackets are delighted with Captain Peel, who animates the men by the exhibition of the best qualities of an officer, though his courage is sometimes marked by an excess that borders on rashness. When the Union Jack in the sailors' battery was shot away he seized the broken staff, and leaping up on the earthworks waved the old bit of bunting again and again to a storm of shot, which fortunately left him untouched.

Our ammunition is running short, but supplies are expected every moment. Either from a want of cartridges or from the difficulty of getting powder down to the works our 12-gun battery was silent for some time. The Admiral (Sir E. Lyons), on his little gray pony, is to be seen hovering about our lines indefatigably. To-day he rode out with Lord Raglan and his staff, and spent some time in examining the progress of our fire from a quarry in a hill overlooking the right attack. Two more 68-pounders were brought up to Captain Gordon's attack, and two more were ordered to be added to Captain Chapman's attack last night, but they could not be got into position in time for the opening of the fire. We have to deplore the loss of Lieut.-Colonel Alexander, R.E., a most energetic and indefatigable officer. On the death of Brigadier-General Tylden he succeeded to the command of the Engineers and the superintendence of the engineering operations and when the works commenced before Sebastopol he devoted himself with such unrelenting zeal to his duties that he seriously injured his health. After the failure of a long day, he used to lie down in his clothes. Yesterday he complained of pains in his head; he retired to his tent as usual last night, and threw himself on his blanket with a leather stock on; an attack of apoplexy supervened, and ere morning he was no more. By his decease, Captain Gordon, R.E., than whom the service does not possess an abler, braver, or more devoted officer, succeeds to the command of the Royal Engineers, and his place in the command of the left attack will be taken by Major Tylden, late Brigade-Major of Royal Engineers. Captain Lovell succeeds to the post vacated by Major Tylden.

The smoke was so thick at intervals to-day that but little could be seen but its external folds. The French fire slackened very much towards 1 o'clock, the enemy pitching shells right in to their lines and enfilading part of their new works. The French fleet was said to be busy hammering about the forts, but as I did not see them I do not assert it to be a fact that they did so. Hour after hour one continuous boom of cannon was alone audible, and the smoke screened all else from view. At 3·15 there was an explosion of powder in the tower opposite to our right attack. The Flagstaff Fort seemed much knocked about by the French. The Redan and Round Tower earthworks fire nearly as well as ever. As it was very desirable to destroy the ships anchored in the harbour bow on, and to fire on the dockyard buildings, our rockets were brought into play, and, though rather erratic in their flight, they did some mischief, though not so much as was expected. Wherever they fell the people could be seen flying up the streets when the smoke cleared. At 3 o'clock p.m. the town was on fire, but after the smoke had excited our hopes for some time, it thinned away and went out altogether. At 3·30 there was another explosion, but whether it occurred in the French or in the Russian lines I could not ascertain, as the winds of our left was covered with vapours of sulphurous smoke and "villanous saltpetre." As our enemies are rather prodigal of powder, and as our ammunition is not over-abundant, they were again admonished to fire more carefully to-day, and our replies were less frequent to the Russians than before, so that it almost seemed to me who did not know the truth that the enemy were overpowering our fire. They kept smartly at work from three guns in the Round Tower work, and from some four or five in the Redan, on our batteries. The Lancasters came out in force to-day. The men begin to understand them, and the true value of the arm is becoming apparent. There is a difficulty in ascertaining where the shot and shell from these strike, so great is the distance of range, but Mr. Hance, R.N., speaks very highly of the gun under his charge, and I believe Colonel Lake, R.A., has been enabled to send in a favourable report of the results. Our loss has been trifling. Yesterday, the 18th, the total of killed and wounded, as well as I can make it out, was as follows:—

	Killed.	Wounded.
Light Division	0	6
First Division	2	3
Second Division	1	11
Third Division	0	1
Fourth Division	0	6
	3	27

Lieutenant Smith, of the 95th, was slightly wounded in the trenches.

Some deserters came in from the enemy. I were forwarded to head-quarters, where they were examined by the interpreters. They declared the town was in a very bad state, that sickness prevailed among the military, and that there were great numbers of killed and wounded from our fire.

These men seemed glad of escaping, and their personal appearance was not nearly so good as that of the men who fought at the Alma. Admiral Kornileff is, they state, dead; he was wounded in the thigh so severely while superintending the fire in the Round Tower battery that he had to undergo an amputation, from the effects of which he died.

The Russians have suffered a severe loss in the death of this officer, whose name may be familiar to some readers in connexion with the Sinope expedition.

OCTOBER 20.

Two 68 pounders were mounted last night in our batteries, and the firing, which nearly ceased after dark, was renewed by daybreak. We are all getting tired of ;his continual "pound-pounding," which makes a great deal of noise, raises much powder, and does very little damage. It is very hard to batter down earthworks. Most people about London have seen the Artillery butt at Woolwich. How long has it lasted our "heavy fire" of artillery! Then, again, the Russians have plenty of labourers. They easily repair at night what we destroy and damage during the day. It is difficult for us to do the same. Our men are worn out with fatigue; the daily service exhausts them, and the artillerymen cannot have more than five hours' rest in the 24. They are relieved every eight hours, but it takes them three hours to get down to their work and return from it to the camp. Our amateurs are quite disappointed and tired out. I fear as are people in England, but they must have patience. Rome was not built in a day, nor will Sebastopol be taken in a week. In fact, we have run away with the notion that it was a kind of pasteboard city, which would tumble down at the sound of our cannon as the walls of Jericho fell at the blast of Joshua's trumpet. The news that Sebastopol had fallen, which we received and England, has excited great indignation and indignation consternation here. The whole army is enraged about it, as they feel the verity, whatever it may be and whenever it may be realised, must fall short of the effect of that splendid figment. They think, too, that the hands of the Allies will be withered in the face of popular delight at the imaginary capture. In fact, people at home must know very little about us or our position. I was much amused at seeing in a recently-arrived journal an account of a "Old Zadan;" the manufacturers of campaign bread sure Zadan, in which the advices us out here to use salt ! milk ! and butter ! in the preparation of what must be most delicious food. Salt is a luxury which is rarely to be had unless in conjunction with porky fiber ; and as to milk and butter, the very taste of them is forgotten. Lord Raglan was very glad to get a little cold pig and ration run and water one night on our march here. However, the hardest lot of all is reserved for our poor horses. All hay rations for baggagers are rigidly refused ; they only receive a few pounds of indifferent barley. There is not a blade of grass to be had—the whole of these plateaux and hills are covered with thistles only, and where the other covering of the earth goes I know not. The hay ration for a charger is restricted to 6lb. daily. Under these circumstances horse-flesh is cheap, and friendly presents are being continually offered by one man to another of "a deuced good pony," which are seldom accepted.

When day broke this morning we saw the Russians actively engaged in throwing up new works at the rear of the Redan, to protect the ordnance stores and buildings. They were in readiness to open on us by the time we commenced fire, at 6 o'clock.

The Garden Battery is very troublesome to us and the French. The latter are pushing up zig-zags and parallels close to the enemy's lines, and expect to be able to get their batteries to within 400 metres of the place. They are exposed to very heavy fire, and the Russians ply them with shell admirably. Every one is now talking of storming. We could have stormed with more chance of success when we first sat down before the place. Yes, we could perhaps; but who was to know it? When we have reduced them to the state in which they were when we came up from Balaklava—I, [a?] Sebastopol minus the batteries, if we can—we shall only have done, it is said, what we could have done then without going to all the labour of making our earthworks and trenches. However, I do not agree with this. No one could have calculated on the misfortunes of the French and on the weakness of their attacks. The very work of silencing these Russian earthworks is productive of the best results, for by the time we do so we shall have reduced the enemy, inflicted enormous loss on their troops, and have damaged the town, and rendered it unfit for defence. So far, indeed, our strategy has not been lost.

At 12.50 a.m.'s fire broke' out behind the Redan, caused by our rockets, shell, and red-hot shot. It looked very promising at one time, but died out towards sunset. From the column of smoke which rose it must have been considerable. At 3·15 p.m. a fire of less magnitude was visible to the left of the Redan, further in towards the centre of the town. Lieutenant Davies, Grenadier Guards, received a severe wound in the right leg to-day while on duty in the trenches, and I regret to add that H.R.H. Prince Edward of Saxe Weimar, who is a universal favourite, and has behaved with the greatest gallantry throughout the campaign, was wounded a moment afterwards, close to the place where Lieutenant Davies had been. His wound is not at all serious, and need not cause the least anxiety to his friends. Our wounded officers are all getting on favourably. Our loss yesterday was 3 killed and 32 or 33 wounded. The First Division had 12 wounded (all Guardsmen) and 3 killed (all of the same brigade) ; the Fourth Division has three men wounded ; the Light Division had 11 men wounded ; the Siege Train had 6 men wounded. To-day we had no fatal casualty, and our loss in wounded must be small ; I have been able to make out very few, but as I do not see the official returns my information may be erroneous :—

	Killed.	Wounded.
First Division	3	17
Second Division	0	2
Third Division	0	1
Fourth Division	0	2
Light Division	0	7
Siege Train	0	7
	3	36

Major Young, R.A., was slightly wounded while in charge of his battery to-day.

I have just heard that the fires we saw to-day were most disastrous. We have unfortunately burnt the hospital, which, the deserters say, was full of wounded men from the Alma and from the batteries. We have also destroyed a small war magazine.

OCTOBER 21.

Any day is alike another, and the scenes of yesterday are scarcely distinguishable from those of to-day. The enemy seemed more afraid of our Lancasters this morning, and we are told they are drawing over towards the French. The latter become more vigorous in their fire, and are doing marked damage on the left of their line. Their enemy in working the new parallels is rapidly producing its r sults, and their works are creeping up hour after hour towards the enemy's walls. Sandbags have been placed on the top of most of the exposed public buildings, to prevent their taking fire. It is evident we must advance our works a little nearer. A truncion was knocked off one of our new 68-pounders, and the gun rendered unserviceable in the right attack, where it was doing good service. The firing lasted on both sides, with sharp intermissions, from sunset to sunrise. One hand with the repeated booms of artillery. The fleet of Shacheboys has come in to Balaklava, with nine trails and ordnance stores—just in time. The Russians slacken fire. There are only three guns from the Redan to-day worked vigorously. The Round Tower and Garden battery are as strong as ever.

The enemy have got up a large gun to lobermann, with which they pitch shot and shell into the camp of the Second Division merely to annoy them. They

... still active and troublesome. There were two explos ans—one in our own works, one in the Russians'—towards noon to-day.

OCTOBER 71.

Last night a battery was finished before Inkerman, and two 18-pounders were mounted in it, in order to silence the less ry ship gun which annoyed the Second Division yesterday.

The steamer Vladimir came up to the head of the harbour, and opened fire on the right attack of our men. She threw her shells with beautiful accuracy, and killed two men and wounded 20 others before we could reply effectually. A large traverse was erected to resist her fire, and she has hauled off. 22 guns have been placed in a conflict to open in this attack by the exertions of the men under Major Tylden, who directs it. They have all begun this morning. There were nearly a dozen silent last night.

On the left attack, under Captain Chapman, traverses and platforms were repaired, and a new battery was commenced. Our men also commenced a new battery, to be armed with 32-pounders, to fire on the shipping below. The site of this is on the left and in front of the left attack, and it will not be further than 500 yards from the place. This is a good distance for red-hot shot, and great things are expected from it.

Lord Dunkellin, Captain Coldstream Guards, and eldest son of the Marquis of Clanricarde, was taken prisoner this morning. He was out with a working party of his regiment, which had got a little out of their way, when a number of men were observed through the dawning light in the ravine in front of them. "There are the Russians," exclaimed one of the men, "Nonsense, they're our fellows," said his lordship, and off he went towards them, asking in a high tone as he got near, "Who is in command of the party?" His men saw him no more. As they were unarmed, they retreated rapidly, but there is no fear of his lordship's safety, for the Russians feed so shot, and merely closed round and seized him ere he could get away. No doubt he will be well taken care of, and forwarded probably to St. Petersburg, for his father was Ambassador at the Court of the Czar, and is said to have once enjoyed his friendship.

The Russians opened a very heavy cannonade on us this morning ; they have always done so on Sundays. Divine service was performed with a continued bass of cannon rolling through the responses and liturgy. The French are terribly cut up by the Garden Battery, more so, however, by their misfortune of last night. The Russians made a stealthy sortie towards morning, and advanced close to the French pickets. When challenged, they replied—"Ingles, Ingles," which passed muster with our allies as bona fide English, they say ; and before they knew where they were, the Russians had charged them, got into their batteries and spiked four mortars. They were speedily repulsed; but this misadventure has mortified our brave allies exceedingly. The night before they lost on a party of men who used becomes pare parted, and they turned out to be Russians. They were too confiding the second time. We are all liable to mistakes. There was a great alarm the other evening. Eleven battalions of Russians crossed the Tchernaya, and deployed towards Balaklava, but we were quite satisfied to leave Sir Colin Campbell to dispose of them. However, at night monastery and cannon opened along the rear, and woke us all up. It turned out the officer of marines on the heights had been told he always would have a clear space left for his guns to play upon in case of attack, and that some newly-arrived Turks, unaware of this arrangement, had trenched on his space, with lights in their hands, whereupon, knowing the Russians were about, he blazed away at the poor "Bono Johnnies," all of whom he fortunately missed.

The French General sent over to-day to ask for assistance in silencing a new battery which has tormented them excessively. He gladly replied "No," and silenced the battery ere round.

No incident of consequence occurred to-day. It was all filled up with volleys of artillery. A Pole and some Russians deserted last night. They tell us that the enemy have lost 3,000 killed and wounded, that the town is in a frightful state—the ships closed, the merchants fled, the goods placed underneath in the cellars, and that the "pointed" balls and shells (Lancasters) do frightful mischief. There are no longer volunteers to work the guns, as there were at first. The men have now to be forced to the batteries. Many poor women and children have lost their lives in this terrible cannonade. It seems incredible that the Russian authorities should have let them stay in the town when they could have easily sent them across by the bridge of boats to the north side. Provisions still continue plenty and water is abundant in the town. Our armament for to-morrow will be, it is hoped, as follows :—Right attack, 21 guns—two 68s ; four Lancaster guns in batteries between left and right ; left attack, 42 guns—total 71; plus 10 mortars, 81. The French have 56 guns; total, 127 for the Allies. The Turks guard the rear, and have about 18 guns in all.

There are now 18 deserters at head-quarters, including a woman, who was taken as she was going down to visit a cousin (sweetheart) in the trenches. Two deserters leaped in through our embrasures. They were Circassian prisoners. They reported that all the people were let loose, as the French are supplied in the Round Tower yesterday must have done more mischief. That which took place behind our 12-gun battery was horrison.

Sir E. Lyons went out to-day in front as usual. There was brisk skirmishing to-day between our sharpshooters, well armed and wounded. No need, but worked several prisoners, and one had through short through the jaws, who cannot speak. The loss of our men was very small. Our artillerymen are very much exhausted ; our fires are bad, and the platforms are much complained of.

OCTOBER 24.

The return of killed and wounded for the 22d of the month, during the greater part of which a heavy fire was directed on our trenches and battery attacks right and left, shows the smallest number of our artil and of their casualties. We only lost one man killed in the Light Division, and two men in the siege train ; of wounded we had one in the First Division, two in the Second Division, one in the Third Division, and 10 in the Siege Train. Lieutenant Brown of the 68th Regiment lost his leg yesterday. Captain Childers, R.A., was killed in his battery. He had just ordered a gun to be fired, and had run to look through an embrasure to watch the effect of the ball, when a shot came in and struck off his head. Mr. Young, of the Artillery, who died on the 23d of cholera, was brother of Sir W. Young, killed at the Alma, and was not the major of the same name in command of a company of artillery in the left attack. The latter was slightly wounded a couple of days ago, but is now quite well. The request made to us by the French that we would direct our fire on the Barrack Battery, which annoyed them excessively, was so well attended to that on the evening we knocked it to pieces and silenced it. The Garden Battery is little better.

Her Majesty's ship Himalaya, Captain Kellock, arrived yesterday, with 300 men returned from Sebastopol.

Dr. Hall has returned from Scutari, and has resumed his duties as P.M.O. of the army before Sebastopol.

The Algiers has made her appearance also, and is

very welcome, as she carries large stores of ammunition.

About 500 men came to-day, as fit for service, from Scutari. They were landed at Balaklava, and proceeded to march out to their camp, but I regret to say that before they had marched many miles—indeed, there are not many to march—more of the poor fellows than it was pleasant to count fell out exhausted, proving that they had not quite recovered from their illness.

The diminution of our numbers every day is enough to cause serious anxiety. Out of 35,600 men borne on the strength of the army there are not more now than 16,500 rank and file fit for service. Since the 10th of this month upwards of 700 men have been sent as invalids to Balaklava. There is a steady drain of some 40 or 50 men a-day going out fro us, which is not dried up by the numbers of the returned invalids. Even the 20 or 30 a day wounded and disabled when multiplied by the number of days we have been here becomes a serious item in the aggregate. We are badly off for spare gun carriages and wheels, for ammunition and forage.

All the prisoners were sent in from head-quarters to the main guard at Balaklava, except two, who are employed with the Quarter-Master General's Staff to point out the sites of the magazines and public buildings which should be destroyed. Our prisoners contradict each other on many points, but all agree as to the damage done to the town and to the multitudes of killed. One did, that the Russian Governor sent in yesterday to Lord Raglan to ask for a day's truce to bury the dead on both sides. The answer was shortly has it that Lord Raglan replied "He had no dead to bury." The Russians in revenge for this are leaving their dead where they fall outside the lines, and also bring them out from the town and place them in the valley frequented by our pickets and skirmishers, who are much annoyed by the stench. This is a new engine of warfare. An ambulance corps under Captain Grant is doing good service now that it has arrived. There are two carts attached to each division, and each cart generally goes into Balaklava twice in the day with sick and wounded. Diarrhœa is still prevalent. Full rations of fresh meat are issued whenever it is practicable, and double allowance of rum to the parties in the trenches. The weather continues to be beautifully mild.

The Tonning brought in Colonel Hood, of the Guards, Lord James Murray, Captain Ellison, &c. Several officers of the Irish Constabulary and of the commissariat departments also arrived in her. The French send out 400 men of each battalion every night to their works, and all the ground in front of them is excavated with trenches, parallels, zig-zags, and approaches. It is evident that if the place falls this winter the French must make a lodgment opposite their attack. We have the military town (suburb) to deal with, and it is so situate that the possession of it would by no means insure the capture of Sebastopol Proper, while the occupation of it permanently would be impossible till the forts and portions of the town which command it are destroyed. Our mortar fire has nearly ceased. The complaints against our fuses are louder every day. The Russians opened a new battery to-day. They have 200 guns upon us and the French, and our fire has been reduced considerably.

THE CAVALRY ACTION AT BALAKLAVA.

OCTOBER 25.

If the exhibition of the most brilliant valour, of the excess of courage, and of a daring which would have reflected lustre on the best days of chivalry can afford full consolation for the disaster of to-day, we can have no reason to regret the melancholy loss which we sustained in a contest with a savage and barbarian enemy.

I shall proceed to describe, to the best of my power, what occurred under my own eyes, and to state the facts which I have heard from men whose veracity is unimpeachable, reserving to myself the exercise of the right of private judgment in making public and in expressing the details of what occurred on this memorable day. Before I proceed to my narrative, I must premise that a certain feeling existed in some quarters that our cavalry had not been properly handled since they landed in the Crimea, and that they had gained golden opinions on the indecision and excessive caution of their leaders. It was said that our cavalry had allowed the Russian guns and gunners to escape, and above all, that at Mackensie's farm-house, with all the gorge as before confusion, and with the certainty of taking many guns and prisoners ; and, above all, that at Mackensie's farm-house, with all the gorge as before confusion, and with the certainty of taking many guns and prisoners, and, above all, that at Mac- kensie's farm-house in front of them ; subsequently, they had been improperly restrained from charging, and had failed in gaining great successes, which would have entitled them to a full share of the laurels of the campaign, solely owing to the timidity of the officer in command. Whether or not these accusations were true, enough of them had reached the ears of our cavalry, and they were indignant and exasperated that they should have lost so many chances, and that they should have to bear this stigma without any just occasion for it ; and, perhaps, the prominent thought in their minds was that they would give such an example of courage to the world, if the chance offered itself, as would shame their detractors for ever.

It will be remembered that in a letter sent by last mail from this it was mentioned that 11 battalions of Russian infantry had crossed the Tchernaya, and that they threatened the rear of our position and our communication with Balaklava. Their hands could be heard playing at night by the travellers along the Balaklava road to the camp, but they "showed" but little during the day, and kept up among the gorge and mountain passes through which the roads to Inkerman, Simpheropol, and the south-east of the Crimea wind towards the interior. It will be recollected also that the position we occupied in reference to Balaklava was supposed by most people to be very strong—even impregnable. Our lines were formed by natural mountain slopes in the rear, along which the French had made some very formidable intrenchments to bar the approaches to the town from the eastward, at the distance of three and a-half or four miles along the French works. These entrenchments, for one mile and a-half in extent, and commanding the roads over the mountains towards Balaklava, were filled by Turks, while the space along the side of the mountains diminishing in height with the slope toward the level of the plain, were held at compact masses of Russian infantry, which had joined the from the base of the ridge on which he stood to the foot of the formidable heights at the enemy's lips. I would see the French trenches lined with R...is...ys.

THE CAVALRY ACTION AT BALAKLAVA.

If the exhibition of the most brilliant valour, of the excess of courage, and of a daring which would have reflected lustre on the best days of chivalry can afford full consolation for the disaster of to-day, we can have no reason to regret the melancholy loss which we sustained in a contest with a savage and barbarian enemy.

I shall proceed to describe, to the best of my power, what occurred under my own eyes, and to state the facts which I have heard from men whose veracity is unimpeachable, reserving to myself the exercise of the right of private judgment in making public and in suppressing the details of what occurred on this memorable day. Before I proceed to my narrative, I must premise that a certain feeling existed in some quarters that our cavalry had not been properly handled since they landed in the Crimea, and that they had lost golden opportunities from the indecision and excessive caution of their leaders. It was said that our cavalry ought to have been manœuvred at Bouljanak in one way or in another, according to the fancy of the critic. It was affirmed, too, that the light cavalry were utterly useless in the performance of one of their most important duties—the collection of supplies for the army—that they were "above their business, and too fine gentlemen for their work;" that our horse should have pushed on after the flying enemy after the battle of the Alma, to their utter confusion, and with the certainty of taking many guns and prisoners; and, above all, that at Mackenzie's-farm first, and at the gorge near Inkermann subsequently, they had been improperly restrained from charging, and had failed in gaining great successes, which would have entitled them to a full share of the laurels of the campaign, solely owing to the timidity of the officer in command. The existence of this feeling was known to many of our cavalry, and they were indignant and exasperated that the faintest shade of suspicion should rest on any of their corps. With the justice of these aspersions they seemed to think they had nothing to do, and perhaps the prominent thought in their minds was that they would give such an example of courage to the world, if the chance offered itself, as would shame their detractors for ever.

It will be remembered that in a letter sent by last mail from this it was mentioned that 11 battalions of Russian infantry had crossed the Tchernaya, and that they threatened the rear of our position and our communication with Balaklava. Their bands could be heard playing at night by the travellers along the Balaklava road to the camp, but they "showed" but little during the day, and kept up among the gorges and mountain passes through which the roads to Inkermann, Simpheropol, and the south-east of the Crimea wind towards the interior. It will be recollected also that the position we occupied in reference to Balaklava was supposed by most people to be very strong—even impregnable. Our lines were formed by natural mountain slopes in the rear, along which the French had made very formidable intrenchments. Below those intrenchments, and very nearly in a right line across the valley beneath, are four conical hillocks, one rising above the other as they recede from our lines; the furthest, which joins the chain of mountains opposite to our ridges being named Canrobert's Hill, from the meeting there of that General with Lord Raglan after the march to Balaklava. On the top of each of these hills the Turks had thrown up earthen redoubts, defended by 250 men each, and armed with two or three guns—some heavy ship guns—lent by us to them, with one artilleryman in each redoubt to look after them. These hills cross the valley of Balaklava at the distance of about two and a half miles from the town. Supposing the spectator, then, to take his stand on one of the heights forming the rear of our camp before Sebastopol, he would see the town of Balaklava, with its scanty shipping, its narrow strip of water, and its old forts on his right hand; immediately below he would behold the valley a and plain of coarse meadow land, occupied by our cavalry tents, and stretching from the base of the ridge on which he stood to the foot of the formidable heights at the other side; he would see the French trenches lined with Zouaves a few feet beneath, and distant from him, on the slope of the hill; a Turkish redoubt lower down, then another in the valley, then, in a line with it, some angular earthworks, then, in succession, the other two redoubts up to Canrobert's Hill. At the distance of two or two and a half miles across the valley there is an abrupt rocky mountain range of most irregular and picturesque formation, covered with scanty brushwood here and there, or rising into barren pinnacles and plateaux of rock. In outline and appearance this portion of the landscape is wonderfully like the Trosachs. A patch of blue sea is caught in between the overhanging cliffs of Balaklava as they close in the entrance to the harbour on the right. The camp of the Marines, pitched on the hill sides more than 1,000 feet above the level of the sea, is opposite to you as your back is turned to Sebastopol and your right side towards Balaklava. On the road leading up the valley, close to the entrance of the town and beneath these hills, is the encampment of the 93rd Highlanders.

6   Russell in his distinctive Crimean outfit

and Generals Estcourt and Airey are equally active. They all visit Balaclava, inspect the lines, ride along the works, and by their presence and directions infuse an amount of energy which will go far to make up for lost time, if not for lost lives.' (1) Lord Lucan told Russell: 'Lord Raglan ought to give you an annuity for *The Times* has poked him up out of a lethargy which was about to be fatal to him and to us all, and he now takes wholesome exercise.' (2)

Russell was also aware, and made his readers aware, of the difficulties under which the Commander-in-Chief worked:

> Perhaps there is no clerk in England who has so much writing to get through, *ipsâ manu*, as the Field-Marshal in command of the forces. I believe his Lordship is frequently up till two or three o'clock in the morning, looking over papers, signing documents, preparing orders and despatches, and exhausting his energies in secretary's work. Such a life could with most men afford little opportunity or energy for action. The system that necessitates such labours on the part of a Commander-in-Chief must be faulty; it certainly is unsuited for the field or for times of war, and is cumbrous and antiquated. (3)

For many weeks the war was a matter of desultory artillery exchanges and occasional night skirmishes. From now on the French were to assume an increasingly predominant role: they brought in reinforcements faster than the British, their lines were closer to the enemy. In mid-February they attacked a Russian strong-point and were driven off with heavy losses. They tried again a month later with the same result. For the British things were quiet enough for Russell to remember, on 28 March, that it was his birthday—and that he was not sure whether he was thirty-four or thirty-five years old. But his eye for significant detail had lost none of its sharpness. On 30 April he wrote to *The Times*: 'There are no fusees for such shells as we have, and we have plenty of fusees for shells which we have not. There are lots of 13-inch shells and no fusees for them, and there are lots of 10-inch fusees and no shells for them. . . . Who sent them out, or who kept them back? Who are the traitors, or the knaves, or the fools?'

At the beginning of May an allied expeditionary force sailed to attack the Russian base at Kertch, 150 miles to the east, and gain command of the waters of the Sea of Azov. It had been on the way only twenty-four hours when it was ordered back. Russell, who had contrived a passage for himself, noted in his diary that it was rumoured there was a peace settlement. But the reason for their recall was less exciting and more typical; General Canrobert had received orders from his Emperor in Paris that all the French ships should be hurried to Constantinople to collect reinforcements.

This gave early warning that the underwater cable that had just been laid between Balaclava and Varna, enabling telegraphed orders from London or Paris to reach the allied commanders within a few hours, would be a mixed blessing, particularly since it made it possible for Napoleon III to confuse and confound his generals with peremptory demands.

The telegraph brought no immediate benefit to Russell and his fellow correspondents. On 23 April he wrote to Delane: 'I have ridden over here [to the British headquarters] today to inquire about the telegraphic communication with Varna and find that no persons can send any messages by the wire without the permission of the Commander-in-Chief and I need not tell you that this permission can not be obtained by me nor should I like to ask for it. . . . I am utterly powerless to make any arrangement here, and I hope that you will be more successful in London . . .'

The authorities continued to show their dislike for Russell in petty ways. In May he was kicked out of his quarters in Balaclava on the orders of Sir Colin Campbell. The action was pointless as well as spiteful since Russell had already taken delivery of the hut he had ordered in Constantinople and men of the Army Works Corps had erected it for him in the rear of the Fourth Division's camp on the plateau:

> It was square, with a sloping roof, with windows about 18 inches square at two
> sides, and it was divided by a partition, thus constituting a room about 8 feet by
> 6 feet, which was the reception, dining room and study; and a smaller section,
> which was to be my bed-room. The material was of zinc and iron plates fastened
> on a stout wooden frame . . . The workmen put up shelves, made a deal table,
> supplied two chairs, and, when I had procured canvas to nail on the walls of the
> room, which were papered before the summer ended, I was installed *en prince*.
> (4)

The hut was poorly insulated and attracted attention from the Russian gunners but, by Crimean standards, this was palatial living, and Russell's chief fear was that the generals would order him to move it away. They never did, however, and the hut remained his 'fixed abode' for the rest of the campaign.

In many ways, as the days lengthened into summer, he was well placed. His accounts of the army's winter discontents were being confirmed by witnesses before the Roebuck committee of inquiry in London. He received encouraging letters from *Times* readers as well as from Delane and Mowbray Morris and occasionally John Walter himself. His debts were diminishing and solvency seemed attainable when London publishers sought permission to bring out a compilation of his Crimean Letters. The weather grew pleasant. He was busy and full of energy and embarrassingly well-provided with material comforts. Delane sent him a telescope and a buffalo robe to keep him warm at night. He was keen for a reunion with Mary and wrote to her on 18 April 1855:

> . . . there is very little chance at present of my being able to get home for the
> whole of this siege is so hopelessly bungled that I don't think we'll see the end of
> it for months. If you come out to Constantinople you must have someone with
> you and even then you could only come up in a ship to see me for a short time
> for I never would expose you to the remarks and disagreeability of camp life.

There is one lady out here and she is a strange woman, perfectly proper indeed but going about with men's trowsers under her clothes strapped over men's boots—Mrs. Duberly, 8th Hussars*—and she is not spoken of very respectfully I can assure you, nor would I wish to expose you to the same remarks . . .

Russell had a strong sense of the necessary modesty of the virtuous woman and a line in the same letter suggests that he was developing an equally strict sense of social position. His father had taken a job as a shop walker in a Liverpool store. Russell wrote: 'As to my father's uneasiness about his position, I of course regret for his own sake—and a little for mine—that he is in what must be considered a post unfit for a gentleman.' The letter shows he was forming professional as well as social ambitions: 'Of my own future prospects I know nothing but of course I never can and never will go into the gallery again. I may succeed in getting something or other when I get home which will relieve me from my uncertain and precarious tenure income from daily exertion though I should always like a certain amount of work.' He was, as always, desperately anxious for news of home and bursting with affection: 'Oh, dearest Mary,' he wrote nine days later, 'how I long to see you—to look at your old phiz once more. Give my love to all the chicks—kiss them and hug them for me and give my love to all friends.'

His Italian servants refused to accompany him to the hut on the plateau because it was subject to bombardment. He sacked them and hired an Armenian who soon left, however, for a safer life in retail trade in Balaclava.

The Crimean was the last time, perhaps, when war was widely regarded as a spectator sport. The Russian commander had invited a party of ladies to watch the fun from the heights above the Alma. Once they were established on the plateau above Sebastopol, the allied camps had many curious visitors. The British called them 'T.G.s'—'travelling gentlemen'—though there were many women among them. Some were friends or relatives of officers. Others, like A. H. Layard and A. W. Kinglake, had more professional interests. On the whole the army gave them a much more friendly welcome than it accorded the newspaper correspondents.

On 19 March Russell wrote in his diary: 'Fenton has landed daguerrotype apparatus.' Roger Fenton, the pioneer photographer, had been commissioned by Thomas Agnew and Sons of Manchester to record the campaign in pictures. He arrived with two assistants, five cameras, seven hundred glass plates for the negatives and a mobile dark room. He stayed nearly four months and built up a valuable record—landscapes of the plateau and Balaclava, scenes in the camps and gun emplacements, portraits of leading figures. Unfortunately, he was not able to take action pictures—his subjects had to freeze in position for the exposure of the plates—and he was fastidiously careful to avoid all unpleasantness. If his camera did not lie, it certainly did not tell the whole truth.

* Fanny, the wife of Captain Henry Duberly, was the most famous of the Crimean wives. Her free-and-easy manner led to gossip but she was widely liked for her cheerful good nature.

On 22 May Russell wrote to Mary: 'My picture was tuk [*sic*] yesterday, but it won't be ready for some time to come.' The result was the finest portrait ever made of him, firmly seated on his camp chair, sturdy and alert, four-square and full-bearded, wearing the miscellaneous uniform that made him so unmistakable a figure. (Plate 6)

The army was also visited by Florence Nightingale and the French chef Alexis Soyer who had revolutionized the kitchens at Scutari and invented a field stove—designed so that the fire would not be visible to the enemy—and demonstrated its effectiveness with a banquet for two hundred. Russell admired Soyer and was amused by him too. He told Delane:

> Soyer is here eating whatever he can get and obstinately deaf to all hints that he ought to come in time to cook the dinner. Miss Nightingale is very ill, poor soul. Soyer dragged her into a battery—the mortar battery out of fire—and put her on the stern of a gun with the elegant expression meant to be neat and well-turned—'Voila! The Child of Peace had her breech on the breech of the Son of War!' (5)

Towards the end of May the expeditionary force sailed again for Kertch and this time succeeded in carrying out its mission. Russell had written to *The Times* about the aborted voyage three weeks before so in theory, if the Russians were getting telegraphed information from London, they should have been warned and ready. In the event, they were neither. The allied force of 15,000 men, French, British and Turkish, met little resistance at Kertch and Yenikale and had no difficulty destroying the forts. The allied navies took control of the Sea of Azov.

Although successful, the expedition was poorly led and marred by looting and vandalism. Russell was so outraged by the smashing of fine houses and a classical museum that he pointed directly in his Letter to *The Times* to the man he held responsible, Sir George Brown, commander of the British contingent. He said no blame could be 'attached to Englishmen or to any British subject, with the exception of the Lieutenant-General, whose apathy or neglect permitted the perpetration of disgraceful excesses.' (6) It was unusual for Russell to attack an individual in his public writings and very unusual for him to do so in terms as strong as this but he felt great shame: 'I don't know what will be thought of the Kertch affair,' he told Delane, 'but to my mind it was beastly, brutal and disgusting.' (7)

While Russell was away his place in the Crimea was taken by a young journalist, W. H. Stowe, who had been sent out to administer *The Times*' Fund at Constantinople. Russell was horrified, on his return, to find his colleague dying of cholera. The army had done nothing for the sick man, refusing him admission to the military hospital on the grounds that he was a civilian. Furious at such bureaucratic heartlessness, Russell had Stowe carried down to the hospital at Balaclava where he died a few hours later. When the news reached *The Times* it provoked a bitter editorial said to have been written by John Walter:

We shall not send out another friend, another valuable life, to a service in which, among other dangers, British inhumanity is to be encountered. Whoever goes out to administer our Fund must expect that, in the event of his sickening in the crowd—and almost everybody there does sicken at one time or another, until he is acclimatised—he will be excluded from the hospitals where he is sent to minister, and deprived of the medical aid which he has, perhaps assisted with the most needful supplies. (8)

On the battlefront much had changed. The British, now very junior partners in the enterprise, had strong French units on either flank. And there was a new ally in the field, a contingent of 5,000 Sardinian troops sent by Court Cavour, Prime Minister of Piedmont, who was anxious to win Anglo-French support for the cause of Italian independence and unification.

By June 1855 the allies felt strong enough to launch their assault on Sebastopol. On the 7th, while the British mounted a diversionary attack, the French took and held one of the main Russian strong-points, the Mamelon. Eleven days later they attacked the key positions on the outskirts of Sebastopol, the British going for the Redan, the French for the more formidable Malakoff. Both attacks were beaten off. Russell, whose account of this action was lost in transit and never found, reckoned that the British had lost 1,500 men killed or wounded and the French more. The army, he said, was disappointed but not despairing. The soldiers were ready to attack again next day but their commanders decided to try to undermine the Russian defences by mines and explosives instead.

It was a good moment to take a break since the allied assault could clearly not be resumed for several weeks. Russell had been feeling 'seedy' for some time, very tired and sometimes feverish; the heat of the Crimean summer did not agree with him. Mary was on her way to Constantinople where he hoped to join her for a holiday.

He was further cheered by a communication from the Fielding Club, a round-robin in which many old friends sent words of admiration and good wishes. The Secretary's introduction said:

The New Secretary of the Home Department of the Fielding trusts that the corresponding member at Balaclava, Kertch, and, in short, at any place between here and Seringapatam, continues in good health, possessed of clear ink, well-nibbed pens, and general serenity, and that he may soon return to his anxious friends and expectant country with all his language and his former spirits.

Thackeray's contribution was especially welcome:

I have just come from the Administrative Reform Association, held in Drury Lane, where I heard your name uttered with enthusiasm, and heard ('heard', by the way, is not pleasing coming twice in this way, but Albert Smith is making a deuce of a row) received with applause. We all wish you back here almost as much as you wish it yourself. I am going to America, so I shan't see you unless you come back soon; but in every quarter of the world,

I am yours very truly indeed,

W. M. Thackeray. (9)

Russell had just arrived in Constantinople when he heard shattering news —Lord Raglan had died, in despair at the failure of the June attacks and worn out by his exertions. On 2 July Russell wrote to Delane:

Chenery goes up tomorrow for a fortnight to take my place . . . I'm deuced seedy and worn out. . . . Poor Lord Raglan. No man ever won so many friends by an inexpressible charm of manner, by perfect polish and exquisite urbanity, but he was hard as marble to all but his own and theirs. Of dear Stowe I have no more to say. He died tranquilly as one who had trust and faith in Heaven. . . . All these deaths have made me very selfish and desponding. Stowe's inexpressibly shocked me. No one but a great General can relieve us and I almost think Heaven is against us.

Providence failed to provide a great general. As Russell had feared, General Sir James Simpson was chosen to command the British army. Russell wrote to Delane on 9 July:

My wife arrived here safe and sound, thank God, on the 5th, and we are now enjoying the breezes of the Bosphorus and small talk together, and indeed I now find more than ever how much I required a holiday and what good it will do me. . . . The army is depressed and officers are flocking down 'sick' in shoals. Everyone is glad to get away who can. By Lord Raglan's death we became, I fear, dwarfed to a mere contingent for Simpson is not the man to sustain our perilous position of equality with the French by dignity of demeanour or blandness or firmness of character. . . . He is a blunt bigoted old Scotsman—a violent military Tory, a hater of the French—and destitute of the charms of manner and fascinating address which gave poor Lord Raglan singular influence over all who were in contact with his person . . .

The Times paid Mary's expenses for the holiday and arranged for her to be escorted on the journey out by John King, who had been engaged by the paper to act as Russell's groom and valet in the Crimea for £8 a month plus expenses.

Russell's holiday lasted more than a month and did him good. 'If I am not a giant,' he told Delane, 'I am at all events a stoutish gentleman refreshed with sleep, wine and society.' (10) He made some attempt to wind up the affairs of *The Times'* Fund, but he was never happy with administration and its attendant paper work and was soon urging Delane to send out someone more businesslike. The first volume of his Crimean Letters had been rushed through the press: 'You will be glad to hear,' wrote Delane, 'that your book makes a very pretty volume and Routledge promises for it a success exceeding that of any of his previous publications.' (11) It was a double delight—his first published book and an advance on royalties of £500. In addition, the same publishers were offering an advance of £700 for a considered history of the war to be written when all was over.

Mary enjoyed the Bosphorus so much there was talk of her taking the children out for the duration of the fighting. She accompanied her husband on his return to the Crimea for a brief look at the battle zone before sailing back to Guernsey.

On the plateau Russell found an army that had largely lost interest in the war. In mid-August the Russians mounted their last attempt to break the allied stranglehold. They attacked on the eastern flank and were beaten back by the French and the Sardinians in the battle of the Tchernaya, generally ignored in English history books because the British were not involved.

The allies now prepared another assault on Sebastopol. On 5 September they opened up a heavy artillery bombardment that lasted for three days. On the 8th the infantry attacked. A powerful French force went for the key Russian strong-point, the Malakoff, while a smaller British force attacked the Redan.

Russell's description of the day's events reveals him as an established master of his craft. The Letter, dated 8 September 1855, was over ten thousand words long, a graphic narrative full of telling detail but informed throughout with a grasp of the strategic pattern. Though he made it, as always, as truthful as he could, it reads like an adventure story.

The French on the right began the assault with four strong divisions:

After hours of suspense the moment came at last. At five minutes before twelve o'clock the French, like a swarm of bees, issued forth from their trenches close to the doomed Malakhoff, scrambled up its face, and were through the embrasures in the twinkling of an eye. They crossed the seven metres of ground which separated them from the enemy at a few bounds—they drifted as lightly and as quickly as autumn leaves before the wind, battalion after battalion, into the embrasures, and in a minute or two after the head of their column issued from the ditch the tricolor was floating over the Korniloff Bastion.

The French succeeded because they attacked in great force and were able to seize their objective before the Russians could bring up reinforcements. The British, as Russell made brutally clear, failed because they attacked with inadequate forces—by a stroke of scarcely credible obtuseness the same two divisions were used that had been repulsed and badly mauled in the attempt three months before—and they were badly led. Most of the blame lay with

Lieutenant-General Sir William Codrington, who had succeeded Sir George Brown as Commander of the Light Division and who was given command of the attack. The senior British generals adopted a passive role:

> . . . a stranger would have been astonished at the aspect of the British Generals as they viewed the assault. The Commander-in-Chief, General Simpson, sat in the trench, with his nose and eyes just facing the cold and dust, and a great coat drawn up about his head to protect him against both. General Jones wore a red nightcap, and reclined on litter, muffled up in clothes, and Sir Richard Airey, the Quartermaster-General, had a white pocket-handkerchief tied over his cap and ears, and fastened under his neck, which detracted somewhat from a martial and belligerent aspect. . . . All the amateurs and travelling gentlemen, who rather abound here just now, were in a state of great excitement, and dotted the plain in eccentric attire, which revived olden memories of Cowes, and yachting, and sea-bathing.

The British fought their way into the Redan but in insufficient numbers to hold it against the inevitable counter-attack. Colonel Windham is the hero of Russell's account, struggling gallantly to regroup his men and appealing repeatedly for reinforcements:

> Colonel Windham saw there was no time to be lost. He had sent three officers for reinforcements, and, above all, for men in formation, and he now resolved to go to General Codrington himself. Seeing Captain Crealock, of the 90th, near him busy in encouraging his men, and exerting himself with great courage and energy to get them into order, he said, 'I must go to the General for supports. Now mind, let it be known, in case I am killed, why I went away.' He crossed the parapet and ditch, and succeeded in gaining the fifth parallel, through a storm of grape and rifle bullets, in safety; and standing on the top of the parapet he again asked for support. Sir William Codrington asked him if he thought he really could do anything with such supports as he could afford, and said, if he thought so, 'he might take the Royals,' who were then in the parallel. 'Let the officers come out in front—let us advance in order, and if the men keep their formation the Redan is ours,' was the Colonel's reply; but he spoke too late—for, at that very moment, our men were seen leaping into the ditch, or running down the parapet of the salient, and through the embrasures out of the work into the ditch, while the Russians might be perceived following them with the bayonet and with heavy musketry, and even throwing stones and grapeshot at them as they lay in the ditch.

Russell remarks that General Codrington 'seems to have become confused by the failure of the attack, and to have lost for the time the coolness which has hitherto characterised him.' Forty years later he stated the case against Codrington more forcefully:

If any officer wishes, in assaulting a great earthwork defended by valiant soldiers, to know how not to do it, he will study the 'arrangements' for the assault of the Redan by Sir W. Codrington. A column of 1000 men, consisting of 500 men from two divisions (the Light and the Second, both of which had been engaged in the unsuccessful assault of 18th June), one column of 500 to lead and to be followed by the other! each composed of 'scraps' of six different regiments! finally no supports! *There* is organised defeat for you! (12)

General Simpson planned to renew the attack next day but it proved providentially unnecessary. During the night the Russian commanders decided to abandon the southern half of the city. Next morning the allied armies saw, to their great relief, that the enemy were burning the city, destroying their remaining ships and retreating across the river, leaving behind the port and naval installations that had been the allies' chief objectives. After a siege of nearly twelve months, Sebastopol had fallen.

In the afternoon French and British soldiers advanced cautiously into the devastated and now deserted city. Russell went in next day and visited the main hospital, describing the scene in a Letter to *The Times* dated 12 September:

In a long low room, supported by square pillars, arched at the top, and dimly lighted through shattered and unglazed window-frames, lay the wounded Russians, who had been abandoned to our mercies by their General. The wounded, did I say? No, but the dead—the rotten and festering corpses of the soldiers, who were left to die in their extreme agony, untended, uncared for, packed as close as they could be stowed, some on the floor, others on wretched trestles and bedsteads, or pallets of straw, sopped and saturated with blood, which oozed and trickled through upon the floor, mingling with the droppings of corruption. With the roar of exploding fortresses in their ears, with shells and shot pouring through the roof and sides of the rooms in which they lay, with the crackling and hissing of fire around them, these poor fellows who had served their loving friend and master the Czar but too well, were consigned to their terrible fate. Many might have been saved by ordinary care. Many lay, yet alive, with maggots crawling about in their wounds. Many, nearly mad by the scene around them, or seeking escape from it in their extremest agony, had rolled away under the beds, and glared out on the heart-stricken spectator—oh! with such looks! Many with legs and arms broken and twisted, the jagged splinters sticking through the raw flesh, implored aid, water, food, or pity, or, deprived of speech by the approach of death, or by dreadful injuries in the head or trunk, pointed to the lethal spot. Many seemed bent alone on making their peace with Heaven.

The war was not officially over but neither side felt any desire to fight on. The Russians fortified their positions on the north bank of the river and the allies made no move to cross. Russell returned to his hut, picked up the diary which he had not touched for weeks and noted: 'I got out of the habit of writing my diary daily owing to my fatal habit of procrastination and thus I have lost the most interesting memorial of the war's most interesting time.' On 19 September he records a visit with friends to a Balaclava restaurant: 'I keep falling in the mud and saying "Well I never was so drunk in all my life."' Next day, the anniversary of the Alma, he watched the presentation of colours and medals to the Light Division: 'I must say I feel a twinge of vanity hurt and pride snubbed when I see fellows who have not been under fire as I have been at Alma and Inkerman receiving medals, clasps etc. Colville, who behaved well at the Alma, came to show me his hideous medal and the Alma clasp. . . . Mail in, No letter from my darling Mary. I'm beginning to get rather anxious about her.'

In October he sailed with an expeditionary force that anchored off Odessa, mercifully refrained from bombarding the town, then went on to seize the port of Kinburn at the mouth of the Bug. He wrote from H.M.S. *Triton*, anchored off Kinburn, on 19 October:

My darling Mary wife,
    I don't know where you are or what complaints you are making of me, but here are a few lines and only a few to assure you I am well and to tell you that I have not heard of you or from you since I left Crimea now nearly a fortnight ago. . . . I have been very much thinking of you lately—why I don't know. I mean that continual fancies about you come into my head in dreams and in day-dreams too. I long to see the children also. . . . I intend to make an effort to get home at Christmas, and really I do expect that the Czar must soon give in or see the seaboard of his empire ruined. Only for the interests of yourself and children, I would go home soon as I am war-sick and tired of shooting, shouting and smoke.

In Sebastopol the allies were completing the destruction of the naval installations. In November 1855 General Simpson was replaced as British Commander-in-Chief by General Sir William Codrington, who quickly made it clear he felt less inclined than either of his predecessors to tolerate the freedom given to war correspondents. Codrington had been hurt by Russell's portrait of him during the last assault on the Redan. Now he lost little time in drafting orders for the expulsion of correspondents whose writings might help the enemy. It was the origin of military censorship in the British army and, typically of the Crimean campaign, it came too late to be of any practical use.

As the end of 1855 approached, with no further fighting in prospect, *The Times* arranged for Frederick Hardman to replace Russell. On 4 December he wrote to Mary: 'Deenyman—Right or wrong I'll leave camp as soon as Hardman arrives and fly straight to your dear arms if I'm not too stout to get into them. . . . I can scarcely believe it. It is like a dream.'

He arrived home between Christmas and the New Year. He had been away for twenty-two months.

Crimean Conclusions

R ussell's work in the Crimea raises the fundamental issue of a free press: How free should it be to publish all the information it gets? Are there not—in times of war especially—matters so vital to the nation's interests that decisions about what to publish cannot be left to the discretion of journalists?

There was no doubt where *The Times* stood. 'The people of England,' it had said, 'will look for safety in publicity rather than in concealment.' In the 1850s the paper was strong enough to maintain its position against all pressures. It was further strengthened by the fact that though Delane and his staff would recognize no obligation to the authorities, they took their obligation to the truth very seriously. They were neither sensation-hunters nor scandal-mongers. They could not be bribed and they would not be deflected. They had a high, even a grandiose sense of their responsibility not to any particular government or party or faction but to what they saw as the best interests of the nation. This attitude, combined with professional zeal and competence, raised *The Times* to a position of unparalleled power and influence during the Crimean War. In a sense, it was too successful. The very completeness of its triumph ensured that no British paper would ever again be allowed such unfettered freedom in time of war.

By twentieth-century standards, Russell's Letters were excessively long and detailed. No modern paper would find space for articles of six thousand words or more, twice a week over a period of many months, all devoted to the same subject. No modern reader would want to know so much, however important or fascinating the story. But the middle class readers of mid-Victorian Britain were made of sterner stuff and Russell kept them relentlessly informed about all aspects of the British army, its composition, difficulties and morale, the disposition of its units, the hopes of its commanders, its relations with its allies. Within a few hours of publication in London the same wealth of information was made available, by the telegraph, to the Czar in Moscow and soon after that to his generals in Sebastopol. It was a reasonable cause for concern.

The most blatant example, the one that caused most trouble, was a passage in his Letter of 4 October 1854, shortly after the allies had arrived outside Sebastopol and just before their first bombardment of the city. Russell gave details of the allied strength in heavy artillery, the effects of Russian gunfire, even the location of the British gunpowder store. By the time it was published in London on 23 October, the bombardment had been tried and failed. Lord Raglan wrote to the Duke of Newcastle complaining that reports of such accuracy and detail 'must be invaluable to the Russians, and in the same degree detrimental to H.M.'s troops.' He demanded that 'something should be done to check so pernicious a system at once.' (1) But he did nothing more than send his Deputy Judge-Advocate, Mr Romaine, to remonstrate with Russell. Russell apologized for disclosing the position of the powder store but pointed out that, when he wrote the article, everyone in the British camp was confident that Sebastopol would be theirs long before his Letter reached London.

Russell pondered the matter further and shared his thoughts with his readers:

Although it may be dangerous to communicate facts likely to be of service to the Russians, it is certainly hazardous to conceal the truth from the English people. They must know, sooner or later, that the siege has been for many days practically suspended, that our batteries are used up and silent, and that our army are much exhausted by the effects of excessive labour and watching, and by the wet and storm to which they have been so incessantly exposed. The Russians will know this soon enough. They are aware of it long ere this, for a silent battery—to hazard a bull—speaks for itself. (NOVEMBER 25 1854)

No power on earth can now establish a censorship in England, or suppress or pervert the truth. Publicity must be accepted by our captains, generals, and men-at-arms, as the necessary condition of any grand operation of war; and the endeavour to destroy the evil will only give it fresh vigour, and develop its powers of mischief. The truth will reach home so distorted, that it will terrify and alarm far more than it would have done had it been allowed to appear freely and simply. (DECEMBER 1 1854)

Lord Raglan was unimpressed. 'I ask you,' he wrote to Newcastle, 'to consider whether the paid agent of the Emperor of Russia could better serve his master than does the correspondent of the paper that has the largest circulation in Europe . . .' (2) For all his anxiety, however, he still held back from action and Russell went on composing his reports in much the same way as before. He sought to justify himself by a number of arguments, none of them entirely convincing. 'It is for the editor on the spot,' he argued, 'to decide what ought to be made public and what ought to be suppressed in my correspondence' (3); but he knew full well that his editor's instincts were all for disclosing, never for suppressing information. His Letters told the Russians nothing, he claimed, they could not learn more quickly from spies or the interrogation of prisoners or by simple observation from Sebastopol. And when the war was over Russian commanders assured him they had learned nothing of practical value from his Letters, though this was more a reflection on their competence than an argument for presenting the enemy with information. The fact remains that Russell's despatches continued to give many details which the Russians could not have got so reliably from other sources. In this respect his Letters were indefensible.

Their publication was only possible because *The Times* was greatly feared by the authorities in London and Lord Raglan was reluctant to act in the Crimea. The Duke of Wellington would not have tolerated the situation for a moment. The other combatants in the Crimea allowed no such licence. All the despatches of the French correspondents went to a government office in Paris to be checked and censored before being passed on to the newspapers. When a young sub-lieutenant of artillery, Count Leo Tolstoy, wrote a powerful and truthful description of life on the Russian side, *Sevastopol in May*, it was censored out of all recognition.

It is undeniable, however, that Russell's Letters did much more to save the British army than to endanger it. There is no evidence that the Russians benefited in any way from his work and there is overwhelming evidence that the British benefited in many ways. His was the voice—for much of the war the only voice—of compassionate concern. As a direct result of his Letters *The Times'* Fund was set up and vital supplies reached the army when they were sorely needed; essential services—supply, transport, medical—were reorganized; anachronistic regulations about uniforms and turn-out were swept away; a more efficient system was introduced for control of the army; above all, the authorities in London and the Crimea were shaken out of their entrenched lethargy. There can be no doubt that Russell, with the weight of *The Times* steadfastly behind him, did more to save what was left of the British contingent in the early months of 1855 than anyone else. It was an outstanding illustration of what a free press can do in the hands of responsible and fearless men. Few incidents in the history of journalism go further to substantiate the claim which Tom Stoppard puts into the mouth of his idealistic young reporter in *Night and Day:* 'No matter how imperfect things are, if you've got a free press, everything is correctable, and without it everything is concealable.'

None of this saved Russell from contumely at the time and criticism later.

His first accounts of the army's incompetence provoked angry denials from Whitehall and outrage at Buckingham Palace. Prince Albert did not modify his view even when the hearings of the Roebuck committee of inquiry confirmed Russell's charges. At the end of 1855 the Prince wrote to Lord Clarendon: 'That detestable *Times* is doing us again mischief which the gaining of three pitched battles could not repair. Mr. Russell ought to be turned out of the camp for giving to the world such an account of the storming of the Redan as he has done; trying to make his reputation as an author by coloring [*sic*] his picture in casting into deep and dismal *shade* everything that ought to be sacred to British honour.' (4)

The Queen was more open to the evidence. In her private Journal for 28 May 1855 she described a talk with Colonel Jeffrys of the Connaught Rangers about conditions in the Crimea:

He described the misery, the suffering, the total lack of everything, the sickness etc., and in no way exaggerated by other accounts I have seen. He knew Mr. Russell of *The Times*, and many things were *not* put down by him, as they would not have been believed here. I told Col. Jeffrys that the misfortune was that by publishing these mismanagements and sufferings, the Russians got encouraged and became aware of everything. He admitted that this was a great misfortune, but that on the other hand they felt certain things *ought* to be made known, else they would not be remedied, and the country must understand what has been going on. (5)

In the Crimea there were many officers who hated Russell, some who believed his strictures had hastened, if not directly caused, the death of Lord Raglan. The general feeling was described many years later by Sir Garnet Wolseley,* who was a subaltern with the 90th Light Infantry in 1855:

It was on my way back to camp along the Sebastopol Aqueduct by the Lower Tchernaya that I saw for the first time Mr. Russell, the justly celebrated 'special correspondent' of *The Times* newspaper. He was not popular with the army, and those officers who had the privilege of his acquaintance were generally looked upon with suspicion as anxious to be made known in England through the columns of the greatest of all daily papers. The consequence was that his friends and those whom he praised were not always those who were the most highly appreciated by the thoughtful men amongst us. I fully recognised even then how much we owed him for his outspoken denunciations of the disgraceful manner in which our army had been sent by the government then in office to the Crimea without land transport of any kind. But at the time I was intensely prejudiced against him, a feeling that was still far stronger against the officers who were his friends. (6)

One of General Buller's aides-de-camp, Captain the Honourable Henry Clifford, described Russell in a letter home:

He is a vulgar low Irishman, an Apostate Catholic (but that is neither here nor there), but he has the gift of the gab, uses his pen as well as his tongue, sings a good song, drinks anyone's brandy and water and smokes as many cigars as foolish young officers will let him, and he is looked upon by most in camp as a Jolly Good Fellow. He is just the sort of chap to get information, particularly out of youngsters. (7)

---

* Garnet Joseph Wolseley (1833–1913) fought in Burma, India, Canada and Africa, as well as the Crimea. After the Ashanti War of 1873 and his campaign in Egypt in 1882, he was so popular that his name became a slang synonym for 'all right' and people would say 'Everything's Sir Garnet'. He was created a Viscount in 1882 and appointed Commander-in-Chief in 1900.

But only two days later Clifford was writing: 'I am delighted with the letters of *The Times*' correspondent. They are not the least exaggerated, if anything under the mark.'

There were many, especially among the junior officers and the ordinary soldiers, who were deeply grateful that there was one man at least who knew what they were going through and was not afraid to tell. Lieutenant Temple Godman of the 5th Dragoon Guards, confronted by a piece of official blundering, wrote to his sister: 'I wish I could see Russell, I would get him to put it all in *The Times*.' (8) Captain Robert Portal of the 4th Light Dragoons wrote home: '... read *The Times* articles and you will get the truth.' (9) And Colonel George Bell of the Royal Regiment noted in his diary on 17 January 1855: 'The press has already told truths that make one's hair stand on end, and if anything is to save a remnant of the army it will be *The Times* newspaper and their special correspondent, Mr. Russell.' (10)

There is less direct evidence from the non-commissioned soldiers because few of their letters have survived, but there can be little doubt what their feelings were. One of the most touching tributes Russell ever received was paid to him in May 1858 when he was reporting the suppression of the Indian Mutiny. Russell was too sick to use his pen and a corporal of the 42nd Regiment, the Black Watch, was sent to take down his Letters from dictation. When he offered the man some payment he was told: 'No! Mr. Russell, there's not a man in the regiment who was out in the Crimea would take a penny from you, sir. Sure, we ought to do more than that for your honour, for you were the true soldiers' friend.' (11)

The Crimean War was the key experience of Russell's life. It gave him fame and if not fortune, at least a financial stability he had not known before. It gave him confidence too. His life from this time on was conditioned by the Crimean experience.

In some ways his success can be attributed to luck. He was lucky to be confronted with the greatest challenge of his career at the moment when his powers were reaching their peak. He was 'on to a good story', a war that commanded the nation's interest and was full of variety and drama, and he soon found himself on to a great scandal—the struggles of the army to survive under what he called 'the debris of old-fogeyism, red-tapery, staffery, Horse-Guardism'. Though he worked under conditions which were always difficult and often dangerous, there were enviable compensations—the freedom to go where he liked, talk to anyone who would talk to him and write exactly what he wanted. He was working, furthermore, for the most influential paper in the world and for an editor who was prepared to give him unlimited space and support.

But most of these considerations applied equally to his fellow correspondents and not one of them rose to the occasion as Russell did. He had scant respect for his colleagues. On 21 May 1855 he wrote to Delane: 'The new correspondent of the *Morning Post* is a purveyor's clerk named Henty. Mr. Wenkstein of the *Daily News* lives on board ship and the *Chronicle* man I know not. The *Morning Advertiser* is represented, I understand, by a Mr. Keane who chiefly passes his time in preparing cooling drinks at Mrs. Seacole's.'* His deepest contempt was reserved for Nicholas Woods of the *Morning Herald:*

> I tell you that he indulges in excessive romance and is therefore likely to beat me hollow in the long run for popular favour. For example his account of the opening of the second bombardment is much more explicit and circumstantial than mine but the difference between us is that I was near the batteries early in the morning and tried to describe what I saw while he was at Balaklava till mid-day and described what no-one saw and what did not take place. I have always done my best to stick to Miss Verity while he has a liaison with her old rival, Imagination. (12)

It was another piece of luck for Russell perhaps that so many of his rivals were so inadequate. But in the last analysis his success was due not to luck but to character—his serious professionalism, his humanity, a capacity for sustained hard work, respect for the truth, physical and moral stamina. The Crimean War was not an easy assignment. Russell was with the army, with two short breaks, throughout the campaign. He witnessed all its main engagements with the enemy. With the exception of Lord Raglan, who never spoke to him, he was acquainted with all its leading figures and scores of lesser ones. He endured longer and worked harder than almost everyone else there. Yet he managed to give an impression of almost unquenchable cheerfulness.

The published letters and reminiscences of officers who served in the Crimea afford many portraits of Russell and their verdict is almost unanimous. George Lawson, an army surgeon, found him 'an exceedingly amusing man'. (13) Captain Portal described him as 'great fun'. Colonel George Bell wrote: 'Russell, *Times'* correspondent, comes in from a stable loft where he dwells to our den of an evening to have a chat, a glass of brandy pawney, and cigar; he tells some droll stories, sings a good song, and is a very jolly good fellow.' Lawrence Godkin, a fellow journalist, noted that: 'He was a welcome guest at every mess-table, from the moment of his arrival in the camp. In his hands correspondence from the field really became a power before which generals began to quail.' (14) And A. W. Kinglake, the historian of the war whose tribute is all the more impressive because he was a partisan of Raglan's, described Russell in these words:

> His opportunity of gathering intelligence depended of course in great measure upon communications which might be made to him by officers of their own free

---

* George Alfred Henty (1832–1902) was a junior officer in the Purveyor's Department in the Crimea and a part-time newspaper correspondent. He later became famous for his boys' adventure stories which gave extreme expression to Victorian jingoism, imperialism and sense of racial superiority.

Mrs. Mary Seacole, an enterprising Creole from Jamaica, ran a store and hotel at Balaclava. She published an account of her life, *Wonderful Adventures of Mrs. Seacole in Many Lands*, in 1857, for which Russell wrote an affectionate preface.

will; and it is evident that to draw full advantage from occasions found in that way, the enquirer, instead of 'enquiring,' must be a man so socially gifted that by his own powers of conversation he can evoke the conversation of others. Russell was all that and more; for he was a great humourist, and more, again, he was an Irish humourist, whose very tones fetched a laugh. If only he shouted 'Virgilio!'—Virgilio was one of his servants—the sound when heard through the canvas used often to send divine mirth into more than one neighbouring tent; and whenever in solemn accents he owned the dread uniform he wore to be that of the late 'disembodied militia,' one used to think nothing more comic could ever be found in creation than his 'rendering' of a 'live Irish ghost' . . . Russell also had abundant sagacity; and besides in his special calling was highly skilled; for what men told him he could seize with rare accuracy, and convert at once into powerful narrative. (15)

Twenty years after the event, reminiscing about the Crimea in his diary, Russell wrote: 'I don't think but for my Irish nature I could have got on so well.' (16)

II

Home and Away

Russell rejoined his family in London at the end of December 1855. It was late in the evening when he arrived home. Mary greeted him, then led him quietly upstairs and threw open a bedroom door to reveal their four young children who burst into song: 'Oh! Willie, we have missed you. Welcome! welcome home!' He was delighted though a little disappointed next morning when he was told this was a popular song and had not been specially composed for the occasion. (1)

Widely acclaimed as 'Balaclava Russell', he had to endure much lionizing. Unfortunately there are no diary entries for this period and no surviving letters so his reactions are not known, but it seems likely that he was, on the whole, glad that the strict house rules of *The Times* prevented him from accepting civic honours. Two months later he noted in the diary: 'I find I am unpleasantly well known principally by my portrait.' (2)

He went to Printing House Square and settled down with Mowbray Morris to try to sort out his expenses for the past twenty-two months. It was a hopeless task. Russell was never particularly businesslike and the Crimean campaign was hardly the best of times for careful accountancy. Morris struggled to make sense of his bills and receipts, then admitted defeat. He sent Russell the sort of letter that every journalist, home from a long stint abroad, must dream of:

Dear Russell,

I think the best way of settling our accounts is to make what tradesmen call 'a clean slate' and to start afresh. Let it be understood that you and the paper are quits up to next Saturday 16th. From that day you will receive a salary of £600 a year, payable monthly by me as long as you remain on my list of foreign correspondents. This sum being exclusive of travelling and other expenses incurred whilst you are on duty abroad. All I ask on my part is that you will render monthly accounts of your expenditure showing a clear balance, that we may both know how we stand. I am sure you will find regularity beneficial in every way. (3)

It was a generous settlement and Russell resolved to do his best in future to keep his accounts in order.

Although all fighting had ceased, the war was not yet officially over and before the end of February 1856 he was on his way back to the Crimea. On the 25th, in France, he wrote in his diary:

On this day two years ago I arrived in France, as well as I can recollect, on my mission to the East. I return now but whether for good or ill, to enhance or to lose the reputation I have won, I cannot say or pretend to dictate. Leaving dear Mary, who will only fret when I am gone, is a sorrow which is alleviated by the reflection that it is for her and the children's benefit that I do so.

He followed the same route as before, overland to Marseilles, then by sea via Malta, Gallipoli and Constantinople. At Gallipoli he called on the old Greek woman who had looked after him: 'The poor old soul was in and seemed very glad to see me indeed. I gave her little child a present and departed.' (4)

By mid-March he was back at work in the Crimea and thinking about his future. He wrote to Mary:

I find myself after two years hard work free from debt, but with only a *dependency* on *The Times*, the managers fully think me most lavish and extravagant* and three-fourths of my gains from the book gone altogether . . . I am very thankful now, but I must confess that I am beginning to 'think' of the future more than I did, or rather I begin to think of it for the first time perhaps in my life as before this my affairs were so involved and so terrible there was no use in thinking about them. . . . We are just *getting* out of that degree of poverty which makes one reckless and are beginning to get a glimpse of the comforts of Society and of riches. Riches are not happiness indeed, but there is great difficulty in living happy without them. (5)

The same letter gives glimpses of his family life during his leave:

I have often thought of the wrong I did poor little Willie when I thought he and Johnnie told a fib and of his exclamation when I asked him why he cried—'Because I thought you were going to beat me'—and I want to efface from their minds the idea that I am a cruel papa. I shall scarcely be sorry if the Fielding is done up now while I am away, for it does certainly keep one out too late of nights and unfits one for the morning's work.

It is obvious from his letters and diary entries at this time that things had been far from well at home. Russell had rapidly fallen into his old habits, spending most evenings at the club. Mary's nervousness and moodiness had increased. Russell

---

* In his diary two days previously he had written: 'A nasty letter from Willans stating that *The Times* was of the opinion that I was very extravagant! Well, God knows I have made nothing out of my bills.'

half suspected that her friendship with Obé Willans had grown rather too close during his long absence. There had been a major row with Willans' wife. On 20 March Russell wrote in his diary: 'I often think of poor weak Mary at home—how helpless she is, how utterly dependent on others. I have trusted Willans more perhaps than any man ought to trust another. My money, my wife, my children, my prospects, all are in his hand.' At this point the entry becomes disjointed. The next line has been scratched out and the lines that follow are spattered with his impenetrable shorthand. He was clearly upset and angry.

A few weeks later he wrote to Mary:

> Do try and keep your accounts straight, and do not depend on others. That is indeed your greatest fault, want of energy—a dislike to do anything that you can get anyone else to do, and too much sedentary 'indulgence' in 'sitting quiet' . . . You are very desponding about our happiness, dear Dot, because I said 'horrid Brompton', but do you know I can't agree with you, and I'm glad to say so and no one shall put it out of my head but that we may be happy yet. Once you wrote me word that you had known a great deal more happiness than bother notwithstanding all my nasty ways and as I grow older I hope to grow better, and certainly we understand each other better than when I used to be a fierce little savage just caught in the web of matrimony and showing my nasty little fangs and champing at the fair keeper who held me so fast and so lovingly. (6)

A month later he was again reprimanding her for her 'want of energy': 'I am indeed sorry to find the children are so little company to you and that neither music, books nor work can enable you to pass the time without deep dejection. If I had nothing to do, I should feel dejected too.' (7) In the same letter he dealt firmly with her relationship with Willans:

> Friendship built on love for another man's wife is of a very dangerous and unreliable nature. . . . I don't believe in Platonic love. It cannot be safe. That is my opinion. . . . Now in all I write, recollect that I entertain no suspicions of him, except that perhaps his feelings are very affectionate towards you, and that it would be best to aid him in preventing their getting beyond control. Under the circumstances, I do, as I have said, disapprove of your continuing to correspond with him, the more so as he sees the impropriety of doing so as long as his wife continues in her present state of mind.

With no active campaigning to report, he told his *Times* readers about the continued destruction of the installations at Sebastopol, discussed the merits of the purchase system for army commissions and came down against it, reflected on the lessons to be learned from the Crimean fighting, and studied the enemy who could now be observed at close quarters.

His Letter to *The Times* of 11 April said: 'As one gets accustomed to the Russian face it becomes less displeasing, and there are undeniably many of them who are exceedingly like Englishmen—more so than any foreigners I have ever seen.' By mid-June he was telling Mary: 'The Ruskis are kind to their animals, and are really very amicable in many respects but they are fanatical in all that concerns their religion. I wish we were a little more in that way. They are kindly, well-disposed, clever and warmly attached to friends and country, and their upper classes are most elegant and accomplished. In many respects they more resemble us than any people in the world and I think we ought never to have been enemies.' (8)

As the weather improved the armies amused themselves with race meetings and amateur dramatics. On 28 March 1856 Russell noted: 'Busy making out my accounts of my month's expenditure. . . . I think this is my 35th or 36th birthday. Heaven has indeed been most gracious to me and has granted me now great prosperity which I trust will be permanent.' Two days later he said: 'It is certain that peace is made they say.' On 2 April the allied guns fired for the last time—to salute the proclamation of peace.

The end of the war did not mean an end to military idiocy. The next day was bitterly cold with fresh snow on the ground: 'Sir W. Eyre [Commander of the Third Division] selected this day to take out his division with tents and in heavy marching order as far as Komara—frost-bites were numerous, hundreds of men fell out and several died—three it is said—positively expired. This is most scandalous and cruel.' (9)

He made no mention of this incident in his reports to *The Times* but his Letter of 11 April reflected his abiding sense of the wastefulness of war:

> Heaven lets looses all its plagues on those who delight in war, and on those
> who shed men's blood, even in the holiest causes. The pestilence by day and
> night, the deadly fever, the cholera, dysentery; the incompetence, stupidity,
> and apathy of chieftains; the strategical errors of great captains; culpable
> inactivity and fatal audacity—all these follow in the train of victorious armies
> and kill many more than the bullet or the sword.

The Crimean War had been costly in men and money and reputations, conducted on all sides with ineptitude. Russell was one of the few to emerge from it with his credit enhanced. In May 1856, at a ceremony to present the freedom of the City of London to Admiral Sir Edmund Lyons, the City Chamberlain spoke of Russell in terms which he remembered with pride for many years: '. . . it is not too much to say that he has elevated newspaper writing to the dignity of history, and the office of an agent of the daily press to that of an unpaid people's ambassador.'

The allied armies sailed for home. Among the last to leave, Russell was in London by July but once again he was not home for long. Delane asked him to cover the coronation of Czar Alexander II in Moscow. Before going, he accepted an invitation to breakfast with the Prime Minister, Lord Palmerston, at his house in Piccadilly. According to Russell's account, the meeting was no great success from his point of view. There were several distinguished guests at table and he did more listening than talking. After the meal they began to disperse:

As I approached to make my bow and retire, Lord Palmerston said, 'Don't go yet if you are not very busy. I want a few minutes' chat with you.'

The interview which followed was rather embarrassing for me, for Lord Palmerston after a few remarks about my correspondence from the Crimea, suddenly asked me, 'What would you do if you were at this moment charged with the command of the British Army? You have been telling us that the French were so much better than we were; suppose you were called upon to organise our Army, beginning with the upper commands in it, what would you do?' I was naturally taken aback, for I never thought that I should be asked such a question, but I said, 'I think their Staff, the *Etat Major*, is very good and we have nothing like it.' 'No,' said Palmerston, 'that is quite true, but we have done very well without it. Remember we are dealing with a British not with a French Army. The nature of the force of the two differs. Recollect that the most effectual recruiting sergeant in these islands is the village constable. We have to depend on voluntary enlistment to fill our ranks, and I look upon the praise given to the results of conscription as stuff and nonsense. I cannot believe that men who are forced to do work of any kind do it better than men who take up the work of their own accord. You will say perhaps that the pressure of poverty and the fear of the village constable, or gamekeeper, operates as a sort of compulsion, but surely you will understand what a difference there is between that sort of pressure and the result of government enactments which compel the people of a country to submit to military service whether they like it or not. No; all you gentlemen forget that our Army is the Army of England, and that it is not the Army of France, and that it never can be, and I hope never will be, anything but what it is. And you know it well, for you told us how well our troops in the Crimea sustained the ancient reputation of our Armies. I will make no comparisons.' And then for about half-an-hour there followed a series of searching questions respecting our generals. Occasionally my host shook his head, sometimes nodded approvingly, occasionally uttered a word or two of agreement. At last, rising, he said, 'I am very much interested in what you have told me, and I hope I shall have the pleasure of seeing you again soon.' I went away with the feeling that I had cut rather a poor figure in the interview, for Lord Palmerston seemed to know more about our Army than I did. (10)

In August Russell travelled across Europe to Berlin, then sailed from Stettin to St Petersburg *en route* for Moscow. The voyage up the Baltic was enlivened by a group of actors and singers from Paris, including the Italian bass Luigi Lablache, who were to take part in the coronation celebrations. Russell wrote to Mary: 'I had to sleep for three nights on deck. The only advantage was that at night after dinner they used to meet on deck and sing deliciously. Poor Lablache had engaged a cabin two months in advance, but when he arrived he found he could not get into it as his belly was so big, and so he had to sit up all night in his chair with his little dog Cigarette.' (11)

The coronation took place on 7 September 1856. It was a brilliant day and a glittering occasion and Russell rose to it. His Letter, 13,000 words long, was published in *The Times* nine days later. 'The Czar is now the Lord's annointed,' it began, 'The great ceremony which has consecrated his power in the eyes of so many millions of his subjects has been performed with rare precision and success, and with a magnificence to which no historical pageant known to me can claim superiority.' His account displayed Russell's matured powers as a reporter more fully, perhaps, than any other piece he wrote: the easy flow of his narrative; a photographic eye that could encompass the broad splendour of the spectacle and focus the next moment on the minutest detail; a flexible command of the English language which made him equally at home with high ceremonial and touches of human irony. He described a parade of veterans of the war against Napoleon I and his surprise that there were no grey hairs among them, a surprise which 'is removed, however, when you see that the veteran who touches his moustache blackens the fingers of his glove; he has had his hair dyed, just as his boots have been polished—for effect.' He noted that the English church in Moscow had not been closed even at the height of the Crimean War, even though the Russians found the congregation praying for the Queen's victory over all her enemies. He found Prince Paul Esterhazy, the Austrian Ambassador, a picture of wonder: 'He is dressed in puce silk or velvet, with a Hussar jacket of the same material, braided all over with pearls. Diamonds flash forth from all the folds of his clothing. His maroon-coloured boots, which come up to the knee, are crusted with pearls and diamonds, and on his heels are spurs of brilliants, which glitter finely in the sunshine. One would almost be proud to be kicked by such a boot, but perhaps such an honour is only reserved for the great and noble.' After the crowning, when the assembled ranks of the Romanoffs went to congratulate the Czar, he noticed particularly 'the feeble frame of the Empress-Mother totters with outstretched arms toward the Imperial son, and passionately clasps and holds him in a long embrace; and tears and smiles mingle together as the little Grand Dukes are seen to clamber up to the side of their father and uncle, who has to stoop low in order to reach the little faces which ask to be kissed.'

Delane was so impressed with Russell's account that *The Times*' first leader was devoted to its praise:

In all his 60,000,000 subjects, in his hundred races, and his names of terror—in that devoted band of servants that stand round the throne of the Czar, he had not on that day a more useful and effective friend than the skilful Irishman who was recording for all the world, on tablets more enduring than brass or stone, the greatness of his power, the magnificence of his Court, the loyalty of his subjects, the devotion of his church, and the simple, natural affection of his family. . . . Our readers will observe, too, that all was to be related with that particularity which truth-telling and truth-craving Englishmen expect from us, and in the course of that very evening, after a long day of incessant wear and tear. How it has been done our readers can judge for themselves, and, if we are not mistaken it will considerably enlarge their ideas of what a stranger in a new country and a new scene, without even the language to help him, can notice and describe, if he has only his eyes and his wits about him, and does not abandon himself to the luxury of idleness.'

The coronation was followed by weeks of celebration—parades and public feasts for the people, operas and dinners and masked balls for the privileged—and Russell recorded all for his readers together with many well-informed discursions on Russian history and society and national character. He was fascinated by costume. At the Ball at the British Embassy on 22 September his eye was caught by a dignitary from Asiatic Russia:

One Oriental gentleman, who carried on his breast a large silver-bound bandolier full of blue paper cartridges, was an object of the liveliest apprehension, and he was sedulously avoided by many persons all night, for it was generally believed that he would blow up with a great crash if a spark from a candle fell on him. He did not go off, however, except in his carriage early in the morning, but a more dangerous person I never saw in a drawing-room; he had at least three-quarters of a pound of powder about him in silver shells.

When the festivities ended, Russell travelled south through Russia to revisit the Crimea. He wrote to Mary:

I have visited my old haunts and stood on the ruins of my hut like Marius amid the wreck of Carthage, have met with all sorts of adventures and have been in all kinds of miseries, but fortunately the weather has been of the most favourable up to this moment. However, I have not enjoyed it. I find that being without news from home I can take no pleasure in anything. Cut off from you, from all news from the outer world and from home, I am in a constant state of nervousness which is far from being pleasant, and I am always imagining all sorts of things which may Heaven avert. (12)

He returned home to find himself more widely respected than ever. His old university, Trinity College, Dublin, made him an honorary Doctor of Literature so for the next forty years he was known, in formal circumstances, as Dr Russell. He overcame his earlier objections to 'horrid Brompton' and settled his family into a new home more commensurate with his new standing in society—18 Sumner Place in Kensington.

The classical terraces of Sumner Place, with their stuccoed facades and Ionic porches and balustraded balconies, had been built in the early 1850s by Charles James Freake, a talented architect and speculator.* The house was spacious and gracious, set among nursery gardens and an expanding network of handsome squares and terraces. Within easy reach of central London and close to the Museum of Science and Art, the area attracted people of affluence and culture. Thackeray and his daughters were round the corner in Onslow Square, only a minute's walk away. Also in Onslow Square were Sir Theodore Martin, parliamentary agent and a prolific writer, and his wife, Helena Faucit, the Shakespearian actress. Douglas Jerrold lived in Michael's Grove. The house in Sumner Place was the nearest thing the Russell family ever had to a settled family home.

On New Year's Day 1857 they gave a big party. Russell's diary, which had been silent for many months, recorded:

> Mrs. Russell's dinner and great ball. . . . A day of great excitement. I went into town and round there till 3.30 when being unable to do any good I came out and made myself generally un-useful. . . . Company began to arrive about ten. There was once an awful alarm—key of cellar gone—found at bottom of stairs. I had to dance—as a general rule women were old, ugly and very dowdy and ill-dressed. Old Thackeray sloped in upon us just before supper. . . . The children stayed up till all hours and of course were very much admired . . .

At the end of the entry several lines are heavily obliterated with ink. Just enough can be made out to be sure they referred to Mary.

The pattern of their domestic distress begins to emerge now with painful clarity. Russell was a loving man who cared deeply for his family and worried about them continuously during the long separations that his job entailed. But when he came home it was never long before he grew irritated with Mary's nervousness and lethargy. He would go out in the evenings to find more enlivening company at dinner parties and his clubs. And this made her even more unhappy. The cycle was to be repeated many times in the coming years as their relationship deteriorated.

There are many obiterated lines in the diary over the next few weeks and though the words cannot be deciphered, the contexts make it clear the they referred to his troubles at home. At one point he utters an uncharacteristically obscure cry of the heart: 'Lord, what are we, or whose slaves are our children and our forefathers that they should anticipate or have bewailed the course of thy dispensations?' (13) On 31 January he noted: 'Alice and Willy fought this morning and are not to go to play

---

* The terrace formed part of the rapidly-expanding estates of the Henry Smith Charity, which still manages the property. The Charity had been founded by a Tudor businessman who left £2,000 for the purchase and development of land in London, the profits from which were to go to the poor.

in consequence. My father and I walked into town. . . . Mary called for me a little before two. I was playing pool and kept her which made her very angry indeed.' On 28 February: 'dined at the Parthenon—played billiards—afterwards upstairs—and so home. How long, Kyrie, how long?' The next two lines are obliterated.

His social life flourished. He spent many evenings at the Garrick Club with his old friends, Thackeray, Douglas Jerrold, Albert Smith, Charles Reade and many more. He had been an enthusiastic but unaccomplished whist player for some time and now fell into the habit of losing money almost nightly. The actor Charles Kean offered him a box at his theatre whenever he wanted: 'It is but a small return,' he said, 'for the many hours of gratification and interest I have derived from reading your admirable letters from the Crimea.' He went to see Kean's performance of Richard III, generally regarded as one of the great interpretations, and commented laconically in his diary: 'Good but peculiar.' And there were endless dinner parties. On 5 January he dined with Mowbray Morris in St James's Street and noted: 'The dinner plain but first rate. Morris after dinner got drunk and began to talk in the most beastly way.' Walking home well after midnight he 'met a woman crying in the snow who said her child was dying. I gave her 3s. 9d. I fear she was an imposter.'

Five days later at a dinner party with Delane an intriguing idea was put to Russell. According to his diary the talk ranged from Herodotus to Louis Philippe and then 'Low said at dinner apropos of Thackeray, "I don't see why Russell should not lecture and make a fortune." Delane, "Nor I indeed." Dasent, "Oh, yes! Put your pride and get your money into your pocket!" This looks serious.'

Several of his friends had been profiting greatly from the middle-class demand, in Britain and America, for lectures that were both informative and entertaining —Dickens with his dramatic readings, Thackeray with elegant discourses on literary and historical subjects, Albert Smith and his never-ending 'Ascent of Mont Blanc' at the Egyptian Hall. Russell could not resist the chance to give further strength to his new-found financial stability.

He went to see Mowbray Morris who said 'he had no objection to my lecturing provided it was not in Albert Smith's style.' In mid-March his contract with *The Times* was ended on the understanding that he would be taken back, if there was suitable work for him, when his lecture tour finished. He secured an agent, Willbert Beale, who booked an extensive programme to begin in London in May and then progress round the country. There would be a series of three lectures, covering the whole Crimean campaign. Beale would pay all the expenses and Russell would get two-thirds of the box office takings. It was a satisfactory deal and should have been a pleasing prospect but the closer the lectures came the more Russell grew to dread them.

His health was not good at this time. His doctor, Richard Quain, had prescribed iron 'to keep my steam up' and forbad him to go to China—*The Times* had asked him to cover the fighting there—on the grounds that it would be too great a strain. He was eating and drinking too much and staying out late most nights. He was worried about Mary's declining condition and the effect that her neurotic moodiness was having on the children. He found it impossible to concentrate.

In April he took himself off to an hotel in Tunbridge Wells to try to find a peaceful atmosphere in which to prepare the lectures. It did not work.

> APRIL 8 . . . dinner roast beef, pint Champagne, pint claret, 2 glasses of brandy as I felt low and queer. . . . Do not work on my lecture as I could not get up to scratch mentally.

> APRIL 9 . . . At 4.15 commenced revising opening part of first lecture, all I have as yet written. Went through it steadily. Dinner roast mutton, pint of Champagne, ditto of sherry, walked out to smoke my cigar. Came in and had some brandy and water and wrote some of lecture. I find an awful repugnance to it, a want of go in my head, a dislike, in fact, to mental labour.

He returned home and things went no better there.

His friends rallied round. Delane amended the script and approved. On the eve of the first lecture a group of Garrick Club men—Charles Dickens, Douglas Jerrold, Albert Smith and others—gathered at the Gallery of Illustration in Regent Street, heard it through and made encouraging comments. But Russell was more terrified than ever as his début approached. His first lecture was due to begin at 3 pm on Saturday 23 May at Willis' Rooms in King Street:

> I peeped into the vast room. Great Heavens! The hall was filled with Crimean officers. I recognised Lord Lucan, Lord Rokeby, Airey etc. etc., all grimly expectant in front, and many familiar faces behind.
> 'I can't go on,' I said.
> 'Nonsense,' said Thackeray, 'I've lectured, so can you.'
> 'I can't do it, I tell you. Go on somebody and say I'm ill. The money will be returned.'
> Just then Deane came up with a bumper of champagne.* I couldn't drink it. I peeped through the doorway again, when suddenly I was seized and run on to the platform by Thackeray and Co. So I unwillingly made my first appearance as a lecturer in rather an undignified manner. (14)

That night, however, he wrote in his diary: 'It went off better than I expected.' There were two more London lectures in the next few days and Russell worked hard on them with his friends. In a letter to Douglas Jerrold's son, Dickens described one of their script conferences:

> It was a bright day, and as soon as we reached Greenwich we got an open carriage and went for a drive about Shooter's Hill. In the carriage Mr. Russell

---

* John Connellan Deane was a fellow Irishman and Garrick Club member—'a fellow of infinite jest and humour', according to Russell.

read us his lecture, and we discussed it with great interest; we planned out the ground of Inkerman on the heath, and your father was very earnest indeed. The subject held us so that we were graver than usual . . . (15)

Douglas Jerrold was a very sick man. A fortnight later, when he was lecturing in Liverpool, Russell heard of his friend's death:

A telegraph from Beale. Good God how frightful. Douglas Jerrold is no more! This was indeed a 'staggerer' to me. I felt sick and nervous—could scarce write or speak—or eat. . . . A large audience. I was very bad and slow and prosy to a degree. The second part went rather better. When I came home the excitement was over. I could only think of Douglas Jerrold. (16)

He lectured in Dublin, then Edinburgh and Glasgow. He was settling to the task but not warming to it. In Edinburgh he commented:

Lecture at 8.30. I was listened to with very great attention indeed but I do not think there was much enthusiasm although I did my best. I begin to find out what I have not the charm of eloquence—even the attractiveness of volubility—yet I laboured under a kind of inward conviction at one time that I could move masses of men. Am I wrong? Vanity says no yet this experience says yes very decidedly. (17)

He spent the whole of August in Ireland, fishing and shooting and wishing Mary were with him 'even though she were to vex me and fret me'. (18) Then it was back to the lecture circuit which took him to most of the cities and many of the towns of England during the next two months. He was horrified by the industrial areas. At Huddersfield he noted 'Population dirty and ugly. . . . There's a statue of Wilberforce to commemorate the abolition of the slave trade. It would have been well if he could have emancipated the miserable drunken crew I see on the streets.' (19) Next day he was in Hull, then York:

There is an air about York like the respectability of a decayed gentlewoman for in spite of Cathedral and Archbishop and canons and chapter and testamentary jurisdiction York is decaying. As to Hull with all its 'glorious' trade and commerce I would much rather have the quiet gentlemanly tone of York than all the wicked wealth of that disgusting city! (20)

In Newcastle upon Tyne he remarked: 'What a country! It seems as if the primeval world was turning up again, fire and cinders, [?] and smoke.' (21)

At Chatsworth in Derbyshire he met Mrs Gaskell and the great architect–gardener Sir Joseph Paxton. At Brighton he dined with the historical novelist Harrison Ainsworth. At Tunbridge Wells he visited his sons, William and John, at their boarding school and found they both had measles. By the end of October the tour was over: 'Arrived in London. The lectures all over and total earnings £1,600!!! Mary quite well, dear old creature.' (22)

During the summer and autumn of 1857, while Russell was preoccupied with his lectures and preparing his book *The British Expedition to the Crimea*, the columns of the newspapers had been dominated by increasingly disturbing reports from India. The soldiers of the Bengal army of the East India Company mutinied, shot their British officers and attacked British civilians. Delhi fell to the mutineers in May. Next month they took Cawnpore and massacred the British. At Lucknow 1,500 British troops and civilians, with five hundred women and children among them, were besieged in the Residency. The causes of the uprising were many and complex but the fundamental reason was the well-founded fear that the growth of British power—the great provinces of Oudh and the Punjab had just been annexed by the Company—threatened the ancient fabric of Indian life, spiritual and social. The rebellion spread across Northern India like wildfire and there were fears that the other great regions of British influence, Bombay in the west, Madras in the south, would soon be engulfed. Lord Canning, the Governor-General, had promised clemency to those mutineers who gave themselves up, but this served only to enrage the British civilians in India and many of the soldiers whose feelings had been inflamed by stories of atrocities committed by the mutineers on captive women and children.*

On 10 November Mowbray Morris wrote to Russell:

I hear that you are not so entirely satisfied with your new occupation as to regard a return to the old one with any aversion. I may also say that the interval that has elapsed since you left us has not produced anything like a conviction that we can do perfectly well without you. Although China goes on very well under the auspices of Wingrove Cooke, yet India is at present a blank, and a blank I fear it will remain unless you fill it. What do you say? Will you go there for a year, salary £600 to be paid to your wife or other nominee at home, and all expenses out of pocket reimbursed.

The Times also contracted to buy £500 worth of three per cent Consols to be held for Russell's family.

It was a difficult offer for Russell to refuse even if he had felt inclined to. But it came at an awkward moment. On 14 November 1857 he wrote in the diary: 'Little Snooks my fifth child born at 11.30. Christened Tempest Makepeace— anniversary great storm and dear old Thackeray.' The birth left Mary weak and ill and six days later the diary described her as 'very feverish, in great panic, much excited,

---

* Charles John Canning (1812–62) was a son of the statesman George Canning. He was Postmaster-General in Lord Aberdeen's government and in 1856 was appointed Governor-General of India. His policies earned him the nickname of 'Clemency Canning'.

with pulse very quick and excited.' He had not dared tell her about the proposal that he should go to India and now, though he had committed himself to the job, he could not break the news. He was made to suffer for it when he came home late on 2 December: 'I found her sitting up although blowing me up awfully. From a letter of Morris she found I was going to India and she was angry I should be away during her convalescence.'

Nevertheless, he went ahead with his plans. Lord Granville, leader of the House of Lords and a close friend of Lord Canning's, asked him to call:

DECEMBER 8 1857 . . . shown in at once to Granville who receives me very cordially and then to talk of India and Indian affairs. He spoke in high terms of Canning and seemed particularly to insist upon it that I must not think him stiff and cold but let our acquaintance improve—'the better you know him the better you will like him.'

Granville wrote to Canning: 'I have told Delane that R. will find you ready to give him all the information you can . . . you would be a born idiot not to be tolerably open, and decently civil to R.' It was clear that Russell could expect very different treatment from the authorities in India than he had been given in the Crimea. But one man at least was dubious. The Foreign Secretary, Lord Clarendon, wrote to a friend about Russell: 'Granville thinks it useful for him to start with good impressions and a good *entré* in his mouth. But imagine all the mischief in store for us from that fellow, who of course will want a second crop of Crimean laurels grown upon the ruin of everybody's reputation.'

On Christmas Day Mary was sufficiently recovered to get up for the family dinner party but had to go back to bed straight after. The next day Russell left:

DECEMBER 26 Left England, home and wife. *Clavi dura necessitas.* An eventful day. My dear Mary looking at me with such a mild grief in her dear old eyes as if suspecting the truth. She came down to the drawing-room. I could not bear to be much with her.

He went into town, then came quietly home again. The children had not been told he was leaving:

I sent my things down privately to the brougham. I found my wife upstairs asleep. I did not disturb her. The children, under Lizzie's care, were playing very happily.* I did not bid them farewell. After a few words with her I stepped out into the street, but not without Alberta seeing me shake hands with Lizzie. And then I was alone.

* Lizzie was a cousin of Russell's who had come to live with the family and look after the children.

The Taking of Lucknow, 1858

He followed the now-familiar route, by train across France to Marseilles and on to Malta, then eastwards. The Mediterranean was rough and Russell, who was often moved to gloomy reflection by the year's ending, drew a parallel with his own life's voyage:

> The last day of the old year and here am I afloat on the ocean of life once more and drifting to India. That ocean is to me as troublous as the sea which is now around me. The beacon light which shone from home is obscured and my course is painful and uncertain. God grant the light may soon break through the clouds. It is very rough, the wind high, the sea rising. How many days of my life lately resemble the scene around us. In this whole ship there is no man perhaps more blessed with wife and friends, above all with children, than myself, but there is none so little gifted with the art of pushing his fortune, of using friends, of making money to store up for the future. And yet I have much to be thankful for in all truth and if my life is spared and that of her I value more than life I will struggle on till the light comes. . . . Goodbye to 1857—a year to me of great expectations and great disappointments. Would that I had news from home—home—home. Heaven help all who abide therein. (1)

Anxiety about Mary clouded his thoughts throughout the journey. 'I am at night distracted by fears about my Mary, and at day filled with horrid thoughts and conjectures,' he confided to his diary of 29 December 1857. Two weeks later he wrote: Oh Mary, dear Mary, I can know no peace till I read those blessed letters which tell me all is well with you. May the great Being who has planted that angel purity and love in thy heart keep it as a shrine where I too may learn to feel the grossness of my nature and cleanse it by prayer. May we soon meet never never to part again. Amen. Amen.' (2) And on 23 January: 'each day now and then seems a year to me when I think of home and letters and news of her I love. The best way of showing my love indeed will be to be discreet, economical, hard-working and frugal so that I may hope not to be separated from her again. She is indeed a child in the affairs and business of life nor am I as to graver interests much wiser.'

He travelled by what was called the overland route to distinguish it from the much longer voyage round the Cape—by sea to Alexandria, by train via Cairo to Suez, then by sea again to Ceylon, Madras and Calcutta. The journey took more than a month and was dreadful, especially after Suez when they had to take on the passengers from another ship. The heat was barely tolerable, eighty-five degrees in his cabin one morning; the stewards were overworked; and Russell did not care for most of his companions. 'It is a ship of awful grumblers,' he told Delane, 'I must add *cum causa* and I don't know how many protests have been drawn up and signed about all manner of things.' (3)

He spent the time learning as much as he could about India, reading everything he could lay his hands on, talking to fellow passengers who were officials of the East India Company and army officers and missionaries. The diary charts his progress:

It is, I fear, rather intruding itself upon me that we are in India by suffrance not by love. . . . What am I to think or to write amid this Babel of many voices—Durand, Temple, Cust, Beacher, Howarth—and Lord help the people among whom Freeling may have to administer justice. He is coarse, prejudiced and ill-bred, but he is honest I think—he won't err on the side of mercy.' (4)

He began to suspect that there was 'pretty much the same distinction of caste between the English in India as prevails among the natives. The civil service is a system of caste . . .' (5)

Alas how miserable is my ignorance, my want of precise and exact knowledge which is the only kind of knowledge which is of use. . . . It is difficult to find out the springs which move the social feelings of the English settlers in India. Here we are not colonists, we are disunited settlers each of whom thinks his neighbour is depriving him of a share of the plunder which but for the neighbour would accrue to him. This is not *ex cathedra* but is merely the expression of a tendency towards an opinion which experience on board the ship leads one to think may be correct. (6)

He observed, with disapproval, the usual ship-board activities: 'There are ladies going out to be married who seem almost anxious to anticipate the ceremony by a cession of rights to their fellow-passengers and gentlemen who seem willing to forget that they have wives at home.' (7) And to Delane he complained: 'I am beset by missionaries. One of them I heard d—g a waiter's eyes because his boots were not blacked and threatening to punch his head because his coat could not be found the other morning at table.' (8)

Russell learned a great deal from the voyage—not so much from what his fellow passengers told him as from his close observation of their attitudes. These indicated many of the things that had gone wrong in India—the widening gap between British and Indian society; a general contempt for the Indian character and way of life; the belief that the British were in India not just to rule and exploit but also to enlighten and convert. Russell did not share their assumptions. He did not believe that the English—or the British—or the Christians—had a natural superiority over all other peoples. To him, might did not automatically imply right. And his strong historical sense told him that the normal processes of change and decay would not be suspended in the special case of the British empire. His work in India was based on these foundations.

He arrived in Calcutta on 28 January 1858. He was met by Delane's brother Captain George Delane who was a member of the Governor-General's body-guard, and taken to the Bengal Club where he was made an honorary member and given a room. Next day he went to Government House and found Lord Canning:

> . . . immersed in books and papers and literally surrounded by boxes, 'military',
> 'political', 'revenue' etc. . . . I was not astonished to find a Governor-General
> of India at such a time worn-looking and anxious and heavy with care; but
> when I learned incidentally, and not from his own lips, that he had been
> writing since early dawn that morning and that he would not retire till twelve
> or one o'clock that night, and then had papers to prepare ere he started in the
> morning, I was not surprised to hear that the despatch of public business was
> not so rapid as it might have been if Lord Canning had a little more regard of
> his own ease and health. . . . (9)

The first purpose of Russell's assignment was to find out if there was any evidence for the horror stories, gruesomely recounted by the British press in India and reflected in the papers at home, concerning the mutilation of white women by the rebel soldiers, the sepoys. He put the matter to Lord Canning who 'entered at large on the subject of sepoy atrocities which he discredited as also mutilations—is sore on the point, why I don't know.' (10)

Although Russell's views were inimical to those of most of the British in India, the civilians more than the soldiers, they were fortunately shared by the men in command. Perhaps Canning was quick to recognize a natural ally in his fight for policies of clemency rather than revenge. Perhaps he merely thought it wise to follow Lord Granville's advice and court the support of *The Times* and its emissary. Whatever the reason, he gave Russell every help. He described the position and his plans, arranged for his travel and gave him a letter for the Commander-in-Chief, Sir Colin Campbell, making it clear that he had no objection to Russell's presence in the British camp. As they parted, he suggested that Russell should visit the Calcutta hospitals and talk to casualties of the Mutiny.

Russell was impressed by the efficiency and cleanliness of the hospitals. Patients told him stories of the fighting at Cawnpore and Lucknow but none of

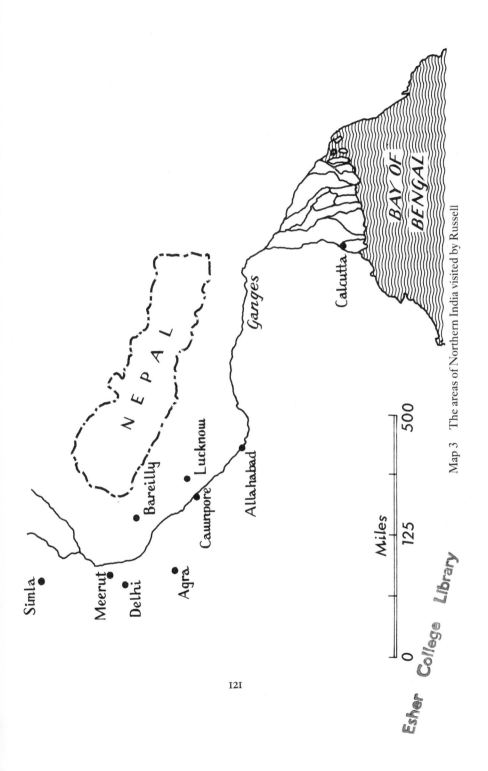

Map 3   The areas of Northern India visited by Russell

Simla

Meerut

Delhi

Agra

Bareilly

Cawnpore

Lucknow

Allahabad

NEPAL

Ganges

Calcutta

BAY OF BENGAL

Miles

0   125   500

121

them had first-hand evidence of atrocities. He questioned many people in the next few days but the most shocking thing he heard concerned the conduct of the British women under siege in Lucknow:

> It is sad to hear that the ladies at Lucknow fought as hard with each other inside as the men did out. The family Gubbins, I think, were detected with stores of champagne and luxuries at the end of the siege . . . the annexation of Oudh . . . seems to have been a tremendous robbery. What about the Crown Jewels and royal menagerie? These are the things that make us heavy with curses. . . . We have a great stewardship and our burdens and responsibilities are not light. (11)

A servant was found for him, a Madrassi called Simon who had been educated by Catholic missionaries, and on 4 February they set off for Cawnpore. They travelled by train for the first 120 miles, then by gharry—a horse-drawn carriage in which the sahib could recline at full length in the shade. At Allahabad he had another meeting with Lord Canning: 'As to Lord Canning's devotion to work, honesty, rightness of purpose, general sagacity, courage and resolution there can be no question. I don't think he vacillates. His jaw says no. But he is cold, haughty, reserved and despises the arts of popularisation.' (12)

On 12 February he reached Cawnpore where Sir Colin Campbell was assembling his forces for the next stage of the campaign. The British were already well on the way to suppressing the Mutiny. Delhi had been retaken and Cawnpore—scene of the brutal massacre of British men, women and children on the orders of Nana Sahib—had fallen two months before. The objective now was to drive the rebels out of Lucknow.

Sir Colin was sixty-six but still very fit and alert, the veteran of fighting that dated back to the Peninsular War, one of the few generals who enhanced their reputations in the Crimea. Capable of great charm and courtesy, he also had an explosive temper but it passed quickly, without leaving resentment. High command agreed with him. He was an able and conscientious commander though so cautious that his more impatient officers nicknamed him 'Sir Crawling Camel'. In the Crimea he had been hostile to the journalists—it was he who had ordered Russell out of his Balaclava quarters—but he was determined not to repeat Lord Raglan's mistake. He welcomed Russell to his headquarters, arranged for him to get a well-furnished tent and a horse and access to the telegraph, invited him to mess with his staff and promised full co-operation.

Within a few days he had formed the habit of chatting regularly to Russell, showing him the reports as they came in, discussing his plans. Perhaps he hoped that by taking Russell so completely into his confidence, he would inhibit criticism. Certainly he put Russell under a deep obligation of friendship and gratitude and Russell must have been influenced by this at times. But it cannot be claimed that he suppressed any vital truths in consequence. He remained his own man, free to write whatever he wanted, sending his Letters off to London with no attempt at censorship or supervision of any kind. And though there were no scandals on the Crimean scale to report, the Letters were often outspokenly critical of the army's behaviour.

He quickly made the acquaintance of the Magistrate of Cawnpore, Mr John Walter Sherer, who was installed at Duncan's Hotel. Sherer gave a picture of Russell at this time in his book *Daily Life during the Mutiny*: 'Coming in one forenoon, I found a strongly-built man of middle stature, with bright eyes and a merry smile, and speaking with a slight Irish accent (and how pleasant a slight Irish accent can be!) and dressed in a frogged and braided frock-coat. This was Russell, with whom we at once seemed to feel at home.' He omits to mention that Russell still wore the full beard he had cultivated during the Crimean campaign. Russell was invited to dine with Sherer's party at the hotel that evening. He regaled them with anecdotes of London literary life and 'it was a great pleasure, when Dr. Russell was called upon (as the phrase is) for a song, to find he possessed an agreeable baritone voice and pronounced his words so distinctly that we could follow them with ease . . . two songs especially pleased us, in one of which the refrain was "We will catch the whale, brave boys" and another "O, save me a lock of your hair".' (13)

Russell was busy during his fortnight in Cawnpore. He interviewed many people and sent *The Times* long accounts of what had happened in and around the city. He was already clear in his own mind that the issues were far from being so black and white as they had been painted. He began, as early as this, publicly to argue the case for moderation in dealing with the rebels. On 15 February he reflected in his diary on 'the growing separation of British and Indians, because the British are no longer corrupt and do not consort with Indian women in the old way.' Nine days later he dined with a group of vengeful civilians and made particular note that 'one fierce-eyed, red-nosed, ferrety, blood-thirsty sort of man—the image of my uncle William—rather boasted of the splendid style in which he hung up niggers.' He was to hear a great deal of this sort of talk in India but he never reconciled himself to it. The habitual, almost obligatory rudeness of the British towards the Indians struck him as both shameful and stupid. He was driven to wonder 'whether India is the better for our rule, so far as regards the social condition of the great mass of the people.' And two years later, in *My Diary in India*, he wrote: 'In fact, the peculiar aggravation of the Cawnpore massacres was this, that the deed was done by a subject race—by black men who dared to shed the blood of their masters, and that of poor helpless ladies and children.' (14)

On 18 February he received 'a dear letter from my own Dot getting well and strong and reconciled to my absence.' On the 27th he scribbled a quick note to her: 'Deenyman darling, Here is your own little chap off from Cawnpore for the march to Lucknow in about ten minutes more . . .'

The great caravanserai moved across the Ganges and into Oudh. The former kingdom, now called Uttar Pradesh, played a key role in the Mutiny. Its annexation in 1856 had greatly increased Indian apprehensions; most of the soldiers of the

Bengal Army came from the region; now it was the centre of the sepoys' final resistance. Lucknow, its glittering capital city, had seen much fighting. The sepoys mutinied there in May 1857, killed many of their officers and besieged the survivors—British officers and civilians, women and children, Indian soldiers who remained loyal to the Company—in the Residency. Four months later a small relieving force fought its way through to them only to become trapped as well. In November Sir Colin led a larger force to the Residency, rescued the besieged and withdrew. Now he was on the march again, this time to restore Lucknow to British rule.

Russell must have found the commissariat arrangements refreshingly different from the Crimea. In India the problem was not one of shortage but the more acceptable one of overabundance. For every fighting man there were six or seven attendants with tents and furniture and provisions of every kind loaded on to an apparently endless train of elephants, camels, ox waggons and a wide assortment of vehicles. Labour was cheap and the tradition was firmly established that the sahib, whose wealth was inexhaustible, should be spared all labour.

The army set out well before dawn to avoid marching in the intense heat of the day:

We got out on the road; where, in silence and order, the Rifle Brigade was plunging with steady tramp through the dust. As the moon sank in the heavens, the line of our march became more like some dream of the other world, or some recollections of a great scene at a theatre than anything else. The horizontal rays just touched the gleaming arms and the heads of the men, lighted up the upper portions of the camels and the elephants, which resembled islands in an opaque sea, whilst the plain looked like an inky waste, dotted with star-like fires. The sun soon began to make his approach visible, and an arc of greyish-red appeared in the east, spreading but not deepening, till the Far-darter himself rose like a ball of fire in the hazy sky. The band of the Rifles struck one of the old familiar steps, and as the light increased, I was able to make out some of my old friends—Ross, Fraser, Reid, and others—and jogged on, side by side, as well as the white mare let me. Her dislike to camels increased every moment, and the approach of one was the signal for a rearing-match. Pleasant beast for a march! Here, for the first time, I observed the significant attendants on our march—the doolys in the rear of the regiments—the long train of covered litters hung from bamboo-poles, and carried by coolies, who, with their reliefs, form a large portion of the column.

The sun was just beginning to make himself disagreeable, when, after several halts, we caught sight of some tents partly hidden in trees. 'Thank goodness! there's our camp. Canter over, and get some breakfast.' And there, sure enough, was our mess-tent pitched; the tables covered with snow-white cloths, our plates, chairs, knives and forks all ready—the curries smoking, and the array of servants standing with folded arms waiting for their masters. (15)

After five nights' march they came to Lucknow. Russell found his first view of the city breathtaking:

A vision of palaces, minars, domes azure and golden, cupolas, colonnade, long facades of fair perspective in pillar and column, terraced roofs—all rising up amid a calm still ocean of the brightest verdure. Look for miles and miles away, and still the ocean spreads and the towers of the fairy-city gleam in its midst. Spires of gold glitter in the sun. Turrets and gilded spheres shine like constellations. There is nothing mean or squalid to be seen. There is a city more vast than Paris, as it seems, and more brilliant lying there before us. (16)

The army camped in the Dilkusha, an area of parkland to the south-east of the city. It was a pleasant spot but within range of the enemy guns and Russell was almost decapitated by a round-shot. He met some old Crimean acquaintances in an encounter described by Sergeant William Forbes-Mitchell of the 93rd Sutherland Highlanders in this book *The Relief of Lucknow*:

On the morning after we had pitched our camp in the Dilkusha park, I went out with Sergeant Peter Gillespie, our deputy provost-marshal, to take a look round the bazaars, and just as we turned a corner on our way back to camp, we met some gentlemen in civilian dress, one of whom turned out to be Mr. Russell, the Times' correspondent, whom we never expected to have seen in India. 'Save us, sir!' said Peter Gillespie, 'Is that you, Maister Russell? I never did think of meeting you here, but I am right glad to see you, and so will all our boys be!' After a short chat and a few inquiries about the regiment, Mr. Russell asked when we expected to be in Lucknow, to which Peter Gillespie replied: 'Well, I dinna ken, sir, but when Sir Colin likes to give the order, we'll just advance and take it.' (17)

There were many people in the city, Russell knew, who had taken no part in the rebellion and he was anxious for their fate. On 4 March he wrote to *The Times*:

Now, I have no sympathy with rebellion, murder and mutiny, but I cannot refrain from expressing a most earnest hope that these unfortunate people, who are at most guilty of a forced neutrality, will not be handed over to a very excited and irritated soldiery, to the fierce Sikhs and to the wild Ghoorkas of Nepal. The time for indiscriminate bloodshedding must cease, let all that the angry civilians of British India can say be said, with the punishment of the mutinous Sepoys and of those actually taken in arms against us. Justice and even vengeance must after a period rest satisfied.

Three days after their arrival Sir Colin sent a strong column under the command of Lieutenant-General Sir James Outram to take up a position to the north of the city.* Three days after that he launched his attack, led by the 42nd, the Black Watch, and a battalion of Sikhs. The plans had been carefully prepared and they worked well. Within a few days the key points of the city were in British hands.

As the final assault began a force of Gurkhas commanded by Jung Bahadur, the *de facto* ruler of Nepal, arrived to reinforce Sir Colin's army. Russell had no respect for their leader—'a cold-blooded murderer'—or for the men, whom he described as 'perfect savages and their ferocity is not redeemed by bravery—badly armed, shod, clad and provided—they are exceedingly dirty.' (18) Their arrival at the precise moment when his men were moving into action was a great embarrassment to Sir Colin who had to preside over a lengthy ceremony of welcome when he was far more interested in the sounds of battle outside and the reports that were coming in to him. Russell noted: 'The brute kept us waiting nearly 45 minutes. He and his men a blaze of jewels, curious to look at. It was a stupid affair and when Sir Colin, to entertain them, set the bagpipers loose at us it became desperate.' (19)

Russell saw a great deal of the action, sometimes from Sir Colin's side, sometimes with the attacking units. He described it vividly in *The Times* and also gave a full account of the looting and destruction that followed:

> In the next court, which was sheltered from fire by the walls around it, our men had made a great seizure of rich plunder. They had burst into some of the state apartments, and they were engaged in dividing the spoil of shawls and lace and embroidery of gold and silver and pearls. . . . Two men of the 90th were in before us, and, assisted later by some of the 38th, we saw them appropriate money's worth enough to make them independent for life. . . . In one box they found diamond bracelets, emeralds, rubies, pearls and opals, all so large and bright and badly set that we believed at the time they were glass. (20)

Russell had no moral objection to looting, which was universally accepted as one of the perquisites of being with the vanguard. His only regret was that he was not able to take full advantage of his chances. In one of the palaces, the Kaiserbagh, a soldier found a boxful of diamonds, emeralds and pearls and offered them all to Russell for a hundred rupees. But he had no money on him: 'I might have made my fortune if I had had a little ready money with me. As it was I loaded myself with jade and got a diamond drop etc. I might have secured a small sackful. I could not believe these things were real which I saw.' (21)

Although he did not condemn plundering, Russell was aware of its disruptive effects, distracting the troops from their military purposes and creating envious ill-feeling between units and individual soldiers. He was glad a few days later when

---

* Sir James Outram (1803–63) had been an officer in the Indian army since 1819. He had built up an impressive reputation as a soldier and as an administrator, playing a leading role—which he later rather regretted—in the annexation of Oudh. He was created a baronet in 1858.

the authorities moved to halt it. And he had nothing but condemnation for the wanton smashing of everything breakable—pictures, ornaments, mirrors, chandeliers—which soldiers seem unable to resist: 'Down came the chandeliers in a tinkling, clattering of glass—crash! crash! crash! door and window, mirror and pendule. Sikh and soldier were revelling in destruction and delirious with plunder and mischief.' (22)

He was even more shocked by the brutality of the British soldiers and their Sikh allies. He knew that the suppression of the Mutiny was being conducted with ferocity. Captured rebel sepoys were blown from the guns, tied across the muzzles of canon and blown apart. There had been many stiffened corpses hanging from the trees on the march. Even so, he was hardly prepared for the cruelty of Lucknow. No prisoners were taken. Mutineers were bayoneted on the spot or worse. Russell was told of one sepoy being roasted alive by the Sikhs: 'There were Englishmen looking on, more than one officer saw it. No one offered to interfere.' (23) He recorded equally savage behaviour by some of the British:

> After the Fusiliers had got to the gateway, a Cashmere boy came towards the post leading a blind and ancient man and, throwing himself at the feet of an officer, asked for protection. That officer, as I was informed by his comrades, drew his revolver and snapped it at the wretched suppliant's head. The men cried 'shame' on him. Again he pulled the trigger—again the cap missed; again he pulled and once more the weapon refused its task. The fourth time—thrice had he time to relent—the gallant officer succeeded, and the boy's lifeblood flowed at his feet, amid the indignation and the outcries of his men! (24)

Russell used the lull after the battle to compose long Letters to *The Times*—the telegraph hastened their journey as far as Calcutta—and to develop his friendship with Sir James Outram, the Company's Commissioner for Oudh: 'so kind, so chivalrous, so good, so generous, his views so elevated, so noble and so just. I think he would make a great Governor-General. I am sure he would.' (25) They held similar views about the most politic and humane ways of dealing with the Mutiny. Neither liked the proclamation that Lord Canning now issued, declaring that since the people of Oudh had supported the rebels their lands would be confiscated though consideration would be given to those who immediately declared loyalty to the Company. It was an unusually harsh move for 'Clemency Canning' to make, based on a mistaken assumption that the fall of Lucknow meant the collapse of all rebel resistance in the province. In fact, the bulk of the rebel forces had escaped from Lucknow and large areas remained under their control. Outram and Russell both realized that it was ridiculous to expect the local chiefs and landowners to declare their allegiance to the Company while powerful rebel units still roamed the area.

Outram decided to go and see Canning and try to get him to modify his policy. Before he left he received a letter of encouragement and support from Russell, to which he replied: 'That letter I shall ever treasure, and so will my family. And I shall treasure it, not because it is the flattering and warmly-written letter of a man of European fame, but because it is the letter of an honest, truth-telling man.' (26)

Russell sent a copy of the proclamation to *The Times* and argued forcefully for policies that would not further alienate the people of India:

My own impression is that there is no foreign Power whatever could maintain an army in India without the aid of a considerable portion of the population. We could not march a mile without their assistance . . . No mawkish sentiments of clemency should guide our conduct; let us be just and politic, and, if clemency be compatible with justice and policy too, let us not be ashamed of being animated by a quality which is one of the grandest characteristics of heroes, of conquerors, and of mighty empires, and which posterity admires more than the valour by which opportunity for its exercise was won. For the Sepoy let there be justice, and, if justice be death, let execution be done, but let us cease to disgrace ourselves by indiscriminate clamouring for 'more heads', and by the foolish talk in which some young men are wont to indulge of 'polishing off every nigger in Oude.' (27)

Delane wrote to him:

I have nothing but to congratulate you on the perfect success with which you have sustained your fame. I feel myself, and hear everybody saying, that we are at last beginning to learn something about India, which was always before a mystery—as far removed from our sight and which was as impossible to comprehend as the fixed stars. The public feeling has righted itself more promptly than was to be expected, and we had before the recess a debate in which the most humane instead of the most bloodthirsty sentiments were uttered. The key to the savage spirit was the 'atrocities', and these seem to have resolved themselves into simple massacre. (28)

This was soon followed by another letter from Delane:

You have done so admirably well that everyone admits that your story of Lucknow equals the very best of your Crimea achievements. It has been fully appreciated and you have not, as you had in the Crimea, a large party interested in running you down and contradicting you. . . . Pray draw £10 on my account and carry it all in gold about you when you next accompany a storming party. It makes one blasphemous to think that you got nothing out of the Kaiserbagh for the want of a few rupees. (29)

13

Indian Conclusions

On 13 April 1858, four weeks after the fall of Lucknow, Sir Colin Campbell led the army north to subdue the rebels in Rohilcund. Russell hated the growing heat of the Indian plains. He lost his appetite, went down with dysentery, and by the time they were ready to set off he was so weak that he had to be carried along in a dooly. He drew a picture of one in his diary (pp. 130–31)—one of his better artistic efforts—and added the words:

> There are two extra bearers who run alongside and relieve the others. They go at a kind of rate upwards of 4 miles an hour, all the time making strange noises and keeping up a kind of chorus of sound like a refrain of a dismal ballad. There is one mistake in the sketch. The disengaged arm is always held at right angles. They catch their breath in short alternate gasps. All night the awful noises of camp—camels loading, tent sticking, peg hitting—resounded: elephants trumpeting, tom-toming of natives, noises of bazar people, shouts and yells of camp servants, syces to each other, packing up. The smell from dead bodies near my tent very dreadful and offensive . . . (1)

Once again the army marched in the cooler hours of darkness and camped during the heat of the day. Russell was soon well enough to dispense with the dooly and try riding on an elephant which he found uncomfortable. On 26 April he noted: 'Then to Serai for breakfast where I was disgusted by finding in courtyard two servants of an officer lying horribly beaten and one with his wife in great grief by his side. They had been licked for something or other by their master. This is a savage, beastly and degrading custom . . .' (2)

On 29 April he had a serious accident. He went to get his horse and was in the way when it was attacked by another horse. He received a fierce kick on his right thigh 'knocking me two yards back and over'. The doctor bled him—'25 leeches were clapped upon calf and thigh'—and he had to resort once more to the dooly.

The army was now in contact with the enemy cavalry, the sowars, and Russell was worried: 'I am every morning in dreadful fear of being cut up by sowars as my doolymen go far out in the open and frequently outside the advanced flankers. This morning I woke up and found no trace of our army in sight.' (3)

13] **April**   ····13 TUESDAY [103–262] ◐ ····   4th Month **1858**

Dirty "Douglas thou hast lied" At night of pain'. In ye morning came in Clifford & he pronounces it to be dysentery in rather incipient stage – nothing to eat. angas water or rice water to drink arrow root – for grub. Orders came out for us to march soon after night fall. Lord help us – I am to go in a dooly as I am unable to ride. Below is ...

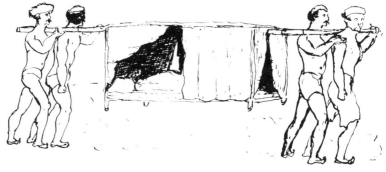

There are 2 extra bearers who run along side & relieve the others – they go at a head space & forward at 4 miles an hour all the time making strange noises ... keeping up a kind of chorus of sound like a refrain of a dismal ballad. There is one mistake in ye sketch – the disengaged arm is always held at ... angles. They catch their breath in short ... gasps. All night the awful noises of camp camels loading tent sticking peg hitting ... elephants trumpeting, – sometimes of natives ... of bazar people – Shouts & yells of camp servants syces to each other – packing up. The smell from dead bodies near my tent very dreadful & offensive – My Mahomedan Kitmutger ... went off this morning refusing to leave Lucknow I think

Typical pages of Russell's diary, written as the army marched from Lucknow to engage th[e]
with neat pen-and-ink sketches.

1858 4th Month   ·· **14** WEDNESDAY [104-261] ··   **April** [14]

Oxford and Cambridge Terms begin

I Left Lucknow at 2 15 in a dooly. crossing field
this the main street over Charbagh bridge, & about 6 o'clock reached
Camp Bunteerah at 6 am. I was seedy enough indeed but
slept well - the motion of a dooly is not disagreeable - We are
under ye command of old Pukur hana - more saw Colin
waits behind - streaming thro' silent deserted streets of city in
clouds of smothering dust was picturesque & disagreeable enough
It is melancholy to travel along so sad & so solitarily - & pred
too Gripes are upon me - Halting at one old place Bun-
-teerah I found my letters beside from Peel's. He was not
looking well . hale & thin, but he said his arm was better. We
had a good deal of talk about Charbong. He said he had a
[illegible] of attacking . thy London [illegible] & puffs in case of
war est. must prove successful - Well there was a prospect of
war with France relating to the refugee question

I nearly forgot to say that I left with regret my monkey
behind me - dead - It was caught in a tree in the Bithin fore
work was very young & tame & whenever I went near him or
her she pulled my whiskers - Poor creature she caught cold &
died just like a christian poor beast - my little pren poney
is famishing -

little [illegible] comes to me forbids animal food - I think
[illegible] or rice water - dine on arrow root - manifest on
steps - have no appetite - Today very seedy & in much
pain indeed -

remaining Indian mutineers. Russell occasionally enlivened the pages of his diary

The next day showed his fear to be well founded. The army defeated a rebel force at the battle of Bareilly. Russell was too ill to see much of the action except for one skirmish which swept altogether too close:

> I could see the 79th firing on my left and was just lying down after watching them on my elbow when there was an awful panic, cries of 'Sowars' and instant flight. Sukeram brought up my horse and, naked to my shirt, leg bleeding, bare head, I scrambled into the saddle and rode towards the road. Dooly came up . . . I was exhausted and just sinking back when there was another panic. Again the sowars charged up. One fellow cut down a bullock driver within 20 yards of me as I mounted my horse—headlong flight and awful confusion. As I rode on I felt as if cut down—thought of many fox hounds—recollect a sweet sense of pleasure and gaiety as I tried to keep my seat. A Highlander caught me—'Where are you hit, sir? A doctor, a doctor.' I remember nothing more—awoke on my own dooly, screaming from spasms on the lungs, felt I was going to die . . . (4)

The providential Highlander was none other than his old Crimean acquaintance Sergeant William Forbes-Mitchell who gave a matching account in his book:

> I was detached with about a dozen men of No. 7 company to find the ammunition-guard, and bring our ammunition in rear of the line. Just as I reached the ammunition camels, a large force of the rebel cavalry, led by Firoz Shah in person, swept the flank and among the baggage, cutting down camels, camel-drivers and camp-followers in all directions . . . we saw Mr. Russell of *The Times*, who was ill and unable to walk from the kick of a horse, trying to escape on horseback. He had got out of his *dooly*, undressed and bare-headed as he was, and leaped into the saddle as the groom had been leading his horse near him. Several of the enemy's cavalry were dodging through the camels to get at him. We turned our rifles on them, and I shot down the one nearest to Mr. Russell, just as he had cut down an intervening camel-driver and was making for 'Our Special Correspondent'; in fact, his *tulwar* was actually lifted to swoop down on Mr. Russell's bare head when my bullet put a stop to his proceedings. I saw Mr. Russell tumble from his saddle at the same instant as the cavalryman fell, and I got a rare fright, for I thought my bullet must have struck both. However, I rushed to where Mr. Russell had fallen, and I then saw from the position of the slain cavalryman that my bullet had found its proper billet, and that Mr. Russell was down with sunstroke, the blood flowing freely from his nose. There was no time to lose. Our Multani Irregulars were after the enemy, and I had to hasten to the line with spare ammunition; but before I left Mr. Russell to his fate, I called some of the Forty-Second baggage-guards to put him into his *dooly* and take him to their doctor, while I

hastened back to the line and reported the occurrence to Captain Dawson. Next morning I was glad to hear that Mr. Russell was still alive, and likely to get over his stroke. (5)

Russell's job put him in frequent danger but he never came closer to violent death than this. Few other correspondents would have resisted the temptation to tell their readers all about it in graphic detail. Russell's Letter to *The Times* made only a passing mention to the sowars' charge and no reference at all to his own escape.

But in his diary, after a night of great pain, he allowed himself a moment of self-pity: 'I was painted all over with tincture of iodine till I was blistered. How my dear Bucky would have shrieked to see me. Such are the chances of a special correspondent in the field. I am bound to say that *The Times* seems to have very little feeling of what I go through, very little indeed.' (6)

This was unfair. Delane's letters were unfailingly concerned and encouraging. Russell's old friend, John Macdonald, now installed in Printing House Square, wrote to him:

> You will be glad to have confirmed to you the assurance that your work has given entire satisfaction here, and that we consider you have amply sustained your old supremacy over all competitors. Some of the electric letters were astonishingly vivid; and so far from joining in the outcry against the wire as unfavourable to literary effect, my decided conviction now is that in competent hands it may be made to yield the most brilliant results. I have not yet been called on to pay the Indo-European bill for telegraphing; but I reckon that altogether we shall not get out of this job for telegrams alone under £5,000. It was, however, one of those occasions on which it would never have done for us to have been content with moving neck and neck with the penny papers. (7)

The telegraph was used to the full in the Indian campaign. The line was run out everywhere the army went, affording immediate contact between the Governor-General and the Commander-in-Chief and the subordinate commanders. Russell was allowed to use it to speed his messages to Calcutta or Bombay. From there, however, the reports had to travel by sea so the time saved was only a few days. On average it took four weeks for Russell's Letters to reach the columns of *The Times*. The cost-conscious Mowbray Morris viewed the telegraph with suspicion. He wrote to Russell:

> The truth is, these telegrams of yours have never repaid the trouble and the cost they have occasioned. Real news in India, or elsewhere, seems to find its way to the general public, and in point of fact it has always reached our agent in Alexandria through the usual channels and as expeditiously as possible, whilst your private telegrams have sometimes, as you know, lingered on the road. . . . If

your telegrams had even once given the only or the earliest information I would not grumble; but as it has happened, the game has not paid for the candle. (8)

The summer heat and the monsoon deluge put an end to active campaigning and this was lucky for Russell since he was in no condition to march with the army. He had to use an amanuensis—'a clear-headed Scots Corporal of the 42nd writing a most excellent hand'—for his Letters to *The Times*. At the beginning of June he set off, with two sick officers and Simon his servant and an escort of a hundred Sikh soldiers, for Delhi and the hills beyond.

In Delhi he was hospitably welcomed by the reinstated British community, and taken to the scenes of the recent fighting. He also went to see the ex-King of Delhi who had been briefly restored to his throne by the rebels and was now a prisoner—'that dim-wandering-eyed, dreamy old man with feeble hanging nether lip and toothless gums.' (9) The ex-King was tried by the British in January 1859, found guilty of abetting the mutineers and exiled for life to Rangoon where he died in 1862.

Travelling along the Great Trunk Road Russell found himself succumbing to the normal symptoms of residence in India, especially in the hot season: 'The population seem for the most part Mussulmans and some of them looked very insolent as I passed, so much so I really felt inclined to try and kick them.' (10) Soon after he noted in his diary, 'All Indians [meaning the British in India] in course of time become anti-nigger.'

Russell arrived in Simla, the fashionable hill station which was already full of refugees from the heat of the plains, on the afternoon of 14 June 1858. The Deputy Commissioner of the Hill States, Lord William Hay, took Russell into his own house until accommodation could be found. At dinner on his second evening there 'a young brute named Mitford . . . excited my wrath by declaring he thought it quite right to burn wounded sepoys and declaring he did not want justice but vengeance—that he hated all niggers. I put him down in great style and Hay thanked me for it afterwards.' (11)

Within a few days a house was found for Russell and Captain Alison, one of his companions on the journey to Simla, at £60 for the season. They soon acquired, in the Indian manner, an army of servants. Alison threw himself into the social round but Russell, incapacitated by his leg, spent long days on the verandah, surveying the Himalayas which he soon found boring, reading Mrs Gaskell's *Life of Charlotte Brontë* which he found fascinating, and studying the flora and fauna of the garden. He practised his marksmanship, potting away at kites and crows, and collected a menagerie. Cages were made and servants and friends brought him an assortment of birds as well as two bear cubs and a small hill monkey. One of the bears disappeared almost immediately. The survivor became very wild and Russell admired the way the monkey gradually tamed it and turned it into a friend.

He spent nearly the next four months in Simla, gradually recovering his health and observing, with more amusement than approval, the behaviour of the British:

There are some hundreds of families who, for the most part, do nothing but talk scandal, promenade for a few hours every evening and wait for ball after ball with eagerness.' (12)

He was particularly shocked by the rigid social code which prevailed among the British in India at that time and for many decades to come—the intense snobbery, the all-importance of precedence and protocol. His lameness and sickness prevented him from going about the town for many weeks and he had to depend for company on people coming to see him:

> I am told that there is one feature about the visits which are paid to me that I am unable to duly appreciate, owing to my ignorance of Indian etiquette. The fact is that, as I have called on no one, I do not deserve to be visited by any one. The rule in India, founded on a state of things which has altogether disappeared, or had been much modified, is that the new arrival shall call on the people at the station, who return his visits in proper form. . . . Awful and unforgiveable offence is sometimes given by strangers who in their ignorance neglect the rules of precedence in paying their visits, or who may be guilty of unintentional omissions. (13)

He had many hours to sit and think, and several pages of his diary are abandoned to nostalgia—the names of old acquaintances and melancholy musings on their fate. He received many heartening letters. Charles Dickens told him all about the bitter row that had divided the Garrick Club—Edmund Yates had written a smearing article about Thackeray and Thackeray persuaded the Club committee to expel him—and added: 'Everybody talks about your letters, and everybody praises them. No one says, or can say, more of them than they deserve. I have been deeply impressed by your suggestions, in your note to me, of the miseries and horrors by which you are surrounded; and I can well understand what a trial the whole frightful revengeful business must be to an affectionate and earnest man.' (14) Delane wrote: 'You will have seen, I hope, how I have backed every one of your suggestions with leading articles. . . . Everybody, too, says and with perfect truth, that it is you who have first made India known to us, described its aspect as its peculiarities, so that we have before our eyes at last the scene of so many exploits and reverses. . . . Tell us something about yourself in your next private letter. You are at least as interesting as India to all of us.' (15) In a later letter Delane revealed that he was following his Crimean practice and ensuring that the franker comments of Russell's private letters reached the ears of authority: 'Stanley [Lord Stanley, the Colonial Secretary] is a very good Indian Minister, and follows very obediently all the good advice you give him. I send him extracts from your private letters and always see an immediate result. It was your first private letter from Cawnpore which led to the order against indiscriminate executions.' (16) Even the undemonstrative Mowbray Morris said: 'For my own part I shall be heartily glad when the cessation of active hostilities relieves you from a perilous mission, which is a source of much anxiety to all your friends.' (17)

Russell received many letters, too, from officers and officials of the Company in India. Although his prime purpose in the hills was rest and recuperation, he sat at the centre of an impressive information network which kept him in close touch with the progress of events and shifts of opinion. The result was a series of powerful Letters to *The Times* on the subject which increasingly occupied his mind—the future of the British in India. These culminated in his Letter of 28 August 1858 entitled 'The Sahib and the Nigger'.

In this he argued that one of the chief causes of the Mutiny and the support the sepoys got from the Indian people was 'our roughness of manner in our intercourse with the natives. It is not a pleasing or popular task to lay bare the defects of one's countrymen but . . . I must say that I have been struck with the arrogant and repellent manner in which we often treat natives of rank, and with the unnecessary harshness of our treatment of inferiors.' He gave examples and pointed out that British acts of brutality generally went unreported and unpunished because the victims were afraid to go to law for redress. He remarked that it was often the household servants who had turned with the greatest ferocity on the white families:

> . . . as a rule the bitterest foes of the Englishman were those of his own house. 'What ungrateful miscreants! They had lived with us for years!' Yes; and each year, ladies and gentlemen, but added to the secret source of bitterness, hatred and malice which your indifference, coldness and harshness were filling up to overflowing. . . . It would be so easy to speak differently, to act with a little more temper and forbearance, that one wonders why this sense of power, which nearly every Englishman more or less enjoys, should need to be expressed so rudely. I do not and I cannot believe the men who tell me it is essential to our rule that we should use brute force on all our dependants.

The British, Russell said, not only supported the Indian caste system but maintained one of their own that was even more rigid and rooted in colour prejudice:

> But while we assist in maintaining caste and custom we abhor colour. . . . There is no association, no intercourse, except of a discreditable kind, between Europeans and natives. Marriages between them now occur only among the lower classes. All society would be frightened from its propriety if at one of its balls there appeared any of those slim, tall, dark-eyed, crepe-haired, and rich-coloured Eurasian ladies, who prove that the older generation of British officers did not disdain alliances now regarded with scorn.

He warned that things were getting worse rather than better: 'The habit of speaking of all natives as niggers has recently become quiet common. . . . Every man of the mute, white-turbaned-file, who, with crossed arms, glistening eyes and quick ears, stands motionless along the mess room table, hears it every time a native is named, and knows it is an expression of contempt.' The article concluded by saying there was much to be proud of in Britain's achievement in India. All might yet be saved but it would require something like a change of heart among the British: 'We must remember that Hindoos and Mussulmans are our fellow-creatures.'

Soon after he sent this Letter news arrived that the East India Company— 'Company Bahadur', the brave company, as the Indians had called it in happier times—was to be disbanded. Henceforth the government of the British provinces of India would be the responsibility of the British government under the Queen. Russell wrote another weighty article pointing out that the Hindu and Moslem civilizations of India were more venerable and in many ways more refined than that of Britain. He particularly warned that the governmental change should not involve any change in the old religious toleration:

> Companee Bahadoor had no particular religion; he was a very mild kind of Christian, respected treaties which contained provisions for the revenues of idols and the preservation of temples, and did not particularly encourage the itinerant expounders of their own faith. . . . But Queen Victoria is a Protestant monarch by act of Parliament. She is *Fidei Defensor* by the Constitution, and she cannot be a Hindu Ranee or Mahomedan Sultana and a Christian Queen at the same time, nor measure her faith by degrees of latitude. (18)

Later he turned to another important problem and devoted an article to 'The British Army in India'. He described the vital role which the loyal Sikh regiments had played in the suppression of the Mutiny and stressed that it would always be impossible to hold India without Indian help:

> . . . it must be remembered that, great as may be the British power in India, it is great only so long as its exercise is consonant with the feelings of the people of India; for I hold that, weak as those myriad millions are in physical resources, in moral courage, in mental vigour, and in true independence of spirit, it would be quite beyond our strength to hold India by armed force. Were it possible to do so, it would be financially impossible. . . . We must learn—and I fear the lesson has not yet been taught, and that it would be unwillingly learnt by many—to conciliate the affections, as I believe we have gained the respect, of the people. (19)

This was his basic message and he hammered it home with all the force at his command in Letter after Letter.

He also used his convalescence to embark on another kind of writing, something he had had vaguely in mind for some time. On 26 May 1858 he had said in the diary: 'I must write the novel. What is it to be about?' A fortnight afterwards he wrote to Mary: 'I shall set about the novel the moment I arrive in Simla and have got the use of my old pin so far as to be able to sit up and write without inconvenience.' But his next letter to her—from Simla—was less sanguine: 'I fear that my novel or whatever it will be won't be very lively considering the influence under which it will be written.' It was the start of a long and painful effort to succeed in the field where his friends, Dickens and Thackeray, had made so great a mark.

There was time, too, to write home and to worry about his family. Towards the end of July he let his feelings explode in an unusually testy letter to Mary:

My dearest Mary,

I enclose your own note to read that you may see I had some good reason to be vexed not with you but with the receipt of such a disgusting little bit of paper sent just one half round the world. What do I out here in India care about Mrs. F. and Mr. H. or where they live or sleep so long as you do not associate with any one whose conduct you do not approve or even suspect to be likely to lead to impropriety. I unfeignedly and deeply deplore that you should have sent Alice, now 11 years of age, to the Foxs. Surely you might have waited for my answer if it was necessary to consult me at all. Well it is all over and done. I can only hope for the best. It is impossible for me to go home till my debts are cleared off, and I hope that you are not adding to them. . . . Your last letter was dated June 9th. In that you never said a word of your intentions of going to Margate or of the fate of the house. I suddenly find you in Margate 'at great expense' but I am still to direct to Sumner Place, and Alice I find on her way to the place I dread. . . . I have been hurt more than you could believe by Alice's silence and by her never showing any wish to write to me. I can scarce help thinking she would do so if she received encouragement or if the idea were suggested to her. As to the boys they are too young yet, and I prefer children to be children as long as possible. (20)

Two weeks later he noted in his diary that he had sent her a 'short but not sweet' letter and added: 'I do really feel savage when my deeny does not attend to her own little chap.' Then, however, he received some family photographs from her and the mood changed:

The only one of the photographs I do not like is poor little Alice's. She is horribly draped—like a woman instead of a girl—and the great staring white division in her hair has a very bad effect. Little Tempest is a regular stunner and my visitors swear he is like me. The boys are very good, but I don't like the expression of weakness about the jaw and lower part of Willy's face. My deenyman is first class and looks scrumptious *but*—there is a but, you see—the artist let you put your left hand out too far, and it is larger than it ought to be in consequence. But its nice old eyes is very expressive. Alberta too is capital. Should you not hear from me for two or three mails after this regularly do not be uneasy because I am going with a small party into the interior of the mountains to see the country. It will do me more good than sticking here at Simla. (21)

His health and mobility were improving. He had already had one short tour in the hills but the 'small party' that was now proposed was a much grander affair, consisting of Lord William Hay and five other Britons, their personal servants and Lord William's official attendants—he was on government business—supported by an army of a hundred and sixty coolies. The expedition lasted more than a month and they travelled in style, at first following the road that a former Governor-General, Lord Dalhousie, had begun as a grand highway to Tibet. The road was never completed and was already falling into decay but it still made for a magnificent march into the higher mountain areas. Lord William dispensed justice as they went and settled local disputes and despatched one or two escaped mutineers to Simla for trial and almost certain execution. They were lavishly entertained by the local rulers and Russell was impressed by some of the 'lovely women' dancers. One day he noted: 'Rajah had come to see Hay drunk this morning and had been sent back in disgrace.' One Sunday the diary records with remorse: 'Played cards in wilful forgetfulness.' It rained a lot but they travelled hard, admired the dramatic scenery and did a great deal of shooting and fishing. By the time they returned to Simla on 5 October Russell could walk several miles 'with trifling inconvenience'.

Half way through the trip he wrote to Mary:

I am very much perplexed what to do in the future education of the children for the time is near at hand when I must look out to get them some foundation at the great public schools which are the best training places to enable them to fight their way through the world. They live in happy days if they have but perseverence, ordinary ability and industry, for nowadays nearly every sort of employment in the state as well as military commissions are open free and without interest or reserve to lads who can pass the examinations. To fit them for these examinations and to give them at the same time sound and healthy education should be our care, and then they must battle their own way as their father did before them. For the girls there is, of course, a more restricted career and greater uncertainty, but they shall have a good education too as long as I can give it to them. . . . I have had some fine shooting of hill partridge off the road, but of course I can't go after the bears and leopards and deer which live in awfully difficult places. Little Simon is still with me and, I fear, does me and *The Times* a good deal but I can't help it. In a few days we shall cross the snow pass and then I shall return to Simla for a few days only ere I get back to the plains . . . (22)

The rains were ending and the Mutiny, too, was nearing its close. But there were still considerable rebel forces at large in Oudh and Sir Colin Campbell—now ennobled as Lord Clyde—was preparing his final campaign. Russell arranged for his menagerie to be transported to Calcutta and set off to join them.

He travelled by way of Meerut where the Mutiny had started seventeen months before and Agra where he was enraptured by the Taj Mahal:

> Here is a dream in marble. Here is the Taj—solid, palpable, permanent; but who can, with pen or pencil, convey to him who has not seen it the exquisite delight with which the structure imbues the mind at its first glance—the proportions and the beauty of this strange loveliness which rises up in the Indian waste as some tall palm springs up by the fountain in a barren wilderness! It is wrong to call it a dream in marble; it is a thought—an idea—a conception of tenderness—a sigh, as it were, of eternal devotion and heroic love, caught and imbued with such immortality as the earth can give. (23)

He reached Cawnpore on 17 October and booked in at Duncan's Hotel. According to John Walter Sherer, Russell was upset to find how viciously the British–Indian papers were attacking him over his articles in *The Times*. But he soon cheered up under the influence of red wine and friendly company and next day 'was quite the life of the evening, full of anecdotes and laughter, again singing some capital songs.' (24)

Sherer was impressed by his capacity for concentration:

> There was one characteristic of Dr. Russell I especially admired, which was that he could not be interrupted. . . . He would be sitting pen in hand, writing his diary or what not. You entered.
> 'I hope I am not disturbing you?'
> 'Not in the least. I am all ears; go on.'
> You went on, told your tale, he listening and answering if necessary.
> You stopped. His eye dropped on his paper; his pen moved; he recovered the thread of his writing without difficulty and with a unembarrassed continuity. (25)

Russell was in Allahabad on 1 November to hear Lord Canning read the proclamation announcing the transfer of control from the Company to the Crown and promising a pardon to all rebels who had not taken part in the murder of Europeans. He found Sir Colin and his efficient Chief of Staff General Mansfield poring over maps and working out their plans. Next morning, before first light, they crossed the Ganges and marched into Oudh once more.

Sir Colin was anxious to give the local chiefs every opportunity of surrendering gracefully. Copies of the proclamation were sent to them to assure them that the old order had changed. Russell admired the Commander-in-Chief's humanity and was shocked, though scarcely surprised, to find it was not always reflected in the attitudes of his officers:

To Flood's tent. One of the 53rd there told us that at Secunderabagh, having
set the place on fire, some sepoys who had been firing on our men made signs to
him of surrender. He told them to come down—first man handed his musket
and he made signs to the man to take off his belt and pouch etc. and so with the
rest. Then he 'fell them in' against the wall and told the Sikhs to shoot them and
it was done and the Sikhs sliced them up, 57 in all. Afterwards the officer
seemed to think he had done a first rate stroke of work. (26)

The campaign was hot and hard and frustrating for the enemy would not stand
and fight. Gradually Sir Colin drove them northwards. During the first week of
1859 there was a brief fight and the last rebel forces were dispersed to seek
uncertain sanctuary across the border in Nepal. By mid-January Russell was back
in Lucknow. 'My mission in India,' he wrote, 'was complete.'

His thoughts were turning towards home and his prospects for the future. He
wrote to Mary:

The miserable thing that strikes me in my position is the fact that it contains no
promotion and no prospect of advance. Unless exiled in a foreign country, I
have reached the height of my profession and station as a newspaper
correspondent. I see men of my own age, colonels or magistrates in the Civil
Service, still pressing eagerly on the path of higher emolument and higher
honour. I have run my race—my tether is stretched to the very uttermost. But
still I am very thankful for its extension. Had I served the government or the
state I never could have obtained such a reputation as I have acquired in serving
The Times. One hardship of my lot is separation from you. Out of twelve years of
married life perhaps five have been spent away from you. But you had an early
experience of the roving nature of my life. (27)

The New Year brought disturbing news. Mary had been very ill and their
youngest child, Tempest, was also sick. Soon after Tempest died and Mary was
heartbroken. Russell wrote to say he would sail home as quickly as he could: 'Dear
Dot, we have a lot of little people to take care of, and I hope you will not forget all
for one. I will say no more now but I hope ere I leave India to hear more from you
and a little longer and a little more cheerful or less sad letters.' (28)

His final Letters to *The Times* repeated and reinforced his message—the need to
win the trust and affection of the Indian people if they were to be reconciled to
continued British rule. 'The sympathies of the people,' he warned, 'are against us.'
Again he demonstrated his ability to take the broad historical view:

Let us not think our empire in India founded on a rock against which the
heathen may rage in vain. Compared with the dynasties which have ruled here,
our race is but the growth of yesterday. Three years have not elapsed since the
kingdom and city from which I write [Lucknow] were the appanage of a dynasty

of which no traces now exist except such as may be found in prison or in exile. Since the beginning of the half century we have broken down great confederations, annexed vast territories, conquered fierce races, and now we have just ridden triumphantly through the wildest storm of treason, treachery and battle that ever tested the nerve, strength and courage of a nation. Let us be thankful, but let us not be over-confident. Above all, let us beware how we rouse that silent, ever-watchful, slow-working, irresistible power, before which no race can maintain its own but by efforts which at last destroy it—the hate of its subjects. (29)

As usual, he expressed his feelings with even more force in a private letter to Delane: 'I believe that India is the talisman now by which England is the greatest power in the world, and that by its loss we lose the magic and prestige of the name which now holds the world in awe. I believe that we can never preserve India by brute force alone except at a cost which will swallow up all the wealth of the home country.' (30) It continued to worry him deeply that most of the British in India still believed they could only hold their position by force and fear:

Among those men are many personal friends of mine whose characters I admire and respect. I get hot in the head and red in the face talking to them every night. I argue that their sentiments are opposed to civilisation, to humanity, to justice, to universal experience, to common sense, and in reply I am told that human nature is nothing, and that I know nothing of India. I recollect that sound legislation in Ireland was resisted by the same cry, and the same armour denied the weapons of reason in the English Parliament. I hope in God they may not be equally successful here.

He allowed himself one note of self-congratulation:

My letters have produced a most material effect on the tone of the Indian press, and as to society, though I undergo a good deal of quizzing, it is more than compensated when I hear one man who threatens to break every bone in his bearer's skin held in check by the half-serious, half-joking remonstrance, 'You had better not or you will have *The Times* down on you.'

Russell's achievement in India was greater than this suggests. His initial inquiries and early reports put an end to the wild tales of mutilation and other atrocities. He gave his readers, as Delane said, a fuller and clearer account of India than they had ever had before; what the country and its peoples looked like; the fascinating variety of cultures; what is felt like to live and march and fight there; the way the British treated the Indians. The later Letters, which were much more concerned with the great issues of policy and attitude than with day-to-day events, marked a new departure in journalism. Until this time correspondents' reports had been regarded as fuel for the leader-writer in London. Now Russell thundered forth on his own in a series of closely-argued articles that were more like editorials than anything else, and the leader-writers of Printing House Square could only pant behind him in support.

In one of his last letters to Delane from India he wrote: 'Can we be just and fear not? I think we can. I do not believe in the innate depravity of nigritude. . . . I am satisfied now, more than I ever was in my life as to the truth of any view taken by me of any one case, that I am right with respect to Indian affairs.' (31)

It is impossible to measure the precise extent of Russell's influence but it was certainly both considerable and beneficial. As *The History of The Times* says: 'The settlement of the Indian troubles without recourse to reprisals, which would rankle for ever, was a high Imperial purpose and one which Russell and *The Times* served with eminent success.' (32)

Editorial Status

Russell said goodbye to Sir Colin Campbell and General Mansfield 'and all the friends among whom I had lived in perfect harmony for more than a year' (1) at the end of February 1859. At Cawnpore there were more farewells and a reminder that the end of the Mutiny did not mark the end of British bullying. He saw a white man attack a group of natives:

> He rushed among the coolies, and they went down like grass, maimed and bleeding. I shouted out of the gharry, 'Good Heavens, stop! Why, you'll kill those men!' (One of them was holding up his arm, as if it were broken.) A furious growl, 'What the — business have you to interfere? It's no affair of yours.' 'Oh, yes, sir, but it is. I am not going to be accessory to murder. See how you have maimed that man! You know they dare not raise a finger against you.' (2)

He stayed with Sir James Outram in Calcutta and secured a passage for himself and some of his Simla menagerie, including the bear cub, on a ship of the Peninsular and Oriental Company. Judging from his letters, he was in an uncertain frame of mind when he took ship. To Delane he wrote: 'Now that it comes to leave-taking I am almost sorry to leave India. Strange as it may appear, there is an attraction on the part of populations disfigured morally by dreadful vices.' (3) But to Sherer in Cawnpore he said:

> I go home to a sick wife, carrying from India no very pleasant memories, a damaged reputation, great popular enmity—the only Englishman, I believe, who ever left India poorer than when he came into it—with nothing to cheer me save the conviction that I did my duty according to the light that was vouchsafed to me, and the damnation of a faint applause awaiting my efforts. But seeing all this were to do again I would do it . . . (4)

There are no entries in the diary for the first half of 1859 so his activities are known only in outline. He reached home at the end of April. Lord Stanley, the

Colonial Secretary, asked him to call, listened to his views on the settlement of India and proffered official thanks for the support he had given to Lord Canning's policies of clemency. He had the usual tussle with Mowbray Morris over his expenses. Routledge commissioned him to write a full account of his experiences which was published the following year under the title *My Diary in India*.

At home he found Mary still pathetically weak from her illness, still mourning the lost baby and more nervous than ever. The kind of life into which she had married was cruelly unsuited to a woman of such a shy, affectionate and dependent nature. She could not cope with the growing family during his absences and, when he was at home, found herself unhappily torn between distress at his convivial habits and the apprehension that he would shortly be off on his travels again. Russell knew what she suffered and did his best to reassure her and restore her confidence. In his last surviving letter to her from India he said: 'My darling Dot, we will have much to talk over when I come back, and wherever I go I will always have you with me again.' (5) It was a promise he was congenitally incapable of keeping but, for the moment at least, he made an effort to stay with the family, resisting pressure from Delane that he join the army of Napoleon III in Italy.

The French Emperor had a formidable fleet and an army of half a million men at his command and there were mounting fears that he would turn them against Britain. Aware that their regular army was inadequate to meet such a challenge, Lord Derby's government encouraged the formation of volunteer units, organized on a regional basis and trained in the rudiments of discipline and marksmanship. It was a popular move. In towns and cities across the country rifle corps sprang up, flaunting a colourful variety of insignia and uniforms, determined to drive any invader back into the sea. The movement was attended by more enthusiasm than military sense and, in an attempt to redress the balance, Russell wrote a booklet *Rifle Clubs and Volunteer Corps*. It was a straightforward, practical piece of work and must have had a deflating effect on many readers when it was published by Routledge in 1859. Enthusiasm, he said, was not enough. If the units were to be effective, they would need strict training and discipline; they should be organized not as Rifle Clubs, with all their implications of sociability and dandyism, but as Rifle Companies, properly officered and regularly drilled; they should be armed with 'the beautiful Enfield rifle' and dressed in uniforms of russet brown or grey;* they should be used, not as independent forces, but in support of the regular army. He cast doubt, even, on the diplomatic benefits of the movement:

---

* Russell argued that these colours were 'certainly the least visible under most circumstances and therefore the best for riflemen'. But more than forty years were to pass before the British army abandoned its red coat and assumed the khaki service dress.

Admirable in many respects as the Volunteer Corps—those 'free rifles'—may be, there can be no doubt that the consciousness of a new kind of strength, or the belief in its possession, will infuse an amount of passion into her political relations which may render the work of British diplomatists more difficult than ever. I am not one of those who think that a state of readiness for war is the best preservative of peace. On the contrary, I believe that a King or a State with a fine fleet or an efficient army is continually tempted to seek occasion for the display of their qualities in active service.

In June 1859 he took his family to Switzerland, hopeful that the mountain air would improve Mary's health and that escape from the temptations of London's club life would help him to get on with his book about India. But he missed the stimulus of lively company. 'I am not in force,' he complained. 'I feel the want of society. I am in a desert.' (6)

They travelled among the mountains, visiting Murren, Interlaken and Chamonix, and Russell did some fishing. He found relief from the intellectual tedium in the conversation of a fellow tourist, John Bigelow, a New Yorker who had trained as a lawyer, engaged in politics, then turned to journalism and bought a partnership in an evening paper. Russell's name and work were well known in the United States. His Letters from India and the Crimea had been generously quoted in the newspapers there and much admired. The two men had many interests and attitudes in common. Bigelow hated the system of negro slavery which formed the basis of the economy of the Southern states and Russell was keen to discover all he could about the great democratic experiment across the Atlantic and the bitter divisions that were now threatening its survival. They formed an immediate friendship.

On 12 August Russell heard from Delane: 'It has occurred to me that if you would take the trouble you could write just as good leading articles as anyone else, and that if you could do so, we could give you well-paid and continuous employment, not dependent on such happy accidents as Indian Mutinies and foreign wars . . .' (7)

The Russells returned to London in early September. Any benefit Mary may have derived from the holiday was immediately undone. She was violently sea-sick crossing the Channel and had a miscarriage a few days later.

Russell immersed himself in the work of a leader-writer on foreign and colonial topics. His first subject was the Italian situation. Many years later in *Retrospect* he recalled his introduction to this new branch of his trade:

I entered the little room which was to be the scene of my struggle with the printer's devil in no very confident spirit, though I had dined pleasantly at mess at Woolwich and was cheerful enough till my eye rested on a formidable heap of cuttings and print neatly piled on the writing-table. I must explain as to the struggle I have mentioned, that when the theme suited me and my pen moved swiftly over the slips, I could generally accomplish my task by 12.30 or 1 o'clock; but sometimes the editor was impatient and the grey matter would not work, and the blurred sheets chided each dull delay of revision or correction enforced by the imp from the printing slab, with 'The editor is sending every moment for your copy, sir!' Sometimes the ready finger would be waiting to seize the top of the page as the pen reached the bottom. I finished my first leader at two o'clock, revised the proof and was about to leave when the messanger said, 'Mr. Delane would like to see you before you go, sir.' And it was nearly three before I was called into his room, where he was glowering across the table at a monkey-faced little man, to hear 'Capital! Well done! Come a little earlier on Sunday!' I turned out in evening clothes and a light overcoat at 3.15 in Ludgate Hill, and, as my baggage was at Woolwich, I slept at the London Bridge Hotel and went down to barracks by the first train next morning. When I entered the ante-room for breakfast and saw the *Times* laid out on the table, I experienced a curious feeling of *mauvaise honte*, mingled with curiosity, but it was soon dispelled by the satisfaction which the appearance of the leader in a prominent place caused me. I read it very carefully, and detected in the garish light of day faults invisible at 2 a.m., but on the whole I was rather proud of my work and rather disappointed no one talked about the *Times'* views of the Italian question at mess or at the club when I went up to town. Next day I had to repair to my workshop in Printing House Square and interest myself in the news just in from China and India. 'I congratulate you. Your article has the real stuff and go of a leader, and you shall see it in the first place to-morrow.' This from Delane. (8)

The initial euphoria did not last long. 'There was a great difference,' he wrote, 'between the absolute freedom of my life in the field, and the dictation from the office.' (9) Delane held his leader-writers on a tight rein, gave them firm instructions and did not hesitate to amend or rewrite their work as he thought necessary. Russell's strengths lay in descriptive and discursive writing, not among the close arguments and weighty judgements of the editorial. He preferred to work from down-to-earth reality—from scenes and incidents he had experienced, from conversations and the details of daily life—rather than with abstract ideas and grand generalizations. He did not enjoy making magisterial pronouncements on matters which he felt he knew too little about.

Before the end of 1859 the chance of another new journalistic venture came his way. A group of friends, led by John Connellan Deane, suggested that the new interest in national security had created a demand for a magazine that would deal exclusively with the defence of Britain and the empire—the army, the navy and the volunteer movement. It should be a weekly, they said, and Russell was the man to run it. Bradbury and Evans, the proprietors of *Punch*, expressed themselves interested in publishing it if Russell would agree to be the editor. He put the matter to Delane who said there would be no objection from *The Times*. Then he accepted the offer.

But Delane was mistaken. He was under the impression, it seems, that Russell had reverted to the position of a freelance contributor. The fact that he was still on the staff made all the difference. The house rule was invoked—that no staff man at *The Times* could work on a regular basis for another paper. On 23 December there was an embarrassing meeting in Mowbray Morris' office:

> Mowbray came down and we entered on business. . . . I was nervous and affected to tears at what I saw in his mind. Delane was silent till towards the close but I could perceive he felt how I was shielding him by throwing aside the question of permission on which I had every right to rely. Eventually it was decided thus. My salary as a member of the staff ceases. I become a contributor and earn as much as I can, Delane and Morris promising to assist me—and whenever I please I revert to my old position on the paper, giving up the editing of the *Army and Navy Gazette*. (10)

Bradbury and Evans offered Russell £25 a week. He replied with a series of counter-proposals which were accepted: he should be paid £15 a week; they should commission him for £1,200 to write a book for them; he should go to America in October to cover the presidential election and write a further book about that for a further commission of £1,200; and if *The Times* asked him to go abroad for them, he should be free to do so without losing his editorship. It is a revealing deal. Russell was anxious for more foreign reporting and increasingly interested in the American situation. He did not want to lose his connection with *The Times*. And he was more concerned to have ready money in considerable amounts than a guaranteed steady income for the future. He was once again in financial difficulties, with the doctor's bills for Mary and the children's school fees adding to the expenses of his own expansive way of life.

In the event he wrote neither of the books he proposed and he did not go to see Abraham Lincoln elected President of the United States. But he remained editor of the *Army and Navy Gazette* for the next forty-one years.

He threw himself wholeheartedly into the job. An old friend, James Cornelius O'Dowd, became assistant editor.* They established themselves in rooms at 16 Wellington Street just off the Strand, the house where Dickens had launched his magazine *Household Words* ten years before. Russell made up a bed on a sofa and spent many nights there in the early months of the magazine's life.

The first issue came out on Saturday 7 January 1860, offering sixteen folio pages for sixpence. 'The time is auspicious', Russell wrote in his introductory article, 'for the establishment of a journal that may deserve to become the organ of the Services, and the means of communication between them and the public, for

---

* O'Dowd, like Russell, had been educated at Trinity College, Dublin, read for the Bar, then turned to journalism. He was assistant editor of the magazine until 1869 when he was appointed Deputy Judge Advocate-General. He died in 1903.

whose interests they exist. . . . In all honour we aspire to be the organ of the Services, so far as they can have an organ at all'. It was a modest prospectus and the magazine fulfilled it conscientiously for more than seventy years, purveying a wealth of detailed and often highly-specialized information, providing a forum for the discussion of ideas, arguing consistently for reform and the improvement of the lot of officers and men.

Russell enlisted the support of army friends as contributors and subscribers. In March he went to see the reforming Secretary for War, Sidney Herbert, '. . . and had a long talk *de ominbus*. He was *very affable*, told me to ask Maynard [Herbert's secretary] whenever I wanted anything, was glad of the success of the *Army and Navy Gazette* etc. etc.' (11) He travelled round Britain, watching reviews and manoeuvres, talking to officers and officials, studying new weapons. Throughout the year the diary shows him hard at his editorial task, 'working like several niggers'.

The Bigelows arrived in London in February after a leisurely excursion round Europe and Russell got his friend elected to the Garrick Club for three months. Bigelow's autobiography gives a few glimpses of the lighter side of Russell's life at this time:

On the 27th of February I dined with William Howard Russell, where I met Delane, the editor of *The Times*, and Romaine, Secretary of the Admiralty. Delane impressed me by the accuracy of his information on a variety of subjects, by his quickness to apprehend and eagerness to appropriate what seemed true and new in what he heard, and the correctness of his scent, in a rambling conversation, for what is reliable. . . . I was astonished to find what an interest all these gentlemen took in the fight between Sayers and Heenan, his American antagonist, which was to come off in a day or two.* They could hardly have seemed more interested if the contest had been between an English and American naval squadron. (12)

On 29 April Bigelow records that 'we walked around to Russell's. I found him and Mrs. Russell at breakfast. Presently Thackeray, who lived in the neighbourhood, came in also . . . discussed the third number of the *Cornhill*, Thackeray's new magazine, which had just come out.' On 2 May Bigelow gave a dinner party at the Garrick where he and Russell discussed the American crisis and the slavery question. Three weeks later the two families took a Fortnum and Mason hamper to the Derby where Bigelow was amazed at the crowds: 'as national a saturnalium,' he noted, 'as the British people have any experience of.'

* Sayers and Heenan fought for the Champion's Belt on 17 April 1860. The fight lasted thirty-eight rounds—two hours twenty minutes—by which time Heenan's face was so battered he could hardly see and Sayer's right arm was broken. The contest was declared a draw.

During the summer of 1860 Russell met another American who was to become a friend. Thackeray introduced him to Samuel Ward, the most eccentric and variously-gifted member of an eminent New York family. Ward, generally known as 'Uncle Sam', was the personification of his nation's ideals of enterprise and adventure. He was forty-six years old and had already lost an inherited fortune in business, made another one in the '49 gold rush, lost that in a few months of reckless speculation, engaged in freelance diplomacy in South America that made him rich again, and settled in Washington to a career as a one-man pressure group that was to earn him the title 'King of the Lobby'. He was deeply cultured and widely read. Russell liked him immediately, finding him 'refined, philosophical and cosmopolitan'—far too much so, he thought, ever to succeed in America. (13)

Towards the end of May Russell was distressed by the sudden death of his old Garrick Club comrade, Albert Smith. A few days later his cab overturned in the street and his thumb was broken. The next day, 1 June, he wrote in the diary: 'I had intended to go to Ireland on Saturday and even to have taken my wife with me which considering her troublesome disposition in travelling showed that I was making great sacrifices.'

Trouble with Mary continued to cloud his private life. She complained a great deal and frequently let him down, forgetting to send the cab for him, keeping him waiting. This much is made clear in the diary but there are many obliterated lines and excised pages and there can be little doubt that most of these referred to his domestic troubles.

The crisis came in mid-October. His father had been visiting them and on the 17th Russell saw him off on the train to Liverpool, then went to Folkestone for a few days' sea-fishing with friends. Next day a telegram brought him rushing back to Sumner Place: 'Alas, what a sight—my life delirious and convulsive . . . a dreadful night of it.' Throughout the week that followed the diary's pages carried the same bleak message: 'Sickness in the house—sorrow' or 'Sickness in the house. Lord have mercy upon us.' Then on 26 October he wrote: 'Soon after 11 this morning my darling after six hours of pain and travail bore me a son. It was in her bosom when I went out to the office in the afternoon and she looked happy though she was a little melancholy.' And next day: 'I was so happy today. Mary did not sleep much but the darling did not seem very unwell. Still her face was puffed, her eyes swollen and her sight almost gone. She adjured me to take the children to divine service—to become a better man. I promised. Please God I will with his help keep my vow.'

The days that followed were terrible ones. Mary's life was despaired of more than once and it was not until mid-November that she began gradually to recover. On 21 December he noted: 'I dined at Garrick first time for weeks.' And two days after that: 'Deenyman better, praise be to God. . . . Thackeray came in and sat with me.'

Thackeray was a pillar of considerate support throughout the weeks of anxiety. At the height of the crisis he would appear outside 18 Sumner Place at an appointed time and Russell would signal from the bedroom window whether he was able to come out for a walk or not. One day they went to Regent's Park Zoo to see the bear Russell had brought from Simla. It did not know him.

On 1 January 1861 the diary records: 'The New Year gives me much indeed to be thankful for—a blessing ineffable in my darling's improved condition. May I be thankful for it and show my thankfulness. She was not so well today.' Russell was still struggling to write his novel—'My story goes on slowly indeed'—and working hard on the magazine. On 3 January he wrote: 'At office all day. But I cannot write sometimes. . . . The labour becomes quite dreadful. I am very capricious in the working of my head battery.'

The prospect of civil war in America was growing. Russell kept himself informed of developments through correspondence with John Bigelow, who had returned to New York to play an active part in the presidential election on the Republican side. Abraham Lincoln, the Republican candidate, won the election convincingly but there was an ominous element in the victory: his votes had come almost exclusively from the populous states of the industrial North. The Southern states, whose economies were based on the cotton plantations and the four million negro slaves who worked them, were more afraid than ever that Northern rule in Washington would destroy their established way of life. Lincoln did his best to reassure them: 'I have no purpose,' he declared, 'directly or indirectly to interfere with the institution of Slavery in the states where it exists. I believe I have no lawful right to do so, and I have no inclination to do so.' His policy, he insisted, was not to abolish slavery, merely to prevent its extension to the new states being opened up in the West, Kansas and Nebraska. His overriding aim was to preserve the Union intact.

In November 1860, after Lincoln's election but before his inauguration, Bigelow wrote to Russell:

Since the election the spunky little state of South Carolina has been making a great deal of noise and splutter, but in a few weeks all concerned in making it will be covered with ridicule that are not covered with infamy. We shall be vexed for the next four months with all the world's theory of the new President's cabinet, and with the rivalries, jealousies and dissentions of office-seekers. When that is over, and the new government is well under way, the world, at least that portion of it which comes in contact with us, will begin to realise the magnitude and the value of the revolution accomplished by the election of Lincoln. (14)

Bigelow's confidence was misplaced. The theory had been developed among the Southern states that under the Union's constitution any state which considered its vital interests endangered by the federal government had the right to secede. In December South Carolina declared itself independent. Within a few weeks ten other Southern states followed suit. In February 1861 their delegates assembled in

Montgomery, Alabama, and united into a new nation, the Confederate States of America. Jefferson Davis of Mississippi was chosen President.

In his inaugural speech Lincoln said: 'No State upon its mere motion can lawfully get out of the Union. I therefore consider that the Union is unbroken and shall take care that the laws of the Union are faithfully executed in all States.' It was to take four years of fighting and the deaths of more than half a million men to bring this about.

The approach of war made Delane look to his dispositions. *The Times* had a correspondent in America, J. C. Bancroft Davis, a New York lawyer who had been sending weekly letters packed with information and intelligent comment for over five years. But Davis was a Republican, deeply committed to the Northern cause, and there was a clear need for a more objective observer who would also be capable of following the campaigns. Russell was the obvious choice. Thackeray told him: 'You must go. It will be a great opportunity.' (15).

The terms offered were munificent—£1,200 a year and all expenses met. Since he owed Mary's doctor £500 it was, as he said in the diary, 'a lucky sort of intervention'. The house in Sumner Place was sub-let at £210 a year. Bradbury and Evans, the proprietors of the *Army and Navy Gazette*, agreed to let him go and gave him an advance of £750 on the book he would write for them about his experiences.

It was arranged that Mary, who was still poorly, would go and live with the Deanes in Bath. The baby, named Colin de Lacy in tribute to Russell's best friends among the generals, would go with her. The other four children were at boarding school.

On 28 February 1861 Russell went to see Delane:

He was very kind and sympathetic. *Most important of all*. He solemnly impressed on me the necessity of not incurring any danger whatever—'If you have the smallest reason to suppose that you will be exposed to any outrage or annoyance let nothing induce you to remain. Come back at once. Do not hesitate. Do not mind the result. I will take care that you are held secure and that you shall not suffer and you may depend on it your interest will be protected here.' (16)

That evening he took his sons, William and John, to dinner at Simpson's and told them about his American trip. Then he went on to the Garrick Club where Thackeray proposed 'a nice little toast in my honour' and someone warned him 'Take care—no fair play—they're treacherous.'

Next day he went to Bath to say goodbye to Mary:

How sad are these partings—how frequent—what lessons they should teach us for the future. If we had prudence, they need not be. Poor deenyman joked with me about an American wife etc. etc. But really and truly she bore up most nobly. . . . Never can I forget the look in those dear eyes and the poor fretted face and the melting lips so tender and so true. . . . I went to the station in a storm of pain. (17)

The American Civil War

He set off for America on 2 March 1861. His ship was due to sail the next evening from Queenstown in Cork Harbour on the southern coast of Ireland. He took the train to Liverpool, then the boat to Dublin, struggling all the way to keep his luggage together and to plan the later stages of his journey: 'All this time I have failed to penetrate the mysteries of Bradshaw. I am quite worn out trying to ascertain how I am to get to Queenstown'.

In Dublin next morning he was piqued to discover he was not universally known in the land where he had first thrilled to hear himself called 'Mr. Russell of *The Times*'. The hotel clerk would not accept his cheque: ' "Don't you know who I am?" "I don't know anything about Mr. Russell of *The Times*". I must confess I was hurt".' (1) But he caught the right train and went on board the paddle steamer *Arabia* at dusk.

They had a rough crossing but Russell was a good sailor. He tucked into four Cunard-sized meals a day and studied his travelling companions, the Americans especially. He was impressed by the bellicose determination of the Southerners and surprised at the disrespect many Northerners showed for their recently-elected leader. One of them said to him: 'Lincoln is a rail-splitter.* I hope he won't be a Union-splitter.'

Russell was embarking on the most difficult period of his career. His previous assignments had been simple by comparison. In the Crimea and India, for all the frustrations he had to face and for all his strictures on British behaviour, there had never been any doubt which side he was on. But in America he was a neutral observer, a dangerous role in any civil war where impartial comment will always look like hostility to the protagonists. And it was not in his nature to remain silent when great moral issues were involved.

He was not helped by the background of Anglo-American relations. It was less than a century since the American colonies had broken away from British rule and fewer than fifty years since the two countries had been briefly at war. The relationship was like that between a stern father and a rebellious adolescent son with radical tendencies. They were still, in a sense, 'family'—sharing a common ancestry and language and religion—but with all the attendant tensions of close

---

* Lincoln was called the 'rail-splitter' because as a young man he had supplemented his income by working as a farm-hand, splitting fence rails with an axe.

kinship. There were many in Britain, particularly among the ruling classes, who wanted America's democratic experiment to fail. The Americans, for their part, were desperately anxious for approval and painfully sensitive to British criticism.

There had been no shortage of censure. In the 1830s Frances Trollope, the mother of the novelist, and Harriet Martineau had both published descriptions of America that contrived to offend Northerners and Southerners alike. Worst of all, Charles Dickens—having been fêted and lionized during a visit in 1842—produced, in the American chapters of *Martin Chuzzlewit*, an account so ferociously contemptuous that he felt unable to return to America for twenty-five years.

The trans-Atlantic animosity subsided in the middle years of the century. There were strong trade links between the two countries: more than one-fifth of Britain's exports went to America; more than three-quarters of the cotton that fed the thriving mills of Lancashire came from the Southern plantations. The British were relieved to see American expansionist energies directed towards the wide-open West and the Mexican South rather than against Canada. By the 1850s Americans were too preoccupied with their internal troubles, the widening split between North and South, to worry unduly over what the British thought about them. British visitors were more understanding and less censorious. In 1860 the Prince of Wales paid a friendly and successful visit. But the undercurrent of mistrust remained strong and the first year of the Civil War was to bring Britain and the United States dangerously close to conflict.

Russell's task was further complicated by the discrepancy between his attitude to the crisis and that of his masters in Printing House Square. President Lincoln, anxious to win the allegiance of the uncommitted central states, did not declare himself wholeheartedly opposed to slavery. Had he done so, *The Times*, whose record on the slave trade and the emancipation of negro slaves in the British possessions had been impeccable, would have had no alternative but to support the Northern cause. As things stood, however, *The Times* was able to adopt an ostensibly neutral stance, leaving itself free to condemn the conduct of both sides in mandarin tones. But it grew increasingly clear that the men who controlled the paper's policies were temperamentally inclined to favour the South.

'*Why* should we be so very anxious to see the Union preserved?' John Walter wanted to know. 'What has it done to command our sympathy?' (2) Mowbray Morris, who had been brought up in the West Indies, actively approved of the slave system and made no secret of his feelings: 'The Northern government and its policy are an abomination to me,' he wrote, 'and I greatly enjoy to hear them abused.' (3)

Delane's approach was more equivocal. He had visited the United States in 1856 but returned with only two strong impressions, that the hospitality was good and the newspapers were deplorable. In his view, however, *The Times*' chief duty was to reflect and inform the opinions of the upper middle class that ruled Britain. This class was ambivalent in its attitude to the American conflict. There was a feeling that the Southerners were the underdogs. They seemed to represent the more attractive Cavalier qualities, brave and dashing and aristocratic, based on a landed and hierarchical society. Their secession, it was argued, was only doing to the Union what the rebellious colonists had done to Britain in 1775. The British establishment took some pleasure and much comfort in the prospect of the destruction of a Union that was rapidly developing into a powerful state and whose notions of manhood suffrage might push Britain further along the road to full democracy. These feelings, which were fully shared by the Prime Minister Lord Palmerston, undoubtedly influenced Delane and he was further affected by the raucous and sometimes loutish tone of many of the Northern newspapers. His main objective throughout the war was to keep Britain out of it and in this he was successful. But he also struggled to give an appearance of judicial neutrality and this led, as fortunes fluctuated and feelings wavered, to many pompous misjudgements and changes of opinion.

Russell, on the other hand, claimed to approach America with a completely open mind:

No man ever set foot on the soil of the United States with a stronger and sincerer desire to ascertain and to tell the truth, as it appeared to him. I had no theories to uphold, no prejudices to subserve, no interests to advance, no instructions to fulfil; I was a free agent, bound to communicate to the powerful organ of public opinion I represented, my own daily impressions of the men, scenes and actions around me, without fear, favour, or affection of or for anything but that which seemed to me to be the truth. As to the questions which were distracting the States, my mind was a *tabula rasa*, or, rather, a *tabula non scripta*. (4)

For all that, there could be little doubt which way his humanitarian inclinations would take him. A month before he left England he wrote to Bigelow:

Every friend of despotism rejoices at your misfortune; it points the moral and adorns the tale in every aristocratic salon. . . . Our people in Europe are so violent that the spectacle does not attract all the attention which should be paid to the most important social and political phenomenon of the later ages of the world, the result of which will be felt for good or evil to the end of time. But no good Englishman feels any sentiment but one of intense respect and great sympathy. (5)

Bigelow and Sam Ward were there to meet him when the *Arabia* docked in New York on 16 March, and they promptly introduced him to his fellow *Times* correspondent Bancroft Davis. New York was under snow but its newspapers gave him a warm welcome, describing him as 'the most famous newspaper correspondent the world has ever seen'. Even the *New York Herald*, which was to become his most virulent scourge, spoke of 'the world-wide celebrity Mr. Russell has gained by his graphic descriptions of the Crimea and the Indian revolt'. But Russell took an immediate dislike to the *Herald's* publisher, James Gordon Bennett, and described him to Delane as 'so palpably a rogue, it comes out strongly in the air around, in his eyes and words'.

American newspapers at this time were written in a much more gossipy and personal manner than most of the British press, and one of them described Russell's appearance: 'He has short iron locks parted down the middle, a greyish moustache and a strong tendency to double chin, a very broad and very full but not lofty forehead: eyes of a clear, keen blue, sharply observant in their expression, rather prominently set and indicating abundant language.'

The day after he landed was St Patrick's Day and, as a celebrated Irishman, he was invited to dine with the Friendly Society of St Patrick at the Astor House Hotel. There was much eating and drinking and speech-making and inevitably Russell was called to his feet. It is uncertain exactly what he said because he could not remember very clearly himself and the papers gave a variety of versions, but he undoubtedly delivered himself of the fervent hope that the Union would survive intact.

The next morning, with a bad headache, he wrote in the diary: 'I am much affected by reading my speech in the papers. O Lord, why did I do it?' One of the papers said: 'This substantial and slightly protuberant figure may stand about five feet seven inches in his boots. . . . As a speaker he is rather nervous and hesitating . . . he is given to humming and hawing before the commencement of each sentence . . . but in the *matter* of his speech we have seldom heard any orator more lucid, compact and self-balanced than Mr. Russell.' (6) *The Times*, however, was not amused. When reports of the dinner reached London Mowbray Morris wrote to Russell: '*I am very sorry* you attended that St. Patrick dinner and made that speech.' (7)

Russell's indiscretion had one beneficial effect—it endeared him, for the time being at least, to the Northern leaders. He took the train to Washington on 25 March and found his sleeping-car full of 'Rowdies and whiskey and fighting'. He booked a room at Willard's Hotel and on his first evening in the capital was introduced to the powerful Secretary of State, William Henry Seward: '. . . very much given to *raconter et badiner*—a subtle quick man not quite indifferent to *kudos*'. (8)

Next day Seward took him to the White House to meet the President:

Soon afterwards there entered, with a shambling, loose, irregular, almost unsteady gait, a tall, lank, lean man, considerably over six feet in height, with stooping shoulders, long pendulous arms, terminating in hands of extraordinary dimensions, which, however, were far exceeded in proportion by his feet. He was dressed in an ill-fitting, wrinkled suit of black, which put one in mind of an undertaker's uniform at a funeral. . . . The impression produced by the size of his extremities, and by his flapping and wide projecting ears, may be removed by the appearance of kindliness, sagacity and the awkward bonhomie of his face; the mouth is absolutely prodigious; the lips, straggling and extending almost from one line of black beard to the other, are only kept in order by two deep furrows from the nostril to the chin; the nose itself—a prominent organ—stands out from the face, with an inquiring, anxious air, as though it were sniffing for some good thing in the wind; the eyes, dark, full, and deeply set, are penetrating, but full of an expression which almost amounts to tenderness. (9)

He was surprised by the folksy informality of the President's manner:

Mr. Seward then took me by the hand and said—'Mr. President, allow me to present to you Mr. Russell, of the London *Times*.' On which Mr. Lincoln put out his hand in a very friendly manner, and said, 'Mr. Russell, I am very glad to make your acquaintance, and to see you in this country. The London *Times* is one of the greatest powers in the world,—in fact, I don't know anything which has more power,—except perhaps the Mississippi. I am glad to know you as its minister.' Conversation ensued for some minutes, which the President enlivened by two or three peculiar little sallies, and I left agreeably impressed with his shrewdness, humour, and natural sagacity. (10)

The Northerners were anxious to win British support and believed *The Times* might do much to help them. Russell was invited to dine with the Seward family and the next evening he went to the White House for Lincoln's first official dinner party, the only man there who was not a member of the Cabinet.

Within a few days he had met and talked to all the leading men of the government as well as the British ambassador in Washington, Lord Lyons, and the General-in-Chief of the Northern armies, Winfield Scott. To anyone accustomed to the ways of twentieth-century journalism it must seem astonishing that he made no mention of these meetings and conversations in his Letters to *The Times*. But his first Letter from America, date-lined 29 March and published in London on 16 April, described New York as 'full of divine calm and human phlegm' and then devoted itself to the strange phenomenon of Washington at the beginning of a new Presidency:

All the hotels are full of keen gray-eyed men, who fondly believe their destiny is to fill for four years some pet appointment under Government. . . . Willard's Hotel, a huge caravanserai, is a curious study of character and institutions. Every form of speech and every accent under which the English tongue can be recognised rings through the long corridors in tones of expostulation, anger, or gratification. Crowds of long-limbed, nervous, eager-looking men, in loose black garments, undulating shirt collars, vast conceptions in hatting and booting, angular with documents and pregnant with demand, throng every avenue, in spite of printed notices directing them 'to move on from front of the cigar-stand.'

Russell saw the humour of the scene but he also appreciated its implications:

> At the very moment when the President and his Cabinet should be left
> undisturbed to deal with the tremendous questions which have arisen from their
> action, the roar of office-seekers dims every sense, and almost annihilates
> them. . . . This hunting after office, which destroys self-respect when it is the
> moving motive of any considerable section of a great party, is an innovation
> which was introduced by General Jackson; but it is likely to be as permanent as
> the Republic, inasmuch as no candidate dares declare his intention of reverting
> to the old system.

In his private letters Russell referred to the 'Willard menagerie'. In its Babel he
found a remarkable range of opinion—out-and-out abolitionists who wanted
slavery abolished at any price, moderate Lincolnians who were prepared to accept
slavery in the states where it already operated but would not accept the breakup of
the Union, many who wanted peace above all and were willing to 'let the erring
sisters go'. He saw much drunkenness and listened to much ill-informed
argument. There seemed to be no unity among the Northerners, no fixed purpose,
and little understanding of the crisis. Their military preparations were amateurish.

The mood of the Southerners was completely different, as Russell confirmed
when he met the commissioners sent by Jefferson Davis to negotiate the terms of
their secession. Lincoln would not see them but Russell spent an evening in their
company, sounding out their attitudes. He found them determined and united,
undeterred by the prospect of war, contemptuous of Northerners who they
believed to be morally degraded by trade and industry. He also found them fervent
for slavery:

> . . . slavery is their *summum bonum* of morality, physical excellence, and social
> purity. I was inclined to question the correctness of the standard which they had
> set up, and to inquire whether the virtue which needed this murderous use of
> the pistol and dagger to defend it, was not open to some doubt; but I found there
> was very little sympathy with my views among the company. (11)

The meeting convinced Russell that war could not be avoided. He wrote to
Bigelow:

> I fear, my friend, you are going to immortal smash. That little lump of
> revolutionary leaven has at last set to work in good earnest and the whole mass
> of social and political life is fermenting unhealthily. . . . The world will only see
> in it all the failure of republican institutions in time of pressure as demonstrated
> by all history—that history which America vainly thought she was going to set
> right and re-establish on new grounds and principles. I fail to discover among

Map 4   The United States of
America 1861

the men I have come in contact with any 'veneration' for anything—it's a useful
bump—good government grows under it. (12)

He decided to visit the South while it was still possible. In Baltimore on 13 April
1861 he heard that the first shots of the war had been fired. The Southerners had
begun to bombard the federal strong-point at Fort Sumter near the mouth of
Charleston harbour in South Carolina. He hurried South, joined forces with Sam
Ward who was on an unofficial one-man peace mission to the Confederate states,
and together they visited Fort Sumter which had surrendered after a
thirty-four-hour bombardment in which no lives were lost. The hero of the hour,

the Confederate General P. G. T. Beauregard, gave them permission to go wherever they liked.

During his tour of inspection Russell was observed by Mary Boykin Chesnut, the wife of a Confederate colonel, who wrote in her diary on 15 April 1861: 'Russell, the English reporter for *The Times*, was there. They took him everywhere. One man studied up his Thackeray to converse with him on equal terms. Poor Russell was awfully bored, they say. He only wanted to see the Forts and get news that was suitable to make an interesting article. Thackeray was stale news over the water.' (13)

Later, when Russell's account in *The Times* had been quoted in the American press, she noted: 'JUNE 4 . . . Charleston people are thin-skinned. They shrink from Russell's touches. I find his criticisms mild. I expected so much worse. Those Englishmen come, somebody says, with their three P's; Pen, Paper, Prejudices; and I dreaded some of those after-dinner stories. About that day in the Harbour, he let us off easily.'

There was little military significance in the action at Fort Sumter and Russell was more interested in the attitudes and opinions of the Southerners. He found them delighted that the matter had now been put to the touch and united in their confidence that they could 'lick the cowardly Yankees'. He also found a widespread belief that Britain's need for cotton would bring her into the war on their side. In fact, though the news had not yet reached America, the British government had just declared itself neutral, to the great annoyance of the Northerners who believed this implied recognition of the separate status of the Confederation. By this time Russell had formed a conviction he was to hold for many years: 'I am more satisfied than ever that the Union can never be restored as it was, and that it has gone to pieces, never to be put together again, in the old shape, at all events by any power on earth.' (14)

The men of South Carolina were the first and the most extreme of the secessionists. Russell recounted one of their more outrageous notions in his Letter to *The Times* dated 30 April:

Nothing I could say can be worth one fact which has forced itself upon my mind in reference to the sentiments which prevail among the gentlemen of this State. I have been among them for several days. I have visited their plantations; I have conversed with them freely and fully; and I have enjoyed that frank, courteous and graceful intercourse which constitutes an irresistible charm of their society. From all quarters have come to my ears the echoes of the same voice. . . . That voice says, 'If we could only get one of the Royal race of England to rule over us, we should be content.'

Russell continued to insist that he heard the idea proposed many times and not always from men whose minds had been excited by drink. But it was not seriously entertained anywhere outside South Carolina and his account aroused a good deal of amusement and ridicule. Mary Boykin Chesnut noted in her diary: 'Russell's letters are filled with rubbish about our wanting an English prince to reign over us.' (15)

Russell was always anxious to get his reports to London as quickly as possible. But throughout the Civil War it took messages a fortnight or longer to make the journey. Slow communication may have had diplomatic advantages—Britain and the North might well have gone to war at the end of 1861 if the leaders on either side had been able to make their feelings known to the other in the heat of the moment—but it was infuriating for the journalist. Russell was particularly worried during his tour of the South. He had no faith in the American postal system and wrote to Bancroft Davis on 2 May: 'I feel that my despatches are hardly safer to hit a steamer than if they should be thrown into the sea in a sealed bottle.' (16) He was desperately concerned, too, for news of home—the last reports of Mary's health had been depressing—and asked Davis to open his letters in New York and telegraph the salient points to him.

From Charleston he and Sam Ward travelled by way of Savannah and Macon to arrive in the Confederate capital, Montgomery, Alabama, just in time for the official declaration of war on 7 May 1861. Russell met the rebel President, Jefferson Davis, that day. He noted in the diary: 'to State Department, introduced to Davis who is interviewing several citizens. Large airy plain room. 'President' on door. He is a very calm resolute man—slight, spare—with extremely wrinkled puckered skin on thin intellectual head—plain in manner, said but little, admitted military spirit of people which exposed them to ridicule.' Russell asked for a safe conduct to protect him on his travels:

Mr. Davis said: 'I shall give such instructions to the Secretary of War as shall be necessary. But, sir, you are among civilised, intelligent people who understand your position, and appreciate your character. We do not seek the sympathy of England by unworthy means, for we respect ourselves, and we are glad to invite the scrutiny of men into our acts; as for our motives, we meet the eye of Heaven.' (17)

While in Montgomery Russell saw slaves being sold at auction in the streets:

The auctioneer, who was an ill-favoured, dissipated-looking rascal, had his 'article' beside him on, not in, a deal packing-case—a stout young negro, badly dressed and ill-shod, who stood with all his goods fastened in a small bundle in his hand, looking out at the small listless gathering of men, who, whittling and chewing, had moved out from the shady side of the street as they saw the man put up. (18)

He described the sale for *The Times* and added:

I am neither sentimentalist nor Black Republican nor negro worshipper, but I confess the sight caused a strange thrill through my heart. I tried in vain to make myself familiar with the fact that I could, for the sum of 975 dollars, become as absolutely the owner of that mass of blood, bones, sinew, flesh and brains as of the horse who stood by my side. There was no sophistry which could persuade me the man was not a man—he was, indeed, by no means my brother, but assuredly he was a fellow-creature. I have seen slave markets in the East. . . . Here it grated on my ear to hear the familiar tones of the English tongue as the medium by which the transfer was effected, and it was painful to see decent-looking men in European garb engaged in the work before me. (19)

Later the same day, he told his readers, he saw a negro girl put up for sale but failing to reach the reserve price of $610. 'Niggers is cheap' was the comment on every side.

During the rest of his tour through the South—which took him to Selma and Mobile, along the coast of the Gulf to the federal outpost at Fort Pickens, west to New Orleans, then up the Mississippi to Baton Rouge, Vicksburg and Memphis——he made slavery and the condition of the negroes his special study. Although he conceded they often looked well cared-for, he could not reconcile himself to the idea of slavery. He believed it debased both slave and slave-owner. The true reason for the system, he had no doubt, was economic. His fiercest criticism was reserved for those, and they were many, who defended it on religious grounds: 'The miserable sophists who expose themselves to the contempt of the world by their paltry thesicles on the divine origin and uses of slavery are infinitely more contemptible than the wretched bigots who published themes long ago on the propriety of burning witches, or on the necessity for the offices of the Inquisition.' (20)

Russell did not disguise his views from his Southern hosts and there were many arguments. On 10 May he noted in his diary: 'I felt very shaky today and had a vague notion that I drank rather too much last night and did not act as I ought to have done, but there is always great excitement in arguing with Americans.'

Sam Ward wrote a series of letters to Seward in Washington, describing the mood and the military preparations of the South. It was a risky thing to do and the only precaution he took was to use the pseudonym Carlos Lopez. But most of the letters got through and they give a lively picture of Russell in action:

Russell is fighting secession sword in hand. He attacks these gentlemen with great vigour—stigmatizes the whole movement as impolitic and suicidal and invariably has the best of the argument. (CHARLESTON, APRIL 19 1861)

Russell continues the good fight—no one can stand against him in a forensic 'set to'. He ascribes will and intelligence to Mr. Lincoln and people change their tone and augur better for the future where assured of his force and intelligence by so competent and impartial a judge. (SAVANNAH, MAY 2)

I hope you have been kind and attentive to Russell who as I wrote you from Savannah fought secession all the way through the South. He is as good a Northern man as you are and when you see his letters about slavery, which will shake all England, you will see that you could have no better ally. He is honest, kind hearted and in controversy the ablest general logician I ever heard converse. (NEW YORK, JULY 7) (21)

Russell's ability in debate was widely known by now. The New York magazine *Harper's Weekly* carried a full-page article about him on 22 June which said: 'In his personal intercourse Dr. Russell unites the charms of experience, genius and sincerity. A willing controvertialist, he rushes into a discussion with the fearlessness of conviction and the generosity of one who feels that he has ideas and knowledge to spare. As an observer, while endowed with a keen relish for enjoyment, nothing seems to escape him.'

Russell and Ward were back in the North by the end of June. It seemed likely that the first major battle would take place soon and Russell was anxious to see it from the Northern side whence he could be reasonably sure of getting his account back to London. Several of his Letters from the South had gone astray. He wrote to Bancroft Davis:

I have just seen a file of *The Times*, my letters have all gone to pot apparently. I miss one from Charleston, one from Savannah, one from Montgomery. There were two from the first two and three from the last. This is going to be a very terrible war if it be fought out. It must end in a compromise I think. The South is not as strong as the North, but its defensive power is enormous. I have a little touch of fever which weakens me but do not say anything about it to them at home. (22)

He was still worried about his family, too. There had been little news from England and what there was had not been heartening. On his return to Washington, however, he received a reassuring letter. On 5 July he wrote in his diary of Mary: 'She is a true woman—never was finer courage, more tender love in this wide world, never, never.'

The tour of the South proved immensely influential. Russell's views on the impending conflict were clearly formed on this journey and he was not to change them. He had been greatly impressed by the unanimity of the Southern whites, their zeal and courage, their conviction that they stood for an admirable way of life, the workmanlike enthusiasm of their preparations for the struggle. 'There is no people in the world', he told his *Times* readers, 'so crazy with military madness'. He was the only non-Southern journalist in the rebel states at this crucial time and so the only one with any claim to objectivity. His reports were read avidly in London and in Washington. Their basic message—that the South would fight and fight hard—went home. 'I don't believe you ever wrote better', Delane told him, 'the interest has been throughout maintained, and the skill with which you managed your Southern raid has delighted everybody here.' (23)

Back in the North after more than two months away he detected some change in the spirit of the people. There was a stronger sense, he thought, of the need to preserve the Union though the feeling was not strong enough to match the intensity of the South. President Lincoln had called for volunteers to sign on for three months with the army and men were flocking to the colours, but Russell noticed that most of them came from the ranks of the recent immigrants, Germans and Irish particularly, rather than from native-born Americans. On moral grounds, which weighed heavily with him, he believed the North was in the right: slavery was an evil; the United States should remain united and whole. He saw that the sheer material strength of the North—its vast superiority in numbers and industrial plant and transport, its command of the sea—was bound to prevail in the end so long as its will held. But he saw, too, that this would entail a long and bitter struggle—so bitter, he feared, that it might never be possible to rebuild a secure and contented Union.

Russell did not return to Willard's Hotel in Washington but took rooms— 'two furnished clothes chests over a water closet facetiously considered apartments'—at 179 Pennsylvania Avenue. They were cheaper and money was a serious consideration once more for he had made a discovery common to travelling journalists: 'I made up my accounts for *The Times* this evening and find I am short a good deal of money. How can this be?' (24)

He was very busy the first three weeks of July 1861 studying General Irvin McDowell's preparations for an attack across the Potomac into Virginia. He got on well with McDowell who talked to him freely, invited him to go where he liked and showed a pleasant sense of humour. 'I have made arrangements,' McDowell told him, 'for the correspondents of our papers to take the field under certain regulations, and I have suggested to them that they should wear a white uniform to indicate the purity of their character.' (25) There was a horde of reporters from the Northern papers but the senior officers had scant respect for them and Russell had no direct competition. The only other British journalist in Washington was Frank Vizetelly, who was primarily an artist and had been sent out by the *Illustrated London News* to record the war in sketches and brief articles.

McDowell also said to Russell, only half-joking: 'I declare I am not quite easy at the idea of having your eye on me, for you have seen so much of European armies, you will, very naturally, think little of us, generals and all.' (26)

He was right. Russell was not impressed by the army of the Potomac. The general had a very small staff and was clearly going to find it hard conveying his orders to the units once the fighting started. He had no reliable maps of Virginia and no clear conception of the enemy's dispositions. Such cavalry as he had was incapable of adequate reconnaissance. The Northern papers were talking of an army of more than 100,000 men 'in the highest state of efficiency', but

Russell reckoned 'there were not more than a third of that number, and those in a very incomplete, ill-disciplined state'. (27) Their training had been perfunctory:

> The officers are dirty, unsoldierly-looking men; the camps are dirty to excess; the men are dressed in all sorts of uniforms; and from what I hear, I doubt if any of these regiments have ever performed a brigade evolution together, or if any of the officers know what it is to deploy a brigade from column into line. They are mostly three months' men, whose time is nearly up. They were rejoicing today over the fact that it was so, and that they had kept the enemy from Washington 'without a fight'. And it is with this rabblement that the North propose not only to subdue the South, but according to some of their papers, to humiliate Great Britain, and conquer Canada afterwards. (28)

There was, indeed, a dangerously euphoric spirit abroad and an increasing hostility towards Britain. The Northerners could not understand why the country that had led the fight against slavery gave their cause so little support. They still resented Britain's declaration of neutrality and they resented even more the magisterial and sometimes derisive tones which the British press, *The Times* especially, adopted in dealing with their affairs. They were suspicious of the troop reinforcements that were being shipped to Canada.

Partly, he thought, as a result of this hostility, Russell was not allowed to stay with the army of the Potomac as the moment of battle approached. In the afternoon of 20 July he was in the Senate, listening to a tedious debate, when a messenger brought him a note from McDowell saying the advance would begin the next morning and they expected to meet the enemy before noon. He rushed out to a livery stable and paid an extortionate sum for a saddle horse. Then he discovered that the only bridge was closed until dawn to all traffic except army supplies. He 'laid out an old pair of Indian boots, cords, a Himalayan suit, an old felt hat, a flask, revolver and belt', ordered a very early call and went to bed.

16

'Bull Run Russell'

When the state of Virginia declared for the South in April 1861, Jefferson Davis moved the Confederate capital to Richmond, only a hundred miles from Washington. As Winston Churchill wrote: 'The two capitals stood like queens at chess upon adjoining squares, and, sustained by their combinations of covering pieces, they endured four years of grim play within a single move of capture.' (1)

McDowell's attack on 21 July was an attempt to make that 'single move' and deliver a crippling blow before his three-months men left for home. The Southern forces under Beauregard were drawn up in defensive positions in front of the railway junction at Manassas, above a small river called Bull Run or Bull's Run. McDowell planned to throw the weight of his attack against the left wing of the Southern army and break through before they could move up enough reinforcements to hold him. It might have worked but for the stubborn resistance of a Virginian brigade commanded by Brigadier-General T. J. Jackson. In the action which earned him the nickname 'Stonewall', he held on till reinforcements arrived. The attackers fell back and, though they were not effectively pursued, the haste and confusion of their retreat turned it into a rout.

Russell saw nothing of the battle. Although he made an early start from Washington, it was nearly thirty miles to Bull Run and the road was clogged with traffic. McDowell's supplies were struggling forward; Congressmen and their wives were on their way to see the fun; to Russell's surprise and disgust, one unit—the 4th Pennsylvania Regiment—was marching away from the sound of gun-fire because their three months were already up. It was noon when he reached the village of Centreville and joined 'a crowd of civilians on horseback, and in all sorts of vehicles, with a few of the fairer, if not gentler sex.' (2) They were picnicking on a hill top, scanning the wooded slopes across the valley, trying to make sense of what little they could see of the action. It was not enough for Russell so he pushed on across country. After three miles he had to rejoin the crowded road and was astonished to see a group of waggons approaching a small bridge against the stream of traffic. He described the scene in a Letter which *The Times* published on 6 August:

By the side of the new set of waggons there were a number of commissariat men and soldiers, whom at first sight I took to be the baggage guard. They looked excited and alarmed, and were running by the side of the horses—in front the dust quite obscured the view. At the bridge the currents met in wild disorder. 'Turn back! Retreat!' shouted the men from the front, 'We're whipped, we're whipped!' They cursed and tugged at the horses' heads, and struggled with frenzy to get past. Running by me on foot was a man with the shoulder-straps of an officer. 'Pray what is the matter, Sir?' 'It means we're pretty badly whipped, and that's a fact,' he blurted out in puffs, and continued his career. I observed that he carried no sword. The teamsters of the advancing waggons now caught up the cry. 'Turn back—turn your horses' was the shout up the whole line, and, backing, plunging, rearing, and kicking, the horses which had been proceeding down the road reversed front and went off towards Centreville.

The Letter goes on to describe how Russell forced his way forward again only to encounter stronger waves of soldiers who had abandoned their guns and equipment in the rush to get away. They were convinced the enemy cavalry was at their heels:

Presently a tremor ran through the men by whom I was riding, as the sharp reports of some field-pieces rattled through the wood close at hand. A sort of subdued roar, like the voice of distant breakers, rose in front of us, and the soldiers, who were, I think, Germans, broke into a double, looking now and then over their shoulders. There was no choice for me but to resign any further researches. The mail from Washington for the Wednesday steamer at Boston leaves at 2.30 on Monday, and so I put my horse into a trot, keeping in the fields alongside the roads as much as I could, to avoid the fugitives, till I came once more on the rear of the baggage and store carts, and the pressure of the crowd, who, conscious of the aid which the vehicles would afford them against a cavalry charge, and fearful, nevertheless, of their proximity, clamoured and shouted like madmen as they ran. The road was now literally covered with baggage. It seemed to me as if the men inside were throwing things out purposely. 'Stop,' cried I to the driver of one of the carts, 'everything is falling out.' '— you,' shouted a fellow inside, 'if you stop him I'll blow your brains out.' My attempts to save Uncle Sam's property were then and there discontinued.

Darkness was falling as Russell rode back through Centreville. He felt sure McDowell would be able to regroup his forces in the area and prevent an enemy advance. But there was no sign of any attempt to stop the rout. He took the road to Washington:

. . . all the road from Centreville for miles presented such a sight as can only be witnessed in the track of the runaways of an utterly demoralized army. Drivers flogged, lashed, spurred, and beat their horses, or leaped down and abandoned their teams, and ran by the side of the road; mounted men, servants, and men in uniform, vehicles of all sorts, commissariat waggons thronged the narrow ways. At every shot a convulsion as it were seized upon the morbid mass of bones, sinew, wood, and iron, and thrilled through it, giving new energy and action to its desperate efforts to get free from itself. Again the cry of 'Cavalry' arose. 'What are you afraid of?' said I to a man who was running beside me. 'I'm not afraid of you,' replied the ruffian, levelling his piece at me and pulling the trigger. It was not loaded or the cap was not on, for the gun did not go off. I was unarmed, and I did go off as fast as I could, resolved to keep my own counsel for the second time that day. And so the flight went on. At one time a whole mass of infantry, with fixed bayonets, ran down the bank of the road, and some falling as they ran must have killed and wounded those among whom they fell.

It was nearly midnight when he regained his rooms on Pennsylvania Avenue. He tried to write his Letter but fell asleep at his desk. He was awakened at six in the morning by the sound of heavy rain on the windows and the more ominous sound of thousands of men tramping wearily through the capital. He hung a notice on his door—'Mr. Russell is out'—and sat down to begin the Letter that was to fill nine columns of *The Times*. It was three o'clock the next morning when he finally put his pen down and handed the sheaf of papers to 'my respectable Englishman', engaged to deliver them to the mail steamer in Boston just before it sailed. Then he slept till late in the afternoon.

The Letter was another descriptive *tour de force*. He confined himself strictly to what he had seen: 'I sit down to give an account,' he began, 'not of the action yesterday, but of what I saw with my own eyes, hitherto not often deceived, and of what I heard with my own ears, which in this country are not so much to be trusted.' He made it clear that what had happened was both a defeat and a disgrace: 'Such scandalous behaviour on the part of soldiers I should have considered impossible, as with some experience of camps and armies I have never even in alarms among camp followers seen the like of it.' In spite of this, and despite the fact that he was writing with the shameful events still vividly fresh in his mind, he was able to take the considered, dispassionate view. Bull Run, he told his readers, was not the end of the war:

> The North will, no doubt, recover the shock. Hitherto she has only said, 'Go and fight for the Union.' The South has exclaimed, 'Let us fight for our rights.' The North must put its best men into the battle, or she will inevitably fall before the energy, the personal hatred, and the superior fighting powers of her antagonist. . . . But, though the North may reel under the shock, I cannot think it will make her desist from the struggle, unless it be speedily followed by blows more deadly than the repulse from Manassas.

The South did not follow up its advantage, and the North was given time to recover confidence and begin to recover its strength. The confidence came all too quickly. Exactly seven days after the battle he noted in the diary: 'The papers are beginning to say there never was such heroism as at Bull's Run!' (3) And a few days later he reflected gloomily that he would almost certainly get into trouble for repeating 'in a mild form' what all the papers were saying the day after the battle.

It was unfortunate for Russell that, because it took four weeks for his account to reach the American papers and their readers, most of them had chosen to forget the full extent of the disgrace before his words came back to remind them. 'We scarcely exaggerate the fact,' said the *New York Times*, 'when we say, the first and foremost thought on the minds of a very large portion of our people after the repulse of Bull Run was, What will Russell say?' They found out on 20 August when long quotations from the Letter were printed in the American papers, together with much violent protestation and personal abuse. Immediately he became known as 'Bull Run Russell'. Some of the Northern papers said he exaggerated the panic; others, like the *Chicago Tribune*, claimed he had not been there and had made his whole story up in his room in Washington; the most vitriolic said he had led the retreat and incited the panic. 'As for running away,' the *New York Herald* declared, 'Mr. Russell himself set the example, and riding a foaming steed, was foremost in the line of retreat.' Only the *New York Times* spoke up in his support: 'He gives a clear, fair, and perfectly just and accurate, as it is spirited and graphic, account. . . . Discreditable as those scenes were to our Army, we have nothing in connexion with them whereof to accuse the reporter.'

On the day he published the Letter, Delane wrote to Russell: 'I can't describe to you the delight with which I, and I believe, everybody else, read your vivid account of the repulse at Bull's Run and the terrible *débâcle* which ensued. My fear is only that the United States will not be able to bear the truth so plainly told.' (4) Mowbray Morris put it more strongly: 'When your description of the Bull's Run affair appeared in *The Times*, everyone said 'Russell will be lynched'—and there was very serious apprehension for your safety entertained even by men not usually given to idle fears.' (5)

There was good reason for fear. For the next six months and more Russell had to endure constant vilification—in the papers, in his mail, in the streets and the camps. His life was frequently threatened and more than once in imminent danger, for there were many armed men about and they were often drunk and some of them had little respect for the law even when they were sober.

On 23 August he wrote: 'The torrent is swollen today by anonymous letters threatening me with bowie knife and revolver, or simply abusive, frantic with hate and full of obscure warnings. Some bear the Washington postmark, others came from New York, the greater number—for I have had nine—are from Philadelphia. Perhaps they may have come from members of that "gallant" 4th Pennsylvania Regiment.' (6) The next day, on a visit to the Washington Navy Yard, he was introduced to 'a drunken Senator for California, named MacDougal, who when not drunk may not be invincibly offensive. He said, "Really now and so it's you. Let me have a good look at you. Well I am quite glad to meet you. Ah well now, I guess you are quite notorious you know . . ."' (7)

On 1 September a soldier of German origin recognized him and levelled his loaded firelock. Russell had the man arrested. In the middle of the month he went to the prairies beyond Chicago to shoot quail with a party of friends and was himself arrested—at the instigation of a malicious 'patriot'—for hunting on the Sabbath.

Russell was not liked by the South either. On 27 July Mary Boykin Chesnut had written in her diary: 'I long to see Russell's letter to *The Times* about Bull Run and Manassas. It will be rich and rare . . .' But when she saw it she was not pleased:

> Russell, I think in his capacity of Englishman, despises both sides. He derides
> us equally, North and South. He prefers to attribute Bull's Run to Yankee
> cowardice rather than to Southern courage. He gives no credit to either side.
> After all, we are mere Americans! . . . In spite of all this there are glimpses of the
> truth sometimes. And the story reads to our credit, with all its sneers and jeers.
> When he speaks of the Yankees' cowardice, falsehoods, dishonesty and
> braggadocio, the best words are in his mouth. (8)

An attack of 'Potomac fever' enabled Russell to lie low for a few days. His doctor gave him a powder which had to be taken every two hours with mint julep—an infusion of whisky, sugar and ice with sprigs of fresh mint. He kept to his rooms, read *Great Expectations* and wrote another Letter, reviewing the new stategic position. 'The first part of the campaign has been played out,' he said. 'That it has ended disastrously for the Federalists is to be attributed, in my mind, to the impatience and ignorance of the politicians who forced the military leaders to precipitate advances for which they were not prepared.' He was unshaken in his belief that the superior strength of the North would tell in the end: 'If the war continues, discipline will do its work with the United States armies, and then the question will resolve itself into one of numbers and position.' (9)

When he was well enough to go out again, he was careful to travel on horseback. He spent much of his time with Lord Lyons at the British embassy and most of the rest with senior army officers who had no quarrel with his description of Bull Run. General McDowell had been demoted to divisional commander but had not lost his sense of humour. He told Russell: 'I must confess I am much rejoiced to find you are as much abused as I have been. I hope you mind it as little as I did. Bull's Run was an unfortunate affair for both of us, for had I won it, you would have had to describe the pursuit of the flying enemy, and then you would have been the most popular writer in America, and I would have been lauded as the greatest of generals.' (10)

Russell also kept his sense of proportion. He had written to Bigelow:

It is not true that I commanded the Confederates in person or led off the Federalist centre; neither did I lie on my stomach disguised as Raymond of the *Times** and kill Beauregard with a pistol tooth pick as he rode insultingly over the battlefield; neither did I say that I had never seen such slaughter at Solferino (where I wasn't) or at Inkerman where I was; nor did I set down the loss of the Federalists at 12,000 (though I do think every way, it was near 1200); in fact anything you may see in print about me, contradict point blank on my authority, even if it be that I am a gentleman who regards his word (for then I should begin to doubt it was so) . . . (11)

And in a subsequent letter to Bigelow he said: 'It was a beautiful exercise of gymnastic vigour, friend B.—that on 21st of ult. The Federalists acted like Irishmen at a fair—ran away when they had knocked down their enemy—afraid of the police coming perhaps.' (12) At the end of this letter he refers to renewed worries about his family: 'My mail July 15 date I received a brief from wife. Still invalid. Great nervous suffering and the latest born not very well.' The baby died soon after.

There was little for Russell to report in the weeks after Bull Run. The South made no more move to attack. In the North a new army commander, General George B. McClellan, set about the laborious task of rebuilding the army of the Potomac. Russell's diary reveals him in a generally reflective and often despondent mood:

AUGUST 27 1861 . . . There is a melancholy fact in the great republic tumbling to pieces. Assuredly it was a great work. But it was of man, not of God. All its greatness and the idea of its life was of man—the principle of veneration did not live in it. There was nothing even in the Washington worship to save it. God and the Queen!

SEPTEMBER 12 . . . I sat and worked a little but there is not much to say unless one draws on his imagination for the news of what is going on elsewhere or goes into terrible deductions. I am satisfied all the party men here are furious with me.

OCTOBER 6 This is the 19th after Trinity, alas! alas! . . . Oh how I long for some certain sure faith. I believe in God the Father everlasting, maker of Heaven and Earth. And then I stop and shudder and doubt. Who shall know? Give me the eyes of faith and the heart of hope and the living life for repentance, oh God all Good.

OCTOBER 7 . . . I am living in an air of danger and only the goodness of Providence saves me. But I feel I have a sort of public duty after all. I am a little apt now and then to think I am indeed what I was called by the City Chamberlain long ago 'the unaccredited ambassador of the people.'

---

* Henry Raymond, a *New York Times* reporter, who left the battlefield of Bull Run too soon and gave his paper an inspiring story of a Union victory.

By mid-September he was seriously wondering whether there was any point in staying in America. He was no longer *persona grata* with the Northern leaders and there was a disturbing discrepancy between his view of the situation and that which *The Times* was advancing in its leading articles. He wrote to Delane on 13 September:

If the remark has been made to me once I heard it fifty times lately 'Why does *The Times* quote the [New York] *Herald* almost exclusively and give its name in the American news particularly after the language it has used towards you,' and I must confess I have not been able to answer the question. By lies, incessant attacks to which I cannot reply, the paper and its congeners have succeeded in creating a dangerous feeling against me. They take me as the exponent of Englishmen, England and *The Times*, and would like to avenge themselves upon me *tria juncta in uno*. . . . *The Times* is regarded on all sides as a Secession print or as an agent which is doing all it can to break up the Union. . . . I don't want to ask you to sacrifice the policy of *The Times* to me, but I would like you, if possible, not to sacrifice me (and no end of children and a wife) to the leaders in *The Times*. . . . The fear of insult makes me hold aloof from such men as Seward, who is at present very wild with Lord Lyons; and the President, whom I met the other night at M'Clellan's, looked as black as thunder. I wish you could—I know you would—help me through and out of my dilemmas. If, on consultation with M'Clellan or Fremont, I find my presence distasteful, so that my mission can no longer be continued with advantage to the paper, it will be best for you to consider what steps to take, what advice to give, and to withdraw me altogether if necessary, though I confess I should not like to give all the rascals in U.S. such a triumph over me and you.

Delane counselled endurance: 'I hope most sincerely, then, that you will endeavour to be patient under the manifold vexations and anxieties of your position, and, *unless there is danger*, not think of returning here where there is nothing to be done.' (13)

Russell replied promptly, pointing out that danger was unavoidable: 'It is impossible to express one's opinions freely or to be on a battlefield in America without risk and danger, and the literary assassinations previously are but the preparations for the execution.' He described his anxieties about his family and his difficulties with the authorities in Washington, then added: 'The Americans, with all their faults, are a prodigious fine people, and I cannot help admiring many things about them, though I am now unwilling to say so lest it should be supposed I did so *pour cause*. It is their cursed Press. . . . I am equipping myself for a campaign and have got a nice cart or ambulance, saddlery etc., but no tent as yet. If I cannot hook on to M'Dowell I shall be in a fix.' (14)

The end of October brought distressing memories of Mary's grave sickness the year before. On 2 November 1861 he wrote in his diary: 'I am low and cast down exceeding. Think of home—sin too. . . . I think of the troubles of this terrible time last year. God forgive me. Kyrie eleision.' A week later he opened his heart more freely than ever before:

I am not a man of reflection. If I were how different would be my position, how deplorable my frame of mind. Whilst I am expected to be jocose, enlightened, wise, witty, well-informed and unflagging in spirits and resources here are dark horrors of memory and present gloom pressing around me. My wife imploring me to come back, duns pressing and all my affairs in one great muddle as well can be. I see no chance of extrication unless by the slow process of paying off debts at the rate of a few hundred, say £600 per annum. Well it would be something if Mary were content and happy. How terrible the disease, the poison of uric acid appears to be—the whole brain is shaken, the system becomes one vast repertoire of various disorders and the mind dwells on morbid images. (15)

There were other reasons for gloom. He continued to receive threatening anonymous letters. The citizens of Philadelphia organized a petition asking the Secretary of State to expel him. Some 'Professor', who is not named, gave an anti-Russell lecture at Willard's Hotel. The *New York Herald* and other papers consoled themselves for the dearth of news by devising fresh ways of abusing him. Scurrilous verses were composed. One of them, *Bunsby Russell on Bull Run*, ended with the lines:

> But reason exists why the battle's chief brunt
> Brought no sight to his eyes, no sound to his ear,
> A Strict Army rule held him back from the front,
> For the old women are kept in the rear!

Another, *Ye Londonne Times Correspondente His Bulle Runne Lettre*, concluded:

> I wish you would lette me come home—
> I'm tyred of alle thyse bustle:
> I wysshe no more ye worlde to roam,
> Yours truly, Billie Russelle.

In mid-November there was an incident that brought Britain and the North close to war. The Southerners, believing that the need for their cotton would bring Britain—and possibly France as well—into the war on their side in the end, despatched two emissaries to plead their cause in London and Paris. The two men, Mason and Slidell, each with an assistant, evaded the Northern blockade and got on board a British mail-packet, the *Trent*, at Havana. As she left for Europe, however, the *Trent* was stopped by a Northern gun-boat and the four Southerners were taken off as prisoners.

Most Northerners greeted the *Trent* incident as a bold and brilliant coup. The British thought it high-handed and insulting to the Union Jack. Specialists in international maritime law were invoked on both sides and came to predictably conflicting conclusions.

Russell heard the news on 16 November. He spent the next two days sounding out opinion as widely as possible, particularly at the State Department and the British embassy: 'NOVEMBER 18 . . . Saw Lord Lyons who was greatly perplexed apparently and unable to make it out at all. He was quite out of sorts, uneasy and perplexed. The orders are that the legation are not to speak of it.' Next morning he started writing his Letter to *The Times*, which he described in the diary as:

> . . . a most difficult task to perform. It is very possible my letter may be the first detailed account of Mason and Slidell in England and, as everything depends on the way in which news is broken, I feel a very great responsibility. God help me. My responsibility is unattended by that which makes me bear it willingly. I have neither position, place, profit nor honour but still looking at *The Times* as something more than private property—a mere newspaper—to the best of my ability I used my position to promote the honour and interests of my country. (16)

He need not have been so anxious. *The Times* published a full account of the incident, carried home by the *Trent*, five days before his Letter appeared. The Letter was printed in full, however, retelling the story in measured terms, describing the Northern people as jubilant but their leaders as 'not so radiant', discussing the legal arguments at length.

The crisis lasted more than four weeks. The British government said the arrests were illegal and demanded the release of the four men, but—influenced by Prince Albert*—it did so in a manner carefully contrived to enable President Lincoln to give way without too much loss of face. Delane described public feeling in Britain: 'It is a real, downright, honest desire to avenge old scores. We have no news here except that the whole Army, Navy and Volunteers are of one mind, and all mad for service in America.' (17) But Russell, though he had suffered more than most at the hands of the Northerners, was not so easily carried away. He wrote to Delane: 'As to this war question, I wish we were entering on it with cleaner hands if it comes to blows. There is too much of a legal subtlety in the points raised by the Government. . . . I am much exercised about the Southern people becoming independent and a slave power—and we the authors of it! That touches me nearly.' (18)

The great question was whether Lincoln's government would back down and release its prisoners. Washington buzzed with rumours and opinions changed

---

* It was the Prince Consort's last and perhaps most valuable intervention in affairs of state. He died of typhoid fever on 14 December 1861.

daily. On 19 December Russell wrote in his diary: 'But with all their fearful brag and bluster, the Yankees will not be such cursed fools as to go to war with us. They are too cute to give us such a chance. No fear of it.' But three days later, in a letter to Delane, he said: 'I don't think these fellows will give up Mason and Slidell in which case God help the world but Old Nick will be unchained for some time to come after.'

At Printing House Square Mowbray Morris was making his contingency plans. He wrote to Russell advising him, if it came to war, to attach himself to the British embassy and try to get to Halifax, Nova Scotia, whence he could cover the fighting from the British side.

Despite the seriousness of the situation—perhaps because of it—Russell was having a more than usually convivial time, theatre-going, playing bowls in a saloon, maintaining his contacts with the army, dining late into the night. He had many friends among the diplomats, British, Russian, Prussian and others; Anthony Trollope, touring North America with a view to writing a book, appeared in Washington; there were amateur theatricals at the British embassy in which Russell and Frank Vizetelly played prominent roles. He made friends with the photographer Matthew Brady and went to the studio on Pennsylvania Avenue to pose for his portrait (Plate 9) in the uniform of a Deputy Lord Lieutenant of Ireland. It is not clear what right he had to this uniform or how he had acquired it but the creases in the cloth indicate a man who had been living well. The diary confirms this: 'DECEMBER 7 1861 Woke up with an intolerable flavour of claret and cold punch combined about me and remained wondering why I did it all. . . . DECEMBER 8 . . . and there was a great deal too much of that horrid whiskey to suit my fancy. . . . I sang all the Irish melodies.'

Much as he hated the prospect of Britain getting involved in the war, Russell recognized that it would at least solve his own immediate problem, for he was still finding it impossible to get any assurance that he would be allowed to accompany the Northern army when it marched, and without such permission he would be virtually unable to do his job. On 27 December, however, the news broke: the prisoners were to be released.

Russell rushed to Boston to try to get an interview with Mason and Slidell but the hand-over was conducted too expeditiously for him. So he went on to New York where he succumbed to another attack of fever. He was nursed by his friends, notably Sam Ward. On 16 January he wrote to Delane:

Ward told me yesterday that a great speculator in the Funds and an enormous millionaire had come to him to ask whether Mr. Russell could not be induced to write more favourable articles for the U.S. so as to influence the *Times* in its general tone, and in that case, said he, 'we could afford to place some hundreds of thousands of dollars at the call of Mr. Russell and his friends.' I told Ward that he had better ask his friend to call upon me and make me the proposition directly, but he said that he would only convey the substance of the conversation to me, whereupon I said 'the gentleman had better communicate directly with the Editor of the *Times*—the answer he will get from me if he comes will not suit him.' Ward further said that 'the gentleman' was anxious to know what it would cost to buy all the *Times* shares, as to which I referred him to the solicitor in London, and expressed an opinion that it might be done by Mr. Chase when he had raised his £30,000,000.

I am now nearly well, but there is a sort of weakness and languor over me that I never experienced before. I hope my next letter for the paper will be better. (19)

There was a move, during Russell's convalescence, to reconcile him to James Gordon Bennett, publisher of the *New York Herald*. But Russell said he would only meet him if he was prepared to apologize for the behaviour of his paper, so nothing came of it and the attacks continued.

He also used his convalescence to try to get his expenses into some order. He wrote to Mowbray Morris: 'I am going to hurl at you next mail all my cheque books and bank accounts up to the end of last year, and henceforth I shall send you in a monthly account, but I got all out of gear in moving by loss of papers etc.' (20) Two weeks later he wrote again, apologizing for the state of his papers: 'my mind was in such an uncertain state as to going home or staying, as to fight or no fight, that I neglected everything down to my health. . . . I am going to see how things are in Canada. . . . I wish I weren't quite so unpopular here, for it is the most difficult thing to stand up in good heart against the cold shoulder.' (21)

Next day he wrote to Delane, announcing his intention to visit Canada 'partly to see how things are going on there and partly to try if change of air and of life will not stir up my liver or whatever else it is which requires stirring up.' He still felt his life endangered: 'if ever I am in another Bull's Run you may depend on it I never get out of it alive . . . it is a dread load round a man's neck to be feeling always that he is disliked and is liable to insult and outrage. . . . It's hard work playing a neutral game unless you're on neutral ground, I can tell you.'

He was warmly welcomed in Canada and much lionized, and gathered material for a book about Canada. He was told by almost everyone that it would be foolhardy to go back to the United States. His health revived but his spirits did not.

For all his moral strength and physical stamina, there was a marked tendency in Russell's nature towards self-doubt and self-pity. Over and over again, the diaries and private letters point to a degree of uncertainty that was never allowed to show in his public utterances. He was a man who needed constant reassurance. Like many of those who give an impressive display of confidence and courage, he was sensitive and vulnerable and prone, when things went badly, to believe he was insufficiently appreciated. He was quick to suspect he was being exploited, that his personal well-being was being sacrificed to the demands of his employers.

He worried about his future. On 22 December 1861 he had written to Delane:
At the verge of 40,* however, a desire to be something for the sake of one's own self and children does spring up in the mind too, and I would go through this very cheerfully if I could see at the end of my labours any *pied à terre*, for I cannot but recollect how my little bit of ground was knocked from under my feet this time two years when I returned from India. Is there a chance of anything permanent for me which shall not necessitate my being a kind of scribbling 'Wandering Jew' . . .? Do consider for me. I am a helpless poor devil and would be nigh friendless save for you and one or two more, none so well able to help me as yourself—none more inclined I know.

He was under pressures, certainly, that would have strained the reserves of the strongest man. The news of Mary continued to be disturbing. His own health was not good—the leg that was injured in India was sometimes stiff and painful and he was susceptible to the American fevers. There was no sign of any abating of the hatred he had endured since Bull Run and he recalled Delane's words to him before he set off for America: 'If you have the smallest reason to suppose that you will be exposed to any outrage or annoyance let nothing induce you to remain. Come back at once.' There was little prospect that he would be allowed to accompany the next campaign. There was no point in transferring to the South for he was disliked there too and would never be sure of getting his Letters to London. Worst of all perhaps, his views were increasingly at odds with those of *The Times*.

All these elements in his character and situation came together at this point to bring about the most unhappy period of his professional life. He made Delane and Mowbray Morris fully aware of his feelings and received from them a stream of support and encouragement. 'Do you remember a Mr. Chaplin,' Delane asked, 'who made acquaintance with you at Washington? He has come back, like everybody else, full of your praises. Indeed, if you knew how large a share you occupy in public attention and what importance is attached to every word you write, you would cease to repine.' (22) But Delane would not, or could not, do the one thing that would have made Russell's position more tolerable. He did nothing to modify the unsympathetic and often abrasive tones of *The Times* when it addressed itself to the American problem and the conduct of the North in particular.

On 16 February 1862 Russell wrote a long complaining letter to Mowbray Morris:

I have now been a year in this country all but a few days and am I fear more and more unpopular each moment I stay here, not personally I do believe and know

* He was, in fact, at the verge of 41 but still chose to regard 1821 as the year of his birth.

among those acquainted with me, but politically and nationally. . . . The tone of *The Times* has been regarded with anger and indignation—it is considered by the Federals as intensely antagonistic and embittered and I am looked upon as the main agent in producing that disposition on the part of the paper. Right or wrong there is no arguing the matter away. If you could see what I have had to bear in railway trains and in the street you would at least give me the credit of no common devotion and endurance—of danger I speak not now. That danger there is and will be increasing instead of diminishing. It is really astonishing how I have escaped hitherto.

He goes on to recount his long and loyal services to *The Times* and the hostility he incurred 'of powerful classes in England'. He talks about his family troubles and his financial problems. He claims that he was only engaged to spend six months in America:

I am writing to you, my dear Morris, as a friend *currente calamo*. Pray bear with me. I'm a huge lump of improvidence and want of forethought, I know. So do you. I would to Heaven I had an ounce of your prudence and excellent sense on such matters. But as I was saying, I calculated that I would be back in September, and then I would go on with my novel, already begun, for which Bradbury and Evans were to pay me literally enormously (and more fools they, perhaps), £1,500 when half done, and share of profits and all sorts of things, and complete other work which would bring me in at least as much again. When I was compromised so far as to be obliged to remain here by regard for your wishes and my personal character matters became difficult at home, but so long as Willans was on the spot he could manage, he said, provided I could come over for a week or two in the winter, though he by no means desired me to abandon my post, as he thought by doing so I would damage my reputation, above all among my friends, such as yourself, Delane, MacDonald and Mr. Walter, at the office. Now that he is away I am in a regular quandary; the word hardly expresses it. I scarcely know what to do. If only I could understand my own affairs! (23)

The distressed state of mind the letter revealed, by its manner as much as its matter, caused something close to consternation at Printing House Square. They had already lost the services of Bancroft Davis who had resigned, through ill health, in December. If Russell left America, *The Times* would be entirely without representation at events of historical importance.

His old friend John MacDonald joined the correspondence: 'Delane doesn't like letters from Canada when he wants them from the Potomac. And Morris is tremendously riled with you for writing long *grumbles* ending in nothing specific. . . . Take the large view of the situation, preserve your good humour unbroken among all the incivilities of the Yankees, the exactingness of Printing

House Square and the trials of being separated so long from your wife and children. Depend upon it, my dear fellow, that is your right and your wise course.' (24)

Mowbray Morris took a sterner line:

> I have but little time to answer your long letter of the 16th Feb. from Quebec; nor do I feel disposed to enter prematurely into the various & very serious points that you have raised touching your connection with the paper, past present & to come.
>
> The present however demands immediate attention, & so I must, at the risk of forming a hasty judgment, tell you what I think your duty demands.
>
> *You must either go to the front or come home.*
>
> You were charged with a mission which cannot be adequately discharged in Canada or New York or even at Washington. It is your business to report the military proceedings of the Federal Army—to chronicle its exploits if any, & in default of these to write whatever could be deemed interesting to English readers. Up to the beginning of this year you did well; but since then you seem to have lost heart & to have thrown us overboard. This cannot last—& so I repeat
>
> Go to the Front or come home. (25)

By the time he received this letter Russell was back in Washington, resuming the struggle to get a pass authorizing him to accompany the army. It was not to be had. He could not even get permission to go with a small expedition to Fortress Monroe.

The end of March brought a new anxiety. It dated from the day, nearly three months before, when the Northern government announced that Mason and Slidell would be released. Russell heard the news that day first from a friend on the British embassy staff, then from at least two other contacts. He had just received a despairing letter from Sam Ward, who was almost distracted at the thought of the war between the North and Britain, so he sent Ward a telegram of friendly reassurance: 'Act as if you heard some very good news for yourself. Dine as soon as you get this.' Somehow or other the *New York Herald* came to hear of the innocuous message and now they, and other papers in their wake, accused Russell of using private information to help his friend to profitable speculation on the New York Stock Exchange. The charge was entirely groundless. The news was not confidential by the late afternoon when Russell sent the telegram; Sam Ward was no longer an active speculator; and the message reached him too late to be put to such use anyway. But it was a new stick to beat 'Bull Run Russell' with and it was put to effective use. It was particularly hurtful to Russell because he greatly prided himself on his incorruptibility, and he knew the strict view his employers took of that sort of back-sliding, and also because it soured—for a time—his relations with the ambassador, Lord Lyons.

He wrote in his diary:

> MARCH 24 1862 One of the saddest days I have had in all my life, and Heaven knows I have had some sad ones, too. Lawley came in to tell me from Monson that

Lord Lyons would not see me today, as I demanded. This is not fair; but even now in my great anger and distress I do not attribute to Lord Lyons any vindictive feeling towards me so much as immense annoyance at the idea of being called to account in Parliament for communicating to me the information at all. He persists apparently in thinking that I acted solely on the words of Monson.

MARCH 25 This morning very seedy. Dear old Rowan came in, and I tried to be gay and failed miserably, I fear. Down to breakfast, could eat nothing. Monson came, and we had a long and to me most painful conversation, because I could not but feel that though he felt that I had only been indiscreet he felt bound to intimate the indiscretion could not be pardoned. Oh, William Russell, where was you sense? Why did not your pride kill you? You on whose character for truth and honour no man ever cast a shadow, because he could not! (26)

Delane wrote regretting the 'indiscretion' and saying 'how keenly we felt the tarnish it cast on a reputation in which we take so warm and affectionate an interest. Remember that of all the weaknesses poor mankind is cursed with, good nature is the most dangerous.' (27) He added: 'This incident makes it all the more necessary that you should not think of coming home.'

But Russell's mind was made up before the letter reached him. He made one more attempt to solve the problem of his pass, putting his case in writing to the President. Nothing came of it. He wrote to Mowbray Morris on 5 April: 'It is obvious that even if I had not your express orders to return home it would not be possible for me to remain out here with the ban of the Government upon me. . . . I have secured a berth on the *China* which sails on the 9th.'

So Russell sailed home and *The Times* was presented with a *fait accompli*. Delane took it philosophically: 'I wish I could think you had done right in coming home so precipitately in the very crisis of the war. It is lamentable that at such a time we should be practically unrepresented. However, here you are and we must make the best of it. I shall hope to see you tomorrow, Ever yours. John T. Delane.' (28)

Mowbray Morris also wrote in a forgiving vein, then set about trying to make sense of the receipts and accounts that Russell brought home. He was still wrestling with them twenty months later. The final bill for Russell's American expenses totalled £1,340.

Russell was lucky his employers took it so well. He had involved them in a great deal of time-consuming correspondence and in the end, ignoring their repeated pleas, had abandoned his post in an abrupt and arbitrary manner that must have seemed ungrateful. He certainly left them very much in the lurch and they never succeeded in finding an adequate replacement for him.

There is no way of knowing what would have happened if he had stuck to his task, but the chances are that the Northern authorities would have relented in the end and allowed him to follow their armies into battle. The Civil War went on for another three years, years which saw many great battles and the emergence of some superb commanders and the emergence, too, of a new kind of warfare. The presence of the world's most able and experienced war reporter during these events would have been of great value to historians and invaluable to *The Times*. He might have saved the paper from some at least of the long series of errors and misjudgements and violent changes in attitude which marred its coverage of the Civil War.

Instead he resumed his job as editor of the *Army and Navy Gazette* and held the magazine on a steadier and more prescient course than that followed by *The Times*. Delane did not ask him to write for the paper on American affairs. Their attitudes had grown too divergent and they grew more so as the war progressed. Occasional entries in the diary over the next few years show that Russell did not alter his opinions and felt no remorse:

> SEPTEMBER 28 1863 . . . Our papers still go on with the pleasant conceit that the hated Northerners are going to lose the game. Charleston is believed to be impregnable but if it goes it is no great loss! Such rubbish. I really believe on the U.S. question the great John Bull has lost his head and is distracted by jealousy to such an extent that has not only ceased to be just and generous but to be moderately reasonable.

> MARCH 10 1865 . . . News of the fall of Wilmington. It looks, as I have prophesied, all up with the South but the end is not yet.

> JUNE 12 1865 . . . *The Times*, after many serious fiascos on the American question, is committing the enormous blunder of threatening the Yankees with the loss of our good opinion if they hang Jefferson Davis. Why, we have been abusing them for four years—can not think worse of them. Had *The Times* followed my advice how different our position would be—not only that of the leading journal but of England! If ever I did state service it was in my letters from America.

7   *The Times* correspondent at the sacking of the Kaiserbagh in Lucknow

8   Russell photographed in Washington in 1861

9a   Forty-three members of the Garrick Club. Russell, moustached,
chalks his cue between the two bearded players on the left

9b   No 18, Sumner Place, Kensington

10a Albert Edward, Prince of Wales

10b Alexandra, Princess of Wales

11   Trentham Hall, Staffordshire, home of the Dukes of Sutherland; demolished in 1905

London Life

Russell was home again by the end of April 1862. He had spent nearly half of the previous ten years out of the country and more than half away from his family. He knew the burden that this imposed on Mary and he now adopted a more settled and conventional mode of life. There were further foreign assignments to come but they would be more widely-spaced and not, on the whole, either so long-lasting or so far-flung. London became the true centre of his life.

The family home was still 18 Sumner Place, but it was often sub-let for short periods as they sought a place that might prove beneficial to Mary's health. She was a chronic invalid but her condition varied greatly. Sometimes she was well enough to play some part in family life and go into society, and there were moments when Russell dared to hope for a complete recovery. Then she would relapse and plunge them back into despair. The boys, William and John, were sent as boarders to Cheltenham College at a total cost of £400 a year. Alice and Alberta were educated at home by a governess except when Mary's condition grew too distressing when Alberta was sent away to friends. As a respectable member of the professional upper middle class, Russell had to support a considerable household. Its precise extent is not clear but it included the governess, a cook, a housemaid, a nurse when Mary was seriously ill, a manservant for Russell and cousin Lizzie who lived with them and received £24 a year for her help.

The maintenance of such an establishment put a heavy strain on his already groggy finances. The perennial hope that his long trips abroad would restore them to solvency was never fulfilled, despite the royalties on his books and his steady income from the editorship of the *Army and Navy Gazette*. In July 1862 there was a rearrangement of the magazine's affairs. Russell bought fifty per cent of the shares and was given an annual salary of £1,212. Two years later he bought the rest of the shares and became sole proprietor. But these transactions involved him in greater debt, the burden of which was borne by his friend Maitland Dashwood who seems to have been always ready to lend him money when it was needed.

His friendship with Delane survived his defection from the American Civil War and in the years that followed Delane gave him a number of special reporting jobs and several books to review, most notably Todleben's history of the defence of

Sebastopol and the volumes of Kinglake's *Invasion of the Crimea* as they appeared.

Towards the end of 1862 he received an unexpected present: 'I saw Morris at 3 o'clock. Such good news. He told me *The Times* had settled £300 a year on me for *life*! And that without any claim on me for labour whatsoever. Just, he says, as a soldier receives a pension for service.' (1)

It was a flattering gesture—no *Times* writer had been honoured in this way before—and the proprietor, John Walter, made it even more remarkable by taking out a £1,000 life insurance on Russell and offering to pay the first five years' premiums himself. Russell was delighted but, as always, what he most needed was ready cash. He worked out his liabilities and was shocked to find they came to £1,800. 'Mary's bills are monstrous,' the diary said. He had to go back to *The Times* and ask if they would give him an immediate advance on the first four years' pension. They finally agreed and on the first day of 1863 he wrote in the diary: 'Saw Morris and received from him £1,200. . . . Had a very stupid evening as far as I was concerned—sent off piles of checks [*sic*] and people were paid by wholesale. Thus I begin this year with nearly all my debts paid off by an advance of £1,200 being the amount of the pension allotted to me for the next four years.'

During the 1860s he extended his activities as a London club man. He was already a member of the Raleigh Club as well as the Garrick. He joined the Carlton, the bastion of the Conservative party, and enjoyed its 'fine grand comfortable air'. (2) Later he was elected to the Marlborough Club whose membership was limited to personal friends of the Prince of Wales. But the Garrick, though he often grumbled about it, remained the focal point of his social life, the haven where he could escape professional and family pressures for a while and find refreshment in the company of like-minded men. Most of his old companions were to be found there regularly, whiling away the afternoons at the whist table, dining and drinking in the evenings, discussing the way of the world, playing whist and billiards late into the night. Thackeray remained the 'Panjandrum' of the place; Dickens was back after one of his resignations; and there was a host of distinguished writers, artists and actors, many of whom were portrayed in the group which H. N. O'Neil painted in 1869 and which still hangs above the fireplace in the billiard room. (Plate 10)

Russell enjoyed every aspect of club life. He ate gargantuan meals and drank hugely—with one dinner at the Garrick he records taking 'half champagne, bottle claret, pint sherry'—and was usually remorseful the next morning. He became preoccupied with the problem of his weight and, though he went occasionally to a gymnasium and the Turkish baths, he could not get it down below thirteen stone which was far too much for a man of barely five foot eight inches. 'I ws too seedy to face gymnasium,' he noted one day, 'but I faced the Garrick.' (3) He was fond of billiards and over-fond of whist at which he invariably showed more enthusiasm than ability. 'Wondered if a club is not an evil thing for a working man,' he wrote in the diary one day after losing four shillings at whist. He had a pleasing baritone voice and was often called upon for an Irish song or some rousing ballad. His party-piece was an old English sea song 'The Greenland Whale Fishery', which told a tale of brave endeavour and tragedy in the cold Northern waters and had to be sung 'with some vigour'.

But the things he most enjoyed were company and conversation. He had a quick mind and ready tongue. Thackeray said it was worth a guinea a day to him to have Russell dining at his table in the Club. The Irish brogue gave added charm to his talk and he had a vast fund of experiences and anecdotes. His relish for argument was tempered by natural courtesy and good humour. Anthony Trollope, who joined the Garrick in April 1862, wrote in his *Autobiography*:

> Of 'Billy Russell', as we always used to call him, I may say that I never knew but one man equal to him in the quickness and continuance of witty speech. That one man was Charles Lever*—also an Irishman—whom I had known from an earlier date, and also with close intimacy. Of the two, I think that Lever was perhaps the more astounding producer of good things. His manner was perhaps a little happier, and his turns more sharp and unexpected. But 'Billy' also was marvellous. Whether abroad as special correspondent, or at home amidst the flurry of his newspaper work, he was a charming companion; his ready wit always gave him the last word. (4)

Russell, too, left some account of his literary contemporaries. 'I can't fancy,' he wrote in the diary, 'how Trollope can catch the attention. He is a burly, rough, boisterous old boy—with great hates and no great likings, *I* think most immensely selfish and a thorough gambler, "a lewd creature" as Charley Synge said. But he is burly in mind, masculine and of tremendous energy and action.' (5)

At a publisher's party he met the American poet Longfellow and described him as 'grey-haired, long-haired, grey-bearded, long-bearded, grey-whiskered, long-whiskered, blue-eyed, sweet-faced—silent.' (6) At another party he found Browning 'very commonplace out of poetry'. (7)

Russell was particularly scathing about the novelist Charles Reade who spent much time at the Garrick Club:

> He was jealous—or may it not be said envious? He had an unappeasable appetite for praise. Every fragment of praise that was not offered to him he regarded as a lost quantity—offered to another it was a robbery. He had a cheerful, robust and simple confidence in his supremacy as master novelist of the age. . . . He dined with me several times, and I met him over and over again at little Garrick dinners, but if he indulged in return banquets I was not among the elect. (8)

---

* Charles James Lever (1806–72) was another product of Trinity College, Dublin. He wrote many popular novels, chiefly about the rollicking hard-drinking society of military men and fox-hunters in Ireland, the style of which influenced Russell in his own novel-writing efforts.

Shortly after Russell's return from America, Thackeray and his two daughters left Onslow Square and moved to a new house at Palace Green, Kensington. But Russell continued to see much of his old friend and the diary records many meetings at the Club and at home: 'Thackeray visited us during his intervallum and says he's going to let his daughter write now, as she gets more and does it better than he does.'* (9)

There was nothing to prepare Russell for the blow which fell on Christmas Eve 1863: 'Boys and girls went to theatre at Romaine's house. Mary went out in bath chair after breakfast and seeing her out of dining room window soon I opened the door and the news came—"My dear friend W. M. Thackeray died this morning—found dead in his bed from the effect of retching violently." Oh my God how soon and untimely!' Next day he called at 'the house of mourning' and dined with friends in the evening: 'Everything saddened by the loss of my poor friend.' The funeral took place on 30 December:

> This day I followed the remains of my dear friend W. M. Thackeray to the grave at Kensal Green. Mary also went in a brougham with Peter. Maitland Dashwood called on me, went together in his carriage. The Thackeray girls and Lady Colville also there. Such a scene! Such a gathering! Dickens, thin and worn, so rejoiced me saying he had lately been speaking to T. on familiar topics.† J. Leech, J. Doyle, Millais—the Garrick almost whipped of its cream but not a [?] noble, not a swell, not one of the order. Little he cared.

It took Russell a long time to recover from the loss. More than two months later he wrote:

> Read a review of somebody's life of my dear Thackeray. Lord how I wish the man who wrote it were dead and he of whom it was written were alive. Never more will the world be to me as once it was. No, not with all the happiness of wife and children—or even if fame and fortune came instead of this dull drab inglorious struggle with the present which leaves no hope for the future. (10)

Thackeray's death brought Russell closer to Charles Dickens, who wrote to him on 3 January 1864:

> Your letter has given me great pleasure, and I most heartily and cordially reciprocate your good wishes for the New Year, and for our meeting oftener in it than in the old one. Howsoever far apart we have been since we laughed and

---

* Anne Isabella Thackeray (1837–1919), the novelist's elder daughter, wrote several novels and volumes of essays.
† The quarrel over Edmund Yates, which had estranged the novelists for four years, had only recently been healed.

rode and talked with poor Jerrold, I have always followed you closely, and have always found new occasions to express my sense of what England owes you for your manly out-speaking and your brilliant description. (11)

Dickens often invited him to stay at his home at Gad's Hill in Kent and he went at least once, in January 1866:

... to Gravesend where Dickens met me driving a basket carriage affair. ... It is about 4½ miles to Gad's Hill, a plain ugly house. ... A very good dinner for about 20 people. ... Then we played billiards. I beat Dickens and Collins beat me and then we went to bed at 2 o'clock. My bedroom charming and comfortable in all ways. He [Dickens] looks old but is hale and vigorous and is only ten years older than myself. (12)

One further letter from Dickens has survived. It was written on 5 March 1867 in Newcastle-upon-Tyne: 'Your letter reached me in these coaly regions last night. I am working my way through a course of 50 readings, and am constantly here, there, everywhere and nowhere. You made me laugh so last night that I nearly choked myself with an oyster. My unforgiveness and vengeance to your charming daughter.' (13)

Russell was beginning to find new friends in very elevated circles. 'Every Irishman loves an aristocrat,' said Oliver St John Gogarty. This was not entirely true of Russell who had been, after all, the chief scourge of the noble commanders in the Crimea, but he had an ingrained respect for the social hierarchy. He was a natural conservative, glad and grateful to live under a monarchical system in which there was respect for established institutions and where 'the bump of veneration', as he called it, acted as a steadying force. But his admiration for the system did not imply uncritical admiration for his social superiors. He was never blind to their individual faults and never afraid to make his opinions known. It was they who sought his company rather than the other way round.

He spent the whole of September 1862 at house parties in the Scottish Highlands, fishing for trout, amusing the ladies with his ineptitude at croquet, hunting deer. 'Gnats and midges insufferable' he noted after a day's deer-stalking, and when he missed a stag at a hundred yards commented Pooterishly 'Deer me, deer me!' But he enjoyed himself enormously and was invited to return next year: 'How I hope I may be able to go—with all my heart *spero*—and if Bucky and Alice could come it would be complete.'

From this time on whenever it was possible he spent at least one month in the late summer of each year fishing and hunting in Scotland or in Ireland. There was never any lack of invitations. His good manners and wit and common sense made him widely welcome and he caused a great deal of amusement by his inability to cope with practical matters like his luggage and the train time-tables. He was constantly teased for his erratic marksmanship and took it in good part: 'I killed a fine stag on Thursday at Kinlochewe,' he told Mowbray Morris, 'and suppose that a more unfortunate antlered monarch of the waste has not been born the present century.' (14)

In September 1863 Russell dined at Apsley House with the second Duke of Wellington and in the years that followed he was often invited for hunting weekends at the Duke's country house near Reading, Stratfield Saye. Here, too, his unpredictable ways with the gun and with appointments made him notorious: 'My dear Doctor,' the Duke wrote, 'I now understand how you escaped being murdered in America—by throwing over appointments, and so late as to make it impossible to catch you in any other way.' (15)

Russell was at Stratfield Saye in December 1865 when Disraeli and his wife were there:

> Dizzy in great force after dinner. Talked of Tycho Brahe, Copernicus, Kepler, Galileo, the Ptolemaic system etc. to our wonder till Calcraft suggested he was lecturing and John Hay shrewdly hit on the real fact that he was only repeating a part of the speech he would have made if he had been elected Rector of the University of Edinburgh. He does not shoot and does nothing at all but spy into books—flat-footed, bad-legged creature. Punch is very like him. (16)

For all these grand distractions, Russell got through a lot of work. Editing the *Army and Navy Gazette* kept him busy: 'It is our own paper now. One works with a will,' he noted in the diary when he became proprietor. (17) He completed a two-volume account of his American experiences, *My Diary North and South*, towards the end of 1862. He was not pleased with it, writing to Bigelow that 'the form of a diary is quite destructive to any sustained interest and I will never be a slave to my daily nonsense and hasty observations again.' (18) The judgement was mistaken. It is a lively and highly-readable book, packed with vivid pictures and shrewd comments, a valuable source of first-hand impressions of the American scene during the first year of the Civil War. The diary form gave it shape and pace. The need to write rapidly, 'dictating from the actual diary word for word as fast as I could', suited his style. The book was a considerable success and things did not work out anything like so well when he abandoned the diary form for the third, companion volume, *Canada, its Defences, Conditions and Resources*. The diary refers several times to his struggles with 'my unhappy book on Canada' and it was not ready for publication until 1865. He also struggled on intermittently and even more desperately with his novel.

Early in 1863 a note came from Delane: 'But you—you who wrote the Coronation at Moscow as never man wrote—don't you feel it is a duty to scribble the marriage of the Prince of Wales? I am sure you do and that you will not let a work so peculiarly your own fall to any other scholar of the school that you have founded.' (19)

The wedding of the Prince and Princess Alexandra of Denmark took place at St George's Chapel, Windsor, on 10 March and Russell's account of the service and the scenes around the Castle filled eleven columns of *The Times* next morning. It was another massive set-piece description which showed that his recording eye had lost none of its sharpness and accuracy. The tone was necessarily deferential, the style at times almost purple. But it was a glittering occasion attended by most of the royalty of Europe and eminent representatives from much further afield, and Russell enlivened his account with many human touches. He noticed the aged Prime Minister, Lord Palmerston, 'as he stepped up lightly into his seat, and looked round him with a brisk joviality, as if about to quell a troublesome member, or evade by a most voluminous reply an awkward question.' He described the entry into the chapel of the Princess Royal, now Crown Princess of Prussia, 'looking as young, as amiable, and as timid as when, with slow steps, she herself was led to the alter at the Chapel Royal, but this time was leading by the hand a fine little boy, who, all unawed by the stately pomp around, dragged on his mother's arm, as he looked behind him at the pageant, and with difficulty brought his little feet to surmount the three steps of the *haut pas.** All have risen as they enter, and the Queen now rises too, and bows to her daughter with a kind and winning smile—the first that has passed across her face since she entered the Chapel.' The Queen, still in deep mourning for Albert, watched the ceremony from a gallery and when the choir began to sing a wedding chorale composed by the Prince Consort 'Her Majesty drew back from the window of the pew, and, after an effort to conceal her emotion, gave way to her tears and almost sobbed, nor did she throughout the rest of the ceremony entirely recover her composure.' *The Times* sold 108,000 copies of its wedding issue, 11 March 1863, almost double its normal daily circulation.

In August 1863 Lord Clyde, formerly Sir Colin Campbell, died. Russell's account of the Westminster Abbey funeral paid tribute to 'one of the best and sternest of England's soldiers, who was also the kindest and best of friends.' (20) Delane wrote next day: 'I should be a beast if I did not thank you for your most beautiful and affecting description of poor old Clyde's funeral. It touched me more than the ceremony itself, which I thought had too much of the undertaker element.' (21)

At the suggestion of the Prince of Wales, Russell had expanded his description of the royal wedding into a book which was published, lavishly illustrated and sumptuously produced, before the end of the year. But he did not meet the Prince until May 1865 when they were fellow guests at a party on board the *Great Eastern*.

The world's biggest ship, Brunel's last engineering masterpiece, had been refitted to hold and pay out 2,300 miles of electric cable. The Atlantic Telegraph company, undeterred by the early failure of their first attempt to link Great

---

* Prince Frederick William Victor Albert of Prussia disgraced himself later in the ceremony by trying to throw things and biting two of his restraining uncles on the leg. He became King of Prussia and Emperor of Germany in 1888, presided over his country's military and colonial expansion, and lived in exile in Holland after Germany's defeat in 1918.

and North America, were resolved to try again. As their preparations neared completion, the directors gave a ship-board lunch party at Sheerness. The Prince of Wales was guest of honour. Russell was there because Delane had commissioned him to cover the cable-laying enterprise. His diary for 24 May records:

> ... was presented to Prince by Lord Alfred after lunch as we were coming back and had a long chat with him about American hotels, shooting, Mexico, Great Eastern etc. He said he was very glad I was going in Great Eastern. 'I'm afraid this Andy Johnson* is a very bad man etc. What a number of vessels there are on this river etc.'—a little constrained on my side perhaps and so we parted and H.R.H. walked aft after half an hour or so.

The *Great Eastern* sailed from the south-west corner of Ireland on 23 July bound for Trinity Bay, Newfoundland. It was a long laborious voyage. They had to pay out the cable very carefully, check it constantly to make sure the electric current was getting through and when it failed they had to steam back and grapple for the cable to locate the fault. Russell did not enjoy it: 'Were you ever taking in an Atlantic cable at the rate of a mile an hour?' he asked Mowbray Morris. 'No? Well then please not to consider anything on this earth disagreeable.' (22) But he worked hard to make himself master of the complicated technical mysteries involved—nautical, electrical and mechanical—and his account over seven columns of *The Times* displayed unsuspected abilities. 'Everyone I have met,' Delane told him, 'is delighted with it and considers it a miracle of lucidity, which on such a subject was not easy.' (23) In the book that followed shortly, *The Atlantic Telegraph*, he gave even more impressive proof of his skill in making a mass of esoteric information not only intelligible to the layman but interesting as well. The cable-laying was not so successful but, as Russell remarked, 'it was one of those glorious failures which mark out the road to ultimate success.' (24) In fact, the *Great Eastern* sailed again the following year and this time the cable was well and truly laid.

The voyage had taken nearly six weeks and it was Russell's longest absence from home since his return from the American Civil War. The children were growing up and, with Mary sick most of the time, the parental burden fell largely on his shoulders.

The diary mentions many family excursions to the theatre and the zoo. When the boys were home from school he did his best to stimulate their interests but

---

* Andrew Johnson had become President of the United States on the assassination of Lincoln in April 1865. A 'poor white' from the South, he hated the cotton aristocrats and had threatened them with revenge. Once in the White House, however, he greatly modified his policies, ran foul of the radical Congress and was impeached in 1868 for 'high crimes and misdemeanours'. He was narrowly acquitted.

found it unrewarding work. He took them to Boulogne but 'they didn't seem much struck with anything'. (25) They sailed down the Thames from Chelsea: 'They didn't know Lambeth Palace and never asked a question all the way to London.' (26) When the elder boy, William, who had the discouraging nickname 'Duffer', was sixteen Russell tried to have a serious talk with him: 'Willie and I talked—he only wants to know what he is to be.' (27)

He found the two girls much more enlivening, Alice who was nicknamed 'Waddy' and Alberta who was often called 'Bludge'. He was very fond of both of them and proud of them too, though they angered him regularly by being late for breakfast and morning prayers and he was far from blind to their physical defects: 'Breakfasted *con tutte*—late. Alice's face is dwindling into a pimple bisected by a tremendous mouth and pointed off by two dark worms of eyes. Bludge is looking prettier in spite of her giant organ of a nose.' (28) The description of Alice must have been exaggerated for she was already, at the age of fifteen, attracting admiration: 'I was quite annoyed with hideous Charley Deane's *tendresse* for poor Alice—he called to her and stared at her with his horrid eyes till it almost drove me to pull his nose.' (29)

Before long it became his duty to introduce Alice into society and act as her chaperon at balls. In 1865 she went with him on his annual jaunt to the Highlands. Early the next year he noted: 'It was past three o'clock ere I got to bed. What a thing to have a dancing daughter. She looked very well with a red and white camellia in her hair.' (30)

In the spring of 1866, when he had to go to Aldershot for a military parade, he took Alice with him and within two weeks she had fallen in love with a man twice her age, Captain Frank Macnaughten of the Eighth Hussars. The Captain had been a member of Lord Raglan's escort in the Crimea—he was one of the cavalry officers with whom Russell had shared the shelter of a stable on the night of the great storm.

It was a considerable conquest for Alice, who was not yet nineteen, for the Captain was in line for an Irish baronetcy. On the day he was told of their engagement, 14 April, Russell wrote in his diary: 'I was at first excited but at least the only thing I thought of was Alice's happiness and her position . . . it remains to be seen what old Macnaughten says and my Lady to the proposal of their son to marry a girl without a penny. I suppose they think he should have a peeress.' But the matter was settled within four days: 'The most important day of my life since I was married. I am to hand over my little darling Alice to another's care and she is to exchange a husband's for a father's love. . . . Frank Macnaughten thinks he will satisfy her with his quick constant love but he is not brilliant sprightly or gay.' The next day he noted that Alice 'looked quite charming in her new bonnet with her new cloak and her radiant face and her lovely liquid rapt eyes. . . . I think she is so young, poor little baby, and I would like her to know her own mind more.'

Mary played no part in all this. In the four years since Russell's return from America her condition had declined, bringing sorrow and suffering to the household, and in December 1865 she collapsed completely. It seems probable that she was suffering from the after-effects of eclampsia, a condition that attacks some women during pregnancy. The symptoms are high blood pressure, retention of fluid and sometimes kidney failure. Mary's physical troubles can be traced from November 1857 when the birth of her fifth child left her feverish and with a racing pulse. Nearly two years later there was a miscarriage. Then in October 1860 the birth of her last child was preceded by weeks of fever and convulsions and followed by an almost mortal sickness. In serious cases such as Mary's, eclampsia leads to premature degeneration with very high blood pressure and kidney damage. After her collapse at the end of 1865 there were occasional days of spontaneous remission when Russell dared to hope for a return to something like a normal family life. Early in the New Year he accepted that there was no further room for hope: 'JANUARY 7 1866 A violent storm of rain and wind burst over us this morning. But that was nothing to the dreadful storm within. The poor sick weak dying creature was most awful—her screams and cries pierced the brain and my heart.'

The attacks diminished in violence but Mary never really recovered. During all the excitements of Alice's engagement in the spring, the diary hardly mentions Mary. Confined to her room, she was unable to show either interest or understanding. Russell decided to send her to a nursing home at Henley-in-Arden:

MAY 1 1866 . . . A servant came over from Captain Macnaughten with a beautiful bracelet for Alice—all the while poor Mary was in the room waiting for her start. . . . I bade my darling wife goodbye—sad sad indeed. I trust she may see her Alice married. It is well they—Alice and Alberta—do not remember all her wonderful love and [?] for them—goodbye sweetheart goodbye.

Nine days after her mother's departure Alice gave her first dinner party which Russell reported 'utterly spoiled by beastly drunken wretch of a waiter who quite played the devil with everything.' (31) A few days later he noted: 'I promised Waddy I would never again say a word to her of coming down late to breakfast.' (32)

As the wedding day approached Alice suffered the usual apprehensions: 'Alice is afraid now and depressed at leaving home! my dear child.' (33) Russell himself was less than joyful. His diary on 7 June recorded baldly: 'Alice Mary Russell and Frank Macnaughten married this day at Holy Trinity, Brompton. I dined at Carlton Club, that is sat at table. Walked to Leicester Square. Home—very very ill.'

War and Bereavement

During the 1860s Prussia, under the guidance of Prime Minister Bismarck, became the leading power on the mainland of Europe. On his first venture as a war correspondent, in 1850, Russell had witnessed the initial repulse of Prussia's ambitions at Idstedt. Now he was to see them triumph.

Bismarck started by avenging the defeat at the hands of the Danes. In 1864 the Prussian and Austrian armies marched together to seize Schleswig and Holstein. Russell deplored Britain's failure to act:

> FEBRUARY 6 1864 . . . The poor Danes are getting a tremendous beating from the Austrians and Prussians in Schleswig. Everyone feels that we are playing a very third-rate fiddle in the face of the world.

> FEBRUARY 8 . . . The Danes are getting it over the head and ears from devils. We confounded Pharisees shake our heads and cry out 'God help them. Very sorry. Can't interfere.'

By the early summer of 1866 Bismarck had engineered the next act of the drama, war with Austria. Delane had a correspondent with the Prussian armies, Captain Henry Hozier, and he wanted Russell to cover the campaign from the Austrian side. Russell more preoccupied than usual with domestic problems, was more than usually difficult. Delane clinched the matter with a persuasive letter, written on 15 June:

> My dear Russell,
> Pray give me a decisive and unmistakable answer as to whether you will go abroad as a 'Special' with one of the armies. Your wife is no worse than she has been for several years. You talk as if you wished to go abroad, and I offer you almost any place you like . . . and so again I ask you, 'Will you go?' and 'When?' You ought to start at once. The Prussians have already entered Saxony and you ought this very day to be beside Benedek [the Austrian commander]. But there is still time if you will go. Say the word. The messanger waits for your 'Yes' or 'No'. But pray let it be 'Yes'. You know how I care for you and your reputation. I

am sure you will lose character if you do not go. Say 'Yes' now. Come and see
me tomorrow and start on Monday. (1)

Russell was in Vienna by 23 June. He had long talks with the Foreign Minister
Mensdorff and was given letters of introduction to Benedek: 'I was quite charmed
with my reception by everyone and felt the force of a reputation.' (2) On the 26th
he dined at the British Embassy and the ambassador's wife, Lady Bloomfield,
wrote in her diary next day: 'I had Russell, *The Times* correspondent, to dinner
yesterday, who is off to Benedek's Headquarters tonight. He is a very amusing
clever Irishman.' (3)

Russell bought a horse, hired an English groom and made friends with Charles
Brackenbury, a young captain of the Royal Artillery who had been sent to act as his
assistant. They made their way to the front and dined one evening with Benedek
and his staff. The Prussians were advancing quickly from the north, under the
command of the brilliant strategist Moltke, and there had already been several
minor engagements.

On 2 July Russell and Brackenbury climbed to the platform at the top of a
sixteenth-century tower in the village of Königgrätz: 'man told us it was *verboten*
but let us up nevertheless—on gaining platform . . . a splendid view of the Austrian
army.'

The diary for the next day reads: 'Awakened at six by a water spout—such a
torrent. . . . The whole Austrian army more than 200,000 strong is out under this
rain.' Below this, in a different ink, he later added the words: 'It is curious. I wrote
the above as my diary lay beside me on the table in bed and went to sleep—woke
about seven—dressed, came in to breakfast intending to go out about horses to
camp when Brackenbury and I heard firing. The Battle had begun. The day never
to be forgotten.'

In his subsequent Letter to *The Times* Russell graphically described what
happened during breakfast:

As we were actually speaking, there came through the fog of the morning the
dull thudding sound which really issues only from the throat of cannon, but
which when first heard leaves one in doubt whether it may not be from the
rumbling of carts, the rolling of a harmless barrel, or the kicking of a horse on a
wooden floor near at hand. We listened. In a few seconds there could be no
question as to the real nature of that tumult. (4)

Brackenbury saddled his horse and rode off to Benedek's headquarters. Russell,
whose horse and groom were away despatching a Letter to London, remembered
the commanding view from the Königgrätz tower and hurried to the platform:

Nothing but a delicate, and yet bold, panorama on a gigantic scale could give a
notion of the extent of the view and the variety of landscape visible from this

tower, and no panorama could convey any idea of such a scene, filled with half a million of men moving over its surface like the waves of the sea or as a fast-driving cloud in a gale—a scene in which every village was vomiting forth fire and smoke, every knoll the scene of murderous conflict, every valley the indiscriminate grave of thousands of men, every cornfield covered with the full harvest of death, and trodden under foot by furious legions before day was done, while the church spire, rising aloft from its blood-stained base and the flames of the little hamlet, seemed to bear witness to Heaven against the wickedness of man. (5)

In many ways it was reminiscent of the battle of Balaclava—from a safe vantage point, covering the whole field of action, with every opportunity to take comprehensive notes, he watched a varied encounter involving cavalry as well as artillery and infantry, the different units in contrasting and colourful uniforms. But the battle of Königgrätz, sometimes called Sadowa, was longer and more complicated than Balaclava and very much bigger. In weight of numbers and fire-power it was not to be surpassed until the First World War.

Russell, who had seen more of war than most of the soldiers there, was impressed and deeply moved. He saw the neighbouring village of Sadowa engulfed by the Prussians: 'The pleasant little village, snug church, hospitable mill—all were burning. It was with surer divination of the coming woe than we had that the poor people had fled in tears or remained in hopeless sorrow in their homes. The heat of this great battle burnt up whatever it touched and sent forth the lava which destroyed as it flowed on all sides.' (6) Austrian officers who had joined him on the platform were more phlegmatic: 'The officers said "Ja so!" and "Hem!" and uttered various other sounds of varied import possibly, smoked their cigars and looked on.'

Russell's experience of war enabled him to recognize the key moment of the battle as it occurred. About one o'clock in the afternoon he noticed the Austrian gunners falling back over the brow of a hill on the right of the line:

I confess the advance of the Prussians in this direction appeared to me
inexplicable and very serious; for, although the left and centre of the Austrians
might be victorious, this movement threatened, by forcing back their right, to cut
them off from Königgrätz. . . . A general who saw what was visible to those in
the tower would have felt uneasiness and have turned his attention to fill the gap in
his line at the centre, and to drive back the Prussians who were doubling up his
right. (7)

Others saw the import of the moment—Bismarck and Moltke. In his book *The Battle of Königgrätz* Gordon Craig wrote:

From another vantage point, on the Roskoberg, Count Bismarck trained his
telescope on the same ridge that was attracting Russell's attention and noticed
that something he had thought was a line of trees was actually moving and that the

Austrian guns seemed to be firing towards it. He handed his glass to Moltke, who took a long look and then put away his red handkerchief with a decisive flourish. He spurred his horse over to the King and said, 'The campaign is decided and in accordance with Your Majesty's desires!' (8)

There was more fierce fighting to come, but before the day was out the Austrians were in full retreat, leaving behind them 13,000 prisoners and 24,000 killed and wounded.

Russell lost his portmanteau with most of his books and papers in the confusion of the retreat. Whenever he stopped, he wrote. He reached Vienna at midnight on 7 July 1866 and spent the next day completing his Letter which was published in *The Times* on 11 July. He told Mowbray Morris: 'it was rather difficult to write and retreat rapidly at the same time, but I did my best.'

The Letter showed no diminution in his powers as a describer of great battle scenes. It was lucid, vivid and accurate, informed throughout by his matured military appreciation. With Hozier writing from the Prussian side, *The Times* was able to record a new kind of 'first' and the *Saturday Review* paid generous tribute:

> For the first time we have had a great battle described immediately after it had taken place by narrators who have followed the fortunes of either army. *The Times* had supplied English readers with a description of the battle of Sadowa as it appeared to an observer on the Prussian side, and also with a description of it as it appeared to an observer on the Austrian side. We have never had this done before with anything like the same amount of fulness and graphic power. (9)

Russell wrote to Delane:

> I think there is a good fight still left in the Austrians but that they are not in good feather. . . . And yet if Austria goes all Europe will become Republican, ruled by plebiscite despots or Cossack. . . . I am beginning to believe in nationalities but it's a bad faith for England. Look at my 'nationality'. I wish they could try a little Paddyocracy over there. . . . I hope you will make allowances for my account of the battle written as it was. I had a better view of it than Benedek anyway though I could not get the details. How well our friend Hozier is doing. I'm proud of him. . . . If I fall avenge me by a few brisk leaders please and take care of the family. (10)

He continued to admire Hozier's work—'at once excellent in narrative, in description, in observation and in research'—and envied him the pleasures of marching with the victors. But he felt called upon, as founding father of the growing band of war correspondents, to draw Delane's attention to one defect in Hozier's methods:

. . . for as to what he saw *propriis oculis* his evidence is beyond question and his statements without a fault. When he proceeds however, to show circumstantially how it was that the Prussian horse got at the Austrian horse through their armour—there being no Austrians without cuirasses at all—or makes a gallant action out of a surprise of Benedek's staff and bodyguard, he is deceived by others, and they ought to be exposed who deceived him. (11)

In subsequent Letters to *The Times* from Vienna Russell analysed the significance and the causes of Austria's defeat. 'When Austria marched from the wreck of Königgrätz,' he wrote, 'she found that the sceptre of the German Caesars had been stricken from her hand.' They were beaten, he concluded, because they had no reserves, there had been too little rapport between Benedek and his subordinate commanders, and above all because the Prussian infantry were armed with the 'needle-gun'—a breech-loading rifle, fired by a striker with a long needle-like point which penetrated the explosive material already in place in the cartridge. The Austrian infantry were still using the muzzle-loaded rifle which was accurate but took much longer to load.

Russell was anxious that the British army should learn the lesson. He wrote to Delane on 9 July:

Let there be no mistake about it. The needle-gun has pricked the Austrian Army to the heart. If we do no *at once* arm our troops with a breech-loader with fixed ammunition (no d—d humbug about 'capping') we are howling idiots and deserve to be smashed in our first fight. . . . Fixed ammunition with its own ignition must be the system, or we lose the greatest advantage of the breech-loader. *Do press this on the authorities if they have the smallest doubt about it.* . . . The motions required for capping are the very greatest drawbacks to firing next to ramrod ramming. Do be urgent, incessant and remorseless about this. It is quite incredible how brave men are cowed by this d—d weapon—cavalry and all. Nor could I, had I not seen, have believed in such tremendous volleys on their front. The needle-gun *trebled* the line of the Prussians—a line of skirmishers made a tolling fire like a regiment firing a *feu de joie*. (12)

Delane made sure Russell's words were circulated and the matter was raised in the House of Commons. 'It was probably the first occasion on record,' said the *Pall Mall Gazette*, 'in which any newspaper correspondent, and that correspondent a civilian, was spoken of by a Minister of the Crown as a person most capable of giving an opinion—and whose opinion was entitled to great weight on a purely military subject.' (13)

Although there was no more serious fighting after Königgrätz, *The Times* retained Russell in Austria for many weeks. With no major events to report, he travelled widely—to Verona and Lake Constance, to Prague and Dresden. He hired a tutor to improve his German and spent much time in restaurants, at the theatre and the opera, visiting museums and art galleries. But the lifting of the spirits which action and hard work invariably brought him quickly wore off and he found himself depressed and lonely.

'I don't dance,' he wrote to Mowbray Morris from Vienna, 'I don't drink beer if I can help it and other people's amusements are beyond my capacity. There is one thing I can do. I can smell a bad smell fearfully well and my life is one demnition "phew!"' (14)

On 16 September he wrote in the diary: 'My Wedding Day anniversary. Twenty years ago. My darling Mary alive but dead to me.'

On 13 October he described a visit to a Vienna picture gallery with a friend: 'Ross was in uniform and attracted the attention of a lovely Pole who was alas nothing better than she should be as he found out speaking to her. They all seem to be as depraved as can be in sexual matters and to have no idea of virtue.' Two days after this he noted: 'had visions, perturbations during the night. How dreadful is this loneliness. I have no friends near me. . . . I want a woman to guide me and to cheer me and all of the world's best half is shut out from me. Sentiment is mischievous.' And six days later, in Prague, he wrote: 'I am becoming in an odd state of mind and body now—for I can not sleep and am much tormented by the devil of sense either within or without, waking up in much unrest and need of sympathy.' (15)

He was home in London by the end of October 1866. Eighteen Sumner Place was sub-let and he lived in rooms in the Inner Temple. In November he took William and Alberta on a sight-seeing trip to Cologne and Paris. On 1 December he visited his wife: 'My darling darling Mary. God what a wreck and ruin. An hour or so of cries, tears and bitter sorrow—the poor sad mind.'

On 1 January he noted: 'This New Year opened upon me in my little garret in Number 1 Tanfield Court, Inner Temple. After my meal of tea and toast, I sat me down at my task, the novel, distracted by smoke, by thoughts that breathed and words that would not burn—the fire would not certainly and it was bitter cold.'

The novel had already been nine years in the writing and he had promised the publishers, Tinsley Brothers of the Strand, that he would have it ready for the presses by the spring. On 7 January he admonished himself: 'Now for my solemn resolve. No cards, no whist till I write my novel sink or swim. . . . To meet Tinsley's demand of three volumes to be ready in April—say this day three months—I must write . . . 277 lines a day.'

But the next day he noted: 'The letters from Henley sad indeed—alas! She is going my poor friend and wife—my only true friend who loved me as no one else did or can or will.'

Mary died on 24 January 1867: 'This morning at 2 a.m. all that remained of my darling Mary's frame-work of the soul was left by pain alone with death.'

Their marriage had lasted more than twenty years, the last fifteen of them increasingly overcast by Mary's physical and mental decline. 'All happy families resemble one another,' Tolstoy wrote, 'but each unhappy family is unhappy in its own way.' Russell's domestic griefs may have been unique but they were not unusual. Many of his friends and colleagues—Thackeray and Dickens, Delane and Morris—endured marriages that were equally, and sometimes more painful than his, and Russell always tried to remember the early years together when they had been poor and the children had been babies and there had been much happiness as well as much love in his home.

Mary was buried in Brompton cemetery, alongside the two boys who had died in infancy, on 28 January—'a drizzling day which yet let fall no drops of pity on us'. Alice could not be there and he wrote to her: 'I do know I tried to do my duty to her and that—Oh with how many a shortcoming—I sought in the best way of my lights to teach you all to love her and that I tried to do my duty to you all. It is no exaggeration of grief to say that a purer or more truthful heart never was filled with human impulses than that which beat in the tender breast that nursed you—a generous "foolish" Irish heart.' (16) Three days later he noted in the diary: 'I am in receipt of some charming letters, so kind tender and just. Somehow one's children seem to feel less than one's friends—or are mine of harder stuff? I don't know. I hope not.'

He searched for a new home for the family and finally took a cottage in Mortlake called 'The Nook'. Once again there were financial troubles: 'as to the calamity of pounds, shillings and pence to come 'tis quite beyond belief—that is, no one can believe I am in such a pickle.' (17)

Bigelow urged him to reform his ways:

> You have now an excellent opportunity for reducing your expenses. I hope you will improve it. You have no occasion to maintain costly relations with the rest of mankind, while you have abundant motives for thrift. . . . You are a very extravagant dog, my friend. Now let me beg you again—for I have preached to you on the subject before—save your money, invest it productively. You would earn enough to make you rich in a few years, if you entertained the same contempt for Mrs. Grundy that she will entertain for you if you grow old and poor. I tell you there is nothing like having a few thousand pounds slaving away in some dark corner for you, instead of you slaving for them; they toiling while you are sleeping. You'll not regret when you are old any of the money you did not empty into the stomach of Tom, Dick and Harry. (18)

It was hopeless to expect Russell to follow such advice. By August of that year he owed Maitland Dashwood a total of £5,035. It was agreed that all Russell's earnings would henceforth be paid straight into a fund at Coutts Bank, one third of it to go to Russell each quarter and the rest to Dashwood until the debt was paid off. Russell's shares in the *Army and Navy Gazette* were his security.

Meanwhile, he resumed his social life at the old pace. The diary records dinners with the Duke of Wellington at Apsley House, with Trollope at the Garrick, and with the Commander-in-Chief, the Duke of Cambridge: 'He is against the abolition of flogging. I let him see I thought it would raise the character of the army.' (19)

The novel *The Adventures of Dr. Brady* began to come out in serial form in *Tinsley's Magazine* while he struggled with the concluding chapters. It finally appeared in three volumes in 1868. Russell had never been happy about it, calling it 'a weary novel' and 'my *bête noire*', increasingly aware that novel-writing was not his forte. On the day the book came out he noted: 'Dr. Brady out! Saw it in the Club and read it. There is frightful bosh in it. Do the public like bosh nowadays? Am I a severe critic?' (20)

He often underestimated his work but in the case of the novel his apprehensions were more than justified. It tells the rambling story of an Irish doctor whose career paralleled Russell's own in many ways—brought up by Irish Protestant grandparents, studying at Trinity College, Dublin, becoming involved with the O'Connell movement for the repeal of the Union, serving with the army in the Crimea and then in India during the Mutiny. But for all his knowledge of the background places and events, it never comes to life. The characters are cardboard; the dialogue is stilted; the story is riddled with wild coincidences, heavy sentimentality and notions drawn from romantic melodrama. It bears all the marks of its long and painful gestation. Even so the public liked it well enough to earn a second edition in the year of publication. Then it disappeared from view.

The months after Mary's death were greatly cheered for him by his daughters, especially Alice who paid frequent visits: 'She is a perfect child just as when she played about my knees or fought with Alberta to sit on them . . . gave us a most animated account of her doings in the hunting field. She becomes wild with excitement as she speaks and is a different being.'(21)

In April 1867 he went to Paris to see the Great Exhibition. Two months later he returned to Austria to describe the coronation of the Emperor Francis Joseph as King of Hungary for the pages of *The Times*.*

He returned home to his second bereavement of the year. His father, staying at Mortlake, collapsed suddenly and died within a few days. On the day of the funeral, 2 July, Russell noted:

Poor dear old man. His life was not happy . . . his latter days were so weary and his reflections so sad. A man of great ability in his way, witty, shrewd, very kind and good-hearted but battered by adversity and quite destitute of prevoyance or energy—morally deficient in boldness, self-reliance and courage, and self-indulgent in his small way—very kind to others too and very fond of me. As to Alice, no idol was ever so worshipped as she by him.

* The Magyars had taken advantage of the Austrian defeat in 1866 to secure a separate and largely autonomous Kingdom under what was called the Dual Monarchy. Francis Joseph remained Emperor of Austria but also became King of Hungary.

After a fortnight on the Scottish moors he returned to Paris to cover the Great Exhibition and admire the brand new boulevards and avenues of Baron Haussmann. He did much theatre and opera-going, saw the cancan danced and took a trip in a balloon for twenty francs—'We were a good deal knocked about and on the whole the sensation not pleasant—view very fine.' Lord Lyons was now ambassador to France and Russell dined often at the embassy. Delane stayed in Paris for several days and complained that he could get nothing to eat. Dashwood was there too and fell seriously ill: '. . . my dear old friend. I was with him today at one o'clock and much alarmed at a sudden set-back and he wished me to go as I was too demonstrative. I am a bad hand at my sensations.' (22)

He was delighted to hear from Alice that he had become a grand-father and soon overcame his initial disappointment that the child was not a boy. At the year's end, home again in Mortlake, he noted: 'It was very pleasant to see my radiant little daughter and her child. I suppose the rough and rather brute process by which she has been much tamed and made so fond was needful.' (23)

Politics and High Society

Russell's circle of acquaintance grew even grander. The visits to Stratfield Saye were resumed, he dined with the Lord Chief Justice and had long conversations with the Duke of Cambridge. At the beginning of April 1868 a note came from Captain Arthur Ellis of the Grenadier Guards, who was equerry to the Prince of Wales: 'I write only a line to say that the Prince desires me to let you know that if there is anything you would like to see him about during the Irish visit you are to call on him at the Castle there—and HRH will be glad to see you.' (1)

Russell met the Prince and Princess at a ball at Dublin Castle on 20 April and dined with them there next day: 'Superb banquet, in all respects magnificent and well done. Prince very gracious.' The friendship developed quickly. By July he was dining at Marlborough House, the Prince's London home.

In the autumn of 1868 Russell made his only foray into politics. The general election, which followed a few months of Disraeli's Prime Ministership with a minority government, was unusual in two ways—the first to be conducted under the new household suffrage, and the first in which Disraeli and Gladstone confronted each other as leaders of the two great parties.

Mr Gladstone, the Liberal leader, chose the issue on which the election was fought—the disestablishment of the Church of Ireland. The Liberals argued that it was unfair to expect the Irish people, poor and predominantly Roman Catholic, to go on maintaining an established Anglican church in their land, and that resentment of this was a prime cause of their discontent. The Conservatives believed the discontent had other and deeper roots and feared that such a concession to Catholic feeling would open the way to Popery and encourage those who wanted to end the Union.

Russell had never lost his interest in Irish affairs and it had been stimulated in recent months by a series of outrages by the Fenians, an American–Irish movement for the violent overthrow of British rule:

NOVEMBER 23 1867 . . . This day the miserable and hapless Fenians, Kellen, Gould and Larkin, were executed at Manchester. Is justice satisfied? Only

God knows! . . . The poor Fenians. Now Ireland is out of the pale of every sympathy.

FEBRUARY 1 1868 . . . Delane and I had some talk about Ireland. He is very ferocious and foolish and narrow in his views—a capital typical man of the English middle class and therefore most dangerous from the power he wields in dealing with Ireland.

FEBRUARY 17 . . . What the Irish want is their own Parliament and they never will be satisfied with anything short of such a Union as Scotland has or with Queen Lords and Commons of Ireland and some day England will be glad to give it.

Russell's views on Ireland and imperialism in general might suggest that he would have been more at home with the Liberals, but he remained a staunch if unconventional Conservative. In August 1868 he became a member of the West London Conservative Association: 'Paid my £20 as member . . . room three-quarters filled by respectable tradesmen . . . I had at last to make a speech and floundered away wonderfully.' (2) He was being vetted as a possible candidate.

At a meeting in Fulham he was chosen to run for one of the two Chelsea seats. His running-mate was Charles James Freake, the architect who had designed Sumner Place and many other handsome streets and squares in Kensington but who was to make himself something of a laughing-stock during the campaign.

At his adoption meeting Russell made a speech arguing that Popery had come to be identified with rebellion in Ireland and that any move to disestablish the Anglican church there and divert its revenues to the Catholic church would only increase the threat to the Union. He expressed great sympathy for the working class but declared himself opposed to compulsory education 'believing that it was not altogether suited to Englishmen'. (3) The voters must have found his election address confusing: 'I come before you,' he said, 'as a Conservative on independent Liberal principles.'

He spent September in Scotland and the campaign opened at the beginning of October. He had formidable opponents—Charles Wentworth Dilke who was at the start of a long career in politics, and Sir Henry Hoare who seized upon Russell's election address: 'Dr. Howard Russell came forward as a Conservative upon independent liberal principles (cheers and laughter). He was very ill when he read the address, but he almost jumped out of bed and said "Confound the fellow, he has jumped into our trousers and is running away with our measures" (laughter and great cheering).' (4)

It was a lively contest with one and sometimes two meetings every night and audiences who expected sizable speeches and believed in taking an active part. Russell soon realized that Freake was a serious liability:

OCTOBER 8 1868 Speech at Pier Hotel, Chelsea. Poor Freake broke down.

OCTOBER 16 . . . went to Swan where there was a respectable meeting, very warm and enthusiastic, to whom I spoke for an hour and a half—too long. . . . Poor Freake more feeble than usual. I will never be able to pull him through.

There was considerable trouble at the Conservative meetings, most of it caused by supporters of the Chelsea Working Men's Electoral Association. It culminated at the Chelsea Vestry Hall on 26 October. Members of the Association managed to infiltrate the meeting in strength and made such a commotion that Freake could not make himself heard at all. According to the account in the *Chelsea News*, when Russell rose to speak 'the Conservatives, rising *en masse*, cheered the honourable gentlemen for many minutes, and when the applause ceased there arose deafening yells, which sounded as though all the incurables from Bedlam, Colney Hatch, and all the Metropolitan Lunatic Asylums had been let loose in the Hall.' When he could make his powerful baritone heard, Russell went for the hecklers:

> You are unworthy the name of Englishman (uproar). You are afraid of argument! You are cowards! (Great uproar which lasted several minutes, and during the interval, in different parts of the Hall, several policemen of opposite opinions were engaged in pugilistic encounters in a manner worthy of Donnybrook Fair). . . . Are you the people who invited us to come forward to discuss our politics? You are a rabble, and I would sooner follow in the march of an army on the road to freedom than serve such a set of cowards (great cheering from the Constitutional party and groans from the Radical portion of the meeting). (5)

The meeting had to be adjourned for twenty-five minutes and then a resolution was carried that Russell and Freake 'were fit and proper persons to represent the Borough of Chelsea in Parliament'. The announcement of this brought further uproar 'when a rush was made towards the platform and it was with difficulty that the Conservatives got safely out of the Hall, the candidates being escorted outwards by a body of police.'

The next issue of the *Chelsea News* condemned 'one of the worst exhibitions of American rowdyism ever displayed in the English metropolis'. But the paper's sympathies were with the Liberals and so, on this occasion, were those of most Chelsea voters. The results were declared on 18 November:

Dilke	7,374 votes
Hoare	7,183
Russell	4,177
Freake	3,929

After speeches from the successful candidates 'Mr W. H. Russell, who was greeted with sundry uncomplimentary demonstrations which he bore good-humouredly, proceeded to say, amid frequent interruptions that he stood before them a beaten but not a discouraged man (Laughter). He had fought a fair fight. . . . He was not discouraged, because there stood behind him (cries of "Freake" and great laughter) upwards of 4,000 electors who were not inferior in wealth or intelligence to those who voted on the other side.' (6)

The Chelsea result was reflected throughout the country: Mr Gladstone was returned to power with 384 seats against the Conservatives' 274.

A year or so later the Chelsea Conservatives approached Russell to ask if he would stand again for them at the next election but he declined. He had not much enjoyed campaigning and suspected, shrewdly perhaps, that he would not make any great mark in the House of Commons. And the cost of running for election had put a further strain on his faltering finances. He was deeply touched and grateful when the Duke of Wellington offered to help with his expenses.

The Prince of Wales had invited him to accompany a royal tour in the eastern Mediterranean and early in 1869 he set off across Europe with the Duke of Sutherland and his son, the Marquis of Stafford. George Granville Leveson-Gower, the third Duke, was to be a close friend for many years. His ancestors had vastly enriched the family by judicious marriages and by their policy of evicting thousands of Highland crofters to make room for more profitable and less troublesome sheep. He was the greatest landowner in the kingdom with more than 1,300,000 acres, and one of the richest men in England with an annual income of over £140,000. His life-style was that of a prince, moving with a great household between his London home, Stafford House, and magnificent country residences at Trentham in Staffordshire, Lilleshall in Shropshire and Dunrobin Castle in the Highlands.

The Duke was a notable eccentric. Fascinated by fire engines, he rarely missed an opportunity to ride out with the Metropolitan Fire Brigade and the Prince of Wales sometimes went with him. He was a railway fanatic too, delighting in driving engines on his Highland Railway and promoting new developments all over the world. Like many members of the Prince of Wales' set and the Prince himself, he had a great weakness for pretty women. Though he was not particularly interested in politics, he had a talent for the flamboyant radical gesture. He was host to the Italian revolutionary hero Garibaldi when he visited London—to the annoyance of the Queen who sternly told her son that his friend 'did not live as a Duke ought'.

Russell and the Duke crossed Europe in seigneurial style with 'directors in attendance, special trains, saloon carriages, ordered banquets, and accommodation bespoken by telegrams from the superior authorities.' (7) The *Milord Anglais* still commanded great respect and when they reached Italy their journey turned into a triumphal progress for *l'amico di Garibaldi*. They sailed from Brindisi and arrived in Alexandria on 23 January 1869. The Prince and Princess of Wales, touring in northern Europe, were to come on later.

Russell had travelled through Egypt on his way to India eleven years earlier but now he had time to study the country, meet its leaders and marvel at the monuments and artefacts of its ancient greatness. He found it all fascinating.

Egypt was part of the crumbling Turkish empire and its ostensible ruler was the Sultan's viceroy, the Khedive Ismail. Although he enjoyed considerable autonomy the Khedive's policies were controlled, and often confused, by the powerful and rival influences of France and Britain. Both countries had vital interests in the area but the chief interest of each was to prevent the other from gaining predominance. It made for complications and uncertainties which centred at this time on the building of the Suez Canal. The French engineer Ferdinand de Lesseps had fought for the project for many years, with the encouragement and support of the French emperor and much obstruction from the British. Now the work was nearing completion.

Russell and the Duke were received by the Khedive, taken to see the barrage on the Nile and then by special train to Ismailia to be shown the work in progress on the Canal: 'M. de Lesseps was of course irresistible. He proves as conquering when he deals with mind as he has done in his conflict with matter.' (8)

On his return to Cairo Russell found time for more sight-seeing and a long talk with the Khedive about Egypt's political problems before the arrival of the Prince of Wales in early February. A few days of receptions and banquets followed and then the royal party embarked on six blue and gold river steamers for a voyage up the Nile. The Prince's retinue included Captain Arthur Ellis, Prince Louis of Battenburg who was then a midshipman, and Sir Samuel Baker, recently knighted for his explorations of the upper Nile and his discovery of Lake Albert. Queen Victoria strongly disapproved of Baker's inclusion in the party—his principles, she said, were '*not good*' and he had, indeed, lived for many years with a girl of Hungarian origin whom he bought in a Turkish slave market—but he had an invaluable knowledge of the country and was an expert hunter. He also knew about provisioning for a princely journey. According to Russell their stores for the five-week voyage included 'a supply of 3,000 bottles of champagne, 20,000 bottles of soda water, 4,000 bottles of claret; and so on as to sherry, and ale, and liqueurs of all sorts.' (9)

It was an amusing journey with endless sight-seeing for the Princess and much shooting for the Prince and a running joke about the dangers of being overtaken by a boat-load of Britons on a Cook's tour a little way behind them on the river. Russell made considerable play with the tourists in his occasional Letters to *The Times* about the trip and in his subsequent book *A Diary in the East*:

> What might not be pardoned to Mr. Cook's Tourists, who were in full cry up
> the river after the Prince and Princess? Some of our companions had come from
> Brindisi with the British caravan, and gave accounts which did not tend to make
> us desire a closer acquaintance. Respectable people—worthy—intelligent—
> whatever you please; but all thrown off their balances by the prospect of running
> the Prince and Princess of Wales to earth in a Pyramid, of driving them to bay in
> the Desert, of hunting them into the recesses of a ruin—enraptured at the idea
> of being able possibly to deliver 'an address' in the Temple of Karnak.' (10)

Thomas Cook, the entrepreneur of organized travel, was not amused. It was his first venture into Egypt and he did not subscribe to the view that there is no such thing as bad publicity. He later wrote to the Prince of Wales protesting against the suggestion that his tourists were more interested in seeing the royal party than the Egyptian antiquities and had his letter published in the magazine the *Excursionist*. (11)

Russell and the Duke of Sutherland left the royal voyagers on 23 February 1869 and sailed back down the river to visit Thebes and the Cairo pyramids and see something of the strange semi-Europeanized society: 'a most wonderful gathering of old girls, very fat', Russell noted in the diary on 2 March.

The Duke had to return home and Russell saw him off at Alexandria, then explored the city: 'Alexandria, out of the great square, has a villainous loathsome look about it by night. Groups of men scowling at the street corners; gangs of armed watchmen howling frightful challenges; discordant music from dingy dens, where all the nations of the world are gambling, drinking and singing; a procession of scavengers, with buckets and lanterns, crossing in and out of the dark alleys towards the sea.' (12)

Despite the squalor and the constant clamour for 'baksheesh', he had fallen in love with Egypt. 'There is a permanent, never-failing pleasure,' he wrote, 'in the consciousness of being alive in such a climate. Pyramids and ruins have defiled before us like a panorama, on which we gazed with a dreamy blissful tranquillity. *Nil admirari* can be best understood in Egypt where there is more to wonder at than in any land of the earth.' (13)

With the help of Murray's *Hand-book* and an Arab servant, Hamed, he made a tour of Palestine, visiting Jerusalem, Bethlehem and the Mount of Olives, then Jaffa and Port Said where de Lesseps showed him more of the Canal workings.

He was in Cairo by mid-March for the return of the Prince of Wales and a hectic round of banquets, parties, firework displays and shows: 'sat behind Princess at theatre and she spoke to me very often and was very gracious indeed.' (14)

At the end of March the party sailed to Constantinople to be lavishly entertained by the Sultan, then to the Crimea where Russell showed them round the battlefields. They visited the farmhouse that had been Lord Raglan's headquarters on the heights before Sebastopol:

... and the sight of it recalled the long dark nights when, candleless, I sat in my tent looking at the bright lights in the windows and listening to the rolling of musketry which came up the ravine and sounded close at hand; the weary journeys through the mud to Balaclava and back; the trials I endured each mail-day when my letters came out; and the great storm which blew tent and all it contained to parts unknown, and forced me to seek shelter in a dreadful den in Balaclava. (15)

They made their way home in leisurely fashion by way of Athens—the Princess' brother was King of Greece—and Albania, Brindisi again and the Hotel Bristol in Paris. It was 10 May when Russell got back to London.

By now he was fully accepted as a member of the Prince of Wales's circle. His diary for the next few months is little more than a list of grand engagements. He dined at Marlborough House, the Prince's London home, and was host to the Prince and others at the Garrick Club. He watched the racing at Ascot in June from the Royal Enclosure, attended the Queen's Ball at Buckingham Palace the next month and accompanied the Prince to the Trinity House dinner: 'I got into trouble because I wore white instead of blue diplomatic pants.' (16)

Although Russell liked to dress smartly and correctly he did not always meet the exacting standards of the Prince in matters of appearance, precedence and protocol. And though he liked to eat and drink well, here again he found himself out-classed by his new friends:

JULY 5 1869 Prince and Princess of Wales Ball at Marlborough House which was very pleasant indeed and where I took too much wine for my comfort.

JULY 18 Such a *fa niente* of a day—*dolce* but for one's thoughts.

JULY 19 I am not making my way in mind or body.

The Prince of Wales's circle was composed mostly of men who were of noble birth or great wealth or both. They were superior in manner, snobbish in attitude and—from the high moral standpoint which Russell shared with the Queen —depraved in their behaviour. There was much gambling on cards and horses. Their conversation consisted generally of gossip and smutty stories. They were greatly given to what they called 'chaff' and practical joking, though these were never directed against the Prince himself. Many of them enjoyed the company of fast women; some preferred that of compliant boys. There were rogues and adventurers among them, card-sharpers and con-men. When public scandal threatened, as it frequently did, they were ready to close ranks and use all the considerable influence at their command to save their friends. 'If ever you become King,' the Queen warned her son, 'you will find all these friends *most* inconvenient, and you will have to break with them *all*.' They took, on the whole, little serious interest in culture or politics or international affairs. Russell was as much out of his element in their company, morally and intellectually, as he was out of his depth financially.

But he could not resist the temptations of high society life. He liked the *réclame* that such connections gave him, the glitter and elegance of grand occasions, the effortless luxury of life in great houses and in the Marlborough Club which the Prince created for his personal friends.

He was welcomed into the circle chiefly because he could bring a much-needed leavening of cultured intelligence and forthright common sense into their talk.

The Prince enjoyed argument and disputation as long as it was held within the bounds of due deference, and Russell could be relied upon to take the unfashionable line on most subjects that came up for discussion and more than hold his own in debate. He was welcomed, too, as a bridge between society and the world of writers and artists. He wrote an account of the Mediterranean tour (*A Diary in the East during the Tour of the Prince and Princess of Wales*) and after that the Prince referred to him as 'my historian'.

When Delane asked him to cover the opening of the Suez Canal in November 1869, he welcomed the opportunity to revisit Egypt and took Alberta with him. In Cairo he made the acquaintance of Nubar Pasha, the Khedive's Foreign Minister. After the opening ceremony, which was attended by the Empress Eugenie of France, the Emperor Francis Joseph of Austria and the Crown Prince of Prussia, he took Alberta on a trip up the Nile. In a letter to Alice he described her sister's eruption into society:

> Bludge is in no state of mind to write to anyone. I should think no one ever made such a plunge out of school into a whirl of pleasure. She finished up Cairo by dancing at the Khedive's and being late for dinner and she has been at balls and parties enough for a season. Spencer Ponsonby and she are great chums and she gets on famously and is as cool as a cucumber. (17)

In the same letter he said he had secured a job for John, his younger son, at Oppenheims, the bankers in Alexandria. The elder boy, William, was already abroad—*en route* for a job with the Imperial Customs in China.

On 20 January 1870 Russell wrote from Cairo:

> Sumner House (I call it) will be free in March, but I really do not see the use of going to the expense of an establishment for *one* person when I could live very well in a bathroom and at my club like a melancholy old widower as I am. I am quite sure Alberta would never get up in the mornings to breakfast and I would undergo the old misery of loss of temper seven days in the week. (18)

The return to England brought a resumption of the social round:

> MARCH 26 1870 . . . dined at Stafford House . . . went to Countess de Grey's assembly . . . returned to the Duke's and had smoke and drink and to Marlborough where the Prince was playing whist and so home—alas 'home'—what a mockery.

> MARCH 27 Very sad and seedy. . . . Now for good resolutions—to drink less wine at dinner—smoke less—eschew spirits.

> MARCH 28 My 49th birthday I believe.* Anyway to act as though this were the new year.

* It was, in fact, his 50th.

The diary makes no mention of his work as editor of the *Army and Navy Gazette*—presumably it was delegated—but he was occupied for a while in preparing a statement of the case of the Nawab Nazim of Bengal who had a large financial claim against the Indian government. He took rooms in St James's Square at fifty shillings a week. He was dismayed but not surprised to find his weight remained obstinately on the wrong side of thirteen stone. On 9 June 1870 he wrote in the diary:

Charles Dickens dead.

I went to Marlborough House and told the Prince of Wales who was playing cards of Dickens' death and he was more moved than any of the company there. Much upset by it.

HRH asked me to go down yachting with him tomorrow.

The Franco-Prussian War, 1870–1

The 1850s and '60s had seen dramatic changes in the newspaper industry. Within a decade the old 'taxes on knowledge' were swept away: the advertisement duty went in 1853, the stamp duty of 4d a copy was abolished two years later, and soon after that the duty on paper was removed. The way was opened for a new kind of national daily paper, cheaper in price and more popular in tone, appealing to a new and much wider public. The unchallenged supremacy of *The Times* was at an end.

The Daily Telegraph set the pace. It first appeared in June 1855, offering four pages for 2d, and the price was soon cut to 1d. *The Times* also reduced its price, to 4d in 1855, then to 3d in 1861 but by this time the *Telegraph* was selling twice as many copies each day and its circulation was growing rapidly.

Men still spoke of *The Times* as 'the leading journal of Europe' and it continued to command respect for the breadth and reliability of its reports and the weighty seriousness of its views, but in several ways its unique influence was being eroded. The arrival of the news agencies, Reuters especially, put an end to its virtual monopoly of foreign news. Delane's chief sources of information at home, Lord Aberdeen and Lord Palmerston, had gone and the new generation of national leaders found less cause to confide in him. The extension of the suffrage meant that the professional upper middle-class readers of *The Times* were no longer the sole source of political power and influence. The men of Printing House Square were aware of all this. John Walter determined to hold the price at 3d—it was not changed for more than half a century—and to do nothing that would impair the established quality of his paper as a journal of record and responsible opinion. But it was clear, when the Franco-Prussian War broke out in 1870, that *The Times* would be facing fiercer competition than ever before.

Since his victory over Austria four years earlier, Bismarck had been working to consolidate Prussia's control over the whole German people. Some northern states had been absorbed, others were brought to heel in the North German

Confederation. The more resistant Catholic states of South Germany were induced, through their fears of French intervention, to enter into defence agreements. Bismarck moved cautiously because he did not want to provoke the Emperor Napoleon III into action until all was ready.

By the summer of 1870 the Prussian army was an efficient and confident machine, shaped by the brilliant Moltke, proved in recent battle. It needed only some open threat from France to bring Bavaria and the other southern states into the Prussian fold on a wave of nationalist feeling.

The opportunity presented itself when a group of Spaniards proposed that the vacant Spanish throne should be offered to the Hohenzollern Prince Leopold, a cousin of the King of Prussia. This was unacceptable to the French who had no wish for a Prussian-controlled presence on their southern frontier. When Prince Leopold withdrew his candidature, the French rashly pressed for Prussian guarantees that the matter would not be raised again. They pushed too hard and Bismarck goaded them to fury by rewording a telegram—the Ems telegram—to give the impression that the Prussian King had snubbed the French ambassador. On 15 July France declared war.

It was the biggest and most decisive conflict in Europe in the hundred years between Waterloo and the start of the First World War. It attracted enormous public interest in Britain and America, and Delane knew how important it was to get the best men into the field for *The Times*. 'The war has come upon us so suddenly,' he wrote to Mowbray Morris, 'that I have been obliged to act at once and yet I fear we shall be out-stripped.' (1) He wanted to send Henry Hozier and his brother John to the Prussian army but they were both British army officers on the Active List and the British government refused permission. 'Our Ministers are in such a pitiable funk,' Delane told Russell, 'that I believe they sit in Cabinet on close stools.' (2)

He had alerted Russell early in July: 'You will have to put your war paint on again if this Hohenzollern folly is persisted in.' It was universally supposed at this time that the French army would march immediately into Germany and most people expected the French to win, so the obvious place for Russell was with the Emperor Napoleon. But Napoleon kept a tight control over his own newspapers and was not prepared to have foreign—and much freer—journalists writing from his headquarters. He would welcome Russell's company, he said, but only on the understanding that he should send no reports to *The Times*. So Russell was ordered to Berlin instead.

He set off on 19 July with a young friend, Lord Ronald Gower, a son of the Duke of Sutherland who was anxious to see some fighting. They had met two years before at Dunrobin Castle where Lord Ronald had found Russell to be 'the prince of good fellows and good companions; the wittiest, kindest, merriest, most unselfish of men. Napier Sturt and he were as good as a play—both full of anecdote; and their arguments together were as amusing as they were endless'. (3)

Lord Ronald was usefully connected. His mother was Mistress of the Robes to Queen Victoria whose eldest daughter, the Princess Royal, had married the Crown Prince of Prussia in 1858. His companionship gave Russell immediate entrée to

Prussian society at the highest level. They arrived in Berlin on 21 July and took the train next day to Potsdam where they were received by the Crown Princess at the New Palace. She took a lively and liberal interest in politics and, like her husband, had no liking for Bismarck. Russell described the meeting in his diary: 'Dear Crown Princess saluted me very kindly—general conversation of the war—dreadful for Prussia—no general in Berlin when the news came—fear of fleet—harvest not in. Oh if England would but join us. Spoke of the French—liked them so much—MacMahon* "What a gentleman he is" . . . said the Prince of Wales had sent her my book etc.' (4)

Back in Berlin they were joined next day by a retired colonel of the Grenadier Guards, Christopher Pemberton, who had been sent by Delane to help Russell. Russell knew him well and greatly respected him:

> Energetic and resolute, he was so in the smoothest, softest possible manner, and he won his way by a curious admixture of strength and ease. . . . No one could be better suited for the work; a ready writer and a capital soldier, bold, courageous, fond of adventure, a sportsman, a good rider. 'Kit Pemberton' would, no doubt, have become king of war correspondents had his life been spared. (5)

They bought horses and Russell secured a waggon for his luggage and hired an English jockey, stranded in Germany when he lost all his money on Hamburg race course, to be their groom. In his book *My Reminiscences* Lord Ronald later wrote of 'Russell's love of heraldry' and told how he had the side of his waggon decorated with the picture of a large goat and the words *Che sara sara*, the emblem and motto of a more eminent Russell family to which he was not related, that of the Dukes of Bedford. It was an act of presumption that quickly led to trouble for the goat was the sign of travelling medicine sellers in Germany and it attracted much unwelcome attention from the soldiers.

On 23 July Russell called on Bismarck and was received 'with the most charming frankness'. Bismarck, in buoyant expansive mood, spent more than an hour discoursing on the situation: 'He spoke with an unreserve characteristic of the man but embarrassing to one in my position.' Russell asked to be allowed to accompany the army into the field and was told: 'You shall go. We make a general rule against newspaper correspondents going with our army, but you shall be an exception, and in a short time you will receive your *légitimation*.' (6)

The suggestion that Russell was being accorded a unique privilege was totally misleading. He was soon to learn that for Bismarck words were nothing more than weapons to be deployed in the service of his political aims.

---

* Marie Edmé Patrice Maurice de MacMahon (1808–93) had fought in the Crimea and against the Austrians in 1859, distinguishing himself at Magenta and Solferino. He was now in command of the French army in Alsace. He was President of France from 1873–9.

Next day Russell and Lord Ronald returned to Potsdam for the christening of the daughter of the Crown Princess. The whole royal family was assembled there, together with Bismarck and many other state notables. The manners of the Prussian court were more formal and rigid than those in Britain and Lord Ronald noted in his diary: 'I was struck by the profound obeisances that the German courtiers made; but the English military attaché, Colonel Walker, far exceeded in his genuflexions any of the Prussian soldiers and courtiers; indeed "he ducked as low as any barefoot friar".' (7)

Russell wrote to Alice:

> Nothing could exceed the reception I have had here. I have been presented to the King; the Queen talked with me for an hour, and I dined with them and all the big-wigs at the Palace at Potsdam on Sunday when the Princess was christened—the Crown Prince, the Princess Royal etc. Everyone is ready to give me every facility to be killed and I am to accompany either the King or the Crown Prince on the field. (8)

It was decided that Russell should accompany the Crown Prince, who was in command of the Third Army on the left of the German line. He was delighted by this for he had already formed a considerable respect for the heir to the Prussian throne: nine months before, at the opening of the Suez Canal, he had described him as 'looking a soldier every inch of all his great height'. (9) But for a while events moved too quickly for the men from *The Times*.

The Crown Prince left Berlin on 26 July 1870. Within a few days, to everybody's surprise, his troops were across the frontier and advancing into Lorraine. Russell and Pemberton had to wait for their official passes. They did not get away until 1 August and then had great difficulty catching up with the army. The trains were crowded with soldiers and military supplies and no one knew where the Crown Prince's headquarters were.

On 4 August Pemberton left to attach himself to the German Second Army in the centre of the line under the command of Prince Frederick Charles. Russell and Lord Ronald pushed on, anxious not to miss the first battles but continuously thwarted by muddy and congested roads and racked with dysentery: 'I shall never forget,' Lord Ronald wrote, 'the magnificent way in which Russell first divided and then sub-divided his last homeopathic anti-dysentery pill. Sir Philip Sydney's generosity to the woulded soldier at Lützen surely pales before Russell's quartered pilule at Vaucouleurs.' (10)

Russell finally found the Crown Prince's headquarters on 6 August two days after the German victory at Weissenbourg. He was exhausted with hard travelling and diarrhoea and his horse, even more exhausted, was miles behind. He could hear the battle being fought only a few miles away at Wörth:

> How this day passed I never knew, for at last nature asserted herself, and I fell into a horrible trance, a waking sleep, which left me conscious of what was passing and

"Our War Correspondent."
(Cartoon reproduced by kind permission of "Vanity Fair.")

12   Caricature of Russell by Carlo Pellegrini ('Ape')

13a   Sir Garnet Wolseley

13b   Sir Bartle Frere

THE ART OF POLITENESS.

Sir Garnet Wolseley: "Pardon me, my dear doctor, if I say that you have been hoaxed by gross exaggerations and transparent untruths."

Dr. Russell: "Forgive me, my dazzling young general, for mentioning that you are a pig-headed ignoramus, and don't know what you are talking about."

(Reproduced from "Fun" by kind permission of Mr. Charles Dalziel.)

13c   Russell's dispute with Sir Garnet

14   Russell wearing the uniform of a Deputy Lieutenant
for the Tower Hamlets

15   Russell's memorial in the crypt of St. Paul's

Sir William Howard Russell LL.D.
The first and greatest of War Correspondents.
Crimea 1854. India 1857.
United States of America 1861.
France 1870. South Africa 1879.
Born March 28.1820 Died February 10.1907.

yet deprived me of power of movement. At four o'clock the sounds of firing had died away. I awoke and went out. Crowds of soldiers in the streets. They reported that their comrades had gained another great victory, that the French were in full retreat, and that MacMahon was utterly routed with great loss. Here was indeed a bitter blow. In half an hour after, up came the grooms with our tired horses. Too late, alas! too late. (11)

He went to the army telegraph office and sent a brief message to *The Times*. Next morning, at breakfast with a jubilant Crown Prince, he persuaded the chief of Staff, General von Blumenthal, to give him a full account of the battle and he used this to compose his Letter. He wrote to Mowbray Morris: 'I never to my dying day will cease to regret that I was late for Wörth but my conscience is quite clear.' (12)

He toured the battlefield and was, as always, moved by the sight of so many dead, the sufferings of the wounded, the long processions of downcast prisoners: 'Is this the work of Princes or the madness of peoples?' he wrote. (13) There was one prince, at least, who shared his feelings: 'I had nearly an hour's talk with HRH [the Crown Prince] in the gateway . . . in which I had many and every reason to admire his sentiments.' (14)

He was impressed by the efficiency of the German army and also by its discipline which saved the French people from random exploitation and abuse. But he noticed, too, the unequivocal way in which every town and village they took was forced to provide money and supplies in precisely the same amounts as those which Napoleon I had exacted from places of similar size when he had marched into Germany.

Many days of hard marching followed as the Germans advanced quickly, often in pouring rain, trying to locate MacMahon's army. Russell wrote almost every day but his Letters had to go through the field postal system which meant they were taking up to ten days to reach Printing House Square. ·

The Germans were astonished when MacMahon, instead of falling back to protect Paris, led his army north to Sedan. Moltke saw his opportunity and swung his forces round in a great encircling movement. By the end of August he had the main French army effectively contained in the fortified city of Metz and MacMahon's army, which had been joined by Napoleon III, trapped at Sedan.

The decisive battle of the war was fought at Sedan on 1 September 1870. It was still dark when Russell was wakened with the message 'The Crown Prince has sent to tell you to come to the battle.' At the top of a hill looking across the Meuse to Sedan he found the King, Bismarck and Moltke—'the three terrible "Fates" before whose eyes the power of Imperial France was being broken to atoms'. (15) Once again he had found a superb vantage-point 'clearer than any battlefield I have ever seen. . . . Never may man see battle in these long-range days in such ease and safety.' (16)

He sat down, a little apart from the commanders, with his telescope, map, watch and notebook:

In the plains below us, in a bend of the Meuse, were drawn up, in most beautiful order, great blocks of cavalry. On the hills above marched the long dark masses of Prussian infantry, their positions indicated by the play of their bayonets and the sun reflected from their helmet spikes. In front of them, from every knoll, and from the edges of detached clumps of trees, spurted continual jets of smoke from literally dozens of batteries. (17)

The French made repeated efforts to break out:

The toils were closing around the prey. Indeed, it occurred to me over and over again that I was looking at some of those spectacles familiar to Indian sportsmen, where a circle of hunters closes gradually in on a wild beast marked in its lair. The angry, despairing rushes of the French here and there—the convulsive struggles at one point—the hasty and tumultuous flight from others—gave one the idea of the supreme efforts of some wounded tiger. (18)

Before the day was over the German artillery had pounded the French into submission. More than 100,000 men were taken prisoner, the Emperor Napoleon III among them. It was the end of his Empire.

Russell posted a short account to *The Times* that night but it was intercepted by French irregulars and never reached London. He spent the next two days touring the battlefield. He saw Napoleon being escorted towards Germany: 'With one hand he twisted the end of his waxed moustache; the other was placed on his hip, rather back, as if to ease off the jolting of the carriage over the rough stones. The Emperor scanned the crowd at each side wistfully. As he passed, I took off my cap, and he at once returned the salutation, as I thought, with an expression of inquiry in his face.' (19) He was affected by the sight and a few hours later he was deeply distressed to hear that his friend and colleague, Colonel Pemberton, had been killed at Sedan as he rode up to a group of French infantrymen he thought had surrendered. In his Letter to *The Times* he wrote: 'I am so shocked and grieved, as will also be as many friends as a young man ever had when they hear it, by this news, that only a sense of duty impels me to continue my narrative.' (20)

With no immediate prospect of further battles, Russell decided to travel to London and deliver the full story of Sedan in person. He wrote as much as he could' on the journey, reached Printing House Square on the evening of 5 September and wrote on through the night. Next morning's paper contained a long, powerful and accurate account of the battle with a nightmarish description of its aftermath. But it was too late. Other London papers had carried the news of the German victory two days before, telegraphed by correspondents who had watched the battle from the north and lost no time in sending the basic facts to their offices. It was clear that the nature of the reporter's job was changing and, if *The Times* wished to survive, it would have to alter its ways.

The most obvious cause of change was the telegraph. American reporters had learned to make lavish use of 'the wire' in the Civil War and now they were in Europe in force, sending their messages along the Atlantic cable with no concern for cost. The battle of Gravelotte, for example, took place near Metz on 19 August and a full account appeared in the *New York Tribune* on the 21st. The Atlantic crossing cost the paper $5,000 but war was a great stimulus to circulation and the important thing, in an area of intense and increasing competition, was to be first with the news. The American lesson was quickly learned by the British popular papers.

They learned more than this from the Americans. Among London's penny papers, especially *The Daily Telegraph* and the *Daily News*, a new style was developing, briefer and brighter than the old journalism, more personal in tone and not so ponderously earnest about affairs, sometimes vulgar and often ill-informed but often amusing and always readable. The new kind of war reporting that emerged from the Franco-Prussian War was in many ways anathema to Russell, directly opposed to all he had stood for. The new war correspondents put speed before accuracy, liveliness before truth. To them reporting was a job and a glorious game rather than a vocation. Their first duty, as they saw it, was to be first; their next was to be entertaining; then, if it was also possible, they might be informative too. Some of them were given to bragging, in print as well as in the bars, of their courage and cunning. They were often ignorant and brash and cheerfully prepared to bribe or cheat their way to a scoop. At one time Russell suspected them of conspiring to obstruct his Letters and telegrams.

Russell was fifty by this time, not so quick on his feet as his competitors and resistant to change. He had been reporting wars for twenty years. He had made his name by it and established high standards of accuracy and probity. So he went on writing long, vivid and thoughtful Letters, and Delane went on printing them. But both realized, as the war continued and other London papers continually beat them to the big stories, that—in the matter of speed—they would have to match their rivals. In fact, Russell and *The Times* had always seen speed as an important element in news-gathering, though they had always regarded accuracy as even more important and they had undoubtedly been slow to recognize the telegraph's potential. The next few months were full of painful reappraisal.

He rejoined the Crown Prince's army as it marched towards Paris. At Rheims he met Bismarck who described for him his meeting with Napoleon after Sedan. The next day, 12 September 1870, he narrowly escaped death at the hands of a group of French peasants. A few miles outside Rheims, his own horse tiring, he accepted a lift in a cart from two villagers. They took him to a hamlet where he was immediately surrounded and questioned by a menacing crowd of charcoal-burners. Their attitude hardened when he told them what he was doing in their country, and he was acutely conscious of a packet of Prussian despatches in his pocket. Fortunately, his groom turned up with the horses in the nick of time. He noted in his diary: 'The day of my miraculous escape from death at the hands of *franc-tireurs* in the village whither the Frenchmen drove me and delivered me to the enemy—never forget the experience. Back to Rheims more dead than alive.' (21)

At Montmirail he caught up with the Crown Prince who gave him a full description of the conversation that had taken place between the King of Prussia and Napoleon III when they met at the Chateau of Bellevue after Sedan. Russell made careful notes and sent the story to *The Times:*

> The Crown Prince closed the door and remained outside, the King and Emperor stood face to face. The King spoke first. God, he said, had given the victory to his arms in the war which had been declared against him. The Emperor replied that the war had not been sought by him. He had not desired or wished for it, but he had been obliged to declare war in obedience to the public opinion of France. . . . The King inquired if His Majesty had any conditions to make or to propose.
>
> 'None. I have no power. I am a prisoner.'
>
> 'And may I ask, then, where is the Government in France with which I can treat?' (22)

A month later trouble arose over this report. Russell was horrified one day to read in the papers a telegram, issued through Reuters and signed by Bismarck, which said: 'The report of the conversation between King William and the Emperor Napoleon, given by Dr. Russell, *The Times* correspondent, is founded throughout upon mere invention.'

Russell rushed off to confront Bismarck who tried to avoid him at first, then attempted to change the subject, then—when Russell would not let go—said he had never authorized the statement. But when Russell asked him to sign a rebuttal he prevaricated further, promising to look into the matter.

Russell returned to the attack next day. Bismarck, who was not used to being tackled so forcefully, now changed his ground. The King, he said, had complained of some inaccuracies in the *Times* story and asked him to issue a denial. Russell wanted to know what the inaccuracies were so that he could correct them himself, but Bismarck could not tell him. Russell said his source was 'the very best authority', there were others present at the interview, and he recorded the information he was given with the greatest care. He reminded Bismarck that he had never misrepresented or abused any of the many conversations that they had had. Bismarck was growing angry: 'I do not care,' he said, 'if you published every word I said to you, but when you hear things from that dunderhead the Crown Prince you should know better.' To which Russell replied. 'Do I understand I have Your Excellency's permission to publish your opinion of the Crown Prince?'

Such is the story as Russell told it many times in later years, and there is no reason to doubt it.* Soon after the confrontation, the German papers published what amounted to a public apology, describing *The Times*' report as only 'slightly inaccurate' and praising Russell as 'one of the best-informed and most conscientious correspondents of the whole European press'.

The Times had stood by Russell throughout and, when the row was over, Chenery wrote an article saying:

> We are well aware that our correspondent is not only incapable of founding statements on his own invention, but very unlikely to be imposed upon by the invention of others. He has been before the public for the last sixteen years, writing under every possible difficulty, in haste, in the confusion of the battle-field or the march, amid the varieties of conflicting rumours, and even of wilful misrepresentation, and his honour and judgement have never been impeached. Indeed, the faculty which is most remarkable in him is his extraordinary accuracy. Both in England and abroad justice has been done to the discernment and the habit of rapid and acute investigation which have kept him from mistakes. . . . Our opinion is that in Count Bismarck's Note we have only an instance of the tendency of public men to give off-hand denials of anything that is inconvenient. (23)

Russell was in no doubt that the root cause of the trouble was ill-feeling between Bismarck and the Crown Prince. He wrote to Alice:

> When Bismarck saw my report he perceived that the King had kept back from him much of what he had repeated to the Crown Prince. He called the King's attention to the report in a German paper. The King said it was 'not accurate' or was 'slightly inaccurate' (if so, the Crown Prince was to blame) and then B., wishing to hit the Crown Prince for his confidences to me, orders a denial to be given and is obliged to disavow it, and to make an *amende* for which he will not forgive me. (24)

In the event, there was forgiveness on both sides. In the letter just quoted Russell added: 'I like the great man personally, and if I were a Prussian I could fall down and worship him for his work.' And Bismarck later wrote: 'The English correspondent at headquarters, Russell, was himself as a rule better informed than I concerning events and intentions, and a necessary source for my information.' (25)

After Sedan, with the best of what remained of the French army trapped in Metz, the German leaders believed the war was all but over. It was only a matter of

---

* Various, but not conflicting versions of his row with Bismarck were given by Russell in *My Diary during the Last Great War* (1874) and by his obituarists in *The Times* and the *Army and Navy Gazette.*

days, it seemed, before a final capitulation. But the garrison and people of Paris, showing more spirit than their leaders, determined to resist. A Provisional Committee was set up and the city was rapidly fortified and victualled in the hope that new armies might be formed in the provinces to march to their relief. The Germans were faced with the formidable task of surrounding the city, beating back all attempts to break out and dealing at the same time with the armies and bands of armed guerillas who sprang up across France.

The Crown Prince established his headquarters at Versailles to the south-west of Paris and Russell settled down to a life that was compounded of great comfort and endless frustrations. Senior German officers continued to treat him with courtesy and consideration, but the area round Versailles was riddled with sentries, patrols and road-blocks and he found himself, like other correspondents, effectively prevented from finding out what was going on. 'You can have no idea,' he told Mowbray Morris, 'of the difficulty of a correspondent *attached to Headquarters*, just not doing anything or going anywhere. Paris is a basin and they won't let you look over the brim if they can help it—and if you ask for passes "it is better not to leave just now".' (26) It was no use seeking help from Colonel Walker, the British military attaché with the Prussians: 'No English correspondent will ever have an easy time of it as long as Colonel Walker is there, depend upon it.' (27)

He had to compose his Letters largely from information supplied by the Crown Prince or his staff officers. And they were still taking an unconscionable time getting to London.

Morris' letters from Printing House Square show a mounting desperation:

Your letters continue to linger from seven to ten days on the road. . . . We have nothing direct from Paris since the 16th but the *Daily News* publishes this morning a letter dated thence the 20th. If things do not mend with us, I shall resign my place in favour of the express manager of the *Daily News* who evidently is more acute than we are here, or else he has the devil's own luck. (28)

I beg you to use the telegraph *freely*. After any very important event, go yourself with all speed to the nearest telegraph station that has communication with London. Send by the wires, not a scrap of a few lines, but a whole letter. This is what the correspondents of the *Daily News* have been doing frequently. . . . The only objection to what I require is that something important may happen in your absence . . . at the worst, run the risk of the consquences, for it is better to do one thing surely and well than many things slowly and indifferently. (29)

It was excellent advice but easier to give than to implement. Russell replied: 'You beg me to telegraph freely. Now in the first place I cannot telegraph at all except by special favour and as yet I do not think other correspondents have had as much luck as I have had in that way, small as my fortune has been. . . . I make my telegrams as long as they will take them. Each must go through the War Council Secretary.' (30)

Russell was hampered by being on the wrong side of Paris, with much disputed territory and the River Seine between him and the Channel ports. Correspondents north of the river found it far easier to get their messages delivered quickly. And the name of *The Times* carried no weight with the French. Russell wrote again:

> The Prussians will give a pass readily enough but that is good only for the line of country they occupy lying back to Germany and so making a tremendous round, whereas the friendly neutrals and Red Cross people pass through the Prussian lines towards England and when they get among the French are let go on their way rejoicing. But the French think *The Times* is next to the King and Count Bismarck himself in potent hostility and they never would let our messengers pass unless their government ordered it and even then the Prussians might fear the seizure of correspondents' despatches with useful information. . . . I write away despairingly every day and trust to the field post one day and to chance another. (31)

Men were employed to act as couriers. Experiments were made with various routes and methods. Before long Russell was spending half his time as Morris' assistant manager in the field. 'We must try to do something great,' Morris wrote, 'before the war is over, to efface the memory of our early defeats. The *Daily News* has beaten us hollow and continues to do so.' He detailed his plans and added: 'But what's the use of all my precautions and plans, without a little luck now and then?' (32) For a while luck continued to elude them. Towards the end of 1870 Russell entrusted his Letter to a French dressmaker, Mlle Penay, *en route* for London on business, and promised her two hundred Francs if it was delivered promptly. She made good time to Dieppe but there the police searched her, found the Letter and put her in prison for five weeks.

The chief thorn in *The Times'* side was the resourceful Archibald Forbes of the *Daily News*. Nearly twenty years younger than Russell he had served five years as a trooper in the Royal Dragoons, inspired—he said—by hearing Russell lecture on Balaclava. He left the army to become a journalist and made his name during the Franco-Prussian War. He was a powerful writer but his greatest strength lay in his powers of organization and improvisation. Attached to the German army holding the northern approaches to Paris, he made full use of his good fortune. For a long time the speed with which he got his stories to London baffled all his rivals but the secret was simple. He had an arrangement with the Telegraph Master at Saarbrücken railway station. His messages got there in a few hours by train and the Telegraph Master wired them immediately to London. They generally arrived within twenty-four hours of posting.

Forbes had another, less scrupulous method. He was on excellent terms with the army commander, the Crown Prince of Saxony, who was in the habit of telling him his plans in detail. Forbes would write a story based on what he was told and telegraph it to London where it was set up in type at the *Daily News* and then held in readiness. The moment the planned operation began, Forbes rushed to the nearest telegraph office and simply wired 'Go ahead'. In this way the *Daily News* was able to appear on the London streets at noon with a full description of the bombardment of St Denis which had taken place that morning.

Forbes revealed this system in a letter to Russell nearly thirty years later (33). But Russell had quickly detected an element of chicanery in Forbes's methods. *The Times* made an attempt, during the siege of Paris, to lure Forbes from the *Daily News*. Russell was glad it came to nothing: 'I have quite altered my opinion of Forbes,' he told Mowbray Morris, 'and would not like to see him on *The Times*. He simply invents and puts false addresses etc. and I find he has a bad character. . . . He is no doubt a good but risky correspondent.' (34) And he returned to the theme two months later: 'I am so glad we escaped having Forbes. He is a low trooper, full of go but a drunken fellow and an audacious liar. He boasted that his Metz telegram was a fiction and that he invented the greater part of it—the man on the white horse firing his pistol etc. "It gives character," he said, "to the scene." This he told me.' (35)

Although he was envious of the speed with which they managed to get their stories home, Russell had no great opinion of many of his fellow correspondents in France—British and American—and acquired a reputation for being stand-offish with them. 'He seemed to have no leisure for friendly intercourse,' said Colonel Corwen, correspondent for the *Vienna Free Press* and several American papers, 'and perhaps, among all these Great Dukes, Princes and Excellencies, I was too small a potato for it, at which I should not wonder, as he served *The Times*.'

Russell was undoubtedly proud of his professional standing and the eminence of his contacts, and his manner may at times have reflected it. In his satire on English pretensions and philistinism *A Friendship's Garland*, Matthew Arnold made affectionate fun of Russell in Versailles:

Dr. Russell, of *The Times*, was preparing to mount his war-horse. You know the sort of thing—he has described it himself over and over again. Bismarck at his horse's head, the Crown Prince holding his stirrup, and the old King of Prussia hoisting Russell into the saddle. When he was there, the distinguished public servant waved his hand in acknowledgement, and rode slowly down the street, accompanied by the *gamins* of Versailles, who even in their present dejection could not forbear a few involuntary cries of '*Quel homme*!' Always unassuming, he alighted at the lodgings of the Grand Duke of Oldenburg, a potentate of the second or even the third order, who had beckoned to him from the window.

Most of Russell's dealings with Printing House Square at this time were through Morris, but at the end of September he wrote to Delane:

> I heard that it is positively the intention of the Prussians to bombard Paris. Now this is, I suppose, a perfectly legitimate operation of war against a fortified city which refuses to surrender, but I confess it is one I do not desire to witness or to chronicle and *after much reflection* I have decided on asking you to send out a successor to these headquarters . . . Of course, if they do not bombard the city but merely reduce the forts my objections fail. (36)

It was a strange stand to take. Russell was particularly fond of Paris and no one could question the strength of his humanitarian instincts in general. But he knew—better than most—what war involved. He knew, too, that the reporter's first duty was to tell what happened, not to turn his back on it. He had always previously based his conduct on C. A. Dana's precept: 'that whatever the Divine Providence permitted to occur I was not too proud to report'.*

Delane discussed 'this silly resolution of Russell's' with Morris, then wrote to Russell to say he was sure the populated areas of Paris would not be indiscriminately shelled.

Russell was not persuaded. He wrote to Morris:

> I am perfectly serious in my declaration to you that I will not have part in such an atrocity as the Bombardment of the City of Paris . . . a city of two millions of men, women and children. Delane says it will not take place. I would sooner break stones on the road—and indeed I could not describe such a piece of work for if I wrote as I felt you would very soon hear of my being ejected by the Headquarters people here. I must write as I feel. As to reputation! I don't think I should lose any. But if I did 'Cui bono'—or 'cui malo'? (37)

For all the strength of his feelings, Russell abandoned his resolution. He stayed with the German army though they did subsequently bombard Paris and destroy many of its buildings. 'As for the bombardment of Paris,' he wrote after the war, 'it was a failure considered merely as it affected the siege, and from that point of view may be deprecated as an act of simply useless severity; but if, as seems certain, it enabled the Germans to set free troops from the investing circle, it was justifiable in the strictest sense.' (38)

---

* Charles A. Dana, the American journalist, was editor of the *New York Sun*. He tried to recruit Russell at the start of the war but it was not possible to write for *The Times* and another newspaper.

At the end of October 1870 the French army in Metz surrendered, freeing 200,000 German soldiers for the siege of Paris. Ultimate defeat was inevitable but the Parisians held out for three more months, in a state of near-starvation but hoping still that one of the provincial armies might break through the ring of steel and march to their rescue. German patience was strained. They hated the guerilla tactics of *franc-tireurs* and were infuriated by the pointlessness of continued French resistance. Their treatment of the French people grew increasingly brutal and once again Delane was called on to soothe Russell's sense of outrage: 'Don't mourn over the brutality of the Germans. I dare say they are very bad—all soldiers are—but what would the French have been if they had been victorious after so many privations! Just imagine them at Berlin or in any German town on the way.' (29)

On 13 December Russell noted in his diary: '*Ave, Caesar! Morituri te salutant*! The King of Prussia is merged into Emperor of Germany.' It was the culmination of Bismarck's plans to unite the German people under Prussian control.

The elderly King William had no wish to become an emperor and the German states had no wish to lose the last vestiges of their independence, but Bismarck—as usual—prevailed. The proclamation ceremony was held in the *Galerie des Glaces*, the Hall of Mirrors, at the Palace of Versailles on 18 January 1871, and in his account, published in *The Times* on 24 January, Russell made it clear that this was the work of one remarkable man:

> Outside the circle, and some distance apart on the left of it, stood Count
> Bismarck—very pale, I thought, but never did man seem more calm,
> self-possessed, elevated as it were by some internal force which caused all eyes
> to turn on the great figure with that indomitable face, where the will seems to be
> master and lord of all.

On 23 January Russell had a stroke of luck. Taking an after-dinner stroll through the streets of Versailles, he met a French friend who swore he had just caught a glimpse of Jules Favre, the Foreign Minister of the Provisional Government in Paris, riding by in a carriage. It could mean only one thing—the defenders of Paris were seeking terms for their surrender at last. Russell confirmed the news with the Prussians and telegraphed *The Times* to give the paper its first scoop of the war. A few weeks before Morris had written in despair: 'No paper has been so badly served as *The Times* during this great war by *all* its correspondents, old and new.' (40) Now he wrote to Russell: 'You have achieved a great success by your telegram of the 24th, announcing Jules Favre's proposals for the capitulation of Paris. We have beaten everybody.' (41)

Paris capitulated on 29 January, and four days later Russell drove into the city with Odo Russell,* a diplomat who had become a close friend in Versailles, and a

---

* Odo Russell, later Lord Ampthill, had been sent by the British government to negotiate with the Prussians at Versailles. Soon after the war he was appointed Ambassador to Berlin.

carriage crammed with bread, meat and vegetables for the staff of the British embassy.

Morris was jubilant now: 'The *Daily News* people are either inexact or silly. . . . As for their being formidable, you need not be afraid of them, and you have a right to assume airs of superiority. Of late we have beaten every one hollow—news of capitulation—terms of peace—details of possession of Valerian—everything important—has been published by us exclusively, and we have beaten the knavish fellows hollow.' (42)

Russell spent the next few weeks between Versailles and Paris, watching with dismay as the French fell into recrimination and anarchy. On 1 March he was at Longchamps to see the Prussian King, the German Emperor, review his assembled armies in a great march-past: 'The roar of the Germans was deep and full of thunder, but not a bayonet quivered in the ranks. . . . Men's eyes filled and flashed and their lips trembled as they spoke of this "historical day"—this "colossal work"—but I declare there was nothing like wild delight or great outward exultation.' (43)

He was determined to get his story to London as fast as possible but he had the greatest difficulty making his way through the threatening Paris crowds to the Gare du Nord. 'I had the honour,' he wrote in his Letter, 'of receiving some impolite epithets and revilings.' But it was more serious than that. He was twice in imminent danger of assault before he abandoned his horse and made his way on foot through quieter streets to the station. He wrote on the train, sent the pages by courier from Calais and telegraphed the rest of his story to London.

He returned immediately to Paris and wrote to Morris: 'So France is now in the hands of the Jews, and a very evil day I fear is rising on Europe and on England. "It can not and it will not come to good".' (44)

The Paris he had enjoyed so much in the high days of the Empire was transformed. The pleasure capital of the world was a shambles, littered with rubble and infested with rival gangs. Russell was there to see the Communists take over the city and drive out the Provisional Government and the regular French soldiers. The Germans, astonished at the French capacity for self-destruction, rapidly withdrew, taking Alsace and Lorraine with them. The war was over and, for a while, 'chaos was come again'. By the end of March 1871 Russell was home in London.

The Franco-Prussian War has been represented as marking the beginning of Russell's decline as a war correspondent. He was getting old, certainly, for such work and he lacked the ingenuity and the unscrupulousness of many of his rivals. But there is no evidence of any falling away in his basic strengths: he had a great capacity still for hard work and an acute eye for detail; he knew how to make and use valuable contacts; his grasp of military and political realities was firmer than ever; his respect for the truth was undiminished. If British journalism was going in other directions, he had no wish—and neither had *The Times*—to follow. And his regard for the health-giving powers of a free press was strengthened. Time and again in the years after the war he argued that the presence of a critical but responsible press might have saved the French leaders, and with them France, from the disaster.

It may have been a mistake to become so much a part of the Crown Prince's establishment, but it is hard to see how he could have avoided it in the circumstances, and the position led him to a number of exclusive stories and gave him a better understanding of Prussia's policies than his competitors could claim. He got on well with the Crown Prince and many of his staff officers and developed a great respect for Moltke and Bismarck, but he could not warm to the Junker manner—stiff and prickly and arrogant, concerned with efficiency and order rather than common humanity. In a letter to Mowbray Morris, he wondered if the paper had been right to support the German cause:

> Our good friends whom *The Times* has done so much to put down the throat of John Bull will be found very indigestible. They have a profound *contempt* for England as a military power. . . . I am quite satisfied—I fear that I shall die with ample reasons for my faith, even if I do not live long—that when France went down we lost our only ally, an ally whom we had much to forgive and much to endure, but who, after all, natural or unnatural, would have stood by us. (45)

A few weeks after the end of the war he received a letter from the Crown Prince's aide-de-camp:

> His Imperial Highness will only be too glad to bestow upon our *charmant franc-tireur Anglais* the Iron Cross. Though a small reward for all the hours of pain and distress, I hope you will keep it as a memorial of this grand campaign and the gallant future Emperor who commanded the Third Army. The Crown Prince wishes you to receive it out of his own hands.

In fact it was the Iron Cross second class, which the Germans distributed widely, and it reached Russell through the post in July 1871.

He received recognition, too, from a more important quarter. It came indirectly, in a letter from Odo Russell who had been visiting Queen Victoria at Windsor Castle:

> . . . I will commit an indiscretion and confide to you that Her Majesty, our Most Gracious, has just spoken to me about *you*—your letters, your powerful support of a great and good cause and the good *you* and the *Times* have done during the crisis, in terms that would make you blush and gratify you as much as it has me. (46)

India Revisited

In May 1870 Russell had written a long letter to Bigelow, describing his personal situation:

> My eldest boy . . . Willie is far from me in China—Imperial Customs Ningpo, £400 a year to begin with and nothing to end on if he does not comprehend Chinese in a term of three years. Johnnie is in the house of Oppenheim, Alexandria, Egypt, on £300 a year on which he can scarcely live. . . . Alice at Dundalk where the 8th Hussars are quartered . . . as young as ever and just as much a child and as happy as the day is long, doing as she likes with her husband even to breaking his pipes and injuring his mathematical instruments and disordering the whole regiment. (1)

The letter discusses the problems involved in looking after Alberta, then goes on:

> Alice advises me to marry. But, my dear, I shall be fifty in a year. I am not sentimental but all the heart I had to give lies under a little patch of grass in Brompton Cemetery. So I am on the lookout for some nice person to act as chaperon and companion to the little—or big young lady, who is a fine spirited vivacious animal with an angelic voice and no application.
>
> As for the father of this lot . . . he is as usual living in a very go-lucky scrambling sort of way . . . improvident perhaps, certainly burdened by others, and so hurried in what he has to do as never to be able to think or work in any way calculated to a substantial reputation or even substantial proofs of present success. He revels in an agony of pleasure which he can not get out of—like a swimmer who has of his own accord leaped into a stream which proves too strong for him.

Soon after he wrote this the excitements of the Franco-Prussian War drove all such problems from his mind for many months. They re-emerged on his return home in the spring of 1871, though the idea of marrying again commended itself more to others than to Russell:

There is a widow besieging me strenuously. Why am I sought after by widows? I don't mean to say 'Yes' though. (2)

Everyone is asking me when I am going to marry. No one asks me 'whom' and until that is settled I have no answer to make. And why should I marry? It is true I have no one to look after me but if at 51 I am not able to look after myself I have not much business to live at all. (3)

But Mary had been dead for more than five years and as a source of support and comfort she had been virtually dead to him for much longer. Russell, always an affectionate man, was still robust and vigorous. There were times, the diary shows, when he felt a loneliness that was almost unbearable. And the diaries for the early 1870s contain some scattered and tantalizing entries which seem to hint at emotional entanglements. In the summer of 1871, when he was showing the Prince of Wales round the battlefields of northern France, he noted on consecutive days: 'AUGUST 15 A day of strange adventures never to be forgotten. AUGUST 16 Never to be forgotten and must be written now.' But if he wrote anything further it has not survived.

The entry for 18 March 1874 describes a late dinner at the Garrick Club and adds: 'I had the resolution to go away at 11.30 and bid goodbye to Hyde Park but found a very cool, or more properly speaking hot reception as I could desire.' And that summer, staying with the Delanes at Ascot Heath, he noted: 'Today gave me one of the sensations of my life.' (4) But once again there is no elucidation.

Fortunately, Russell was busy enough to save him from brooding too deeply.

He wrote two books about the Franco-Prussian War—a personal account, *My Diary during the Last Great War*, and a study of its strategy, *The Campaign of 1870–1*. He worked intermittently on a promised contribution to Collins' *National History of Great Britain*: an awful literary catastrophe for me' (5) which weighed on his spirits almost as heavily as the novel had done.

The connection with the *Army and Navy Gazette* was maintained. Sometimes he was actively involved as editor, more often he delegated the work. In August 1871 he took R. J. Wood into partnership. Three years later J. Routledge was appointed editor, but Russell continued to keep a supervising eye on the magazine and often wrote articles for it.

His income was high but his spending, as always, out-reached it. His style of living is indicated by an inventory of the wine in his cellar—'178 bottles claret, 2 sherry, 291 champagne, 58 port' (6). As the children dispersed, he sub-let the house at 18 Sumner Place and lived in rented rooms in central London but continued to maintain a considerable establishment. The diary speaks of a German cook at £18 a year, 'a nice little housemaid' at £14 and a butler/valet who was paid £45 a year plus beer money. Early in 1872 he had to raise a loan of £4,000 from Coutts, the bankers, to be repaid at the rate of £600 a year. The Duke of Wellington stood security.

In the summer of 1872 Alberta became engaged to Richard Edmund Longfield who belonged to an Irish landed family with a fine Geogian house, Longueville, at

Mallow in County Cork. On 13 July Russell noted: 'Longfield père told me he would give Dick £1,000 a year and settle £600 a year on Alberta. I told him I had no money but at my death she would have the Trust Fund as Alice would make no claims to it and the boys would be provided for. . . . Alberta sang very well in the evening.'

They were married at Holy Trinity, Brompton, on 19 September, and the young couple set off for a Continental honeymoon, leaving Russell in deeper money trouble than ever:

OCTOBER 3 1872 Seedy. Bills of Alberta's pounding in fast and furious—ah me.

OCTOBER 9 To Garrick and paid two very dear dinner bills, £7 9s. This is more than I can bear.

JANUARY 4 1873 . . . Evelegh's bill £151 17s 6d for doing up 18 Sumner Place due—nearly did up me.

With both daughters married and William working in China, his problems as a parent centred on his wayward younger son John. The job with Oppenheims did not last many months and John was back in London by the summer of 1872, sponging on his father and infuriating him with his feckless behaviour. Russell ordered him out of the house in mid-December but he was back again before the month's end. The trouble continued into the New Year: 'APRIL 5 1873 . . . Saw John at 11. He was sullen, silent and uncandid. . . . I fear he is beyond help and have little hope. Brighton, Cheltenham, Bonn, Woolwich, Paris, Alexandria, the same story—idleness, self-indulgence, gambling and constant promises . . .'

Russell was away from London for most of the year, and towards the end of it he found John a job with General Gordon, who had just been appointed Governor of the Sudan. The Khedive, whose influence Russell used in securing the appointment, had ordered Gordon to suppress the slave trade in the Sudan, an arduous task in hostile circumstances. Gordon took a small staff of Europeans with him and soon found them unsatisfactory: 'The utter helplessness of my staff is lamentable,' he wrote, 'I have driven them like a herd before me. . . . You might as well have two ladies as Anson and Russell.' (7) By August 1874 Anson was dead and John Russell was at Gondokoro, too ill to be moved. Gordon nursed him till he was well enough to begin the journey home and wrote a reassuring letter to his father:

I deeply regret my harshness to your son, and I wish I could have helped him. . . . Nothing but the state of his health, his inexperience making it worse, induced me to wish to be rid of him. You may therefore put down to me, as I have said, the blame, and not to your son, who, I think, if he was in a healthy atmosphere, would do good work. (8)

Russell continued to enjoy the grand life. In May 1871 he took Alberta to Buckingham Palace to be presented to the Queen: 'Queen asked Sydney who I was . . . very graciously disposed, smiled at or on me.' (9) Soon after he was invited by the Prince of Wales to meet again the Prussian Crown Prince and Princess. A few weeks later he accompanied the Prince of Wales on a visit to Ireland in the royal yacht.

When the Prince became dangerously ill with typhoid fever towards the end of 1871 and the whole nation and anxious, Russell was more affected than most:

DECEMBER 12 At 2 a.m. crowd of 30 round Marlborough House. Policeman on duty. Two servants in little lodge where book is kept, four or five outside. Lord H. Lennox passed in—as we waited in came telegram borne by wild-looking man. HL opened and read it—'Restless night—no sign of improvement.' Alas! we passed out into cold grimy London. My poor Prince.

Russell's feelings about his friend were always mixed—respect, admiration and affection compounded with irritation, disapproval and occasional disgust—but at the moment of crisis he remembered only the firm foundations of their friendship. He wrote to Alice:

My darling Waddy.
   I have been very unhappy about the Prince. Had he died the nation would never have known what excellent qualities he had for they only saw the faults in his character. . . . I believe he will rise from his couch an altered man. Every day I had a line or telegram from Sandringham—I do not put my trust in Princes but I do feel a very strong attachment to his person. (10)

The danger was over early in the New Year and Russell was soon able to see the Prince again:

MARCH 2 1872 . . . in presently came Prince, wheeled in chair, with Princess very lovely and thin and radiant. She is a dear dear little woman. PW fat white bald but his eye bright and clear and 'settled'. . . . We all paid respects, shake hands in turn. PW very kind and shook mine warmly. I was so moved to see him. . . . Prince passed several dishes—ate less than before. . . . He is full of fun as ever.

Four days after making this entry in the diary, Russell set off abroad with the Duke of Sutherland and 'two tin boxes, one uniform case, two handbags, cane and umbrella, hat box, fur coat, rifle, bath, fur boots and mackintosh'. They went to Paris which Russell found 'like a faded old courtesan in the rags of her former splendour', then through Italy: 'It is great to travel with a Duke anywhere and it is luxury of motion indeed when in Italy your Duke is *the* friend of Garibaldi.' (11)

They went on to Egypt to renew old friendships, then back to Italy to see the excavations at the Forum in Rome and join the Prince of Wales who was on a convalescent trip. Russell's hopes that the Prince might be reformed by his sufferings were disappointed: 'Alas! am so sorry to see him frivolous as ever.' (12)

Russell travelled widely during the 1870s, often abroad, regularly to Ireland, to Scotland each summer for the shooting, to a succession of noble houses —Stratfield Saye, Belvoir Castle, Sandringham. He spent four months of 1873 covering the Vienna Exhibition for the *New York Times*. The following year he was in Egypt again, where the Khedive consulted him about his mounting financial troubles. Russell, predictably, had no useful advice to give about this but he did express his belief that Egyptian society would be the healthier for a free press: 'Great advantage of free press is that one gets at the truth. It may be mixed with falsehood but the truth can be got at. Here truth is at the bottom of a well which is full and deep with muddy waters and no divining machine.' (13)

He met de Lesseps again—'dear old firebrand'—and found him angrier than ever at British obstructionism. He also came across the brand of racist brutality that had so outraged him in India. At a dinner party in Alexandria he heard a man called Day 'recounting exploits in the way of punching Bedouins and shooting at them with rifles . . . he took to shooting at them with bullets and hit one through the back. "Brutal," exclaimed I, "Horribly brutal," and so to bed. Now this good man Mr. Day should simply be had before the magistrates in any civilised country.' (14) On the idea of Egypt's independence, he noted: 'That is a question which will spring on us some day like a lion out of ambush.' (15)

While in Egypt he heard of the death of Mowbray Morris. Theirs had been a long and sometimes close association and Russell owed much to Morris' conscientious management, especially of his finances. But he had never really liked the man, finding him cold and coarse: 'Morris,' he once wrote, 'is unfit to deal with men of warmer and quicker natures than his.' (16) He had seen little of Morris in the three years since the end of the Franco-Prussian War and now he noted rather callously in his diary: 'MAY 15 1874 News of Mowbray Morris' death! Is he much regretted? How the links in the worn-out chain are snapping. I am tugging heavily at my anchor in a rough sea.'

Russell still wrote occasional pieces, usually book reviews, for *The Times* and several of Delane's sharp little notes have survived:

I don't think you have given yourself anything like time enough to write this last article. It is full of small points of detail but contains no such general summing up of the book as the public will naturally expect. (17)

I publish your article on Russia and Khiva tomorrow. . . . I send you a bundle of slips to write upon for I can't abide the paper you use. It seems intended for the other end of the human animal. (18)

They saw much of each other and the friendship even survived a strange incident which occurred in September 1873 when they were travelling with friends on the train from Inverness to Dunrobin. The talk turned to the exact day of the death of Napoleon III earlier that year. Russell said he could easily settle the argument by referring to his diary:

> It was taken out. But I could not find my glasses. Delane who sat near me said 'I will read it for you.' I had not an idea that I had ever said or written a word against him in my life but I said 'It would be better not' jokingly, but as they were eager as to the date I handed over page January 14 to him. *Turn and see!* (19)

The entry, which Delane read out to the compartment, said, 'I look on Delane as a dangerous guide though my very good friend. And he lies so.' Russell was mortified:

> Never could be greater astonishment than mine when he read it out—my backbone grew red hot I am sure. He behaved like an angel—read it aloud again—handed it to Ronny, to Hartington! Lascelles! How *they* enjoyed it but Ronny, I think, entered into my feelings.

In *The Importance of Being Earnest* Gwendolen says, 'I never travel without my diary. One should always have something sensational to read in the train.' But the incident was altogether too sensational for Russell and he went over the matter in his diary next day:

> SEPTEMBER 14 1873 Slept but little—queer in my inwards—every way. . . . The more I think of yesterday the more I am petrified. Delane said the Duke told him so I don't in the least doubt it was H.R.H. who *lied so* and that when I wrote in my haste I was wrong. But what millions of chances against such catastrophe! Certain that for 20 years Diary not a word could be found such as that of January 14. Written after contention with H.R.H. when I was flatly contradicted and told my authority was wrong and when I was hot as to Khiva* and believed Russians meant mischief and was wroth because J.T.D. took it so coolly and considered them contemptible. . . . I wonder how I should take such an entry? It is well we don't read what our friends write of us.

On the offending page of the diary Russell added a footnote: 'What a gross injustice to dear Delane—and to my regard for him!' But Delane was not offended. Two years later we find him writing to Russell: 'There never were two people, one of whom liked the other so much as I have always done yourself, who see so little of each other abroad yet live so near.' (20)

---

* The Russians had just annexed the state of Khiva, south of the Aral Sea in Central Asia. It is now part of Uzbekistan.

The affair confirmed Russell in his suspicions of the Prince of Wales. On the day before the embarrassing scene in the railway carriage, preparing to leave Abergeldie Castle where he had been shooting with the Prince, he had written in the diary:

On the whole not sorry to leave. The Prince's caprices—the high whist—practical jokes do not at all suit such an elderly poor gentleman as I am and O.M.* is not pleasant or profitable and Aylesford is an ass. . . . The Prince does not improve. His love of trifles grows on him—so does his self-will—his indifference to feelings of others in spite of his real kindness and goodness of heart. There is a riddle. He must have amusement. He never reads—not even a newspaper except a pet par here and there—or a French novel. He loves whist—hates losing—or paying—says he 'Be sure you get your money from Hartington' and yet he lets me go off minus £11 he owes me. He is very quick and observant—his memory is frightfully good—but he only looks at the outside of things. His language is not bad but he permits filthy words in others and seems to like it. (21)

Early the next year, after dining at Marlborough House, he noted:

PW rather disagreeable and chaffy. He is becoming very fond of innuendo and sly references He attacked me sharply as to article in *Army and Navy Gazette* and told me 'You had a few friends left in the Brigade of Guards. You have none now.'. . . I defended myself. . . . After dinner he walked off arm in arm, I may say, with the slimy little Jew Lawson to the Gaiety where he had a rendezvous to see N. Farrer etc. As a punishment I was not asked but told to meet PW at Marlborough at eleven. I didn't go till 12.15 and he was gone. (22)

There was much about his aristocratic friends that Russell disliked and he was painfully conscious of the contrast between the lives they led and those of England's poor. Walking back from a day's shooting with the Duke of Cambridge in East Anglia, on 15 January 1873, he noticed the anonymous graves of a workhouse:

There they lay, these warriors of labour whose toil had created the wealth I saw around me, without a stone or even a wooden cross to mark their resting places and identify them from the beasts that perish. I do not think I have ever been in any country where the humblest of the dead were ever treated with such contumely. . . . I wish those who own the soil were more considerate for those poor ones who till it for them.

---

* The Hon. Oliver Montague, a young cavalry officer who had an enduring romantic passion for the Princess of Wales.

He had scant respect for many of the Prince's friends. In June 1875 Colonel Valentine Baker, commanding officer of the 10th Hussars and brother of the African explorer, was charged with assaulting a young woman in a railway carriage. The Marlborough Club seethed with excitement:

> Everyone with a theory—some that it is a plant which is nonsense, others hysteria, others bad Baker. Duke's orders to suspend him. It is a dreadful scandal and I am inclined to think all probability is against him but immense efforts will be made to get it 'squared'. . . . Baker's old adjutant very zealous but not, I fear, very judicious at vindicating B at girl's expense. A.E. [Arthur Ellis] says P.W. very unlucky in his friends, b—s, violators, cheat card sharpers . . . (23)

On this occasion, however, the best efforts of the 'old boy network' came to nothing. Colonel Baker was convicted and sentenced to twelve months' imprisonment.

By this time Russell was deeply involved in the Prince of Wales' plans for a state visit to India. Sir Bartle Frere,* a veteran of Indian administration under the Company and the Crown, was in charge of the arrangements and the Prince wanted Russell to join his suite as 'historian' and press representative with the title of Honorary Private Secretary. *The Times* offered him £300 a month plus expenses to act as their special correspondent. The rival London papers complained vociferously but nothing was done about it and the matter continued to rankle with other journalists covering the tour, especially Archibald Forbes.

Discussion of the trip went on throughout the summer of 1875. Russell found himself alone in his attitude towards imperialism: 'I had everyone against my view. I hold that we can not *go on* holding India by bullet and bayonet.' (24) At Balmoral in September, the Princess of Wales, who was distressed that she could not go too, made him promise to write her 'nice long letters to me direct, all to myself'. (25)

Russell kept a special India Diary—from the beginning of October 1875 till May the following year—and it is far more revealing than the formal account which he wrote for publication *The Prince of Wales' Tour: A Diary in India*.

They sailed from Brindisi on the royal yacht *Serapis* on 16 October. Russell's wardrobe included a levee dress (coat and blue trousers); full dress (white trousers with gold stripes); evening dress and a cocked hat; day dress and an Indian helmet; undress uniform; patrol uniform; an alternative evening dress (white vest, white tie, white collar); and what he called his *Serapis* mess dress.

It was a pleasant voyage, with visits to Athens and Cairo, much card-playing and deck-tennis, the Prince stalking the deck and potting away at passing birds. Russell

---

* Sir Bartle Frere (1815–84) joined the Bombay civil service in 1834 and worked in India for the next thirty-three years. He distinguished himself during the Mutiny and was appointed to the Viceroy's Council in 1859. Later he became Governor of Cape Colony and High Commissioner of South Africa.

was angered when he heard the Prince had been told by the British government to give a chilly reception to the child ruler of Hyderabad, the Nizam: 'Sir Bartle Frere gave me the Nizam papers to read which filled me with disgust—to bully this wretched scrofulous bandy-legged boy to come to Bombay as a mere exhibition of tyrannical force and spite. . . . Oh shame! Can there be any generosity left in the race?' (26) He even allowed a hint of his feelings to appear in the bland pages of his official book: 'It is well sometimes that we have no foreign critics, no external public (in Europe or Asia) to bear upon our conduct in India.' (27)

Russell formed a deep respect and liking for Sir Bartle, though he argued repeatedly against his conviction that the British had a divine mission to rule India and convert its peoples to Protestant Christianity. During the extensive tour, amid all the splendid ceremonies and endless banquets, Russell noticed with dismay that British attitudes had changed little in the eighteen years since the Mutiny. 'Horrid British snobs in attendance', (28) he noted in Northern India, and towards the end of their journey he commented: 'It is so much to be regretted that the Prince has never had a talk with a peasant. What a flood of light the *ryot* [peasant] could let in! He has never even spoken to a *Baboo* [native clerk]!' (29)

One of the Prince's aides-de-camp was a Royal Navy lieutenant, Lord Charles Beresford, who wrote in his *Memoirs* many years later:

Dr. W. H. Russell, the famous war correspondent, who in his letters to *The Times* during the Crimean War did so much good service, was a most delightful companion. He is remembered by all who knew him, both for his talents and for his sympathetic and affectionate disposition, and his unfailing sense of humour. He was one of my greatest friends . . .

The Prince having requested him to provide himself with a uniform, Dr. Russell designed a kind of Ambassadorial dress of great splendour, with so generous a gold stripe to his kersey breeches, that we told him he had gold trousers with a white stripe inside. These effulgent garments unfortunately carried away when the doctor was climbing upon an elephant, on his way to a Durbar. I executed temporary repairs upon his person with safety pins; and implored him not to stoop. But when it came to his turn to bow, bow he must; the jury rig parted, and a festoon of white linen, of extraordinary length, waved behind him. Fortunately, the assembled Indian Princes thought it was part of his uniform. (30)

The ill-luck with horses, which had lamed Russell on his first visit to India, had not left him. Beresford recalled:

At Main Mir, during the ceremony of a great review of the troops, Dr. Russell, who was riding among the suite mounted on a half-broken Arab, was suddenly heard to shout 'Whoa, you villainous brute!' At the same moment, several of the suite were knocked endways. The Arab then got the bit in his teeth and tore away past the Prince down the whole line. Dr. Russell's helmet was jerked to the back of his head, his *puggaree* [muslin scarf worn round the hat] unfurled in a long train floating behind him, he vanished into the distance and we did not see him again until dinner time. (31)

They were royally entertained everywhere they went and the Prince enjoyed himself slaughtering big game of all shapes and sizes—wild boar, tigers, bears. In February 1876 they were hunting in the Terai jungle of southern Nepal and on the 14th Russell wrote in his diary:

> . . . saw bear tearing through long grass and then dropping in it. Prince came down nearly opposite to me so that the bear was between us. . . . I called out 'Bear right before you Sir.' In another moment out it came. Prince fired and I think hit it. It fell for an instant, then ambled to the bank near me, not 20 yards off. I fired and hit it but it went on a little and was hit by Probyn, I think, in the head and lay dead. . . . Prince asked me if I fired and I did not venture to say I had hit as I found he claimed it, perhaps rightly.

Russell was not a natural courtier and the need always to defer to the Prince was a considerable strain. But his discretion could be relied upon. A note in the diary for 2 March 1876 reads: 'At 7.30 Prince went round to see Jung's ladies.* I was requested to say nothing about it so I will not.'

It was a very busy time for Russell. He had to attend all the formal occasions and take notes of the long repetitive speeches. He telegraphed reports to *The Times* and then composed fuller descriptions for his Letters. Delane was appreciative and reassuring: 'I am very sorry,' he wrote, 'to hear of the indignities offered to the natives. But what could you expect with such a suite? My only wonder is that nothing worse has occurred.' (32) But the Prince was not the easiest of masters, constantly niggling about details, blaming Russell for every tiny error—even misprints—in *The Times*' reports:

> FEBRUARY 20 1876 . . . I am so sick of the mail coming in and the Prince's very captious criticisms . . . at small mistakes.

> FEBRUARY 22 . . . Prince sent for me to bother and potter about little matters in *The Times*. It is most trying but I am now very case-hardened and laugh the matter off outwardly—mistakes are most annoying.

There were limits to Russell's patience, though, and he was readier than most to make his feelings plain to the Prince. One night on the voyage home, when Russell had retired early to his cabin, he was summoned by a messenger to join the Prince's company:

* Sir Jung Bahadur, the Prime Minister and effective ruler of Nepal, had led the Gurkha forces which helped the British to take Lucknow in 1858.

I put on smoking suit and went to saloon where I found him, Hardinge, Annesley, Knollys, Gough etc.. 'We have sent for you to improve our minds—we want to be instructed etc.' I resolved not to try impossibilities. I said 'I have been writing all day, was tired etc.' so he said 'You have nothing to write about now.' 'Your Royal Highness must allow me to be the best judge of that.' 'Oh! there's a rebuke.' (33)

The Prince's respect for ceremonial and his insistence on correct procedures and costume was another source of irritation. At Gibraltar the Prince, who had been initiated into the Order of Freemasons seven years before to the great annoyance of the Queen, presided over a Masonic ceremony for the laying of a foundation stone for a new market place. In his diary Russell spoke of the 'most stupid vulgar ludicrous ceremony, surrounded by fussy imposters in ridiculous toggery . . . Prince of Wales very solemn and impressive. . . . he insisted on my going.' (34)

It had been a long trip and Russell felt tired and jaded before the end. They stopped in Spain where he had a long talk with the King, then in Portugal where the King kept him up till after three in the morning 'discoursing in clouds of baccy. . . . Lord I am so tired. Kings are bores after an hour or two.' (35)

The next day the Prince was host to the Portuguese royal family on board the *Serapis:*

After the King had gone Glyn [Captain of *Serapis*] came to the bridge where I was and asked me to hold the Star of his Order which was coming off. I stuck it in buttonhole of coat. At that instant up came W [the Prince of Wales] and saw it at once. 'You should not make a jest of these things etc.' He evidently regards them as holy. Holy orders I suppose . . . (36)

But on one occasion at least, on the voyage home, Russell was able to score off the Prince:

APRIL 4 1876 . . . I came to lunch without necktie. H.R.H. observed it and sung out at once so I ran down to my cabin, put on tie, buttoned up patrol jacket over it and came up. After a time he thought he would catch me and said 'Have you a cravat?' 'Yes Sir.' 'Let me see.' I opened amid great applause.

They landed at Portsmouth on 11 May 1876. The final weeks of the voyage had been clouded for Russell by the news from home. He had stood surety for one of his in-laws, Peter Burrowes, and now found himself called upon to find nearly £500 to meet his debts. And John Thadeus Delane, his oldest and closest friend, was seriously ill.

The diary over the next months charts the decline of the once all-powerful editor:

AUGUST 9 1876 . . . Delane and I at aquarium. Poor friend. He was low and miserable indeed—the dinner was bad—nothing pleased him. Alas! He was ill, very ill. 'My dear Russell! I am done! I am done!' He said this several times varied with 'Dear Billy, it's all up with me!' He knew more of himself than we did. He went to the office about 10.30. 'I can't give them a chance. I can't afford to be away.'

APRIL 10 1877 Called on Delane. Ah me! how broken he is to be sure! thin, old, bowed, speaking slowly, with glassy eye. Why will he not give up and go away ere it be too late?

JUNE 1 . . . Delane and I dined at Garrick, very very sad, when slowly and his eyes filled he said 'If I should not say it to you to whom should I say it? I am done.' Alas! Alas! We talk of going abroad together. It would be very wretched for me but I would go could I do him any good.

OCTOBER 22 . . . to Delane whom I found in the old chair in the old room but oh! so changed in everything else—no papers! no piles of proof! no mess of letters! no editor's work in fact. Well it was to me a sad interview indeed. I am very fond of him and he was ever my champion—guide sometimes—friend always.

Worn out by the strain of editing *The Times* for thirty-six years, Delane retired in November.

Russell had other troubles too. He found himself accused of accepting £500 from one of the Bengal Princes, the Nawab Nazim, to promote his claims for compensation from the Indian government in the British press. The accusation was groundless. Seven years before he had written a statement of the Nawab's case for use in the law courts but he had written nothing in the papers about it and had received no payment. The affair soon blew over. His family problems were more intractable.

Alice and Alberta were busy with their own families but both the boys were home again. William, who was on leave from the Chinese Imperial Customs, had married and Russell deplored his choice: 'Constance is quite a poor weedy thing—no repose, no manner—lively enough in a soubrette sort of fashion but of no "use" to a poor man—in bad health—not well-instructed or adroit. Although she must have seen I disliked it, she would take up my diaries one after the other and open them.' (37) John, back from the Sudan, was even more troublesome: 'John sullen—he always thinks he is the most ill-used of men.' (38)

Russell offered to pay his passage to the colonies and a modest weekly allowance 'against starvation' but he made no move to leave home:

FEBRUARY 19 1877 John turned out at 11.50 and began some rubbish about a headache which made me furious and I turned on him savagely. He is incurable

and in the middle of my speech he smiled. I could not help calling him a
grinning fool.

MAY 15 A most wretched time. I resolved never to see John if he came in after
hours. This he invariably did, often in drunk and Stephens letting him in. He
never came to dinner and I never saw him at breakfast. So our life.

At the end of May, however, Russell arranged a job for John in the consular
service and took lodgings for him until a post was found abroad.

He worked hard, amid all these distractions, on his official account of the Indian
tour. The Prince of Wales took a close interest in its progress:

APRIL 10 1877 . . . At 3.30 went to Marlborough House to see PW by
appointment. He pounced at once on book and soared over pages as merlin over
field till he swooped on unhappy titlark of an error as to uniform, buttons,
names, orders—saying justly 'My dear Billy, if worth mentioning at all let it be
stated correctly' . . .

The Prince's corrections and Russell's own concern for accuracy gave the
publishers a trying time and they wrote to him in remonstrance: 'Your elaborate
corrections have far exceeded all our previous experience or conception. The
printer's account has just come in—cost of original composition of the whole
volume £94 2s 4d; cost of corrections and cancelled matter £473 17s!!!' (39)

The book was published in 1877, a fat handsome volume which gave an
exhaustive and discreet but readable account of the journey with a great deal of
background information about the places visited.

In September 1877 Russell was at Dunrobin Castle in the Highlands. He wrote
to Alice: 'The house is full, 30 to 36 to dinner every day, and it is surely the
greatest comfort in the world for a poor devil like me to be at home in such a place
and to be treated as if I were a prince.' (40) General Ulysses S. Grant was in the
company, having recently completed his second term as American President, and
in the same letter Russell said: 'He turned out to be very modest and very shy but
most agreeable and far better than we heard he was likely to prove. His wife is
hideous.'

At Trentham on 1 January 1878 he noted: 'Sweet (to me) are the uses of
aristocracy! Here I have all that wealth can command and taste suggest but above
all what I value most the friendship of a very fine character and the most charming
society possible—books, the sports of the field, seclusion, liberty—all are mine.'

Russell was a frequent visitor to Trentham during these years and it seems likely
that, some time in the mid-1870s, he formed a long-lasting relationship with a
member of the Sutherland household. No documentary evidence has survived,
either in the public records or in family papers, but an elderly woman, who lives in
England, has no doubt at all that her father was the eldest of three children born to
Russell and a woman whose name is unknown. The three children were, it seems,

brought up in the household and employed there for some time. Their mother was either a close friend of the family or an employee, possibly a governess.

In his sexual and social attitudes Russell was very much a man of his time. He undoubtedly suffered, as many Victorians did, from the conflict between the demands of a vigorous and affectionate nature and the rigid conventions of social life. He needed a loving relationship with a woman but was too puritanical to adopt the promiscuity of the Marlborough Club. In December 1874, for example, he was writing to the papers to protest against the incursion of the cancan and the exhibition of near-naked women at some London theatres. (41) As a respected member of society he could not contemplate the idea of marrying a servant. But his character was such that any attachment he formed was sure to be serious and enduring even if it did not involve marriage. And if he did form such an attachment, he would certainly keep it as secret as possible. With friends like the Sutherlands, it would not be difficult to cover his tracks and, at the same time, make sure his 'secret family' were well cared for.

There is no explicit mention of such a liaison in his diaries, but three widely-separated entries hint at a relationship to which he owed covert loyalty. On 9 March 1876, during the tour of India with the Prince of Wales, he noted: 'Poor, ill, miserable. I was off to bed before supper to my tent indeed. I met a lot of auld lang syners. Very heavy flirt with a large cavalry woman decidely handsome. Poor Ada. I am very sorry. What can I do?' On New Year's Day 1883, he wrote: 'God knows I can make no prospect this year—I care not to look forward. What can I say of the past? And yet I began 1882 with some hope—some chance of escape. Alas! I only thought then of some escape for her and of some ease for myself from the tension.' And later the same year, when he had fallen in love with the Italian Countess Malvezzi, he wrote: 'NOVEMBER 6 1883 . . . I am thinking of her and of the other her and of the trouble and am in pain to boot all day.'

But there is no further clue in any of his papers as to the identity of this 'other her' and no mention of children.

During 1878 he paid several visits to Paris, breakfasting with *The Times'* correspondent, Henri de Blowitz,* and visiting Lord Lyons at the British embassy. Towards the end of the year he dined with the Prince and Princess of Wales at the Café Anglais and found himself involved in a quarrel between the Prince and his old friend, Lord Ronald Gower. It seems, from Russell's diary, that Lord Ronald had written an angry letter to the Prince, complaining that the Prince had accused him of being a member of an association 'for unnatural practices'. The Prince sought Russell's help as a go-between and in preventing the row from becoming public knowledge. Russell defended his friend's reputation and provoked a princely outburst:

---

* Henri de Blowitz (1825–1903) was Russell's successor as *The Times'* most influential correspondent. He became Paris correspondent in 1875 and three years later, at the Congress of Berlin, scored one of his greatest coups by getting details of the Treaty to London in time for them to be published as the document was being signed.

'I'm d—d if I stand this sort of thing any more. People take advantage of my position and accuse me of all sort of things. It's been on now for two years—one woman writes to ask me if I had taken away her character—a man writes to ask me if I accused him of cheating at cards and another writes to know if I had called him a b—. It's really time to put an end to this sort of thing.' He did not say how. (42)

It is not clear how much Russell was able to help in the dispute but he succeeded in retaining the friendship of both antagonists.

The turning of the year found him, as usual, in a gloomy frame of mind—'very sad and anxious about the future'. (43) He was in debt again and forced to borrow a further £850 from Maitland Dashwood: 'The load of debt on me is killing. That is the demon power which binds me.' (44) He had been losing again at the whist tables:

'. . . my fondness for playing cards is a remarkable illustration of the futility of experience in correcting men's failings or vices. It has been uniformly and for years attended by ill-fortune and I do not play well so "luck" and play are against me and yet I go on.' (45) Although he spent much time at his London clubs and visiting his many friends, he was often lonely: 'I dined at home *solus cum solo*. . . . Oh Lord! It is not good for man to be alone.' (46)

On his birthday, 28 March 1879, he noted: 'Am I 58 or 59 today? Anyway too old for any future now.' But he was, in fact, on the eve of his last campaign as a war correspondent.

The Last Campaign

'Nothing but Zulu Zulu Zulu. It's a miserable business.' When Russell wrote this in his diary—on 6 March 1879—the British army had already suffered a terrible defeat at the hands of Cetewayo's Zulu warriors. One thousand two hundred men of Lord Chelmsford's army had been wiped out in their isolated camp at Islandlwana:

FEBRUARY 11 1879 . . . Great disaster to British in Zulu country on 22 January. Chelmsford obliged to retreat. 24th cut to pieces and lost Colour! Forty officers killed. I was knocked all of a heap.

The Zulu War was the beginning of a fierce struggle for control of South Africa that was to go on for twenty-five years. To the east the Zulus, highly organized and militaristic, had found an ambitious and inspiring leader in Cetewayo. In the south and around the coast the British, concerned for their long sea route to India, ruled the provinces of Cape Colony and Natal and maintained naval and trading bases at Simonstown and Durban. Uneasily sandwiched between these two were the original European settlers of the region, the Dutch Afrikaners—the Boers—who had trekked north from the Cape forty years before to escape British control and establish independent republics beyond the Orange and the Vaal rivers, the Orange Free State and the Transvaal. There were frequent clashes with the resurgent Zulus, and the British made no secret of the fact that they would only feel completely safe if they could bring the Boer areas under their control in a federation.

The first moves towards federation had already been made. In 1877 the Boers asked for British military help against the Zulus and the British exploited this to annex the Transvaal. Russell's old friend, Sir Bartle Frere, now the Governor of Cape Colony and High Commissioner for South Africa, sought to use the continued Zulu threat to further the cause of federation. In December 1878, in defiance of his orders from London, he issued an ultimatum—demanding the disbandment of the Zulu army—which Cetewayo was bound to reject. The war followed swiftly and inevitably.

In May 1879 Russell heard that Sir Garnet Wolseley, whose successes against the Ashanti in West Africa had made him a national hero, was being sent to South Africa to assume command. He determined to go with him. *The Times*, edited by Thomas Chenery, already had correspondents in the field. So had the *Standard* which Russell next approached. He came to an arrangement, finally, with *The Daily Telegraph*:

> MAY 27 1879 . . . Lawson* came about three and at once closed, explained situation, he had plenty of people out but if I was bent on going he would be happy to have my services, not to do rough riding work or bother about telegrams but to do my old world sort of correspondence with reminiscences and a general view of affairs and as much light reading as I pleased to put in, to remain out as long as I pleased.

He was offered £200 a month which had to cover all his expenses.

They sailed from Dartmouth on 30 May. Sir Garnet Wolseley, who had met Russell in the Crimea, had no time for war correspondents. In his *Soldier's Pocket Book*, published in 1869, he had derided them as 'the race of drones . . . those newly-invented curse to armies, who eat the rations of fighting men and do not work at all', and his opinions had been in no way modified by what he saw of the correspondents in Ashanti. But he respected Russell, particularly for his work in the Crimea, and a friendship was formed strong enough to survive their opposing views on imperial and military matters.

On the voyage to the Cape Russell did his homework assiduously. Sir Garnet gave him all the unclassified background papers to read:

> JUNE 9 1879 . . . The Blue Books [official government documents] are not edifying reading but in fact the most vital parts of our transactions never see the light as they are kept back and published in 'confidential reports' and kept dark. For many years Cetewayo kept on digging away at the Natal Government to interfere with the Boers of the Transvaal and all we did was to say we would make representations at Pretoria and to urge him to rest in quiet.

> JUNE 10 . . . read Blue Books. The wonderful way in which Sir Bartle Frere is involved in the shedding of blood and cattle-lifting excites my admiration. I observe we always punish others for our own faults. . . . We are forever talking of the peace and order which prevail under a Government which is forever at war somewhere or other. . . . Mr. Gallagher who looks after Webber's horses says 'There's not a black alive I don't know the thricks of' and thinks himself superior to all the coloured races together . . .

---

* Edward Levy-Lawson (later Lord Burnham) was the son of the founder of *The Daily Telegraph* and became the paper's proprietor in 1885.

At Capetown Russell breakfasted with Sir Bartle Frere at Government House, hired a manservant at £7 a month, then travelled on—with Sir Garnet and his staff—to Durban and Pietermaritzburg. On 29 June he went to church to hear Bishop Colenso preach a 'very fine' sermon. Colenso had been Bishop of Natal for more than twenty-five years, becoming a master of the Zulu language and the leading white spokesman for the Zulus in their disputes with the Boers and the British.*

On 6 July they heard that Lord Chelmsford, determined to restore his reputation before he could be replaced by Sir Garnet, had routed the Zulu army at Ulundi. The war was virtually over. Russell, like Sir Garnet, had arrived too late and there was little for him to report. This was the greatest of his troubles in South Africa but it was not the only one. Ironically, the only war to which he assigned himself turned out to be the most unsatisfactory from his point of view. He was nearly sixty years old and many years had passed since his last campaign. His general health had not been good and his right leg, injured during the Indian Mutiny, was often lame. He was not fit for hard travelling in such an inhospitable land. And the list of his luggage, given in his diary, shows he had no intention of travelling light. It included three portmanteaux, two boxes of clothing, his Deputy Lieutenant's uniform and a uniform case, a helmet case, various rifles and shot guns and their cases, two swords, five order and decoration cases, cigar cases and a cigarette holder, a despatch box, one Gladstone bag and one hand bag and many other effects among them—as always—the Prayer Book that Mary had given him when he was setting off for the Crimea.

Leaving most of this impedimenta behind, Russell journeyed about Natal during July, visiting camps and hospitals, talking to soldiers and correspondents, and feeling unwell: 'Oh dear me, my poor bones. . . . It was so cold.' Back in Pietermaritzburg by the end of the month, he had to take to his bed: 'JULY 30 . . . What a small place the world is. In comes a man to see me. "It's 21 years since I attended you for this very leg." It was Ross of Simla.'

Sir Garnet marched north to capture Cetewayo and disperse what was left of the Zulu army. Russell stayed behind at the Queen's Hotel, recuperating and receiving visitors:

AUGUST 3 1879 Bishop Colenso came at lunch time and was interesting. He insists on Cetewayo being returned.

AUGUST 17 . . . Bishop Colenso called and had long talk after church insisting on impolicy of destroying Cetewayo whom he regards as the only man able to rule the Zulu *indunas* [district chiefs]. We walked to the Club together, his form towering above me and I saw that most people saluted him.

---

* John William Colenso (1814–83) was born in Cornwall and educated at Cambridge. He was a distinguished mathematician and a controversial theologian, risking deposition and excommunication for his objections to the doctrine of eternal punishment.

Russell formed a high admiration for Colenso: 'What a grand nature in a noble presence. I believe a more straight, direct, truth-loving, justice-worshipping man never walked this earth or any other.' (1) They held similar views on colonialism, and Colenso, with his unrivalled knowledge of the South African situation, had a powerful influence on Russell's thinking. At the end of July Russell wrote to the Commander-in-Chief of the British Army, the Duke of Cambridge:

> The Zulu settlement proposed by Sir Garnet will not be lasting or safe. He is reviving the chieftain and tribal systems we want to crush and he is destroying the power of the only man who could keep their chiefs in order. This war was *ev*itable and it was not necessary nor does it consolidate our power. . . . There is no future of a great imperial kind like that of Australia for South Africa. Sir Bartle has caused more man and woman killing and blood shedding in a few months if he be responsible for this war than Cetewayo did in all his reign, and the murders of the wounded prisoners are too horrible to think of. I'm glad I didn't see what I hear of for my pen could not have been stayed no matter what the result. (2)

By mid-August Russell was well enough to set off by waggonette to join Sir Garnet and the main British force. It was a rough journey, affording long hours for reflection and nostalgia. He wrote to a man he had not seen for many years:

Blaaw Kranz. August 23 1879
Dear Max Müller,
   From this wretched outspanning place I am inspired to write to you by a chance encounter with a countryman of yours. . . . And my memory went back to the ancient days and I saw through wreathes of tobacco smoke and dim memorial cloud the face of my young friend in that little crib of mine aloft in N.1 New Court, Middle Temple, as he, leading a tuneful choir, gave his admiring audience wild *burschen lieder* and charmed their young spirits with 'Krambambouler! Krambambouler!' etc. How ill it has fared with me and how well with you since then. . . . Now I am on my way to meet Sir Garnet if I can and see what he is going to do in the way of settling the difficulties which lie in his path. The idea of a great South African Empire seems to me a wild chimera. We did a wicked thing in annexing the Transvaal but we shall do a foolish thing is we try to weld these colonies by force or fraud into a self-supporting dominion. The Kafir is too much and too many for us. The climate is too much for the European. Unless he is content with the hardest life and the most joyless existence in a land vexed by cruel vicissitudes of droughts, rains, heat and cold, he must be discontented and disappointed.

On the journey Russell followed his usual practice of closely questioning everyone he met, Boer farmers and British soldiers. He was again told that some of the Zulu wounded had been killed after Ulundi and reported this to *The Daily Telegraph*, incurring the hatred of many officers. The Boers were surly and restive, already planning to get rid of the British:

> SEPTEMBER 25 . . . It is good to look through foreign specs at times methinks. Boer meeting passed off all well as far as order goes but gave no promise of settling dispute by compromise. They will be content with nothing short of independence. Their language defiant—presence of GW and troops irritates them. . . . It was a most unwise thing not to wait till Boers entreated us to take over the country.

He joined Sir Garnet's headquarters in September and marched with the army. Sir Garnet had lost none of his distrust of journalists, though he made an exception for Russell, and was keen to institute a system whereby officers on his staff would act as newspaper correspondents. Russell saw this would never work satisfactorily. He wrote to the editor of *The Daily Telegraph*:

> It seems to me that however desirable it may be for newspapers to obtain early exact and official information, and however tempting it may be to newspaper editors to secure the services of able official persons as their correspondents, it is absolutely impossible to expect honest criticism, uncoloured statements, or even full information from men whose career and position are at the mercy of those whose acts and conduct they are called on to chronicle and analyse, and I am sure that one of the highest functions of journalism is thus subjected to paralysing influences to the great detriment of the character of the Press and the ultimate corruption of its judgements and destruction of its influence. (3)

Archibald Forbes, who had arrived on the scene long before Russell, had become a national hero after Ulundi when he rode more than a hundred miles to the telegraph station at Landman's Drift to despatch his story. The papers at home, particularly his own paper, the *Daily News*, acclaimed 'the ride of death'. But Russell was impressed neither by Forbes' achievement nor by his flattery:

> OCTOBER 2 1879 . . . Forbes refers to me in a letter to *Daily Telegraph*, 16th August I think, as 'father of our profession'. Oh Lord! What a nice family I have. They clamour at home for a VC for him! He was, I hear, quite drunk at most stations where he arrived on his ride—he had an escort through all the dangerous places—and jumped horses all along, and yet his famous ride was really of 105 miles from 4.30 p.m. to 2.30 p.m. next day. But *I* can't crab *him*!

News reached them that the British Resident in Cabul had been killed by the Afghans:

What a dreadful blow to the Government! I fear it will be followed by worse. Well! If we will go empiring it all over the world we must expect such startling news and deeds. And we are talking of a Burmese War and a Maori War! Queen Victoria's reign has been an incessant record of bloodshed. (4)

In South Africa the British were dealing now with two enemies—the scattered remnants of the Zulu army, and rising hostility among the Boer farmers who, with the Zulu threat removed, wanted the British to leave. There were weeks of hard marching. Russell wrote home:

On the veldt near Lydenburg. . . . I am on my way with two officers to meet Baker Russell's column and very hard times we have of it—all tinned meat living and biscuits and they mouldy—no bread whatever, bad water and brandy at 18s a bottle of the vilest description. . . . My health is, I think, better than when I set out and I am certainly more cheerful than I was but that is a long way off being jolly. (5)

He was particularly distressed by the poor state of the British units and wrote to Edward Lawson of *The Daily Telegraph*:

As to this army no words can express the shame which would fall upon us if we were to be engaged with any foreign army in serious warfare with such battalions. It would need years of careful weeding and training to make them fit for campaigning. The disorders on the line of march whenever there are grog shops or canteens or any places to be broken into are scandalous, and this place has been the scene of disgraceful orgies, which the officers seem to be unable to prevent and afraid to punish. (6)

He sent an account to the *Telegraph*, published in London on 21 November 1879, giving examples of house-breaking, robbery and assault by British soldiers, and criticizing the commanders for their inaction:

For my own part, I think the military authorities have been culpably remiss and negligent in the discharge of their bounden obligation to maintain discipline and to protect the property and secure the peace of well-disposed loyal citizens. What the reasons or motives for their indifference may be I do not pretend to surmise, but I am sure they are pursuing a course which must lead to most serious consequences if they gloss over or pretend to ignore the excesses which in Natal and the Transvaal are covering the army with odium and disgrace.

He denounced 'the easy way in which the military chiefs have treated the serious evils which the Duke of Wellington or Lord Clyde would have stamped on with an iron heel.'

The article had considerable repercussions. The Duke of Cambridge wrote to Sir Garnet Wolseley drawing his attention to the charges and asking for his reply. Sir Garnet denied the allegations in general, claiming that Russell had accepted the word of ignorant or biased informants, but promised to hold an inquiry. The inquiry was perfunctory and failed, predictably, to uphold Russell's charges. But he did not withdraw them and the argument rumbled on for several months.

The question is now impossible to resolve and was probably unanswerable then. No army behaves impeccably when it finds itself operating in difficult conditions in largely hostile country. Russell, concerned for the underdog and anxious for the reputation of the army, demanded the highest standards. Perhaps he expected too much. Perhaps he was too ready to believe the stories of men, mostly Boers, who had no love for the British and were eager to discredit them.

Whether he was right or wrong, the incident shows his moral courage undiminished by the years. He was still ready to speak the truth as he saw it whatever the dangers to his position or popularity:

> OCTOBER 4 1879 . . . Argus very offensive in tone towards Boers—all sneers and jibes . . . talked of annexation and I expressed opinion very forcibly.

> OCTOBER 5 . . . He vexed me by falling foul of the Boers because they were cruel to natives. Good God! What are we?

At the top level, between Russell and Sir Garnet, the controversy was conducted with great civility and did nothing to impair their friendship. 'Both have only one object,' Sir Garnet wrote to him later, 'the good of the State. Both, being human, are liable to error, and are influenced by passions at times in a manner which we regret afterwards. You stung me—I am sure most unintentionally—in the most susceptible point, and I endeavoured to hit out straight in return.' (7) A cartoon in *Fun* magazine (Plate 14) accurately reflected the incident which was rounded off two years later at the Royal Academy dinner:

> APRIL 29 1882 . . . It happened that Sir Garnet and I met near the doorway and I was talking to him of Ireland and my views etc.—we met very cordially—when the Prince [of Wales] passing through, caught sight of us and immediately burst out laughing and said 'What you two! You two are friends, I see,' and went on. But Sir Garnet went after him, 'I beg your pardon, Sir, I did not quite understand what you said.' 'Oh nothing! Only I was glad to see you were friends' and went off. The general came back and said 'I wonder what he means. 'I'm sure I don't know' said I!'

On 8 December 1879 Russell was riding his pony well ahead of the army column, approaching Pretoria, when a Cape storm blew up suddenly as he was crossing a ford:

A flash of lightning struck the water, my horse reared violently, lost his footing, threw me over his shoulder, and I fell under him. My right leg was caught by the stirrup; my left leg was under the horse's shoulder; his neck lay over my chest, preventing me from rising. There was I on my back, with my head just up, supporting myself with my right hand on the bottom of the river, and with my left jogging the reins to make the poor beast rise—the water slowly rising with the pouring torrents—I was drowning. (8)

He managed to free himself at last, struggled clear of the water with his horse and crawled to a nearby house where an old Scottish farmer put him to bed. Sir Garnet found him there next day: '"I thought my last day had come, and that my body would never be found," I said to him. "My dear fellow," was his characteristic reply, "I would never have left the country until I had found you, and I would have given you a jolly good burial".' (9)

It was the end of all active campaigning for Russell. He sold what was left of his kit by auction in Pretoria, dined with Sir Garnet and set off on 23 December on the long trek to Capetown. He was given a small escort and could ride again, though only painfully. It was intolerably hot and dusty during the day. When they camped on the veldt at night they were plagued by mosquitoes and sandflies and then by the bitter cold. In the towns and villages the Boers were inhospitable, the bed bugs insatiable: 'DECEMBER 31 1879 . . . I dined on biscuits, brandy and water—and so ushered in 1880. It is all like a horrid nightmare—moonlight and daylight all the same, waste treeless grassless dusty rocky sandy waterless—by night a grey indistinct sea-like expanse. Not a soul visible hour after hour . . .'

He reached Capetown on 6 January and was welcomed by Sir Bartle Frere at Government House. Next day he met the captured Cetewayo: 'I am satisfied he never dreamt of invading Transvaal or Natal. . . . Lobengula and the Matabele will be our next victims.'* (10)

He stayed as Sir Bartle's guest and, for all the disparity of their views, retained great affection and respect for him. They rode out together in the Governor's carriage on 12 January and Russell noted: 'It is almost amusing to see the dear old codger looking out right and left for people to bow to—he quite understands popularity-making.' And the next day, the day he sailed for home, he wrote in the diary:

Africa is the grave of great expectations but it makes them too. Sir Bartle and I had two long talks *de Frere et omnibus rebus Frereribus*. He has as much real nobility of governing about him as any one I ever met but he is also bigoted in his belief that he can do no wrong, very angry with Gladstone and not well with Wolseley.

* The British seized the mineral-rich Matabeleland in 1888 and five years later Lobengula was sent into exile, where he died in 1894.

Russell's six months in South Africa had left him terribly wasted and he spent the voyage resting and recovering his strength. 'I am fattening up enormously,' he noted but it was a slow process. Six months later his weight was still only twelve stone eight pounds, well below his metropolitan normal.

As usual, he came home to a variety of troubles. The row over the conduct of the South African army continued. Lady Wolseley snubbed him; the Dukes of Wellington and Cambridge were cold; on 13 March 1880 he recorded: 'Prince of Wales at Westminster Hospital dinner said in reference to my "criticism" he was convinced "our army was as brave and well-disciplined as ever it was!" Eheu!'

He was incensed by the demands of the Inland Revenue: 'I have all the risks of a soldier and none of his honours and I am obliged to put my life in jeopardy to turn my pittance. As Editor and Proprietor I am ready to pay but as special war correspondent, I say, it is infamous in the state to come down on me the moment I land and take the money from my purse.' (11)

And he had lost his greatest friend. He heard the news of Delane's death during his last days in Capetown. 'The pain I feel now is incurable,' he wrote to Delane's sister, 'It is now more than thirty years since he began the friendship which on his side was marked by the greatest kindness, and on my side, I know, by affection and gratitude, and now I feel the last link in the chain which bound me with and to the past is gone.' (12) To Lawson of *The Daily Telegraph* he wrote: 'I only know that during my absence the strongest link which bound me to the past has been snapt, and that I have lost in Delane the earliest, oldest, truest and best of friends with whom I quarrelled only to find the *redintegratio amicitiae* which illuminated my life had become warmer and stronger than ever, and was, with Thackeray's affection, the comfort of my existence for many a year of trouble.' (13)

From his personal point of view, the venture to South Africa had not been a success and Russell knew it. Now he came home to find his family dispersed, the last of his true friends gone and the prospect of a lonely old age more threatening than ever. On 28 March 1880 he wrote despondently in his diary: 'I believe I am 60 years old today. I may be only 59. At 30 man suspects he is a fool. Knows it at 40 and reforms his plan. At 50 chides his impotent delay. At 60—?'

23

The Last Years

South Africa was Russell's last venture as a special correspondent but it was far from marking the end of his working life. Despite advancing years and declining health, he was still to do much travelling and write three more books and numerous magazine articles and maintain an active role on the *Army and Navy Gazette* as joint proprietor and frequent contributor for another twenty years.

In the spring and summer of 1881 he went on a jaunt to the United States and Canada with the Duke of Sutherland and a group of friends. The Sutherlands were having serious domestic trouble. The Duke's womanizing was unabated and his wife found solace in High Anglicanism: 'The Duchess is far gone in Ritualism,' Russell wrote to Alice from Dunrobin, 'and we are flooded with parsons.' (1) The trip may have been arranged, in part at least, as an escape from the all-pervading piety at home, but the Duke's declared purpose was to study the rapidly-developing railway systems of North America. The party landed in New York on 25 April and visited Washington where Russell noted 'a vast change for the better' in the twenty years since his last visit. They went on by way of Montreal and Toronto to Chicago, then west to California, returning through Las Vegas, Denver and Kansas to sail from New York again in early July.

Russell's description of the rout at Bull Run had not been forgotten by the Americans but feelings had moderated. During their visit to Washington the party was received by the newly-installed President, James Garfield,* who told Russell: 'You brought us very bad news but we have since discovered it was true. I guess you were very sorry to be the bearer of it.' Russell concurred. There was only one threatening incident, at dinner one evening in an hotel, when a card was brought across to Russell on which someone had drawn the figure of a man fleeing from distant cavalry with the words 'Russell at Bull Run' underneath. He turned the joke against his critic by drawing a pair of disappearing legs in front of the fugitive figure and writing beneath it 'The last man of the Federal Army on that occasion'. (2)

---

* James Abram Garfield (1831–81) had been the commander of a volunteer regiment at the start of the Civil War. He won the presidency for the Republican Party in 1880, assumed office in March 1881 but was shot by a dissapointed office-seeker in July and died two months later.

The American press took a close interest in the distinguished visitors and Russell was much interviewed and described:

> In appearance Mr. Russell is typical of the average cultivated Englishman. About the medium height, his rotund but not burly form is highly suggestive of the best of living. Slightly bald, his hair has turned gray, while the kindly lineaments of a somewhat roseate face are dominated by a highly intelligent but reserved expression of the eye. He wears a gray moustache, is scrupulously neat in dress and is a delightful conversationalist. (3)

When they made fun of him it was without the former rancour:

> If Dr. Russell of the London *Times* had nothing to entitle him to distinction as a journalist but the amount of baggage which he carries on his travels, no one could dispute his right to be regarded as the most remarkable member of the profession. That portion of the doctor's worldly effects which follow his perambulations of the globe would fill an ordinary freight train. (4)
>
> After an exhaustive investigation of the wine list, the Doctor made an ineffectual effort to sing a song, and fell into a peaceful slumber. (5)

Russell assured his interviewers that he was not planning to write about the trip, that he was travelling purely for pleasure 'and I am attaining my object admirably', but he kept full notes and when it was over his friends persuaded him to write a book about their journey. It was published the next year in two volumes —*Hesperothen: Notes from the West*, a relaxed and readable travel book, packed with stories and enlightened comment, displaying considerable knowledge of North American society and an observant interest in the flora and fauna. He noted with approval that the habit of spitting was on the decline and, without approval, that the incidence of confidence-men seemed to be on the increase. He was impressed by the way the freed negroes were being integrated in the northern and western states but concerned for the fate of the American Indians.

In July 1882 he set off on a longer and more eventful trip: 'This Egyptian desire is strong on me', (6) he noted at the start of the voyage. He spent ten months away from home and had the frustrating experience of being very close to a battle without being able to witness and report it. It was an important period in Egyptian history, a time when the British were being drawn, reluctantly but inexorably, towards a complete take-over.

His old friend, the Khedive Ismail, had gone, destroyed by the weight of his debts to Britain and France. Ismail's son, Tewfik, was the new Khedive, faced with an intractable situation. The landed classes feared that any attempt to reform the system would threaten their wealth and standing. But many army officers were inspired by nationalist feeling to demand social reform and an end to foreign domination. In 1881 the officers, led by Arabi Pasha, staged a revolt and forced a new and revolutionary government on the Khedive. In June 1882 there was rioting in Alexandria and more than fifty Europeans were killed. The British Prime Minister, Mr Gladstone, who had been vainly hoping that the Sultan of Turkey would act to restore the situation, was forced to send Sir Garnet Wolseley and an expeditionary force to Cyprus, ready to move in if it was felt that British interests, especially over the Suez Canal, were threatened.

Russell arrived in Egypt as these events moved to their climax. He saw British ships bombarding the rebel-held forts of Alexandria. Among the British he found the old Indian spirit very much in evidence:

AUGUST 23 1882 . . . The Alexandrian tone against Arabi and the Arabs vindictive. They must be punished as rebels—everybody must be shot. . . . Sanguinary conversation at dinner. Officer said he would hang 100 Mahometans guilty or not for every man killed on 11th June i.e. he would hang 6,000 men!

SEPTEMBER 8 . . . I received a great pile of papers. It makes me sick to read them. We are quite changing our national character or showing its worst side for no Gascons could be more braggart and vain and the special correspondents vie with each other in gasconade. The *Times* man is too feeble.

When Sir Garnet landed his army Russell tried hard, though in vain, to get permission to march with them: 'SEPTEMBER 12 What a sight to have beheld our army moving out this night to bivouac on the desert under lovely sky. Alas! Why was I not with them? This is my last chance perhaps. My very last.'

The battle of Tel el Kebir was fought next day. The British took Arabi by surprise at dawn and routed his army. Thousands of prisoners were taken and within twenty-four hours Cairo had fallen and the rest of the rebel soldiers, including Arabi, were captured. Russell hurried to Cairo, watched the disarming of the captives, had an interview with the Khedive and got first-hand accounts of the battle from the British officers for an article for the *Army and Navy Gazette*. It was a decisive and comparatively cheap victory but Russell was far from jubilant: 'SEPTEMBER 25 Got up at five and wrote—nice fresh breeze—wonder what cats in ruins live upon? I cannot write. I have very small sympathy with this war and it does not move me.'

A few days later the Khedive made a triumphant entry into Cairo and saluted the British as they marched past: 'SEPTEMBER 30 . . . What will history say of all this? I doubt present voices. Why are we encouraged to occupy and annex? Is there to be no *quid pro quo*?' There was no doubt in his mind that Sir Garnet's victory implied a complete assumption of control by the British: 'What hypocrisy to pretend that there is no annexation when we control the finances and officer the army and organise and command police!' (7) His sympathies were with the defeated Arab nationalists and the poor peasants.

He was troubled by rheumatism and went to stay at an hotel at Helwan-le-Bains near Cairo:

NOVEMBER 13 . . . What a strange place this is. The desert—these miserable *fellaheen* villagers—such rags, such houses, with such a life. The carts watering our streets—special police at the gate—electric bells to the bathrooms. The poor *fellaheen* care for nothing at all but living—that is a hard problem for them.

He wrote to Max Müller:

Here I am in the strange place which the caprice of nature in causing a sulphur spring to rush out in the desert, and the fancy of Ismail Pasha that he would create a Harrogate in the land of the Pharaohs have made a winter resort, contrary to all the traditions of the Bedouins and wild animals, hitherto its sole inhabitants. I open the lattices of my comfortable hotel window and look out on the Pyramids of Darshour, the mounds of Memphis and the works of Cheops, and in the village at which I stop when I want to cross the Nile I see from the hotel bus, if you please, the 'houses' and the people just as they were I am sure—minus the turbans—in the time of Menes. . . . I think I shall winter out here. I have no home—all my bairns are away and married and are busy with their own concerns and I have only to await the end, if not quite 'pauper indigens', certainly 'exul'. But I trust I may live to pay that Oxford visit and make the acquaintance of your household. (8)

He spent a further six months in Egypt. He made another trip up the Nile. In Cairo he made friends with a member of the Egyptian ruling house, the Princess Nazalé, who fascinated him with stories about the outrageous behaviour of her male relatives. He went to the opera and the theatre and endured regimental dinners: 'APRIL 25 1883 . . . Leith's Citadel dinner. 79th. Oh Lord! the bare long draughty room, naked walls, terrible mess dinner and the infernal pipers, eleven of them. I was nearly lunatic and thought I would never get off.'

It was a life of leisure and luxury. Lord Dufferin, the British ambassador to Turkey, had been sent to Cairo to assess the situation and he and Lady Dufferin insisted that Russell be their guest in the Cairo embassy.* He grew deeply fond of both of them—a feeling that was completely reciprocated—and sailed with them when they returned to Constantinople by way of Rhodes and Smyrna. Lord Dufferin gave him a temporary appointment as his secretary at twenty-five shillings a day and encouraged him to write his memoirs: 'MAY 6 1883 . . . Dufferin talked to me seriously of my duty to myself and the world to leave a record of what I have seen—says I should dictate only when the vein was on me.'

* The first Marquis of Dufferin and Ava (1826–1902) was a distinguished diplomat and pro-consul. He was Governor-General of Canada from 1872 to 1878, then ambassador to Russia, then to the Turkish Empire. He was Viceroy of India 1884–8.

He returned to Egypt in mid-May to say goodbye to his friends: 'MAY 23 1883
. . . Princess Nazalé. It is quite ridiculous but there is no doubt of my being quite
tender towards her and I felt deep regret at leaving her.'

In Alexandria he went to see his prodigal son John, recently appointed British
vice-consul there, and his wife Georgina:

> MAY 27 . . . the poor woman was a scarecrow. A low sweet voice, an excellent
> thing in woman, is not enough to atone for want of face, figure, manner, birth
> and money. She is, I am led to think, very good-natured but deplorably and
> utterly 'common' outside. She may be of a very fine inside but there is no
> outward ray of light hid under so ordinary a bushel.

He gave Georgina £5 to buy a dress and John £70 towards his rent and general
expenses and left them to each other: 'she and John have been so long in solitude
together they are all in all to each other and desire no other company. Well, it's
best so . . .' (9)

He made a slow sight-seeing journey home, visiting Rome, Paris and the Hague
where he was enraptured by the art galleries: 'It is a place in which to spend many
days in deliberate exploration.' (10)

It had been a long trip and, as so often with Russell, the rich living had not
improved his health. He was overweight again and increasingly rheumatic; he was
often lame; and his bronchitis was so bad that coughing sometimes kept him awake
throughout the night. He found writing more and more difficult: 'I fancy I must be
losing all power of composition for I felt difficulty today in regard to common
sentences.' (11) And during his absence there had been much distressing news.
His most generous creditor over many years, Maitland Dashwood, died in June
1883 and a few days later he heard of the death of Bishop Colenso of Natal. On his
trip up the Nile he had been deeply shocked to read in the British papers that his
elder daughter Alice, the mother of five children, had run away from home to live
with a land agent, Frederick William Thornhill. He was so upset that at first he
would not write to Alice. She was divorced by her husband, on the grounds of her
adultery, in February 1883. Four weeks later Russell received a letter from her
saying 'it seems so unnatural that there should be silence between two who had
been ever so near each other'. (12) He did not reply, however, for a further two
months—until he heard from Alberta that she had visited Alice and found her sick
and low-spirited: 'Too late she feels the horror of the pit. "We have tasted the
bitterness of sin" were her words. How I do love her and wring my heart by
suppressing it all. I did not take long to decide—to go at once.' (13) But he did not
hurry home and it was two more months before he met his erring daughter again
and was reconciled to her. She married Thornhill at the end of the year.

In November 1883 Russell himself fell in love. He was in the Scottish
Highlands, fishing and shooting, when the house-party was joined by Lady
Anglesey and an Italian noblewoman who played the piano charmingly, the

Countess Antoinette Mathilde Pia Alexandra Malvezzi. They had been prepared for her arrival by a letter which spoke of 'a fair Italian Countess who plays delicious dreamy melodies'. (14) Russell's diary for this period is disjointed —many pages are blank, others have been torn out—but enough remains to suggest the course of events:

> NOVEMBER 6 1883 We shot the Glen . . . charming day—lunched at Donald Macrae's, milk and whisky. I am thinking of her and of the other her and of the trouble and am in pain to boot all day.

> NOVEMBER 8 Off to shoot at 11 and could not get a word to the Countess and did not like to provoke comment by staying behind. I was left in the middle of the wood till 1.45 and walked off to the road, leaving a piece of paper on stick.

> NOVEMBER 10 At Rugby at 7 a.m., an hour late. Telegram 'presence needed' and so had to go on. Goodbye sweetheart! goodbye! Heavens how strange it seems, incredible! And yet in the madness and folly such ineffable pleasure.

It was an unsuitable match on many counts. Russell was sixty-three, a Protestant and, for all his fame and grand connections, a commoner. Antoinette was thirty-six, a member of an ancient and noble and very Catholic family: 'They were the great family of Ferrara,' Russell wrote to Alice, 'till the states of the church were overturned and, siding with the Pope, the Malvezzis and the Bentivoglios, their cousins, were driven into exile.' (15) Despite all this, the courtship was rapid and smooth. Within a few weeks she took him to meet her parents in Paris: 'JANUARY 23 1884 . . . I explained as well as I could what I hoped to do for Antoinette on my death—some £250 a year to £300 if all went well and he was quite content . . . my darling honey. How good and kind and loving she is. Heaven watch over her and make me worthy. I shall try, I hope.'
In a letter to Alice he gave a fuller description of the negotiations:

> I was presented to Count and Countess Malvezzi and sister Peppina on Sunday and there was a *Conseil de famille* at which I heard for the first time that I was expected to give a pledge that the children, if any, of the marriage were to be educated as Catholics or otherwise the marriage would not take place according to the rites of the Roman Catholic Church and no other ceremony would be binding in the eyes of good Romanists. . . . There was Madame Walewska, Princess Poniatoroska, Count Bentivoglio d'Aragon etc. all at me, but I positively refused to go further than to promise that the girls should be of their mother's faith—the boys being of mine. It was very funny, the grave wrangle over a very remote contingency but they looked as if the world was coming to an end and I was very glad that the poor little woman herself was not at it. (16)

They were married in February 1884 at three separate ceremonies—a civil one on the 16th and two days later an Anglican service at the British embassy, followed by a ceremony at the Roman Catholic Church in the Place d'Eylau St Honoré. Then, their union trebly assured and doubly blessed, there was a reception at Lady Anglesey's Paris house where Russell noted 'I nearly died of hunger and excitement'. He told *The Daily Telegraph* correspondent that he would rather go through ten campaigns than endure such an ordeal a second time.

Despite their wide disparities in age and background, the marriage was a success. Antoinette—who soon came to be known as 'Toney' or 'Titi'—gave Russell's life a stability, a foundation of care and affection, that he had not known for many years. His social life continued but at a gentler pace. She was introduced to all his friends—she was presented to the Queen at Buckingham Palace in May the following year—but from this time on most of his evenings were spent contentedly at home. She took charge of his finances and quickly brought them to order. He played no whist for many years after his wedding. When rheumatism made writing difficult for him, she wrote at his dictation. For the first time in his adult life he could rely on the loving attention of a capable woman and he was deeply grateful. At the end of their first year together, instead of his diary's usual melancholy reflections, he spoke of his '*annus mirabilis*' and noted: 'JANUARY 1 1885 ... On the whole my circumstances are not so bad as many a New Year's Day has seen them for I have cleared off that dreadful debt nearly.' And a year later he wrote: 'JANUARY 1 1886 ... Was ever man so 'blessed' in a dear wife?'

They were both inclined to overweight and mild hypochondria and spent much time in the years that followed at the spas of Europe—Bath and Harrogate, Aix-les-Bains and Marienbad. They took the waters, submitted themselves to mud baths and massage, and Russell tried electrical treatment—'my galvanic torture'—for his bad leg. Nothing seemed to do much good.

Russell was distressed by the deaths of old friends during the 1880s—the Duke of Wellington and Lord Ampthill (formerly Odo Russell), Anthony Trollope and 'dear little Wilkie Collins', Lord Lyons in 1887 and the Duke of Rutland the next year:

MARCH 5 1888 The Duke of Rutland is dead. . . . To me the Lord of Belvoir was ever most gracious, pleasant, kind and hospitable . . . a little of a voluptuary, a great deal of a sportsman, gun and hound. What a smoker! Jim Macdonald told a Frenchman who asked 'Pourquoi est-ce que M. le Duc fume des cigares si énormes?' that he was obliged by his patent of Dukedom to smoke his own length of cigars every day.

In 1886 he became a Freemason. He had been going to join more than thirty years before, in Malta on his way to the Crimea when the call to join the ship intervened, but he had done nothing about it since. Very occasional references in the diary suggest that he had little respect for the movement, and even though he now joined it he did so with little enthusiasm:

APRIL 6 1886 The Drury Lane Masonic Lodge met at three and I was admitted a master mason . . . a most tedious business and Oh Lord!—well, no matter.

FEBRUARY 8 1887 . . . at the Freemasons (Drury Lane Lodge), 300 strong, most trying. I never shall be a good mason—sense of ludicrous too great.

The Russells led an active life. There were regular visits to Ireland to see Alberta and her five children. Old friendships were renewed—Russell went to stay with Max Müller and his family in North Oxford, Dion Boucicault gave them the use of a box at his theatres—and new ones were formed. They met Henry Irving, the leading actor of the time, and he too sent them tickets for his plays. They made friends with the ex-Empress Eugénie of France, whose son had been killed in the Zulu War, and visited her at her house in Farnborough. And Russell was introduced to Colonel John Thomas North, an engineer–entrepreneur who had made a quick fortune developing the nitrate resources of Chile.

The Colonel, a man of great energy and acumen and *bonhomie*, was in London in early 1889 to raise money for new ventures in South America. Russell met him at a dinner party in late January and was immediately captivated. He had been planning to take Antoinette to Egypt but the Colonel soon persuaded him to change his plans and join the party he was taking to Chile. The party, composed with an eye of favourable publicity for the Colonel's schemes, included Melton Prior, the artist and war correspondent of the *Illustrated London News* whom Russell greatly disliked: 'He is the most insufferable conceited snob I ever met.' (17) But Russell was keen to see a part of the world he had never visited and the Colonel was both persuasive and generous: 'Colonel North—"You want some money?" "Yes, I shall need some before I go." "Well, say a thousand." Turning to the old book-keeper, "Fill in a cheque for £1,000 in favour of Dr. Russell."' (18)

Antoinette was a poor sailor and spent most of the voyage 'in bed with her marmoset' but Russell enjoyed the journey and found South America fascinating—its abundance of exotic plant and animal life, its peoples and their problems, and the struggle between the Chilean President Balmaceda and Colonel North over control of the rich nitrate fields. He heard the President tell North: 'You want to get for thousands what is worth millions.' It was true and in the end North got it.

The Russells travelled home through Panama, where de Lesseps was having even more trouble than he had had building the Suez Canal, and New York, where Russell saw his old friend John Bigelow and visited the Military Academy at West Point. They were back in London in July and Russell settled done to write an account of the trip, *A Visit to Chile and the Nitrate Fields of Tarapaca*, which was published in 1890. Lavishly illustrated by Melton Prior, it made a handsome volume. Russell used his usual diary form and wrote in a style that was much more flowing and graceful than that of his earlier works. But he contrived to include, in a pleasantly digestible form, a mass of information about Chile and her neighbours, their political and economic conditions and the disputes between them, as well as a detailed description of the nitrate workings and an assessment of the industry's potential.

Once again his homecoming was shadowed by family trouble, this time concerning John, whose wife Georgina had confirmed Russell's unfavourable view of her by running off to rejoin the man she had been living with before her marriage. John, who was now vice-consul at the Dardanelles, divorced her and married again in Constantinople in November 1890. William was doing better. He was promoted to full commissioner of the Chinese Customs in 1889, with a rise of £400 a year, and his wife produced one daughter.

When they were in London the Russells lived in rented rooms but in considerable style. A long article by Harry How which was published in the *Strand Magazine* at the end of 1892—an 'Illustrated Interview' with Russell—describes their rooms overlooking Victoria Street. Each of them, dining room, drawing room, Russell's study, and the intervening corridors, were crammed with mementos—muskets from the Crimea and matchlocks from India, spears and assegais from South Africa, ink pots and paper-weights made from shells and bullets from the Franco-Prussian War. The walls of each room were covered with oil paintings —family portraits and Landseer's 'Horseman and Hounds' among them—as well as countless sporting guns, fishing rods, swords and scabbards, inscribed photographs from friends. The writing table in the study was a wedding present from the Prince of Wales. The drawing room carpet was a present from the Prince's suite. 'Dr. Russell,' How wrote, 'is of medium height, strongly built, wearing a white moustache, and possessing a head of wavy, silver hair. He is now lame from injuries received by his horse falling on him in the Transvaal. He took me from room to room, and as he narrated the little incidents associated with his treasures, it was all done quietly, impressively free from any boastfulness.' (19)

Early in 1892 Russell paid his last visit to Egypt. Antoinette went with him and they were joined for a voyage up the Nile by Alberta and her husband. On 7 March Russell wrote in his diary:

Such a strange experience. For an hour or more I had a kind of delirium, a waking trance. I sat in my chair on deck, wide awake but quite away from what was passing around me and seeing and speaking and listening to people quite in bodily presence who were, I knew, dead and gone. I tried to escape from it and could not—very queer and unpleasant.

He took Antoinette to meet Nubar Pasha and Princess Nazalé in Cairo, then they made their way home by way of Naples, Capri, Rome and Malta. They had both grown fat—he was fourteen stone seven pounds, she was thirteen stone eight—and they spent the whole of August trying the various cures of the German spas.

That September the Duke of Sutherland died. Russell had seen much less of him in recent years, partly because of his own marriage, chiefly because there had been serious trouble in the Sutherland household over the Duke's affair with another woman. Relations between the Duke and the Duchess were severed completely by the mid-1880s and the family dispute continued even after the death of the Duchess in 1888, for the Duke alienated his children by marrying the other woman soon after. Russell was deeply distressed by the collapse of the family whose friendship and hospitality he had enjoyed for so many years. When he heard of the Duke's death he wrote in his diary: 'My heart is exceedingly heavy. . . . For six and thirty years he was my friend and I can only say I loved him more than any man on earth, and during that time there was never a cloud in the sky under which we moved—he in his place and I in mine—separated by nothing that caused friction or discontent between us.' (20)

As the proprietor of an influential military magazine, Russell was obliged to maintain good relations with the Duke of Cambridge, who had been Commander-in-Chief of the British Army for more than thirty years. The Duke was pompous, overbearing and reactionary—increasingly resistant to reform of any kind. Henry Labouchere had ridiculed him as 'standing at the head of his troops, his drawn salary in his hand'. But the Duke had a liking for Russell, even though they disagreed on almost every important subject, and often invited him to dine. Russell went dutifully and had to suffer much laboured teasing. It became particularly galling when the Duke took to regaling the company with the story, heavily dramatized and false in most of its details, of how he had ordered Russell's tent to be removed from his lines when they were camped near Varna on the way to the Crimea: 'He delights in the tale and laughs over it and then adds "We're good friends now, eh?" The greater part is imaginary.' (21) Russell endured repeated retellings: 'Duke quite affectionate. "You didn't mind my little chaff yesterday about your tent, eh? Did it to please him, you know. Eh?" Such chaff—lead and paving stones.' (22)

With the Prince of Wales his relations were ambivalent. At times he was in high favour and invited to Sandringham and Marlborough House, at others he felt the chill of royal disapproval:

MAY 5 1885 . . . A. Ellis wrote 'The Crown you use on your wife's paper is rapidly driving the PoW stark staring mad.'

FEBRUARY 10 1886 . . . The Prince of Wales gave a farewell banquet to the Duke of Edinburgh at Marlborough House. I not asked—so am out of it.

MARCH 23 Queen's Drawing Room . . . Queen gracious to Antoinette and gave her hand which I am afraid A. kissed. . . . Arthur Ellis told me Prince was inveighing against me furiously. He must have some one to gird against. I am sorry, but I cannot help it.

MARCH 1 1887 . . . to levee and we got into second pen—Prince said (so sympathetically) 'You should have come in a bath chair.' 'No, Sir! on an Imperial bicycle.'

SEPTEMBER 26 At Perth 7.15. Kit Teesdale ran from station to say P.o.W. desired to see me and out he came on platform. 'It is a long time since I saw you' etc.—very gracious to Titi—fat and brown, with a cough.

JANUARY 19 1891 What a good fellow he is! He tied on my muffler as I was leaving and the Princess and Maud came to see us off.

FEBRUARY 3 . . . HRH let off some gas about newspapers as usual and, of course, had his ancient tilt at poor A and NG [the *Army and Navy Gazette*].

JANUARY 2 1895 . . . Tum Tum, dear Prince, full of tricks—a snowball on my hat, *par example*.

He gave occasional dinner parties at the Garrick Club for the Prince of Wales and half a dozen friends. He still went, though much more rarely than before, to the Carlton and Marlborough Clubs. He could still be shocked by the scandalous conduct of the Prince's friends. 'It is beyond belief,' he wrote in his diary on 13 October 1889 when news reached the Carlton that Lord Arthur Somerset, superintendant of the Prince's racing stables, had been arrested at a homosexual brothel in Cleveland Street. There was even greater consternation when it became known that the Prince's eldest son, Prince Albert Victor—'Prince Eddy'—had been to the establishment: 'It is believed the Prince knows about Eddy. It would appear that Holford must have gone with him to the house, not aware, let us pray God, of its repute or purpose.' (23)

Russell heard all the court gossip and there was no doubt in his mind that Queen Victoria's relationship with her Highland servant John Brown had been more than platonic. When Brown died in 1883 Russell noted:

> . . . there will be a quiet satisfaction in many hearts I could specify. As far as I know the man was an insolent and adroit peasant, a cunning coarse gillie who had found the weak spot in a woman's nature when the Queen was bereft of her only friend, companion and counsellor, but there must be some quality we do not understand or know which makes such a one as the Queen regard his death as condemning her to a second widowhood. Arthur Ellis asserted often to me it was physical . . . (24)

A few weeks later, when he was reading J. R. Green's *Short History of the English People*, he commented: 'Lord, what a world. Are we better than we were—when? any time. Green gives a pretty account of Bess. Arthur Ellis gives or gave a pretty account of Victoria and John Brown to me. England believed in Elizabeth's perfect purity. Well, what will history say of 1861–83?' (25)

Throughout the final years of the century Russell maintained a lively interest in public affairs and did much intermittent writing. The running of the *Army and Navy Gazette* continued to exercise him until he was over eighty. He worked at his autobiography, *Retrospect*, and the diary says he sent 'handsomely-bound copies' to a few friends early in 1895 though none of them can now be traced. The same year saw the publication of his last book *The Great War with Russia* which gave an informal and personal account of his Crimean experiences forty years before.

In May 1895 he was summoned to see the Prime Minister, Lord Rosebery:

MAY 10 . . . at 3.15 to 10 Downing Street. . . . Rosebery came in, 'My dear Billy,' carrying a stick—somewhat puffy, he sat down on sofa, pointed to another corner of it, talked of health, told me he had forgotten what he had to say at the meeting of Liberal Club the other night, 'I don't like it at all' etc.. Then a very pretty speech—he had always considered that my great services in the Crimea had never been sufficiently or at all recognised.

A Knighthood or the C.B.

Two weeks later he heard that it was a knighthood:

MAY 25 At Breakfast comes telegram (no! five minutes after) 'Sir Billy Russell K.B. Love and congratulations'. . . . I told staff only as I am rather shy of being Sir Billy'd. . . . At lunch S., despite my 'don't', proposed health of Sir William Russell. . . . My thrushes' and blackbirds' nests robbed of their young by some infernal cruel wretch.

Letters and telegrams of congratulation poured in, many of them saying the recognition was long overdue. On 18 July he took the train to Windsor and joined the eighteen men who were to be similarly honoured, among them his friend Henry Irving, the first British actor to receive a knighthood. His diary describes their reception at Windsor Castle and the lunch they were given, 'excellent champagne—lunch simple and good', but breaks off before the ceremony which was performed by the Queen.

In January 1901 Queen Victoria died and the Prince of Wales succeeded at last to the throne. Russell wrote to him and a few weeks later sent a letter to Queen Alexandra on the thirty-eighth anniversary of her wedding:

MARCH 14 1901 Charlotte Knollys sends an 'immediate' by special messenger to summon me to Marlborough House to see the Queen who was much pleased with my letter . . . the Queen, all black, no ornament, came forward with both hands stretched out, 'I am so glad to see you! Sit down. Will you have a high chair?', then with her own hand she took a high back and drew it to a sofa. 'Will that do?', helped me to it and sat down on the sofa on my left and there we sat and I listened to the dearest lady I ever saw as she spoke of the change that she hated, of her new life, of Marlborough House that she loved so, of the great gaunt palace like a prison . . .

Two days after the coronation of King Edward VII in August 1902 Russell went to Buckingham Palace to be invested as a Commander of the Royal Victorian Order:

At 12.55 I was at the Palace in my dinner-dress, as commanded, and mounted the grand staircase helped by two gentlemen-at-arms to the Grand Gallery. Arthur Ellis rushed at me at once: 'Take them off! Take them off and hide them somewhere,' he exclaimed. He meant my medals. I had forgotten the rule that when one is to receive a decoration he must appear as if he never had one before; so I pocketed my honours and resolved not to sit on them. Then I joined the crowd, and we were all dressed in single file and each was given a card with his name on it for the Lord Chamberlain, who was in the Throne Room next to us on the right of the King, who was seated on a chair of state with a high cushion before him. I don't know how many were before me—six or seven. When I hopped in the King said, 'Don't kneel!' and as I did not halt at once, he said, 'You must not trouble to kneel, Billy! Stoop!' Dighton handed him the riband and badge, and Edward VII slipped it over my head and gave me his right hand to shake. (26)

Old age and the bestowal of public honours did nothing to moderate Russell's unfashionable views on the great issues of the time. On the imperial question he continued to express himself forcibly:

JANUARY 4 1884 The wretched newspapers clamouring over Egypt, calling on the Government to annex. Whatever *we* do is the work of the Elect. And the disgusting politicians caring for nothing but the gain or damage to the party in the business. Who cares for right or wrong—for *fellah* or native? Things rank and gross in nature possess the world.

NOVEMBER 17 1892 . . . The hypocrisy of the religious pretences put forth by the Christian gentlemen, whose maxims I admit are the most potent persuaders, disgusts me and for my own part I believe the Mwangas and Rubaregus are far more likely to be admitted by St. Peter into the Colonial Paradise than the sanctimonious scoundrels, Protestant and Papist, who are filling Uganda with their precious practical followers of the Sermon on the Mount. (27)

MAY 29 1893 [dining with the Duke of Cambridge] . . . HRH and all the company attacked me for saying I thought we should leave Egypt, that it was no good to us, it was against honour etc. Thereupon 'What about the French in Tunis? Who will walk in when we leave? etc.'

MARCH 25 1894 The *Observer* clamouring for more land-grabbing. What a maw the British lion has to be sure. He will choke at last or die of indigestion—or vomit up some of his meals—what a nasty sentence!

SEPTEMBER 23 1895 . . . Prince [of Wales] and King of Greece attacked me about my views of the evacuation of Egypt.

At the end of 1895 Dr Jameson of the British South African Company led a raid into the Boer republic of the Transvaal, hoping to inspire a rebellion and open the way for a British take-over. It failed completely but stirred up an international crisis when the German Emperor sent his congratulations to the Boer leaders. Russell thought the whole business 'most discreditable to us' (28) and was angry at the reluctance of the British government to punish either Jameson or his master, Cecil Rhodes.

When the Boer War broke out in 1899 it came as no surprise to Russell. Although he had no sympathy with the British aims, he was concerned for the reputation of the British army which made a poor showing in the opening encounters. He followed the progress of the war closely, keeping a press cuttings book about it, and wrote a long article for *The Daily Telegraph* which was published on 9 January 1900. He attacked 'the vulgar and vaunting conceit of our insular egotism. . . . We seem to imagine that we are not only actually, but naturally and permanently, the greatest country in the whole world.' There was nothing unusual, he pointed out, in a British army suffering early reverses. It would give rise to less concern if British history books paid more attention to our past defeats and set-backs instead of chauvinistically ignoring them. But history, he went on, also gave reasons for optimism. England seemed to rise the greater from each successive disaster: 'We seem to require some measure of misfortune to call forth the latent powers of our people.'

The other great and continuing issue of the period was Ireland. The mounting demand for independence was expressed in intense political debate at Westminster and, increasingly, by Fenian outrages throughout the United Kingdom. Russell spent many weeks each year in Ireland, visiting Alberta and her family at Longueville in County Cork, staying regularly at Adare Abbey in County Limerick, the home of the fourth Earl of Dunraven, 'the most generous, pleasant and delightful of friends'. (29) He never lost his love for his native land though he grew more and more despairing about its destiny. Many of the comments in his diary would apply with equal force, a century or so later:

APRIL 13 1875 . . . I read the Irish papers with much grief. . . . The study of revenge for wrongs long done is more powerful than reason and immortal hate masters every sense.

APRIL 4 1882 Horrors on horrors accumulate. This murder of Mrs. Smythe caps the ghastly file! It is a disgrace to belong to such a race. . . . These wretches are not human or rather they are so human as to be worse than the wild beasts.

MAY 31 1884 . . . I think there must be design to drive the English into furious reprisals on the Irish population and thus provoke outrage and excite sympathy to create an impossible gulf between the races, quite wide enough as it is. All very sad.

JANUARY 19 1887 . . . I really am becoming Fenian. The stupid ferocity of the respectable British organs in dealing with Irish questions sickens and revolts me.

He had little respect for the British press in general and grew to hate *The Times*:

MARCH 6 1893 The bitterness of *The Times* is unbounded. It is the most violent partisan paper in England or for that matter in the three kingdoms. Its rancour v. Gladstone and Harcourt is fiendish.

FEBRUARY 8 1894 . . . I am disgusted with *The Times*. It now represents the worst side of the Saxon character—greed, selfishness, arrogance, intolerable conceit—chauvinism *in excelsis*.

The last years of his life brought many afflictions. Crippled in both legs, he could only walk with the aid of sticks and towards the end had to be pushed round in a bath-chair. He was deaf in one ear and short of sight, rheumatic and bronchitic, a prey to insomnia. His sons died within a few months of each other—William in China in 1898, John in Constantinople early next year. A grandson, Captain Kenneth Macnaughten of the Royal Fusiliers, died at Khartoum in 1903. His oldest surviving friend, Max Müller, died in 1900.

But he and Antoinette still travelled frequently—to Ireland, to Droitwich for the waters, to Brighton and Dover for the sea air. His interest in public affairs was not confined to wars. He followed the Oscar Wilde trial closely: 'Unutterable abominations of Wilde fully reported Central Criminal Court. Oh shame where is thy blush.' (30) He took a keen interest in the Dreyfus case which was dividing the French.* His dislike of Jews had grown stronger and he had no doubt that Dreyfus was guilty. On 21 October 1898 he dined at Marlborough House and met a young officer of the 4th Hussars, Winston Churchill, who had already made a name for himself as a war correspondent in Cuba, India and the Sudan. He did not relinquish his control of the *Army and Navy Gazette* till the end of 1903. The following February found him writing to John Bigelow and vigorously condemning

* Alfred Dreyfus, a French artillery captain and a Jew, had been convicted of spying for Germany and sent to Devil's Island. His family's long fight to establish his innocence was finally won in 1906.

Britain's 'silly and needless aggression' in Tibet. He continued to keep his diary during 1904 though the entries were sparse and written in a shaky meandering hand. The final entry, still quite legible, was made on 21 December that year: 'The shortest day of a terrible year—and the blackest fog I ever saw.'

Antoinette looked after him with practical devotion and there was a large assortment of grandchildren to cheer and console him. They were particularly fond of the last grandchild, Evelyn, Alice's daughter by her second marriage. They wrote a series of newsy and loving letters to Evelyn, and Antoinette's letters, though few of them are dated, give a picture of Russell in his final decline:

SEPTEMBER 14 1902 . . . Grand Papa is not so bright as I should like him to be, he is fretful and must be very carefully handled!

Grand Papa seems well, bless his little heart. His friend Willie Beecher and his tiresome old wife are coming for a couple of nights. The two old cronies will sit together and tell each other stories and enjoy themselves.

. . . he is very rampageous and irritable. I can't do anything with him. He sings songs at dinner and calls me a bl—y fool when I object to his taking half a tumbler of whisky! . . . I am really getting frightened when I think of what may come into his poor old head to do.

DECEMBER 27 . . . poor Grand Papa, he gets more feeble and broken every day—it makes me so dreadfully sad to witness this irresistible work of nature!

This last letter was sent from 202, Cromwell Road, London S.W. The Russells had moved often in the last years—between rented rooms in West London and hotels in the spa towns and seaside resorts—but it was here, in the Cromwell Road, that William Howard Russell died on 10 February 1907.

Final Reckoning

Russell had been seriously ill for some weeks before he died, and the newspapers were ready with their obituaries. On Monday 11 February 1907 they offered their readers many thousands of words, recounting his career in detail and praising him as an honest and convivial man, a leading and formative journalist. *The Times* spoke of his independence of judgement and the self-effacing nature of his reports: 'he had none of the uneasy craving to keep his individuality before the public which characterises so many of the profession'. It described his achievements in the Crimea at length but thought his finest work might be found in his Letters during the Indian Mutiny. *The Daily Telegraph* stressed his natural good nature and geniality: 'no man had more friends, and it is doubtful whether he leaves a single enemy behind him'. The most perceptive assessment was that of the *Manchester Guardian*, probably the work of J. B. Atkins who was the paper's London editor and who was to be Russell's first biographer:

> What distinguished Russell was that he remained an open-eyed and frank critic when those whom he criticised might have made it much more comfortable for him to shut his eyes or hold his tongue. . . . He was an entirely honourable and patriotic journalist, and it probably never even occurred to him to ask himself whether the conclusions he came to would accord with the popular passions of the moment.'

All the papers—even the *Army and Navy Gazette*—gave the year of his birth, erroneously, as 1821.

Russell was buried at Brompton cemetery beside Mary, his first wife, and their two sons who died in infancy. Among the many wreaths was one from the King and Queen with the words 'For Auld Lang Syne'.

His will showed that, for all Antoinette's careful management, he had never become a rich man. The gross value of his property was put at £4,340. The bulk of it, together with his personal belongings, was left to Antoinette, with smaller bequests to Alice and Alberta and £100 set aside for his granddaughter Evelyn. But they were none of them needy and Antoinette had a settled income of £890 a year from the profits of the *Army and Navy Gazette* which she continued to receive until her own death in 1918.

Within days of the funeral Lord Ronald Gower, Russell's companion in the first days of the Franco-Prussian War, wrote to *The Times* (1) to support the idea of some permanent memorial in St Paul's Cathedral and suggesting that 'it should take the form of a bas-relief portrait, either in bronze or marble, and that the names of the campaigns which Sir William so graphically described should be engraved beneath the likeness'. A fund was organized and two years later, on 9 February 1909, a memorial bust in bronze—portraying Russell in a campaign cloak, writing in a note-book—was unveiled in the crypt of St Paul's. The ceremony was performed by Field-Marshall Sir Evelyn Wood who had been a subaltern in the Crimea. The inscription listed Russell's chief campaigns and used the phrase that has been employed ever since to denote him—'The first and greatest of war correspondents'.

That he was the first newspaper correspondent to turn the reporting of war into a serious profession is a matter of historical fact. Whether he was—and remains—the greatest is a matter of opinion, and strong claims could be advanced for many of his successors. Fair comparison is not possible. Russell enjoyed advantages that were denied war correspondents in later years: he suffered many hindrances but not the ultimate one of military censorship; he worked at a time when it was still possible, from a good position, to see the changing shape of a battle and much of its detail as well; the frequent incidence of war in his time made it possible for him to develop an expert knowledge of weapons, tactics and strategy that many a professional soldier might have envied. His achievement can only properly be measured against those of his contemporaries and in this context there can be no doubt that in the years of his prime—at the Crimean War, in India, and during the initial stages of the American Civil War—his work was unrivalled. He had advantages here too, most notably that of working for the most fearless editor of the world's most powerful newspaper. But the chief sources of his pre-eminence lay within himself—in his dedication to the work, the sharpness of his observation, an appraising intelligence which enabled him to find the truth in a welter of conflicting evidence, his broad historical sense of the strategic and political implications of the events he had witnessed, the courage with which he set down his impressions and judgements.

Many of his contemporaries and most of the correspondents who came after him—reporting the Boer War and the First World War—went to their work with their minds already made up on the main issues. The British cause was just, they believed, and the British soldier was best. What they sought was not the truth, certainly not the whole truth, but stories that would confirm their own and their readers' prejudices. It made for reports that were exciting, and heartening to both their readers and their circulation managers, but it also led to gross misrepresentation. Many of them were carried away by the idea of the war correspondent as a war hero and ran great risks—Forbes on his ride from Ulundi, Winston Churchill escaping from the Boer prison camp—to promote their own glory. Almost all of them fell willing victims to the national mood of the moment, fuelling its propaganda with such fervour that Senator Hiram Johnson could tell the American Congress in 1917: 'The first casualty when war comes is truth.' Later in the twentieth century when wars became more ideological—the outstanding example is the Spanish Civil War—reporting grew increasingly distorted by political partisanship.

William Howard Russell was refreshingly free of most of the failings that are generally attributed to the journalist. He was serious, not superficial. He saw himself as an observer of events, not a participant. Although he suffered great discomforts and many dangers in his campaigning life, he rarely referred to them—even obliquely—in his despatches. And though he was never afraid to give his opinions, they were not based on narrowly nationalistic or political attitudes. His judgements sprang from two strong and complementary qualities: a realistic view, based on his reading of history and his maturing experience, of the way men and armies and nations behave in moments of stress; and high standards of what constituted decent, civilized, humane conduct.

He was not a great writer, in no way comparable in this respect to many of those who practised his craft in later years—Rudyard Kipling and Winston Churchill in the Boer War, George Orwell in Spain and Evelyn Waugh in Abyssinia, Ernest Hemingway and Alan Moorehead in the Second World War, and many more. Russell's style was often pedestrian, sometimes clumsy and occasionally over-blown. But it was always clear and forceful. His readers, even those who were at first outraged by his reports, came to feel they could trust his word and rely on his judgement. It gave him an influence that no other British journalist has ever had.

For many years, through the *Army and Navy Gazette*, he urged much-needed reforms on the British army. He was instrumental, after Königgrätz, in bringing the importance of the 'needle-gun' to public attention. His Letters from India during the suppression of the Mutiny did much to bring opinion at home back to sanity and humanity. Those from the Crimea told the British people, for the first time, what was happening to their army, inspired a massive effort to save the survivors while there was still time, and led directly to the fall of the Aberdeen government. It is doubtful if any journalist anywhere can show such a record of achievement.

And—in public at least—he made nothing of all this. In all his subsequent writings about the Crimean War he never once suggested that he had a hand in bringing down a government. Perhaps he felt it was more becoming to let others make his claims for him and, certainly, as the years passed there were many to do so. Among the tributes that were paid to him during his lifetime, two gave him particular pleasure. The first was spoken by the City of London Chamberlain immediately after the Crimean War: 'it is not too much to say that he has elevated newspaper writing to the dignity of history, and the office of an agent of the daily press to that of an unpaid people's ambassador.' The second, by Sir Evelyn Wood, appeared nearly forty years later:

William Howard Russell dared to tell his employers, and through them all English-speaking peoples, that our little army was perishing from want of proper food and clothing. He probably made mistakes as his statements, often hurriedly written, were necessarily based on incomplete information. He incurred much enmity, but few unprejudiced men who were in the Crimea will now attempt to call in question the fact that by awakening the conscience of the British nation to the sufferings of its troops, he saved the remnant of those grand battalions we landed in September. (2)

Russell was a man of many apparent paradoxes—a man of wars who had no liking for war; a loyal patriot who hated the prevailing national passions of his countrymen; conventional in his ways but often boldly unfashionable in his views; a tough, resilient campaigner who could also be deeply sensitive and vulnerable; a man who relished the aristocratic life without ever losing his sympathy for the poor, oppressed peoples of the world. He founded a new branch of his profession but to the end of his life was not sure whether to be proud or ashamed of it, preferring to think of himself always as a working journalist, a 'special' rather than a 'war' correspondent. All those who met him regarded him as naturally cheerful and convivial, the best of good company, but the diaries and letters reveal him as an anxious and apprehensive man, the frequent victim of self-doubt and depression: 'It is a misfortune,' he once wrote in the diary, 'when a man is of a radiant, shining, grinning aspect, as people think he must be "jolly" i.e. happy.' (3)

For all his private gloom, however, it was a principled and productive and, for the most part, a happy life. His success was based on two fundamentals: his uncompromising quest for the truth, and his belief that a society can only hope to be just and healthy if it is blessed with an independent and critical and courageous press. 'All that a newspaper correspondent wants,' he wrote in the early stages of the Crimean campaign, 'is to see what is done, and to describe it to the best of his ability.' (4) It sounds easy enough. It is surprising how rarely it is achieved.

Notes

Apart from his own printed writings in newspapers and books, the chief sources for Russell's life and work are to be found in the Archives of *The Times*. All his surviving diaries, fifty volumes of them, are there and so too, unless otherwise attributed, are all the letters that passed between Russell and his *Times* colleagues.

The other important sources are documents in the possession of two of Russell's great-grandchildren, Mrs David Simonds of Pangbourne and Colonel R. J. Longfield of Gillingham, Dorset. Unless otherwise attributed in the notes, all the letters quoted from Russell to his daughter Alice are from Mrs Simonds' collection, and all those from Russell to his first wife, Mary, and to Max Müller are in Colonel Longfield's keeping.

Quotations from Russell's autobiographical fragment *Retrospect* are taken from three sources: J. B. Atkins' biography of Russell; a series of articles printed in the Anti-Jacobin magazine in 1891; and the typed transcript of some pages which can be found in Mrs Simonds' collection.

The initials RA refer to the Royal Archives at Windsor Castle.

Chapter 1
1. G. M. Young, *The Liberal Mind in Victorian England*.
2. Diary, 17 July 1882.
3. Ibid., 26 March 1858.
4. Ibid., 26 September 1879.
5. Diary, 28 April 1878.

Chapter 2
1. *Retrospect*. Quoted by Atkins, Vol. 1, p. 3.
2. Diary, 28 March 1896.
3. Ibid.
4. *Retrospect*. Quoted by Atkins, Vol. 1, p. 5
5. Ibid., p. 6.
6. Ibid.
7. Ibid., p. 7.

8. Ibid., p. 9.
9. Ibid., p. 11.
10. *Strand Magazine*, July–December 1892, p. 570.
11. Ibid., p. 571.
12. Diary, 20 June 1890.
13. *Strand Magazine*, July–December 1892, p. 570.
14. *Retrospect*. Quoted by Atkins, Vol. 1, p. 14.
15. *Dublin Express*, 11 February 1907.
16. *Retrospect*. Quoted by Atkins, Vol. 1, p. 3.
17. *Strand Magazine*, July–December 1892, p. 571.
18. Diary, January 1867, various entries.
19. *Retrospect*. Mrs Simonds' collection.

Chapter 3

1. *Retrospect*. Mrs Simonds' collection.
2. Ibid.
3. Ibid.
4. Quoted in *The Times*, 11 February 1907.
5. *Retrospect*. Mrs Simonds' collection.
6. Ibid.
7. Ibid.
8. Ibid.
9. Ibid.
10. Ibid.
11. *Retrospect*. Quoted by Atkins, Vol. 1, p. 26.
12. Quoted by Atkins, Vol. 1, p. 24.
13. *Retrospect*. Mrs Simonds' collection.
14. Greville's *Journal*, 8 May 1841.
15. *Retrospect*. Quoted by Atkins, Vol. 1, p. 115.
16. Ibid., p. 25.
17. Delane to Russell, 20 January 1843. Quoted by Atkins, Vol. 1, p. 27.
18. *Retrospect*. The *Anti-Jacobin*, 14 February 1891.
19. Ibid. Mrs Simonds' collection.
20. Ibid. The *Anti-Jacobin* 14 February 1891.
21. Ibid.
22. Ibid. Quoted by Atkins, Vol. 1, pp. 43–4.
23. *The Times*, 4 October 1843.
24. Ibid., 8 October 1843.
25. *Retrospect*. The *Anti-Jacobin*, 21 February 1891.
26. Ibid.

Chapter 4

1. *Retrospect*. Quoted by Atkins, Vol. 1, pp. 47–8.
2. *The Times*, 11 February 1907.
3. Samuel Smiles, *The Lives of George and Robert Stephenson*, Ch. 15.
4. *Retrospect*. Quoted by Atkins, Vol. 1, p. 51.
5. Ibid., p. 50.
6. *Times* Archives.

7. *Retrospect*. Quoted by Atkins, Vol. 1, p. 53.
8. Ibid. The *Anti-Jacobin* 14 February 1891.
9. *The Times* Archives.
10. *Retrospect*. Quoted by Atkins, Vol. 1, p. 56.
11. Max Müller, *My Autobiography*, Ch. 6.
12. Russell to Mrs Müller, October 1901. Quoted in *The Life and Letters of Max Müller*, Ch. 4.
13. *Retrospect*. Quoted by Atkins, Vol. 1, p. 60.
14. Ibid. The *Anti-Jacobin*, 7 February 1891.
15. Quoted by Atkins, Vol. 1, p. 73.
16. *The Times*, 6 and 7 February 1852.

Chapter 5

1. Atkins, Vol. 1, p. 92.
2. Ibid., p. 114.
3. Mowbray Morris to Russell, 3 December 1852.
4. *Retrospect*. Quoted by Atkins, Vol. 1, p. 100.
5. Ibid., p. 105.
6. Ibid., pp. 105–6.
7. Diary, April 1852. Quoted by Atkins, Vol. 1, pp. 113–4.
8. *Retrospect*. Quoted by Atkins, Vol. 1, p. 112.
9. Ibid., p. 119.
10. Ibid.
11. Ibid., p. 120.
12. *The Great War with Russia*, pp. 3–4.

Chapter 6

1. The book is now in the possession of Russell's great granddaughter, Mrs Simonds.
2. Russell to Mary, 12 March 1854.
3. Ibid., 16 March 1854.
4. *The Great War with Russia*, p. 6.
5. Russell to Delane, 8 April 1854.
6. Ibid., 18 May 1854.
7. Ibid., 7 May 1854.

8. Letter to *The Times*, 19 May 1854.
9. Russell to Mary, 5 June 1854.
10. Letter to *The Times*, 1 July 1854.
11. Ibid., 20 June 1854.
12. Russell to Delane, 23 June 1854.
13. Russell to Mary, 19 August 1854.
14. Letter to *The Times*, 4 September 1854.

Chapter 7
1. Letter to *The Times*, 14 September 1854.
2. *The Great War with Russia*, p. 25.
3. Ibid., p. 41.
4. Ibid., p. 29.
5. Ibid., p. 23.
6. Letter to *The Times*, 19 September 1854.
7. *The Great War with Russia*, pp. 31–2.
8. Ibid., pp. 73–4.
9. Ibid., pp. 171–3.
10. Letter to *The Times*, 26 October 1854.
11. Ibid., 27 October 1854.
12. *The Great War with Russia*, p. 220.
13. Letter to *The Times*, 5 November 1854.
14. Russell to Delane, 9 November 1854. Quoted in Atkins, Vol. 1, p. 175.
15. Russell to Mary, 8 November 1854.

Chapter 8
1. Russell to Delane, 5 November 1854. Quoted by Atkins, Vol. 1, p. 175.
2. *The Life and Letters of E. L. Godkin*, Vol. 1, pp. 103–4.
3. W. M. Thackeray to Lady Stanley, 4 December 1854.
4. Delane to Russell, 4 January 1855.
5. Russell to Mary, 29 December 1854.
6. Russell to Delane, 17 January 1855.

Chapter 9
1. Letter to *The Times*, 6 March 1855.
2. Russell to Delane, 28 January 1855.
3. Letter to *The Times*, 28 February 1855.

4. *The Great War with Russia*, pp. 283–5.
5. Russell to Delane, 19 May 1855.
6. Letter to *The Times*, 28 May 1855.
7. Russell to Delane, 16 June 1855
8. *The Times*, 6 July 1855.
9. Quoted in Atkins, Vol. 1, p. 230.
10. Russell to Delane, 9 July 1855.
11. Delane to Russell, 24 July 1855.
12. *The Great War with Russia*, p. 294.

Chapter 10
1. Raglan to the Duke of Newcastle, 13 November 1854.
2. Raglan, *Crimean Papers*. Quoted by Hibbert in *The Destruction of Lord Raglan*, Ch. 11.
3. *The Great War with Russia*, p. 250.
4. RA G39/17, Prince Albert to Lord Clarendon, 2 October 1855.
5. RA, Queen Victoria's Journal.
6. *The Story of a Soldier's Life*, Vol. 1.
7. Henry Clifford, VC: letter of 19 January 1855.
8. Warner, *The Fields of War: A Young Cavalryman's Crimea Campaign*.
9. Captain Robert Portal, *Letters from the Crimea*.
10. Major-General George Bell, *Rough Notes by an Old Soldier*.
11. *My Diary in India*, Vol. 1., Ch. 2.
12. Russell to Delane, 15 May 1855.
13. *Surgeon in the Crimea*.
14. *The Life and Letters of E. L. Godkin*. Vol. 1, pp. 101–2.
15. *The Invasion of the Crimea*, Vol. 6, pp. 237–8.
16. Diary, 30 March 1874.

Chapter 11
1. Interview with Russell in the *Strand Magazine*, July–December 1892.
2. Diary, 25 February 1856.
3. The letter is transcribed into Russell's diary.
4. Diary, 7 March 1856.
5. Russell to Mary, 13 March 1856.
6. Ibid., 7 May 1856.

7. Ibid., 6 June 1856.
8. Ibid., 18 June 1856.
9. Diary, 3 April 1856.
10. Quoted by Atkins, Vol. 1, pp. 261–2.
11. Russell to Mary, 20 August 1856.
12. Ibid., 5 November 1856.
13. Diary, 6 January 1857.
14. Interview in the *Strand Magazine*, July–December 1892.
15. Charles Dickens to Blanchard Jerrold, 26 November 1858.
16. Diary, 9 June 1857.
17. Ibid., 24 June 1857.
18. Ibid., 10 August 1857.
19. Ibid., 15 September 1857.
20. Ibid., 17 September 1857.
21. Ibid., 24 September 1857.
22. Ibid., 31 October 1857.

Chapter 12

1. Diary, 31 December 1857.
2. Ibid., 16 January 1858.
3. Russell to Delane, 23 January 1858.
4. Diary, 25 January 1858.
5. Ibid., 9 January 1858.
6. Ibid., 15 January 1858.
7. Ibid., 14 January 1858.
8. Russell to Delane, 23 January 1858.
9. *My Diary in India*, Vol. 1, pp. 113–16.
10. Diary, 29 January 1858.
11. Ibid., 2 February 1858.
12. Ibid., 10 February 1858.
13. Quoted by Atkins, Vol. 1, pp. 293–4.
14. *My Diary in India*, Vol. 1, p. 164.
15. Ibid., pp. 233–4.
16. Ibid., pp. 253–4.
17. *The Relief of Lucknow*, p. 117
18. Diary, 23 March 1858.
19. Ibid., 11 March 1858.
20. Letter to *The Times*, 20 March 1858.
21. Diary, 14 March 1858.
22. Letter to *The Times*, 20 March 1858.
23. *My Diary in India*, Vol. 1, p. 301.
24. Ibid., p. 348.
25. Diary, 18 March 1858.
26. Outram to Russell, 8 April 1858.

Quoted by Atkins, Vol. 1, p. 310.
27. Letter to *The Times*, 25 March 1858.
28. Delane to Russell, 8 April 1858. Quoted by Atkins, Vol. 1, p. 311.
29. Delane to Russell, May 1858.

Chapter 13

1. Diary, 13 April 1858.
2. Ibid., 26 April 1858.
3. Ibid., 4 May 1858.
4. Ibid., 5 May 1858.
5. *The Relief of Lucknow* pp. 150–1.
6. Diary, 6 May 1858.
7. MacDonald to Russell. Quoted by Atkins, Vol. 1, pp. 311–2.
8. Mowbray Morris to Russell, 17 January 1859.
9. *My Diary in India*, Vol. 2, p. 60.
10. Diary, 10 June 1858.
11. Ibid., 15 June 1858.
12. Ibid., 10 July 1858.
13. *My Diary in India*, Vol. 2, p. 128.
14. Dickens to Russell, 7 July 1858. Quoted by Atkins, Vol. 1, pp. 333–4.
15. Delane to Russell, 8 July 1858.
16. Ibid. Quoted by Atkins, Vol. 1, p. 342.
17. Mowbray Morris to Russell, 17 July 1858.
18. Letter to *The Times*, 8 September 1858.
19. Ibid., 1 October 1858.
20. Russell to Mary, 28 July 1858.
21. Ibid., 13 August 1858.
22. Ibid., 14 September 1858.
23. *My Diary in India*, Vol. 2, p. 264.
24. Quoted by Atkins, Vol. 1, pp. 296–7.
25. Ibid.
26. Diary, 8 November 1858.
27. Russell to Mary, 21 December 1858.
28. Ibid., 4 February 1859.
29. Letter to *The Times*, 15 February 1859.
30. Russell to Delane, 20 January 1859.
31. Ibid., 15 February 1859.
32. *The History of The Times*, Vol. 2, Ch. 15.

Chapter 14

1. *My Diary in India*, Vol. 2, p. 405.
2. Ibid., p. 408.
3. Russell to Delane, 23 February 1859.
4. Russell to Sherer, undated. Quoted by Atkins, Vol. 1, pp. 364–5.
5. Russell to Mary, 4 February 1859.
6. Quoted by Atkins, Vol. 1, p. 372.
7. Delane to Russell, 9 August 1859. Quoted by Atkins, Vol. 1, p. 372.
8. *Retrospect*. Quoted by Atkins, Vol. 1, pp. 373–4.
9. Ibid., p. 375.
10. Diary, 23 December 1859.
11. Ibid., 21 March 1860.
12. *Retrospections of an Active Life*, Vol. 1, p. 256.
13. *University of Rochester Library Bulletin*, Vol. 12, No. 2, p. 27.
14. Bigelow to Russell, November 1860. Quoted by Atkins, Vol. 2, p. 6.
15. Diary, 19 February 1861. Quoted in the *North American Review*, Vol. 166.
16. Ibid., 28 February 1861.
17. Ibid., 1 March 1861.

Chapter 15

1. Diary, 3 March 1861.
2. Quoted in *The History of The Times*, Vol. 2, p. 366.
3. Mowbray Morris to Mackay, 4 September 1862.
4. *My Diary North and South*, Vol. 1, pp. 7–8.
5. Russell to Bigelow, 4 February 1861.
6. Quoted by Atkins, Vol. 2, pp. 8–9.
7. Mowbray Morris to Russell, 4 April 1861.
8. Diary, 26 March 1861.
9. *My Diary North and South*, Vol. 1, pp. 54–5.
10. Ibid., pp. 56–7.
11. Ibid., p. 94.
12. Russell to Bigelow, *circa* 14 April 1861. Quoted in *Retrospections of an Active Life*, Vol. 1, p. 347.
13. *A Diary from Dixie*.

14. *My Diary North and South*, Vol. 1, p. 153.
15. Ibid., p. 244.
16. *The Historical Outlook*, Philadelphia, Vol. 16, No. 6, p. 252.
17. *My Diary North and South*, Vol. 1, p. 251.
18. Ibid., p. 244.
19. Letter to *The Times*, 6 May 1861.
20. *My Diary North and South*, Vol. 1, pp. 231–2.
21. Ward's letters are quoted in the *University of Rochester Library Bulletin*, Vol. 12, No. 2, pp. 23–33.
22. Russell to Bancroft Davis, 25 June 1861. Quoted in *The Historical Outlook*, Philadelphia, Vol. 16, No. 6, p. 253.
23. Delane to Russell, undated. Quoted by Atkins, Vol. 2, p. 71.
24. Diary, 18 July 1861.
25. *My Diary North and South*, Vol. 2, p. 187.
26. Ibid., p. 213.
27. Ibid., p. 145.
28. Ibid., pp. 157–8.

Chapter 16

1. *A History of the English-speaking Peoples*, Vol. 4, Book 11.
2. *My Diary North and South*, Vol. 2, p. 224.
3. Diary, 28 July 1861.
4. Delane to Russell, 6 August 1861.
5. Mowbray Morris to Russell, 14 August 1861.
6. *My Diary North and South*, Vol. 2, p. 299.
7. Diary, 25 August 1861.
8. *A Diary from Dixie*.
9. Letter to *The Times*, published 10 September 1861.
10. *My Diary North and South*, Vol. 2, p. 306.
11. Russell to Bigelow, 27 July 1861. Quoted in *Retrospections of an Active Life*, Vol. 1.

12. Ibid., 3 August 1861. Quoted in *Retrospections of an Active Life*, Vol. 1.
13. Delane to Russell, late September 1861. Quoted by Atkins, Vol. 2, p. 77.
14. Russell to Delane, 14 October 1861.
15. Diary, 9 November 1861.
16. Ibid., 19 November 1861.
17. Delane to Russell. Quoted by Atkins, Vol. 2, p. 88.
18. Russell to Delane, 20 December 1861. Quoted by Atkins, Vol. 2, p. 89.
19. Ibid., 16 January 1862. Quoted by Atkins, Vol. 2, p. 91.
20. Russell to Mowbray Morris, 7 January 1862.
21. Ibid., 26 January 1862.
22. Delane to Russell, February 1862. Quoted by Atkins, Vol. 2, p. 93.
23. Russell to Mowbray Morris, 16 February 1862.
24. MacDonald to Russell, 24 March 1862. Quoted by Atkins, Vol. 2, pp. 96–7.
25. Mowbray Morris to Russell, 6 March 1862.
26. Diary. Quoted by Atkins, Vol. 2, p. 105.
27. Delane to Russell, 15 April 1862. Quoted by Atkins, Vol. 2, pp. 112–13.
28. Delane to Russell, undated.

Chapter 17
1. Diary, 13 November 1862.
2. Ibid., 25 March 1866.
3. Ibid., 26 June 1868.
4. Anthony Trollope, *An Autobiography*, Ch. 8.
5. Diary, 4 January 1873.
6. Ibid., 7 July 1868.
7. Ibid., 7 January 1874.
8. *Retrospect*. Quoted by Atkins, Vol. 1, pp. 107–8.
9. Diary, 10 October 1863.
10. Ibid., 6 March 1864.
11. Dickens to Russell, 3 January 1864.

From a typed copy in Mrs Simonds' collection.
12. Diary, 25 January 1866.
13. Dickens to Russell. From a typed copy in Mrs Simonds' collection.
14. Russell to Mowbray Morris, 3 October 1864.
15. Second Duke of Wellington to Russell, 26 March 1866. Quoted by Atkins, Vol. 2, p. 128.
16. Diary, 7 December 1865.
17. Ibid., 29 July 1864.
18. Russell to Bigelow, 25 February 1863. Quoted in *Retrospections of an Active Life*, Vol. 1.
19. Delane to Russell, undated.
20. *The Times*, 24 August 1863.
21. Delane to Russell, 25 August 1863.
22. Russell to Mowbray Morris, 24 July 1865.
23. Delane to Russell, 20 August 1865. Quoted by Atkins, Vol. 2, pp. 125–6.
24. *De Profundis:* Russell's account in the *Fortnightly Review*, 1865, Vol. 2.
25. Diary, 1 August 1864.
26. Ibid., 22 August 1865.
27. Ibid., 26 August 1865.
28. Ibid., 5 March 1864.
29. Ibid., 26 August 1862.
30. Ibid., 17 January 1866.
31. Ibid., 10 May 1866.
32. Ibid., 20 May 1866.
33. Ibid., 31 May 1866.

Chapter 18
1. Delane to Russell, 15 June 1866. Quoted by Atkins, Vol. 2, p. 135.
2. Diary, 24 June 1866.
3. Lady Bloomfield, *Reminiscences of Court and Diplomatic Life*.
4. Letter to *The Times*, published 11 July 1866.
5. Ibid.
6. Ibid.
7. Ibid.
8. *The Battle of Königgrätz*, p. 133.
9. *Saturday Review*, 14 July 1866.

10. Russell to Delane, undated but probably 11 July 1866.
11. Ibid., 13 August 1866. Quoted by Atkins, Vol. 2, p. 143.
12. Ibid., 9 July 1866.
13. Quoted by Atkins, Vol. 2, p. 142.
14. Russell to Mowbray Morris, 14 September 1866.
15. Diary, 21 October 1866.
16. Russell to Alice, 28 January 1867. Mrs Simonds' collection.
17. Diary, 20 March 1867.
18. Bigelow to Russell, undated. Quoted by Atkins, Vol. 2, p. 147.
19. Diary, 16 March 1867.
20. Ibid., 9 March 1868.
21. Ibid., 14 April 1867.
22. Ibid., 22 November 1867.
23. Ibid., 26 December 1867.

Chapter 19

1. Ellis to Russell, 1 April 1868. *Times* Archives.
2. Diary, 10 August 1868.
3. *Chelsea News*, 15 August 1868.
4. Ibid., 10 October 1868.
5. Ibid., 31 October 1868.
6. Ibid., 21 November 1868.
7. *A Diary in the East*, p. 24.
8. Ibid., p. 71.
9. Ibid., p. 142.
10. Ibid., pp. 145–6.
11. Swinglehurst, *The Romantic Journey*, p. 75.
12. *A Diary in the East*, p. 317.
13. Ibid., p. 261.
14. Diary, 21 March 1869.
15. *A Diary in the East*, p. 552.
16. Diary, 3 July 1869.
17. Russell to Alice 2 December 1869. Mrs Simonds' collection.
18. Russell to unknown (probably Alice), 20 January 1870. Mrs Simonds' collection.

Chapter 20

1. Delane to Morris, 15 July 1870.
2. Delane to Russell, probably 18 July 1870.
3. Lord Ronald Gower, *My Reminiscences*, Vol. 1, p. 315.
4. Diary, 22 July 1870.
5. *My Diary during the last Great War*, pp. 13–14.
6. Ibid., pp. 22–3.
7. *My Reminiscences*, Vol. 1, p. 332.
8. Russell to Alice, 26 July 1870. Quoted by Atkins, Vol. 2, pp. 169–70.
9. *The Times*, 30 November 1869.
10. *My Reminiscences*, Vol. 1, p. 355.
11. *My Diary during the last Great War*, p. 69.
12. Russell to Mowbray Morris, 9 August 1870.
13. Diary, 7 August 1870.
14. Ibid., 9 August 1870.
15. *My Diary during the last Great War*, pp. 195–6.
16. Ibid., p. 196.
17. Ibid., p. 192.
18. Ibid., p. 205.
19. Ibid., p. 226.
20. Letter to *The Times*, published 6 September 1870.
21. Diary, 12 September 1870.
22. Letter to *The Times*, published 24 September 1870.
23. *The Times*, 14 October 1870.
24. Russell to Alice, undated. Quoted by Atkins, Vol. 2, p. 213.
25. Bismarck, *Erinnerungen und Gedanken*.
26. Russell to Mowbray Morris, undated.
27. Ibid., 5 January 1871.
28. Mowbray Morris to Russell, 23 September 1870.
29. Ibid., 28 September 1870.
30. Russell to Mowbray Morris, 20 October 1870.
31. Ibid., 23 October 1870.
32. Mowbray Morris to Russell, 10 October 1870.
33. Forbes to Russell, 13 July 1899. Quoted by Atkins, Vol. 2, p. 220.
34. Russell to Mowbray Morris, 31 January 1871.

35. Ibid., 7 March 1871.
36. Russell to Delane, 28 September 1870. Russell transcribed the letter on the front pages of his 1870 diary.
37. Russell to Mowbray Morris, 13 October 1870.
38. *The Campaign of 1870–1*, p. 285.
39. Delane to Russell, 13 February 1871.
40. Mowbray Morris to O'Meagher, 17 October 1870.
41. Mowbray Morris to Russell, 25 January 1871.
42. Mowbray Morris to Russell, 6 February 1871.
43. Letter to *The Times*, published 2 March 1871.
44. Russell to Mowbray Morris, 3 March 1871.
45. Ibid., 6 December 1870. Quoted by Atkins, Vol. 2, pp. 227–8.
46. Odo Russell to Russell, 12 March 1871. Quoted by Atkins, Vol. 2, p. 226.

Chapter 21

1. Russell to Bigelow, 21 May 1870. Mrs Simonds' collection.
2. Russell to ?, 28 January 1872. Mrs Simonds' collection.
3. Ibid., 11 October 1872. Mrs Simonds' collection.
4. Diary, 18 June 1874.
5. Ibid., 4 January 1874.
6. Ibid., 3 November 1872.
7. Quoted by Charles Chenevix Trench in *Charley Gordon*, p. 80.
8. General Gordon to Russell, 21 July 1875. Quoted by Atkins, Vol.2, p. 251.
9. Diary, 9 May 1871.
10. Russell to Alice, 17 December 1871. Mrs Simonds' collection.
11. Diary, 10 March 1872.
12. Ibid., 1 April 1872.
13. Ibid., 9 April 1874.
14. Ibid., 6 May 1874.
15. Ibid., 5 May 1874.
16. Ibid., 8 May 1865.
17. Delane to Russell, undated. *Times* Archives.
18. Ibid., 1875. *Times* Archives.
19. Diary, 13 September 1873.
20. Delane to Russell, 10 August 1875. *Times* Archives.
21. Diary, 12 September 1873.
22. Ibid., 5 January 1874.
23. Ibid., 19 June 1875.
24. Ibid., 29 May 1875.
25. Ibid., 7 September 1875.
26. Ibid., 15 October 1875.
27. *The Prince of Wales' Tour*, p. 77.
28. Diary, 5 March 1876.
29. Ibid., 8 March 1876.
30. *Memoirs*, Vol. 1.
31. Ibid.
32. Delane to Russell, 23 February 1876.
33. Diary, 23 March 1876.
34. Ibid., 17 April 1876.
35. Ibid., 6 May 1876.
36. Ibid., 7 May 1876.
37. Ibid., 8 February 1877.
38. Ibid.
39. Quoted by Atkins, Vol. 2, p. 264.
40. Russell to Alice, 7 September 1877. Mrs Simonds' collection.
41. *The Times*, 7 December 1874.
42. Diary, 30 October 1878.
43. Ibid., 1 January 1879.
44. Ibid., 4 January 1879.
45. Ibid., 18 May 1879.
46. Ibid., 16 January 1879.

Chapter 22

1. Diary, 26 June 1883.
2. Russell to the Duke of Cambridge, 31 July 1879. RA 035/77.
3. Russell to Edward Lawson, 8 September 1879. Quoted by Atkins, Vol. 2, p. 296.
4. Diary, 26 September 1879.
5. Russell to ?, 18 October 1879. Mrs Simonds' collection.
6. Russell to Edward Lawson, 8 September 1879. Quoted by Atkins,

Vol. 2, pp. 283–4.
7. Sir Garnet Wolseley to Russell, 13 June 1880. Quoted by Atkins, Vol. 2, p. 306.
8. *Strand Magazine*, July–December 1892.
9. Ibid.
10. Diary, 7 January 1880.
11. Ibid., 21 May 1880.
12. Russell to Miss Delane, 9 January 1880. Quoted by Atkins, Vol. 2, pp. 293–4.
13. Russell to Edward Lawson, 13 January 1880. Quoted by Atkins, Vol. 2, p. 297.

Chapter 23

1. Russell to Alice, 27 August 1880. Mrs Simonds' collection.
2. Atkins, Vol. 2, p. 314.
3. *St Paul Pioneer Press*, 25 May 1881.
4. Ibid.
5. *New York Star*, 8 May 1881.
6. Diary, 21 July 1882.
7. Ibid., 25 December 1882.
8. Russell to Max Müller, 20 November 1882. Colonel Longfield's collection.
9. Diary, 28 May 1883.
10. Ibid., 23 July 1883.
11. Ibid., 23 June 1883.

12. Quoted in the Diary, 15 March 1883.
13. Diary, 16 May 1883.
14. Ibid., August 1894.
15. Russell to Alice, 23 January 1884. Mrs Simonds' collection.
16. Ibid.
17. Ibid., 7 September 1889.
18. Ibid., 4 February 1889.
19. *Strand Magazine*, Vol. 4, July–December 1892.
20. Diary. Quoted by Atkins, Vol. 2, pp. 329–30.
21. Diary, 24 May 1893.
22. Ibid., 7 January 1895.
23. Ibid., 23 November 1889.
24. Ibid., 30 March 1883.
25. Ibid., 1 July 1883.
26. Russell to Alice, August 1902. Quoted by Atkins, Vol. 2, p. 346.
27. Russell to Moberly Bell, 17 November 1892. *Times* Archives.
28. Diary, 9 May 1896.
29. Ibid., 1 April 1896.
30. Ibid., 3 April 1895.

Chapter 24

1. *The Times*, 20 February 1907.
2. Sir Evelyn Wood, *The Crimea in 1854 and 1894*.
3. Diary, 1 January 1863.
4. Letter to *The Times*, 19 May 1854.

Bibliography

Arnold, Matthew. *A Friendship's Garland*. Smith, Elder and Co., 1871.
Atkins, John Black. *The Life of Sir William Howard Russell*. John Murray, 1911.
Ayerst, David. *The Biography of a Newspaper*. Collins, 1971.
Barnett, Correlli. *Britain and Her Army, 1509–1970*. Penguin, 1970.
Bell, George. *Rough Notes of an Old Soldier*. Day and Son, 1867.
Beresford, Lord Charles. *Memoirs*. Methuen, 1914.
Bigelow, John. *Retrospections of an Active Life*. Baker and Taylor (New York), 1909.
Blake, Robert. *Disraeli*. Eyre and Spottiswood, 1966.
Bloomfield, Lady Georgiana. *Reminiscences of Court and Diplomatic Life*. Kegan Paul, Trench, 1883.
Brogan, D. W. *The Development of Modern France*. Hamish Hamilton, 1947.
Brogan, Hugh. *The Times Reports the American Civil War*. Times Books, 1975.
Butterfield, Margaret. 'Samuel Ward, alias Carlos Lopez', *University of Rochester Library Bulletin*, vol. XII, 1957.
Catton, Bruce. *The Penguin Book of the American Civil War*. Penguin, 1960.
Chaudhuri, Nirad C. *Scholar Extraordinary: The Life of Max Müller*. Chatto and Windus, 1974.
Chesnut, Mary Boykin. *A Diary from Dixie*. Houghton Mifflin (Boston), 1949.
Churchill, Winston Spencer. *My Early Life*. Odhams Press, 1948.
  A History of the English-Speaking Peoples. Cassell, 1956.
Clifford, Henry. *Letters and Sketches from the Crimea*. Michael Joseph, 1956.
Clissold, Stephen. *Chilean Scrap-Book*. The Cresset Press, 1952.
Compton, Piers. *Colonel's Lady and Camp-Follower*. Robert Hale, 1970.
Cook, Sir Edward. *Delane of The Times*. Constable, 1915.
Craig, Gordon A. *The Battle of Königgrätz*. Weidenfeld and Nicolson, 1965.
Crawford, Martin. 'British Travellers and the Anglo-American Relationship in the 1850s', *Journal of American Studies*, August 1978.
  'Anglo-American Perspectives', *New York Historical Society Quarterly*, July 1978.
Croker, John Wilson. *The Croker Papers*. Batsford, 1967.
Crowe, Sir Joseph. *Reminiscences of Thirty-five Years of My Life*. John Murray, 1895.
Dasent, Arthur Irwin. *John Thadeus Delane*. John Murray, 1908.
Dickens, Charles. *Martin Chuzzlewit*. Penguin, 1975.
Duberly, Fanny. *Journal Kept During the Russian War*. Longmans, 1856.
Fawkes, Richard. *Dion Boucicault*. Quartet, 1979.
Fitzgerald, Percy H. *The Garrick Club*. Elliot Stock, 1904.
Forbes-Mitchell, William. *The Relief of Lucknow*. Folio Society, 1962.
Furneaux, Rupert. *The First War Correspondent*. Cassell, 1944.
Gernsheim, Helmut and Alison. *Roger Fenton: Photographer of the Crimean War*. Secker and Warburg, 1954.
Gibbs, Peter. *Crimean Blunder*. Frederick Muller, 1960.

Godkin, Lawrence. *The Life and Letters of E. L. Godkin*. Macmillan, 1907.
Gower, Lord Ronald. *My Reminiscences*. Kegan Paul, Trench, 1883.
   Old Diaries. John Murray, 1902.
Grenville, J. A. S. *Europe Reshaped, 1848–78*. Fontana, 1976.
Greville, Charles Cavendish Fulke. *The Greville Memoirs*. Longman, Green, 1874–85.
Hibbert, Christopher. *The Destruction of Lord Raglan*. Longmans, 1961.
   Edward VII. Allen Lane, 1978.
   The Great Mutiny. Allen Lane, 1978.
Hudson, Derek. *Thomas Barnes of The Times*. Greenwood Press (Westport, Connecticut), 1973.
Kinglake, A. W. *The Invasion of the Crimea*. William Blackwood, 1863–87.
Knightley, Phillip. *The First Casualty*. Quartet, 1978.
Lawson George. *Surgeon in the Crimea*. Constable, 1968.
Magnus, Philip. *King Edward VII*. Penguin, 1975.
Müller, Max. *My Autobiography*. Longmans, Green, 1901.
Müller, Mrs Max. *The Life and Letters of Max Müller*. Longmans, Green, 1902.
Nye, R. B. and Morpurgo, J. E. *A History of the United States*. Penguin, 1955.
Portal, Robert. *Letters from the Crimea*. Warren and Son (Winchester), 1900.
Richards, Eric. *The Leviathan of Wealth*. Routledge and Kegan Paul, 1973.
Robinson, Ronald, Gallagher, John and Denny, Alice. *Africa and the Victorians*. Macmillan, 1961.
Russell, William Howard. *The War*. G. Routledge, 1855–6.
   The British Expedition to the Crimea. G. Routledge, 1858.
   Rifle Clubs and Volunteer Corps. Routledge, Warne and Routledge, 1859.
   My Diary in India. Routledge, Warne and Routledge, 1860.
   The Wedding at Windsor. Day and Son, 1863.
   My Diary North and South. Bradbury and Evans, 1863.
   The Atlantic Telegraph. First published 1865; reprinted David and Charles, 1972.
   The Adventures of Dr. Brady. Tinsley Brothers, 1868.
   A Diary in the East During the Tour of the Prince and Princess of Wales. Routledge, 1869.
   The Campaign of 1870–1. R. Bentley and Son, 1871.
   My Diary During the Last Great War. Routledge, 1874.
   The Prince of Wales' Tour. Sampson Low, Marston, Searle and Rivington, 1877.
   Hesperothen; Notes from the West. Sampson Low, Marston, Searle and Rivington, 1882.
   A Visit to Chile and the Nitrate Fields of Tarapaca. J. S. Virtue, 1890.
   The Great War with Russia. Routledge, 1895.
Seacole, Mary. *Wonderful Adventures of Mrs. Seacole in Many Lands*. James Blackwood, 1857.
Smiles, Samuel. *The Lives of George and Robert Stephenson*. Folio Society, 1975.
Strachan, H. F. A. 'The Pre-Crimean Origins of Reform in the British Army', University of Cambridge Ph.D. thesis, 1976.
Stroud, Dorothy. *The South Kensington Estate of Henry Smith's Charity*. The Trustees of Henry Smith's Charity, 1975.
Swinglehurst, Edmund. *The Romantic Journey*. Pica Editions, 1974.
Taylor, A. J. P. *Bismarck*. Hamish Hamilton, 1955.
   Essays in English History. Penguin, 1976.
Thackeray, William Makepeace. *The Letters and Private Papers*. Oxford University Press, 1946.
The Times. *The History of The Times*, Vols. 1 and 2. The Office of The Times, 1935 and 1939.
Tolstoy, Leo. *Tales of Army Life*. Oxford University Press, 1943.
Trollope, Anthony. *An Autobiography*. Oxford University Press, 1947.

Vizetelly, Henry. *Glances Back Through Seventy Years*. Kegan Paul, Trench, Trubner and Co., 1893.

Warner, Philip. *The Fields of War*. John Murray, 1977.

Wilkinson-Latham, Robert. *From Our Special Correspondent*. Hodder and Stoughton, 1979.

Williams, Francis. *Dangerous Estate*. Longmans, Green, 1957.

Wolseley, Sir Garnet. *The Story of a Soldier's Life*. Constable, 1903.

Wood, Sir Evelyn. *The Crimea in 1854 and 1894*. Chapman and Hall, 1895.

Woodham-Smith, Cecil. *The Reason Why*. Constable, 1953.

  The Great Hunger. Hamish Hamilton, 1962.

  Florence Nightingale. Fontana, 1964.

  Queen Victoria. Hamish Hamilton, 1972.

Woodruff, Philip. *The Men Who Ruled India*. Jonathan Cape, 1954.

Index